Hodder

VOCATIONAL

A-LEVEL

Travel & Tourism

■ **GILLIAN DALE** ■ **HELEN OLIVER**

Hodder & Stoughton

A MEMBER OF THE

Orders: please contact Bookpoint Ltd, 78 Milton Park, Abingdon, Oxon OX14 4TD. Telephone: (44) 01235 827720, Fax: (44) 01235 400454. Lines are open from 9.00–6.00, Monday to Saturday, with a 24 hour message answering service. Email address: orders@bookpoint.co.uk

British Library Cataloguing in Publication Data
A catalogue record for this title is available from The British Library

ISBN 0 340 781 998

First published in 2000
Impression number   10 9 8 7 6 5 4 3 2
Year   2005 2004 2003 2002 2001 2000

Typeset by Wearset, Boldon, Tyne and Wear
Printed in Great Britain for Hodder & Stoughton Educational, a division of Hodder Headline Plc, 338 Euston Road, London NW1 3BH by J.W. Arrowsmith, Bristol.

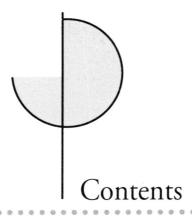

Contents

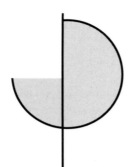

Acknowledgements

The authors would like to thank the following for case study material and interviews:

Canvas Holidays
Deloitte & Touche Consultancy
Explore Worldwide
Marketing Manchester
National Trust
Saga Holidays
SAS Event Manangement
Youth Hostel Management

The author and publisher would like to thank the following for permission to reproduce copyright text and illustrative material:

© Times Newspapers Limited, pp. 51, 54, 123, 128, 135, 224, 239, 260, 307; Adama Bah, from Tourism Concern *In Focus Magazine* (summer 1999), p. 142; *Air Miles* Travel Promotions Ltd., p. 286; ASA, p. 290; Bath Spa Project, p. 265; British Airways Holidays, p. 247; Columbus Publishing, p. 167; Corbis, p. 315; *Daily Mail*, p. 276; Deloitte & Touche Hospitality and Leisure Consulting, p. 87; Dianne P. Laws (1996), *International Tourism Module 3: tourism impacts*, p.5, MSc Tourism Management by Distance Learning, School of Leisure and Food Management, Sheffield Hallam University, p. 122; East of England Tourist Board, p. 102; easyJet Airline Co. Ltd., p. 216; *Financial Times*, pp. 16; First Choice Holidays PLC, p. 242; Frances Kennedy in *The Independent*, p. 124; Glastonbury Festival Leisure, pp. 365, 366; Go, p. 300; Inghams Travel, p. 187; ITC, p. 291; Life File/Emma Lee, p. 316; Lonely Planet Publications, p. 172; Mary Evans Picture Library/G. van de Gucht, p. 7; Oldham Metropolitan Borough Council, pp. 283, 284; ONS, pp. 9, 41, 60, 65, 244, 245; Permission for reproduction granted by Harrogate International Centre, p. 10; Ryanair, p. 237; SeaFrance, p. 268; The Blakeney Hotel, Norfolk, p. 32; The British Tourist Authority, pp. 36, 193; *The European*, p. 127; *The Guardian*, pp. 118, 125; The National Trust, pp. 11, 114-15; The Science Museum, p. 8; *The Sunseeker*, p. 97; Thomas Cook Holidays, pp. 162, 297, 310, 323, 324; Thomson Holidays, p. 175; Tourism Concern, p. 101; *Tourism Intelligence Quarterly*, p. 62; *Travel Trade Gazette*, pp. 40, 44-5, 46, 55, 189, 264; *Travel Weekly*, 55, 67, 168, 191, 195, 198, 204, 217, 218, 219, 236, 267; Virgin Holidays, pp. 85, 248, 269; *Woman and Home*, pp. 190, 239; ZanzibarNet, p. 281.

CHAPTER 1

Investigating travel and tourism

Aims and objectives

At the end of this chapter you will:

- **be able to define travel and tourism**
- **understand how and why tourism has developed**
- **know the current structure of the travel and tourism industry and its key features**
- **know the size of the industry and its importance to the UK economy**
- **have an understanding of the range and types of employment opportunities in the industry**
- **plan your own career and know how to pursue it**

Introduction

This unit introduces you to the travel and tourism industry and provides you with an understanding of the industry as a whole. You will investigate what the industry consists of today and how it has developed. This knowledge will help you with all other units – by showing you how it all fits together.

Some people describe the travel and tourism industry as the world's biggest industry; others say it is the fastest growing. This means that there are an increasing number of employment possibilities for you. You will investigate the type of jobs available and the best ways of finding employment after your Vocational A Level.

First, we must establish what is meant by the travel and tourism industry. Some students expect the course to be simply about holidays – but we will soon establish that the industry is made up of many elements and that leisure travel is only one part!

An investigation into the development of the travel and tourism industry is essential for an understanding of today's industry. You will gain an understanding of how life has changed since the end of the war, and how this has affected people's expectations, in terms of travel. Changes in socioeconomic circumstances, increased technology and new products have all led us to have higher expectations. Many people now think that they 'need' a holiday; it is no longer the luxury that it used to be.

Today's industry is made up of many parts, for example, transportation, accommodation or attractions. It is a very fragmented industry, unlike many others. You will investigate the components of the industry and how they work together to make up the UK travel and tourism industry. Some of the organisations are commercial organisations, aiming to make a profit. Others may be voluntary or government organisations. Through investigating different organisations you will gain an understanding of the features of the industry today.

As it is made up of so many parts and it is growing so rapidly, travel and tourism has become the world's largest industry. You will investigate exactly how big the UK industry is and how it contributes to our economy.

Finally, we examine what opportunities are available to you after your Vocational A Level. You will investigate the range of employment possibilities available to you, both in the UK and abroad. It is hoped that you will use the final part of this chapter to plan your own career and organise what you must do to achieve your goals, be it more training, higher education or producing a CV and going for interviews.

Defining travel and tourism

DID YOU KNOW?

The World Tourism Organisation (WTO) decided that the problems of defining tourism were so great that they needed an International Conference. They held this in 1991 and their definitions were accepted by the United Nations in 1993.

So you have decided to study for a Vocational A Level in travel and tourism. But what do you understand by the travel and tourism industry? Hopefully before enrolling on this course you have understood that you will not just be finding out about holidays and exotic destinations. The industry covers much more than those areas.

There is no single definition used by government, the industry and academics. EdExcel describe travel and tourism as 'the whole phenomenon of people travelling away from home, whether for business or for leisure, and the industry that supports this activity.' Following is a simple version of the definition given by the Tourism Society in 1976.

 The temporary short term movement of people to destinations outside the places where they normally live and work, and activities during their stay at these destinations; it includes movement for all purposes, as well as day visits or excursions.

The key points of this definition are:

- Tourists must return home.
- They only go to their destinations for a short time (usually one or two weeks).
- Tourism can only take place away from your everyday environment.
- Everything you do as a tourist is included in the industry (activities during your stay), e.g. staying in a hotel or visiting a theme park.
- Whatever your reason for travel (visiting a friend, study, or a business meeting), it is part of the industry.
- If you go on a day visit or excursion you are also part of the tourism industry.

You may find some definitions that include day visitors as tourists and others that put them in a separate category. Although this may not be important in the majority of cases, it is relevant when comparing statistics between countries. The WTO therefore clarified this point – tourists are those who stay overnight; those who return home within 24 hours are excursionists or day-trippers. The term visitors includes all tourists and excursionists.

KEY TERMS

Tourists: temporary visitors who stay overnight.

Excursionists: visitors who stay for less than 24 hours.

Visitors: all tourists and excursionists.

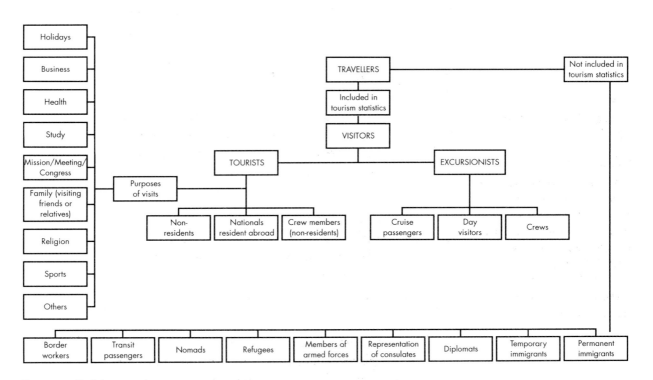

Figure 1.1 Defining a tourist

Source: WTO

In 1997 25.5 million overseas visitors came to Britain, spending more than £12 billion.

KEY TERMS

Domestic tourism: UK residents taking trips or holidays in the UK.

Outbound tourism: UK residents taking holidays outside the UK.

Inbound tourism: overseas visitors that come to the UK.

Types of tourism

When you think of tourism you may think of the traditional two week holiday in the sun. This is called **outbound tourism** – you are travelling out of the UK, your normal place of residence. However, most of the tourism in the UK, and the world, is in fact **domestic** – people travelling within their own country. **Inbound tourism** covers those overseas visitors who travel to the UK. These are very important to the UK economy, as we will see later. Incoming tourists bring money into our economy and provide jobs.

Why do people travel?

We know from the previous definitions that travel and tourism does not simply cover holidays. People travel for many reasons and these can broadly be placed into three categories:

- leisure (holidays)
- business
- visiting friends and relatives (VFR)

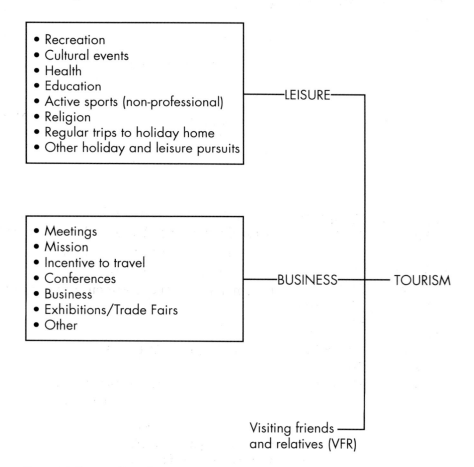

Figure 1.2 Purpose of travel

Source: Adapted from WTO material

Leisure travel

Leisure travel is the most important of the aforementioned categories and includes all recreational travel. Examples include a sports, cultural, religious or study holiday; a city break or clubbing in Ibiza.

Business travel

Business travel includes all travel for business reasons. This may be a meeting, a conference, exhibition or trade fair. The traveller does not normally pay for his or her own travel arrangements when travelling on business – this is covered by the company.

Visiting friends and relatives (VFR)

VFR accounts for many of the tourist trips within the UK. Examples include a visit to grandparents for a day or staying with friends for a week. You may find that this category is often included as part of leisure travel, as it is a form of holiday/recreational activity.

 **DID YOU KNOW?**

The World Travel Market is the annual business event for those employed in the travel industry. In 1998 nearly £9 billion of business was conducted over the four day event held at London's Earls Court.

(All figures in millions)	**TRIPS**	**SPENDING**
Holiday	70.8	£10,355
Business	15.4	£2,475
To visit friends or relatives	41.4	£1,635
Other	6.0	£610
All purposes	133.6	£15,075

Table 1.1 *Purpose of domestic tourism, 1997*

Source: BTA website

DID YOU KNOW?

The British Tourist Authority's aim is to promote Britain to overseas tourists. Visit its website at www.visitbritain.com to establish how it does this. The English Tourism Council's aim is to support the business of tourism in England

As you can see from Table 1.1 when the British travel within the UK it is usually for a holiday. Holidays accounted for 70.8 million trips in 1997. Trips to see friends or relatives accounted for 41.4 million trips, whereas business travel accounted for only 15.4 million trips. However, the amount of money spent on each trip varies greatly.

 # ACTIVITY

Using the definition given by the WTO, decide whether the following people are part of the tourism industry, and if so, which of the following categories they fit into:

- tourist, excursionist or neither
- incoming, outgoing or domestic
- leisure, business or VFR

1 Kate decides to take a year out before going to university and backpacks around Europe for 6 months.

2 James commutes to Edinburgh from his home 20 miles away every day for work.

3 Giovanni has lived in Rome all his life. He comes to Brighton for a month for an English language course.

4 Sue and Claire spend a week clubbing in Majorca to celebrate completing their Vocational A Level.

5 A hotelier from Malta wants to increase his business. He spends a week at the World Travel Market to try and meet British tour operators.

6 Jack decides to go to London for a day to gather material for a Vocational A Level assignment on tourist attractions.

7 Sheila flies to Zurich on the 0700 hours flight from London Heathrow. She has a morning meeting but is home by 2000 hours.

ACTIVITY

Examine the statistics in Table 1.1: Purpose of domestic tourism, 1997. Calculate the amount of money spent on each trip for the three different purposes of travel: leisure, business and VFR.

Discuss your answers with a colleague. Explain why each category differs so much.

Visit the British Tourist Authority website. Gather the statistics for the overseas visitors to Britain. Once again you will see that the average spend per trip varies greatly. Which type of tourism do you think the British government wishes to encourage the most and how will they do this?

The development of travel and tourism

At the end of the twentieth century the tourism industry employed 1.7 million people and contributed £52,524 million to the economy (BTA, 1997).

In order to fully understand the travel and tourism industry as it is today you must investigate its development; including why and how this has occurred.

The growth in travel and tourism has taken place predominantly during the twentieth century and in particular since the end of the Second World War. This will be the period on which we focus in this section. However, it is important to understand the origins of tourism, and so we will briefly outline tourism development up until the World Wars, before investigating the development of the last century.

Early tourism

Travel as we know it today is predominantly for pleasure. This is, however, a recent phenomenon. The original purposes for travel three thousand years ago were for war, religion or trading. Travelling within the UK was uncomfortable; roads (tracks) were basic and there were dangers of highwaymen.

Travel and the Roman Empire

Road transport developed with the Romans, but even so, tarmac was unknown. At this stage, the basic form of the facilities that are provided today began to develop. Accommodation in the form of staging inns (a precursor to the motel) arose to provide for the weary traveller. Catering services, as we call them today, existed at these inns.

The Roman Empire allowed for international travel for trade, and also to visit friends and relatives who may have been 'administrators' in another part of the empire.

Travel became more 'domestic' following the collapse of the Roman Empire. With the onset of the Middle Ages (alternatively known as the Dark Ages) travel became more dangerous. However, the numerous 'holy days', the origins of the public holiday, usually entailed a festival or pilgrimage. Until 1830 there were 33 Saints Days in the holiday calendar – many more than today!

Early transport methods

Until the mid 1600s transport methods for the majority were either on foot or by horse. The wealthy could be carried in a litter or ride in a wagon. The sprung coach of the early 1600s greatly improved transport. By 1815, with the development of tarmac, the road system as we know it today began to develop with public transport being provided by charabancs and horse drawn carriages in the latter half of the 1800s.

The concept of the 'Grand Tour' emerged in the early seventeenth century. Travel for education was considered to be necessary for young men. The cultural centres of Europe were visited for pleasure. Shortly afterwards, the idea of 'taking a cure' at a Spa developed social status and such places as Bath, Harrogate and Buxton developed as fashionable resorts for the wealthy. Health, education, pleasure and social activities were now acceptable reasons to travel.

Figure 1.3 *An early horse and carriage (c.1700)*
Source: G. van de Gucht/Mary Evans Picture Library

Nineteenth century developments

The idea of travel for pleasure was now established. However, other conditions in the nineteenth century further encouraged the growth of travel and laid the foundations for the mass tourism of the twentieth century. These included:

- The development of the railways. The first railway was built in 1825 and was the basis for early tour operations. It was also the major contributing factor to the development of seaside resorts, as people could get there easily.
- Steamships led to greater sea travel and the establishment of the Dover to Calais route thus encouraging overseas tourism.

- The urban life that had developed as a result of the industrial revolution had become unhealthy and unpleasant. Workers longed to escape from city life.

- The population also wanted to escape their monotonous routines dictated by factory work and working life.

- Although leisure time remained restricted, the Bank Holiday Act of 1871 created four public holidays per year. In addition, workers had Sundays free, but they were encouraged to think of Sunday as a day of rest or worship.

Figure 1.4 *A steamship, from the early nineteenth century*

Source: The Science Museum

Early twentieth century developments

In the first half of the twentieth century the travel and tourism industry continued to grow. Steady improvements in transport, outgoing attitudes and the fact that the continent was politically stable all contributed. At this time, passports were not required.

The French Riviera became popular as a winter destination with approximately 50,000 British visitors in the pre-war years. The First World War prevented travel temporarily. However, it also resulted in increasing curiosity about foreign countries and more overseas travel in the inter-war years. The car (developed in 1908 by Henry Ford) began to take over from the railways as the main form of transport.

Commercial air services began between the wars, in 1919. However, the London to Paris price of £16 was nearly a month's wages! It was not until the post-war years that the aviation industry really developed, and this was a direct result of technological advancements in aviation during the war, and a surplus of aircraft. At this stage, although outbound tourism was emerging, domestic tourism was predominant, to the seaside and, later on, to the holiday camp. Suntans became a status symbol and the beautiful Victorian resorts of Scarborough and Brighton became even more popular. The holiday by the seaside was firmly established in the British culture.

Developments since World War Two

The tourism industry has grown phenomenally since 1945. The conditions of the nineteenth century provided the basis for the explosion of tourism after the wars. We will now examine those factors that have contributed towards the mass tourism of the twentieth century.

Socio-economic circumstances

Car ownership

We now take for granted the private transport provided by the private motor car, with 70% of households currently having one or more cars (ONS, 1977).

It was not until this century, however, that the motor car became a popular mode of transport. In 1908 Henry Ford developed his popular T model in the USA. Due to factory production (economies of scale) the cost of the car was reduced and became affordable for the masses. As a result the car was no longer only for the upper and middle classes and soon began to threaten the railways as a preferred mode of transport.

1919	250,000
1929	1.5 million
1951	2.2 million
1960	5.5 million
1970	11.6 million
1987	17.9 million
1990	20.2 million
1994	21.2 million
1997	22.8 million

Table 1.2 *UK car ownership*
Source: Social Trends, ONS

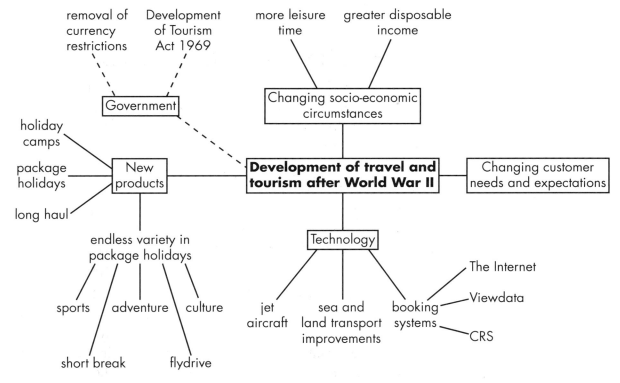

Figure 1.5 *Reasons for the development of travel and tourism in the UK*

ACTIVITY

Refer to Table 1.2. Draw a line graph to show the increase in car ownership. Be careful to draw this to scale and label the axis correctly.

Consider the impact of this increase on the railways.

The BTA publish statistics comparing modes of transport for domestic holidays. Establish the trends in the post-war years.

Car ownership increased six-fold in the ten years following 1919. There are now ten times as many cars on the road as in 1951. It is estimated by the Office for National Statistics that there are now nearly 23 million cars on the roads in Great Britain.

With the increased popularity of the motor car the railways and other public transport systems have suffered from a lack in demand.

Impacts of increased car ownership

1 Congestion and pollution
  The result of 23 million cars on British roads is congestion and high levels of pollution. The 1990s were a period of increased environmental awareness and of the government encouraging use of public transport. However, the high cost of public transport compared to that of the car has meant that to date these efforts have had little success.

2 New products
  Tour operators have to adapt their products to the changing transport methods. Packages can now be bought to cater for those who wish to travel with their own car within the UK. Short break holidays are commonplace; caravaning has emerged as a new form of holiday. In addition, outbound tour operators have developed the fly-drive package and 'self-drive' touring and camping packages, all of which allow total flexibility. Tour operators and regional Tourist Boards have also 'packaged' their local attractions to suit the visitors with cars (see Figure 1.6).

3 Increased access to the countryside and attractions
  The transport network throughout the UK has developed in conjunction with, and perhaps because of, the increase in car ownership. The motorway links across the UK are also now extensive and as a result, day trips are much more accessible. The countryside and associated leisure pursuits have also grown in popularity.

A Driveabout Tour From Harrogate Through JAMES HERRIOT COUNTRYSIDE

Figure 1.6 *A local attraction: James Herriot Driveabout Tour Source: Harrogate Borough Council*

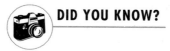

DID YOU KNOW?

There are approximately 22 million visits to the Peak District National Park each year. 90% of visitors arrive by car.

ACTIVITY

Investigate how far you can travel from your home town within two hours.

Establish the attractions that are within this two hour radius (natural and man-made).

Divide the class into groups. Each group will investigate the development of one of these attractions since 1945. Produce your findings as a display.

To what extent do you think the development of these attractions is a result of increased car ownership and improved road networks?

Figure 1.7 Reasons for an increase in leisure time

YEAR	NO. OF MEMBERS
1900	250
1910	650
1920	700
1930	2,000
1940	6,800
1950	23,402
1960	97,109
1970	226,069
1980	1,010,251
1990	2,031,743
1998	2,488,718

Table 1.3 *National Trust membership*
  Source: *The National Trust, 1998*

Increase in leisure time

The increase in leisure time can be attributed to several factors (see Figure 1.7) all of which contribute to the fact that we have more time to pursue leisure activities than was available to our grandparents. How we spend this time varies greatly, depending largely on age, tastes, income and expectations. The result is an increase in the demand for facilities and attractions for us to visit.

It was not until 1908, when the Holidays with Pay Act was introduced, that it became a legal requirement for employers to give their staff **paid holidays**. Prior to this, paid holidays were very rare.

Since 1908, the annual amount of paid holiday entitlement has gradually increased. By 1951 66% of manual workers were allowed two weeks holiday every year and by 1970, 52% had three or more weeks. 94% of UK employees now receive at least four weeks paid holiday per year. Many employers have systems of holiday entitlements according to the length of employee service. New employees may only receive the minimum entitlement, whereas established employees may be rewarded by extra days.

The impact of paid holidays on the travel and tourism industry has been fundamental. Workers can now take time off work and still receive an income. The increased holiday entitlement throughout the last century has contributed to the explosion in tourism, with an increasing number of people now taking more than one holiday per year.

The **working week has been shortened** to a norm of 37 hours, compared to a 50 hour working week in the 1950s when working on Saturdays, for at least half a day, was considered to be normal.

Some employers now offer flexitime as a staff benefit. This is of great benefit to the travel and tourism industry, allowing for long weekends and coinciding with the increasing popularity of short breaks, both domestic and European.

Labour saving devices result directly in increased leisure time. In the period following World War Two, washing was a weekly activity that generally took up a whole day. Although machines were used, clothes had to be moved from machine to mangle and hung out to dry, as automatic washing machines and tumble dryers did not exist. Similarly, the preparation of meals was time-consuming. Microwaves, ready-made meals and dishwashers are phenonoma of the last 20 years only. Maintaining a household was traditionally considered to be a full-time job, and was usually carried out by women.

The **longer life span** of the population combined with the current trend for early retirement means that there is an increasing demand for tourism and other leisure activities for the 50 year plus age group. The profile of such people is attractive to tour operators. They are often wealthier than younger people, because they may have finished paying their mortgage and their children will have left home. Due to healthier lifestyles, this age group are fitter than a century ago and they also have the time to take several holidays a year.

CASE STUDY *Saga Holidays*

Saga began when its founder, Sidney De Haan OBE, first offered holidays in Britain for retired people in 1951. The holidays were low cost, good value, and were sold direct to customers. At a time when most commercial organisations failed to recognise the retired market as having value, Saga grew quickly, expanding its products and passenger volume.

During the 1950s, 60s and 70s, Saga's development reflected the increasing sophistication and affluence of its retired customers, as Mediterranean holidays, cruises, long haul holidays, special interest tours, short breaks, etc., were added to the British holiday portfolio. Saga continued to sell these holidays principally through direct mail, so that as it grew the company developed a very extensive mailing list. As the number of affluent retired people in Britain has increased, so Saga has introduced more and more sophisticated holidays to meet these customers' aspirations.

In 1995 the company lowered its qualifying age limit from 60 to 50, thereby increasing its potential market in the UK from 11 to 19 million people. Today, Saga's product range covers a broad spectrum of different types of holiday in the UK, Europe and the Mediterranean, worldwide and cruises. Customer preferences vary enormously and this is reflected in the diversity of holiday brochures – Saga customers can experience anything from a week at the traditional seaside resort of Bournemouth to a walk in the Borneo rainforest, a Caribbean cruise on our cruise ship, Saga Rose, or the ultimate round the world adventure.

ACTIVITY

Discuss the possible reason(s) for the success of Saga Holidays.

Research the percentage of the population over 50 years of age. How is this changing?

DID YOU KNOW?

On average, people in the UK have 40 hours free time per week.

Although unemployment appears to have stabilised in more recent years, there is still an unemployment rate of just under three million people at the start of the twenty first century. The unemployed do however, have leisure time, although they may not necessarily have a lot of money for making use of tourism attractions or products.

ACTIVITY

Interview people of your parents' and grandparents' generation. Ask questions to establish the following information:

How much leisure time did they have per week when they were your age?

What labour saving devices did they have, if any, in their households?

When did they first have a car?

When did they first use a telephone?

Details of their first holiday – where did they go, how did they get there and what was it like?

Increased disposable income

Disposable income refers to money left over after all necessary expenditure on food, the mortgage, clothing and bills, has been paid. There has been a general trend in the UK for disposable incomes to rise. Average household disposable incomes rose by over 55% between 1971 and 1996. This has resulted in increased expenditure on leisure activities, including travel and tourism.

Technological developments

Technological changes in travel and tourism began with the Industrial Revolution and the use of steam power. Since then, new products have been developed continuously, from TV and telephone systems to cash point machines and personal CDs. Changes in technology are affecting us all. Consumer goods that are commonplace today, simply were not used ten years ago, for example the Internet, mobile phones and digital TV.

The travel and tourism industry has developed as a direct result of technological developments – we would not have been able to travel without the technology of steam in the nineteenth century and that of the aircraft in the twentieth century. Technology is, however, making the industry increasingly sophisticated. We can now book holidays by telephone or even via the Internet, and we can also pay by either debit or credit card. Travel agents use sophisticated computer reservation systems to book flights, holidays and any extra services that customers may require.

As has been already mentioned, the surplus of propeller aircraft available after the war was a major factor in the development in tourism. However, for air travel to become available to more of the population, the prices needed to be lower. This began to happen during the 1950s as aircraft became larger and faster. The most significant development for air travel was the introduction of jet aircraft during this period and

ACTIVITY

Analyse the table and graphs below. What conclusions can you draw from these?

1. **Food, housing and leisure trends**
% of total expenditure spent on:

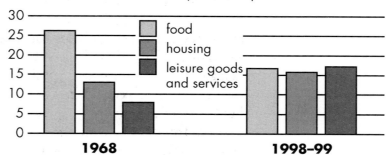

Legend: food / housing / leisure goods and services

1968   1998–99

2.   UK Average household weekly spending

	1998–9		1968	
	£ per week	% of total expenditure	£ per week (1998–99 prices)	% of total expenditure
Leisure	£59.80	17	£21.13	9
Food & non-alcoholic drinks	£58.90	17	£63.90	26
Housing	£57.20	16	£30.74	13
Motoring	£51.70	15	£25.41	10
Household goods & services	£48.60	14	£28.81	12
Clothing & Footwear	£21.70	6	£21.54	9
Alcoholic drink	£14.00	4	£9.92	4
Personal goods and services	£13.30	4	£6.21	3
Fuel & Power	£11.70	3	£15.01	13
Fares & other travel costs	£8.30	2	£6.35	3
Tobacco	£5.80	2	£12.59	5
Miscellaneous	£1.20	0	0.73	0
Total Expenditure	**£352.20**		**£242.34**	

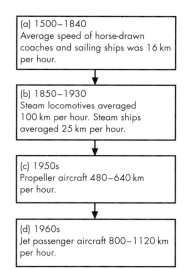

(a) 1500–1840
Average speed of horse-drawn coaches and sailing ships was 16 km per hour.

(b) 1850–1930
Steam locomotives averaged 100 km per hour. Steam ships averaged 25 km per hour.

(c) 1950s
Propeller aircraft 480–640 km per hour.

(d) 1960s
Jet passenger aircraft 800–1120 km per hour.

Figure 1.8 The world has become smaller: reductions in travel times
Source: The Business of Tourism

in particular the Boeing 707 in 1958. Air travel was now fast, safe, comfortable and, relative to ten years earlier, it was cheap. The new jets had speeds of 800 to 1,120 km per hour, compared to the 480 to 650 km per hour of the propeller-driven aircraft.

Further technological developments occurred in 1969 with the jumbo jet (Boeing 747). This aircraft had several impacts on the package holiday market:

- It was possible to fly further in less time, thus making long haul destinations more accessible.
- The increased capacity (400 seats) on the jumbo jet also meant that the price per seat was reduced, thus lowering package holiday prices further.
- As jumbo jets began to be used more, the smaller aircraft were available for charter operations.

Long-haul travel was less exhausting and, as a result, business travel increased. The ocean liners now had competition and the introduction of the jet aircraft resulted in their demise.

Changes in booking systems

Bookings in the period following World War Two were simple to take, as airlines and travel operators had charts on the walls of their offices and took bookings either by telephone or through written enquiries. As demand for travel grew, these businesses developed reservations departments. Teams of people were required, sitting in large rooms wearing headsets, taking orders from agents or directly from the general public. Booking forms had to be signed by the clients and sent to the tour operators in order to secure the booking (many tour operators still have reservations teams as the general public still prefer to talk to someone about their holidays).

With the development of computers, tour operators and airlines developed their own systems. Initially these were just used 'in-house' (a sophisticated version of the wall-chart) and travel agents still had to telephone to make bookings.

It was not long, however, before the tour operators linked their system into terminals in the agencies through which bookings could be made, known as **viewdata systems**.

The move by Thomson to accept bookings only via viewdata meant that without viewdata, travel agencies could not make a booking with the UK's largest tour operator. As a result, viewdata became essential to the travel agent.

By today's standards, viewdata could be regarded as simple and out-of-date technology. It comprises a screen that displays information transmitted by public telephone lines. In the late 1980s however, the move to viewdata was a huge leap forward. By 1987 85% of all package holidays were booked through this system and it is estimated that there were 23,000 terminals distributed in travel agencies throughout the UK. Despite being unsophisticated in terms of its speed and lack of flexibility, it remains the main tool used by tour operators to sell their holidays today, because travel agents have this technology and many are reluctant to invest in newer systems.

Whereas the viewdata system was really developed by tour operators, it was the airlines who developed **computer reservation systems (CRS)**. Airlines started to use computers in the 1950s to store and change the huge amount of information that they needed access to: flight times, fares, seat availability and passenger reservations. At this time the CRS was used internally by the airlines and if agents needed the same information they used the OAG (then Reed) publications and then telephoned the airline to make a booking. Today travel agencies have direct access to the airlines information via the CRS.

The market leader in the UK for CRS is Galileo. Sabre, Worldspan and Amadeus are also used throughout the travel trade. Today there is a wealth of information available on all these systems.

As you read more about technology in the travel trade you will come across the term global distribution system **GDS**. This is a system which links up several CRS's and presents the information together to the user, usually the travel agent.

DID YOU KNOW?

OAG is the travel industries' leading provider of information. It is best known for its flight guides, but it does also publish, amongst others, a *Cruise and Ferry Guide*, *Hotel Travel Index* and a *Guide to International Travel*. Much of this information is now also available on CD ROM. For more information on OAG, access the website at www.oag.com.

CASE STUDY *Dirty tricks?*

In January 1993 the general public were made aware of a campaign apparently being launched by British Airways against Virgin Airlines. Information made available to BA through their computer technology was being mis-used. The aim of the campaign appeared to be to undermine Richard Branson's airline by reducing his profits and credibility. The campaign was based on the fact that Virgin, like many smaller airlines, could not afford to develop its own reservation system and so rented space on another. Virgin, in fact, uses the BA system BABS. This meant that BA were able to access the details of Virgin's clients and offer them alternative flights on BA. BA staff persuaded clients to switch flights through offering extra perks, such as free airport limousine transfer. Richard Branson took BA to court and in January 1993 was awarded £610,000 in damages. BA was publicly humiliated.

Source: Adapted from Financial Times, *12 January 1993*

ACTIVITY

Galileo is the leading CRS/GDS in the UK. Use the Galileo website at **www.galileo.com** to research the company and its products.

Who founded the company and when?

Where is its UK base?

Establish what it does and where?

What is the company's vision?

How many travel agencies are connected to Galileo?

What information/products does it provide them with?

CASE STUDY *UK travel agents and the Internet*

Surveys show that 84% of travel agencies have Internet connections and awareness of the net within the trade is high. However, few have a website and simply use the Internet for browsing or for E-mail.

One exception is Co-op Travelcare. They have their own website at **www.holidaydeals.com** and have recently offered a late availability centre at the same site. Offers from tour operators, airlines, car hire companies, Eurostar, Le Shuttle cruise and ferry operators are available to all. The Co-op search facility interacts with databases from Thomson, Airtours and First Choice, with the result that late availability details can be found easily and cheaply. The result is that this website handled £300 million of holidays per year in 1999.

Unless travel agents are more proactive and develop their own sites, consumers will access the other networks available or book directly with operators. Travel city (**www.travelcity.com**) is a website run and owned by Sabre. This site offers all its CRS facilities, which one could normally only access through a travel agency, direct to the public. Sabre hopes to gain a share of the on line ticketing revenues, estimated to be worth $8 billion.

Expedia (**www.expedia.com**) is Microsoft's own Internet-based ticketing system. Through this site, international flights can be booked on line, using a credit card. Started in 1997, it is now the fifth largest agency in the world, and takes an average income of $3m per week.

Source: Adapted from Insights, *March 1999*

The Internet is clearly a development that may change the face of travel and tourism reservations and the role of agencies. Home shopping may cause travel agents either to fade away or force them to offer a specialised service.

Product development and innovation

The holidays available at the end of World War Two are incomparable to the variety, comfort and style of those available at the beginning of the twenty first century (look again at your results of investigation to the Activity on page 13, where you interviewed people of your parents' and grandparents' generations).

Billy Butlin was one of the first entrepreneurs to respond to the needs of the holiday-maker. When he purchased his first site in Skegness in 1936, he can hardly have imagined the way in which holiday centres would evolve to include Warners' Pontins and Center Parcs today. The decline of the holiday camps was a direct result of the rise of the package holiday overseas in the late 1960s. Today the latter remains the most favoured holiday product, although it has become increasingly sophisticated and varied.

CASE STUDY *Butlins*

When Billy Butlin was on holiday in Skegness he came across a group of miserable holiday-makers, sitting on a bench in the rain. They had nowhere to go, it being the custom to stay away from the 'boarding' house from late morning until late afternoon. He saw the opportunity for providing for these people, and opened up his first holiday camp in Skegness in 1936. The appeal of Butlins was that it provided, on one site, all the facilities and entertainment a family could wish for, including childcare, swimming lessons, bingo and ball-room dancing. Full-board accommodation was provided in the all inclusive price of £3.50 per week.

Although this price was in fact initially too expensive for manual workers, the post-war period saw a huge rise in demand for this style of holiday. Between 1945 and 1960 the holiday camps were at their peak, catering for about 60% of the holiday market. Butlin built other camps to cater for the demand and competitors emerged – Pontins and Warners. These three companies operated a total of 44 camps between them in 1970.

By the 1970s the decreasing price of the package holiday and the desire for sunshine led to the decline of the holiday camp.

Butlins today

The Rank Organisation purchased and re-launched Butlins in the 1990s. It closed many camps, but re-launched five as Holiday Worlds. All were upgraded by improving, and in some cases replacing, the accommodation and designing all weather facilities.

Approximately £50 million has been spent at each centre to revitalise the product for the more demanding consumer. The Holiday Camps of the twenty first century are now called Family Entertainment Resorts, aiming to attract the short break market and opening all year round. By the time improvements have been finished, it is estimated that the Rank organisation will have invested around £350 million in Butlins in a little over a decade. This is in response to consumer demand for:

- high quality
- short breaks
- year round operation

Source: Adapted from Insights, *July 1998*

As can be seen from the Butlins case study, today's holiday-makers are a long way removed from the 'hi-de-hi' consumers that went to Butlins 50 to 60 years ago.

The development of the package holiday

Thomas Cook is often cited as being the first person to organise a package holiday. He took his passengers by train from Loughborough to Leicester in 1841 for a temperance meeting (i.e. promoting abstention from alcohol!).

KEY TERM

Package holiday (also known as an inclusive tour): a combination of transportation, accommodation, transfers and any ancillary services (e.g. car hire or insurance) sold at one price.

ACTIVITY

Find out more about the first package holiday on the Thomas Cook website.

DID YOU KNOW?

In 1998 approximately 84% of the package holiday market was by air travel (source: www.thomson-holidays.com).

It was the faster cheaper air transport, however, that led to the growth in the numbers of people travelling, and they chose to travel by an air package holiday due to its ease and safety.

Vladimir Raitz, is the person who first organised a package holiday as we know it today. In 1949 he used a DC3 to carry 32 holiday-makers to Corsica at a price of £32 and 10 shillings. His package included return flights, transfers to the hotel, accommodation (in tents) and full-board. By chartering a flight and filling every seat, he managed to lower the price for every passenger. He established Horizon Holidays in the same year and carried 300 passengers, and by the end of the 1950s he was chartering planes to Palma, Alghero and Perpignan, Malaga, Tangier and Oporto.

Package holidays such as these were recognised to be profitable operations by many other entrepreneurs, with the result that by the early 1960s package holidays to the Mediterranean coast were an established product. Although the Spanish coast and Balearic Islands received most of these tourists, Italy and Greece were also beneficiaries.

New hotels had been built to accommodate the tourist boom. In comparison to the simple accommodation of British guest houses and holiday camps, this was luxurious. However, in many other respects, and by today's standards, these holidays were simple. Excursions and entertainment were minimal. The excitement and change of being abroad was in itself sufficient attraction to those travelling.

Further factors encouraged the development of the package holiday in the 1970s:

- The lifting of the government restrictions that would only allow the equivalent of £50 per person to be taken abroad.
- Longer paid holidays in the 1970s encouraged people to take a second holiday.
- The wide bodied jet appeared in 1970, reducing airfares further (see previous section on technological developments).

Changing consumer needs, expectations and fashions

This has led to many developments in package holidays. The last two decades have seen continual development of the variety of package holidays available. The simple sun holidays of the 1960s no longer appeal to today's customer, and the changes that have been made by the Rank Organisation to satisfy today's consumer exemplify this. The basic accommodation and lack of flexibility that characterised the holiday camps of the post-war period are no longer suitable for the consumer of the twenty first century.

Today's traveller requires flexibility. Although demand for the package holiday remains high, the packages have been adapted to allow for flexibility. Holiday-makers wish to choose the type of accommodation, the board basis, the type of transport and the length of holiday.

The development of fly-drive packages in the 1970s reflected the demand for independence within a package. The growth in self-catering and increased demand for car hire also reflects our changing travel and tourism needs. More and more people now travel independently rather than booking a package holiday. This reflects consumers' growing confidence – many people are well travelled and so do not need the security of the package deal.

PROFILE *Paris Travel Service (PTS)*

Prior to its purchase by Airtours, Paris Travel Service was one of a group of specialist companies belonging to the Bridge Group. Founded in 1955, PTS was the market leading tour operator offering holidays to Paris.

The brochure for this product is noteworthy in that it is able to offer a totally flexible package for their clients:

- **A choice of transport – Eurostar, flight or coach. 16 airport departure points.**
- **A range of accommodation from budget to 5 star. Within each rating approximately 20 hotels are offered, in different areas of Paris.**

Optional extra services also mean that customers can be as independent or 'packaged' as they wish:

- **Overnight hotels in the UK if required.**
- **Extensions to Venice on the Orient Express.**
- **Optional transfer service.**
- **Meal vouchers if required.**
- **Discounted metro pass.**

DID YOU KNOW?

About 3 million people take short breaks in addition to their main holiday.

The second holiday

As our leisure time increases and our disposable income rises, the phenomenon of the second holiday has emerged. Ski-ing developed in the 1970s as a second (winter) holiday and the 1980s saw the development of the short break market. Although this has benefited the domestic market, the overseas city break is now commonplace, with all major operators producing a 'cities brochure.' Thomson Holidays added nine new destinations to its 2000 brochure and claims a 30% increase in sales.

City breaks also reflect the fact that although we now travel overseas more, it tends to be for shorter periods of time. The average length of stay of holidays has reduced.

Other types of holiday

While beach holidays remain the most popular type of package holiday, other types of holiday have emerged. Culture, sporting and adventure holidays are now all catered for. Adventure holidays, which include specific activities such as hiking or white water rafting, have become particularly successful.

As has been stated, beach holidays remain the most popular form of package holiday. However, consumers also now want activities at their resort. Many beach holidays therefore offer particular activities, for example, parascending, sailing, scuba diving and other water sports.

In terms of destinations, there has been continual growth in the long haul sector. This has resulted from the development of the jumbo jet and the fact that we can now travel more cheaply and quickly to such destinations as the Caribbean, the USA and Kenya. Charter flights to long haul destinations started in the 1970s, bringing prices down further.

Due to the growth of the long haul sector, the **winter sun** holiday has become common place. It is now no longer necessary to have your sunshine holiday during the European summer. **Cruising** has also developed as a mass market product; it is no longer the preserve of the wealthy (Airtours launched its first cruise in the early 1990s).

The **all-inclusive holiday** saw a rapid increase in popularity in the 1990s.

Quality and customer service

Throughout these developments, the consumer has increasingly demanded higher standards of quality and customer service. Today's tourist is well travelled and aware of his or her rights. Tour operators therefore have to be increasingly aware of consumer rights and European legislation.

Environmental awareness

Consumers are becoming increasingly environmentally aware, as some holiday destinations have been damaged or ruined by tourism. The Costas of Spain, the first mass tourism destinations, suffered a decline in the 1980s when people became aware of alternative destinations and the fact that the Spanish environment was dominated by high-rise buildings and provision for tourists. Not only was the environment unattractive, but there was very little of the 'real Spain' to be found. In response to this the Spanish Tourist Board began to market inland Spain, so that it could continue to attract tourists.

Budget airlines

The development of low cost airlines was a major development at the end of the 1990s. Their low costs, brash marketing techniques and ticketless travel is changing the face of the aviation industry today. Some of the formalities of air travel are being removed, and this has caused

DID YOU KNOW?

The growth in consumer programmes, in particular *Watchdog*, has changed the face of British tour operating. Some tour operators believe that customers take their notebook and video camera on holiday, rather than sun lotion and beach towel. The programme is believed to have encouraged a complaint culture.

ACTIVITY

As you can read in the article from *Travel Weekly*, all-inclusive holidays have become a very popular holiday product. However, some do not in fact include 'all', as the name implies. Some may include all meals, drinks, sports, entertainment, children's clubs and even local language lessons. Others restrict the inclusive elements to some sports (often windsurfing, but not waterskiing!) and only locally produced drinks.

ALL-INCLUSIVES

Club Med introduced the all-inclusive concept to the Mediterranean in the 1950s. But only since mass-market operators warmed to the idea has the all-inclusive concept gained widespread popularity.

Throughout the Mediterranean, hotels are switching from half board to all-inclusive arrangements in a bid to boost business.

In the Caribbean, where the concept is well-established, the number of all-inclusive properties continues to expand rapidly. The Dominican Republic's accommodation base is almost entirely sold as all-inclusive.

The trend has spread well beyond Jamaica, St Lucia, Antigua and Barbados. While Clubs International recently introduced an all-inclusive safari option in Kenya, Kuoni is featuring 'cash-free' packages in Mauritius this year.

Kuoni deputy managing director Sue Biggs said that while there was little sign of all-inclusives' popularity abating in the long-haul market, operators needed to constantly update the product.

"We need to keep innovating because once clients go all-inclusive they get hooked," she said. "It is a very relaxing holiday because after you have paid in the UK you really don't need to take any money."

According to Biggs, it remains crucial that operators make clear to customers what an all-inclusive holiday offers. "It most certainly isn't the right holiday for people who want to get involved in local culture, cuisine or sightseeing," she said. "But if the client wants swimming or watersports, or to get some sunshine, then it's a perfect holiday."

Gather five different all-inclusive brochures. Compare the packages to establish what is included and what is not. Which package do you think actually offers the best value for money?

Why are all-inclusives in Africa so much cheaper than in the Caribbean countries?

concern amongst some major airlines, who appear to be losing business. British Airways has responded to this concern by focusing on business passengers. Budget airlines have made European destinations even more accessible for the consumer and has also contributed to the growth in short breaks and independent travel.

ACTIVITY

The variety in package holidays available to you in the twenty first century is endless. Using a variety of up-to-date brochures, select holidays for the following clients. Remember to justify your choices.

	DESTINATION	REASONS
Sally and Alan want to get married overseas.		
A group of four students wish to go on an adventure/activity style holiday. They want to stay within Europe.		
Sanjay and Natalie wish to spend a cultural weekend away.		
The Gee family need a fortnight away. They will take their children, aged 9 and 15 years, with them. However, there must be plenty for them to do.		
John and Gillian are in their 50s. They are looking for a walking holiday with a group of like-minded people.		

Note: although you will find brochures in the travel agents, there are also many direct-sell tour operators, i.e. they sell directly to you rather than through a travel agent. You must look in the Sunday newspapers or specialist magazines to find their advertisements. Alternatively, look them up on the Internet or the in the *TTG Directory*.

DID YOU KNOW?

The *TTG Directory* publishes a list of UK tour operators by their specialist activity and destination.

Future developments

The pace of change in tourism is speeding up all the time. Further changes in consumer expectations, transportation methods and other technology will ensure continued development in travel and tourism in the future. It is, however, highly unlikely that the rate of tourism growth established since the Second World War will be sustained over the next 50 years.

While it is expected that our traditional sunshine holidays will remain popular, long haul travel is expected to grow, as is the demand for active and healthy holidays. To date, the threat of skin cancer has had little impact on the sun lover, apart from the purchase of higher factor sun protection lotions. The risks may yet cause future generations to change our established habits.

Our increasingly high demands are likely to result in improved holiday accommodation. More flexibility may be offered through package holidays, but it is perhaps more likely that we will choose to travel either independently or on a 'pick and mix' basis.

Advances in computer technology will allow for this increasing flexibility and independence. Virtual travel will allow us too 'check out' resorts and then book each item (transport, accommodation, etc.) independently. We will be able to pay via a screen in our own homes. These changes could fundamentally alter the role of both the travel agent and tour operator.

ACTIVITY

In groups discuss the impact that you think the Internet will have on the travel trade. How many people do you know that:

- Have access to the web?
- Use it regularly?
- Have purchased a holiday over the web?
- Would purchase a holiday over the web?

DID YOU KNOW?

By December 1998 there were 4,251 tourism sites recorded in the Internet directory (*www.internet-directory.co.uk*).

Looking further into the future

Changes in transport technology, whilst continuing to develop, are not likely to change much in the near future. A development that has an impact on the industry, similar to that of the jet aircraft, is unlikely to happen until space travel becomes a reality. The US aircraft industry is researching the possibility of aircraft capable of leaving and re-entering the earth's atmosphere. Such a development would reduce the flight time from London to Sydney to just over an hour. Similar advances with sea vessels and road and rail transport are also currently being researched. At some stage in the future we may be able to cross the Atlantic by sea in just two hours and travel overland at 300 mph.

We may, however, not wish to leave home. Virtual travel – experiencing travel through a computer screen while sitting in one's armchair – may appeal to some. For those that are unable to travel at the present time, be it due to disability or lack of finance, this would be a wonderful opportunity.

Structure of the travel and tourism industry

When defining the travel and tourism industry at the beginning of this chapter, we established that it includes everything a visitor does during their stay. As we know, this makes the travel and tourism industry very large. More importantly for this section, however, it also makes it extremely fragmented. Everything from the hotel in which you stay, the transport used, the ice-cream you eat, souvenirs bought and the meals you eat become part of the industry.

It is a much more wide-ranging industry than most, as there are few industries in the world that are linked to so many different kinds of products and services.

❝ Tourism is of vital importance to the nation's economy and it touches on every aspect of national life. But tourism is also a highly fragmented industry, made up of 120,000 businesses as well as a huge number of government departments and agencies, local authorities and national bodies covering everything from transport to heritage, all with an interest in tourism. ❞

Source: Mr Alan Britten at the launch of the English Tourism Council in July 1999

In this section we will look at all the components of the travel and tourism industry, and we will also establish their motives. For example, are they a commercial organisation, aiming to make a profit or are they provided by government organisations to provide a service? Alternatively, are they a voluntary organisation? The aims of organisations within each sector – how and if they generate money and the expectations of those involved in them – will also be raised.

We will examine each of the following components:

- tourist attractions
- accommodation and catering
- tourism development and promotion
- transportation
- travel agents
- tour operators

Once we have established the structure of the industry, how it functions and examined the key organisations, we will be able to investigate the **features** of this constantly changing industry (see page 53).

Commercial and non-commercial organisations

But first we must understand the different types of organisations. These are commonly referred to as the private, public and voluntary sectors. Each has differing objectives, methods of generating or receiving money and the people involved in them (stakeholders) have differing expectations.

Private sector organisations

Most organisations within travel and tourism belong to the private sector. These organisations can be large companies, such as British Airways and the tour operator Thomson Holidays, or small businesses owned and run by one person, such as the local tour guide or a tea shop. The one thing that they all have in common is that their main aim is to make a profit. Although they will all have other aims, (for example, to increase turnover or provide good customer care) if their main aim of making a profit is not being fulfilled they will simply cease trading.

The travel and tourism industry is dominated by private sector companies, most of which are small or medium sized. All theme parks, hotels, restaurants, travel agencies and tour operators in the UK are privately owned. Many of these may be sole proprietors (a one person business), for example, independent travel agencies, ski instructors, a blue badge Guide or a local coach company. Others are large Public Limited Companies (PLCs) which are owned by the general public who have shares in the company. British Airways, for example, used to be owned by the government but is now a PLC.

Unless the company makes a profit, the shareholders do not receive their share of the profits (dividends.) Other PLCs include The Tussauds Group (who own Alton Towers), Forte and the three major tour operators – Thomson, Airtours and First Choice.

Public sector organisations

Public sector organisations receive their funds though local or central government and, broadly speaking, are aiming to provide a service. Examples include the Tourist Boards and English Tourism Council, some local visitor attractions (for example, museums or galleries) and English Heritage. British Rail was a public sector service until it was privatised in the mid-1990s.

Funds for public sector tourism organisations come either from central government via the Department of Culture, Media and Sport (DCMS) or through local councils. The stakeholders of such organisations do not judge the organisation in terms of financial success; their objectives are more likely to be concerned with such issues as numbers of tourists, quality, and environmental issues.

ACTIVITY

The Department of Culture, Media and Sport (DCMS) is the part of the government responsible for tourism. It also looks after the arts, sport and recreation, the National Lottery, libraries, museums, film, broadcasting (TV), press freedom and regulation, the built heritage and the royal estate. It has its own website at **www.culture.gov.uk**.

Access the website of the DCMS.

Who is the Secretary of State (i.e. the Minister in charge of the department) and what is the aim of the Department?

How much money does the DCMS receive from the government and how do they spend it?

Voluntary sector organisations

Voluntary sector organisations often have charitable status. Many are run by volunteers, although some have paid employees. Many voluntary organisations are pressure groups, for example, Green Peace and Tourism Concern. Others, for example, The National Trust, aim to preserve and protect historic buildings and landscapes and some museums are run on a voluntary basis.

This sector supplements activities that are not provided by the public and private sectors. They do not aim to make a profit, but many do need to generate an income in order to support their campaigns.

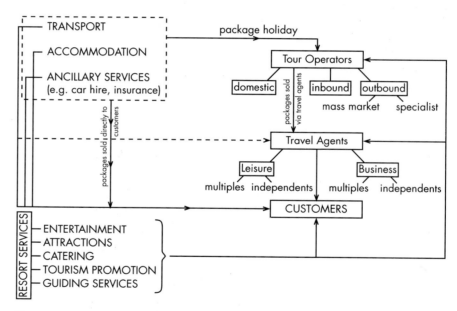

Figure 1.9 Component parts of the travel and tourism industry – and how they interact

ACTIVITY

Using their Annual Reports and Accounts research three organisations either from the college learning resource centre or via the Internet. Research one each from the public, private and voluntary sectors. (E.g. the English Tourism Council, Thomson Holidays or The National Trust)

For each organisation, note its objectives and how it is funded (or how it generates money).

Compare the organisations. Discuss how the expectations of those involved in the organisations (stakeholders and shareholders) may differ.

Tourist attractions

Man-made attractions

When you think of a tourist or visitor attraction, you may automatically think of a theme park, a museum or a famous historic site. These are all man-made attractions. Some may have been developed with the aim of making a profit from tourists, for example a theme park. Others attractions have existed for longer and aim to preserve beautiful or historic building and objects. They may also wish to educate, for example, the Victoria and Albert Museum, the Tate Gallery and the National Museum of Film and Photography.

MILLIONS	HISTORIC HOUSES	GARDENS	MUSEUMS & ART GALLERIES	WILDLIFE	OTHER	ALL
England	58.82	12.88	63.31	19.84	165.38	320.23
N. Ireland	0.60	1.10	0.94	0.48	6.20	9.33
Scotland	7.24	2.04	10.19	2.32	27.04	48.82
Wales	2.44	0.31	2.74	1.01	12.01	18.50
UK	69.10	16.33	77.18	23.66	210.63	396.89

Figure 1.10 Visits to attractions 1997

	THOUSANDS
1 Madame Tussaud's, London	2.799
2 Alton Towers, Staffordshire	2,702
3 Tower of London	2,615
4 Natural History Museum, London	1,793
5 Chessington World of Adventures, Surrey	1,750
6 Canterbury Cathedral	1,613
7 Science Museum, London	1,537
8 Legoland, Windsor	1,298
9 Edinburgh Castle	1,238
10 Blackpool Tower, Lancashire	1,200
11 Windermere Lake Cruises, Cumbria	1,132
12 Windsor Castle, Berkshire	1,130
13 Flamingo Land Theme Park, Yorkshire	1,103
14 London Zoo	1,098
15 Victoria and Albert Museum, London	1,041
16 Drayton Manor Park, Staffordshire	1,002
17 St. Paul's Cathedral, London	965
18 Kew Gardens, London	937
19 Roman Baths and Pump Room, Bath	934
20 Thorpe Park, Surrey	912

Figure 1.11 Top 20 attractions charging admission in 1997

Source: WWW.staruk.org.uk

ACTIVITY

Visit the BTA website at www.visitbritain.com to update the figures shown in Figures 1.10 and 1.11. You may also like to visit the English Tourism Council's website at www.english-tourism.org to compare the information available.

Natural tourist attractions

Attractions can also be natural. The beaches of Northumberland, the lakes of Cumbria and wilderness of Scotland are all natural attractions. In order to protect the UK's natural attractions, many areas have been designated as National Parks, Areas of Outstanding Natural Beauty (AONB) or Heritage Coasts. Other natural attractions include long distance paths and nature reserves.

Events as attractions

Tourist attractions may also be one-off events, for example, local fairs, festivals or shows. National one-off events that are visitor attractions include Glastonbury, the London Proms and the Edinburgh Festival. For the business traveller, trade shows are key one-off attractions: the Boat or Motor Shows, the World Travel Market or the Ideal Home Exhibition all attract the business visitor to the UK.

Shopping as a tourist attraction

Shopping remains a popular leisure activity for the British public. The development of American style malls ensures that shopping also continues to attract visitors from abroad. Bluewater is the latest shopping development in the UK. Located near Dartford, it has 320 shops, cafes, bars and cinemas, as well as a man-made lake which offers ice-skating and boating facilities.

 DID YOU KNOW?

Alton Towers was the number one admissions charging attraction for six consecutive years at the beginning of the 1990s.

 ## ACTIVITY

Theme parks in the UK attracted approximately 10 million visitors in 1997. This figure has been consistent up to the end of 1998, but there is concern that the market has now reached its peak.

Write an article for the BTA website, promoting British theme parks to overseas visitors. You will need to detail the rides available and additional services, such as catering, accommodation and shopping, that will enhance their visit. The following resources may help you:

- www.bpbltd.com (Blackpool Pleasure Beach)
- www.thorpepark.com
- www.alton-towers.co.uk
- www.legoland.co.uk
- *Insights* – market profile of UK theme parks, September 1998.

ACTIVITY

To check your knowledge of the UK visitor attractions and those in your local area, create a table similar to the one below. You will need to investigate visitor attractions in your local area. Although you may know some of the local visitor attractions from your own general knowledge, the attractions that appeal to you may not necessarily be the same as those that the overseas or day-trippers visit. You will therefore need to visit your local Tourist Information centre or its website, to ensure that you have examples of each category.

Which are the most popular visitor attractions in your area? Number the examples you have given in order of importance.

For each visitor attraction in your local area, identify whether it is in the private, public or voluntary sector.

	THREE EXAMPLES OF NATIONAL SIGNIFICANCE	A LOCAL EXAMPLE	PUBLIC/ PRIVATE/ VOLUNTARY
Historic house			
Garden			
Museum			
Art gallery			
Wildlife attraction			
Theme park			
Ancient/historic monument			
Religious building			

Accommodation and catering

ACTIVITY

Working with a partner, write down as many different types of accommodation as you can think of, for example, hotels, B&B, etc.

Compare your answers with other members of the group, to produce a comprehensive list.

As you can see from the list you have just produced in the previous activity, the range and variety of accommodation available to the travel and tourism industry is enormous. Some of the accommodation will be serviced (i.e. providing meals and housekeeping); others will be non serviced (self catering). Some accommodation will be single establishment (for example, a local B&B provider); others will be part of a chain of establishments (for example, Forte, Best Western and Moat House).

Business accommodation

The facilities provided in each establishment will be aimed at different travellers' needs. The business hotel will either be near an airport, a motorway junction or in the centre of a city. It will provide access to computers, desks in bedrooms, conference rooms and meeting facilities. Some hotels also provide a business suite where business people can go to use facilities, others provide facilities within the individual's room.

With the increasing emphasis on healthy lifestyles, many hotels now provide leisure facilities, such as gyms and swimming pools to help the busy executive stay in shape. The emphasis throughout will be on professional, fast but efficient service.

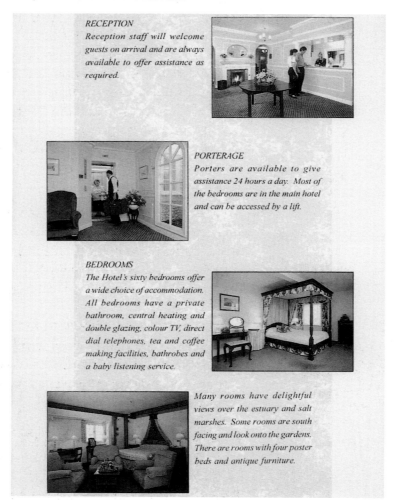

RECEPTION
Reception staff will welcome guests on arrival and are always available to offer assistance as required.

PORTERAGE
Porters are available to give assistance 24 hours a day. Most of the bedrooms are in the main hotel and can be accessed by a lift.

BEDROOMS
The Hotel's sixty bedrooms offer a wide choice of accommodation. All bedrooms have a private bathroom, central heating and double glazing, colour TV, direct dial telephones, tea and coffee making facilities, bathrobes and a baby listening service.

Many rooms have delightful views over the estuary and salt marshes. Some rooms are south facing and look onto the gardens. There are rooms with four poster beds and antique furniture.

Figure 1.12 Accommodation for the leisure traveller: The Blakeney Hotel
Source: Brochure for the Blakeney Hotel

Accommodation for leisure travellers

In contrast, the hotel aiming at the leisure traveller will want to be located away from the hustle and bustle of a business environment, in order to create a relaxed and friendly atmosphere (see Figure 1.12). Additional hotel features for the leisure traveller are very different from those for the business traveller – a log fire is more important than access to a PC!

Accommodation rating systems

As the tourist has become more and more demanding, accommodation providers have had to raise standards, offer flexible services and additional facilities. The range in standards of hotels and the variety of additional facilities they offer means that a system is required to enable the public and tour operators to book accommodation safe in the knowledge that certain standards are adhered to.

Until the year 2000 there were several hotel grading systems, provided by the motoring organisations (AA and RAC) and the National Tourist Boards, using a variety of symbols, inclusive of crowns, stars and keys. The AA, RAC and English Tourism Council (formerly the ETB) have now harmonised their schemes into one. It consists of two symbols, stars and diamonds. Hotels are now given between one and five stars by an inspector. Their award depends on 71 elements, covering all aspects of the visitors experience at the hotel in question. This includes cleanliness, services provided, bedroom comfort, food quality and public areas. The diamond rating will be awarded to guest houses, inns, farmhouses and B&Bs. The Scottish and Welsh Tourist Boards continue to offer separate schemes.

Almost all accommodation providers belong to the private sector. Their primary aim is, therefore, to make a profit. There are no public sector accommodation providers in the UK, unlike Spain and Portugal, where 'Paradores' have been established. These are government-owned buildings that have been converted into high quality tourist accommodation.

Youth Hostels Association (YHA)

The YHA is unique in the UK in that it provides accommodation within the voluntary sector. For a sample *YHA Vocational A Level Teacher Information Pack*, contact the YHA direct.

CASE STUDY *YHA: a force for sustainable tourism*

Recently voted one of the top ten places to stay in the *Observer* newspaper's Travel Awards, the Youth Hostels Association (England and Wales) has come a long way since its humble beginnings in 1930.

Formed as a joint initiative between rambling, cycling and youth organisations to meet an increasing demand for simple accommodation by walkers and cyclists, the YHA started life as a volunteer-run organisation with 6,000 members, and basic 'makeshift' accommodation funded by donations and grants.

Today, the YHA boasts a network of 230 Youth Hostels, spanning rural and urban locations, and over 13,000 beds throughout a rich variety of buildings – from converted medieval castles to purpose-built centres, with en suite rooms, located near the Millennium Dome and Granada Studios in Manchester. Funded by 260,000 contributing members, overnight and meal sales, it now has 1,000 paid staff, and a turnover of £28 million. As one of the top five accommodation providers in the UK, it is a major contributor to the tourism industry and a leading national charity.

However, YHA is not just an economic force. While others have recently discovered the concept of 'sustainable tourism', YHA's aim from the start has been to instil a knowledge and love for the countryside, and an understanding of the deeper values associated with our environment and heritage. YHA accommodation is a means to this end. Available to every age group – to individuals, families, groups and foreign visitors – Youth Hostels serve the educational and recreational needs of all. They signify good value accommodation, which is friendly, comfortable, dependable and secure. And, with YHA's continuing programme of re-investment and modernisation, they are set to remain a sustainable force in UK tourism for years to come.

ACTIVITY

Research the YHA in more depth. What are its objectives? How does it generate revenue/how is it funded? What are its stakeholders' expectation?

Catering establishments

These, as with accommodation establishments, vary in range, standards, quality of service and the facilities offered. Similar to accommodation, they are also dominated by the private sector. Examples range from the international chains of fast food restaurants that now dominate our high streets to local cafés and restaurants.

Tourism development and promotion

Tourism is developed and promoted by both commercial and non-commercial organisations at national, regional and local levels (see Table 1.4).

	ORGANISATION	**EXAMPLES**
National level	British Tourist Authority National Tourist Boards	English Tourism Council Welsh Tourist Board Scottish Tourist Board Northern Ireland Tourist Board
Regional level	Regional Tourist Boards	Cumbria Tourist Board East of England Tourist Board Heart Of England Tourist Board London Tourist Board Northumbria Tourist Board North West Tourist Board South East England Tourist Board Southern Tourist Board West Country Tourist Board North Wales Tourist Board Mid Wales Tourist Board South Wales Tourist Board
Local level	Tourist Information Centres	Brighton TIC Cambridge TIC Skegness TIC Windsor TIC
	Guiding services	Blue Badge Guides Guide Friday

Table 1.4 *Examples of the organisations that promote and develop tourism within the UK*

With the exception of Blue Badge Guides and Guide Friday, all the above organisations are partially funded through the Department of Culture, Media and Sport (DCMS) and form part of the public sector.

British Tourist Authority (BTA)

The British Tourist Authority was established under the Development of Tourism Act (1969). The BTA's responsibilities are as follows:

- To promote tourism to Britain from overseas.
- To advise government on tourism matters affecting Britain as a whole.
- To encourage the provision of tourist facilities and amenities in Britain.

It is funded primarily through grant-in aid from the DCMS. However, it also generates some of its own income through activities within the travel trade, publications and some public and private sector interests.

DID YOU KNOW?

In 1999 the BTA received a grant of £35 million from the DCMS. It generated another £16 million from its own activities.

In 1999 the BTA spent its money on:

● Promotional programmes, which encourage overseas visitors to extend their stay, visit new destinations or visit in low season periods.

● Running 43 offices in 36 countries.

● Providing an information service within these countries offering details on all parts of Britain.

● Market research and publication of results.

● Liaison with the travel trade to encourage sustainable development.

● Developing databases.

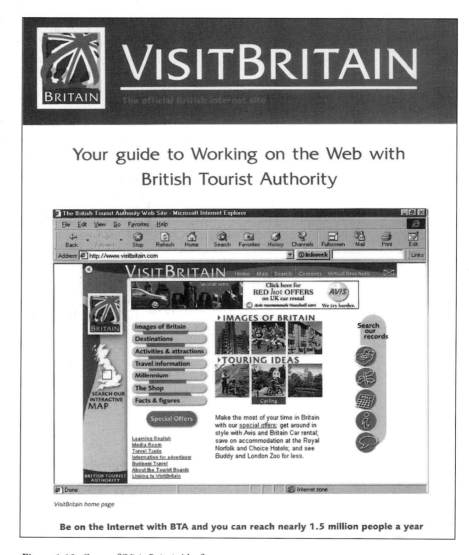

Figure 1.13 *Cover of 'Visit Britain' leafleat*

Source: BTA

Promotion by National Tourist Boards and the ETC

National Tourist Boards have traditionally promoted their own country. The Welsh Tourist Board (WTB), Northern Ireland Tourist

Board (NITB) and Scottish Tourist Board (STB) continue to do this. They have broadly similar objectives:

- Maximising the income and jobs generated by tourism.
- Creating a positive image of their country as a tourist destination.
- Advising the government and other public bodies on tourism matters.
- Encouraging sustainable development.
- Research.

The English Tourist Board was replaced by the English Tourism Council (ETC) in 1999. Its role is somewhat different. It supports the business of tourism by setting quality standards, researching markets and ensuring sustainability. The promotion of England is now carried out by the Regional Tourist Boards.

Promotion of domestic tourism

The ten Regional Tourist Boards in England have now taken over the promotion of domestic tourism. In Wales the three Regional Tourist boards support the WTB in this role. Similar to the BTA and National Tourist Boards, the Regional Tourist Boards also receive grants, but must supplement these with commercial activities, such as subscriptions from their members, selling publications, inspecting accommodation, running training programmes and conducting research.

ACTIVITY

Locate on the map below the ten Regional Tourist Boards in England plus the three in Wales.

Promotion of local tourism

Local tourism is promoted through both private and public sector organisations. Each town is now likely to have a Tourist Information Centre (TIC), whose aim is to provide visitors with information and support local providers. Run by the local councils, it is not the aim of the TICs to make a profit, however, they can no longer afford to provide their services free of charge. Their grants from the ETC (and formerly the ETB) have been continually reduced and so they now need to supplement their income. Once again this is done by charging for maps and other publications. The TICs may also charge for services, for example, the book-a-bed-ahead scheme (BABA), facilitating conferences, organising local Blue Badge Guides or arranging transfers.

ACTIVITY

Visit your local TIC to establish the following information:

What services does it offer?

How many enquiries does it receive per year? Are these predominantly received by post, across the counter, by telephone or E-mail?

Do the staff think that the Internet will change their role?

Local tourism is also promoted by private enterprises, for example, Blue Badge Guides, coach touring companies and all the attractions that encourage visitors. The increase in tourism has greatly encouraged the development of guiding services. One such company is Guide Friday who now operate in over 30 destinations and carry 1.4 million customers per year.

CASE STUDY *Guide Friday*

Guide Friday began with one bus in Stratford Upon Avon, showing visitors the delights of the town and Shakespeare's houses. This was 25 years ago. Since then it has grown steadily, expanding into Cambridge, then Oxford, Bath and Edinburgh. Others followed after research, trial and some error.

Guide Friday mainly expands into heritage destinations with high visitor numbers. It works closely with local authorities, TICs, hotels, attractions, coach companies and tour operators. Brochures are produced at great expense and advertising is carried out nationally rather than regionally. The vehicles are the main marketing tool – it is felt that the traditional feel and ease of recognition adds to the business. There is considerable customer loyalty, with visitors moving around the country using Guide Friday to see each city. This loyalty is monitored by offering a discount with each tour ticket for the customer's next tour.

Each tour operates in the same way, with tour tickets being valid for a whole day, thus allowing customers the flexibility of jumping on and off at places of interest en route.

ACTIVITY

Why has Guide Friday chosen destinations with high visitor numbers and why does the company work so closely with other organisations?

Give two examples of how Guide Friday caters for today's customers who demand high levels of service and flexibility? Explain why customer loyalty is so important?

Compare the objectives of Guide Friday with those of your local TIC.

Transportation

Although air transportation is certainly the most important form of transport for the package holiday market (holidays by air account for approximately 84% of all package holidays), we will also consider land and water transportation within this section.

The components of transportation are far reaching, including all of those services shown in Figure 1.14.

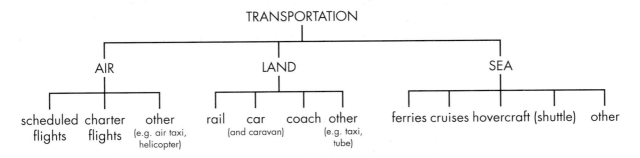

Figure 1.14 *Transportation systems*

As we have seen in the section on the development of travel and tourism, it is the changes in transport that have stimulated much of the development of the travel and tourism industry. While the changes in transport did not occur as rapidly in the latter half of the twentieth century, there were still significant changes that had an impact on the travel industry. One of these was the development of the Channel Tunnel, a second was the emergence of budget airlines (see section on development of travel and tourism in this chapter and in Chapter 4 for more details).

Sea travel

Since P&O initiated a commercial route across the Channel, several alternatives to that simple ferry crossing have been developed. Two companies now compete on the short sea ferry crossing from Dover to Calais. However, they have been faced with strong competition from the hovercraft and shuttle. In addition, numerous other ferry crossings are offered from other channel ports to destinations as far away as northern Spain.

Cruise travel has also fundamentally changed. Now offered by mass market tour operators, it is no longer only a form of travel for the wealthy.

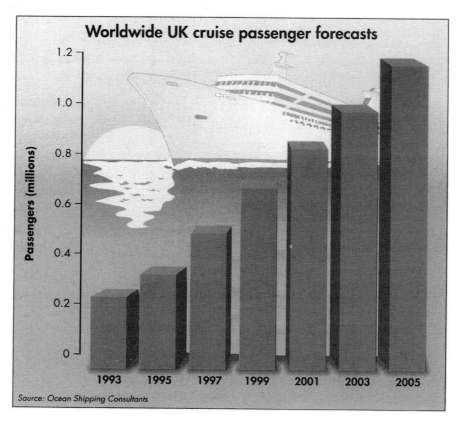

Figure 1.15 *Worldwide UK cruise passenger forecasts*

Source: TTG

The Mediterranean is considered a great cruising area because of its ideal climate, art and history, and the short distances involved. It is also possible to visit three continents – Europe, Africa and Asia – in a single cruise. As a result, the Mediterranean attracts 330,000 UK cruise passengers a year, which accounts for more than half the UK cruise market.

Air travel

Air travel is provided by scheduled or chartered flights. Although air taxis and helicopters are also air travel, they account for only a small percentage of the total. Scheduled airlines are those that run to a regular timetable throughout the year and will depart regardless of the number of passengers on them. All major airlines are scheduled and in Britain these include British Airways, Virgin Atlantic and British Midland. The emerging budget airlines – Go, Easy Jet, Ryanair and Virgin express – are all scheduled airlines. Most countries tend to have their own scheduled national airline, known as the flagship airline (for example, Air France, Quantas, Air New Zealand, Lufthansa and Cathay Pacific). These may be public sector, as is the case with Air France, or privatised, as is the case with British Airways.

Charter aircraft are usually contracted for a specific holiday season and run to a timetable set by the tour operator. For example, each major tour operator will need aircraft seats between May and October for its 'summer sun' passengers going to the Mediterranean. They therefore fill aircraft that they contract (buy) for this period. By filling every seat, they can bring the price per person down and offer a relatively cheap package holiday. Many charter airlines are now owned by the tour operators (for example, Britannia, Airtours and JMC).

Travel on land

Land transportation in the travel and tourism industry is dominated by the private car. With 70% of households having one or more cars, this is the preferred mode of transport for domestic holidays. However, as discussed on page 000, tour operators have adapted to customers preferences for flexible packages overseas by providing 'self-drive' package holidays.

Rail transport within the UK has changed phenomenally in the last ten years. The privatisation of British Rail in the mid-1900s has meant that each area of the country now has different train operators.

Coach operators are also adapting to the changing consumer needs. Although tours of Europe by coach remain popular, more fly/coach holidays are being put into the operators' brochures. Long haul fly/coach holidays in the US, Canada, Australia and New Zealand have been established for many years now. The main UK coach operators are Cosmos, Crusader Holidays, Insight, Leger, Shearing, Trafalgar and Wallace Arnold.

Great Britain

	ONE CAR ONLY	TWO OR MORE CARS
1961	29,000	2,000
1971	44,000	8,000
1981	45,000	15,000
1991	45,000	23,000
1997	45,000	25,000

Figure 1.16 Households with regular use of a car in the UK
Source: ONS

PROFILE *Club Cantabrica*

An express coach journey involves overnight travel, of between 12 and 22 hours, to your destination on a 'luxury coach' with facilities such as a hostess, video, reclining seats, snacks and drinks and a toilet. Companies such as Club Cantabrica are increasingly playing airlines at their own game by aiming to attract new custom with business class-style seating and enhanced on-board service. To compensate for the longer journey times, they are offering cheaper holidays and claim that they can offer greater comfort than that provided by an airline.

Based in St Albans, Hertfordshire, Club Cantabrica has a winter ski and summer sun programme. 25 coaches are fitted out to a high standard for its operations to the Costa Brava, the South of France and the Italian Riviera. The Spanish programme has four departures per week and offers holidays of 7, 10 and 14 nights. Accommodation is in campsites, mobile homes and apartments.

Justin Poole, the Club Cantabrica ski sales manager, claims: 'Ours is a road version of a quality air product, with coaches designed and built for mountain work. We offer a £60 to £90 saving on an air ski package.'

Source: Adapted from Travel Trade Gazette, *17 Feb. 1999*

ACTIVITY

Do you agree with Justin Poole in the Club Cantabrica Profile? Do you think that an express coach is a 'road version of a quality air product'?

What impact will the development of budget airlines have on express coach companies?

Why do you think European coach tours are so popular with the Americans?

Travel agents

As the name agent implies, travel agents sell travel products and services on behalf of others. A travel agent does not, therefore, normally 'produce' anything. They act as the link between the client and suppliers, such as tour operators, airlines, hotels and ferry services. These suppliers are known as 'principals'.

The principals produce products such as:

- cruises
- flights
- domestic holidays
- city breaks
- Le shuttle
- winter sun
- summer sun
- activity holidays
- short breaks
- touring holidays
- ferry crossing
- Eurostar
- sports holidays
- camping holidays

The aim of the travel agency is to sell these products on behalf of the principals, in return for which they receive commission. They may also sell a range of ancillary services in order to increase their commission levels (i.e. their income). These may include insurance, car hire, airport car parking or an overnight stay at an airport hotel.

ACTIVITY

Name one principal for each of the afore listed travel products.

Multiple and independent travel agents

In recent years travel agents have been referred to as holiday shops – indicating their status as a retail outlet, just like any other shop on the high street. As with other shops, travel agents vary in size and the type of products they offer. A useful comparison could be food outlets. While most towns now have a Sainsburys, Asda, Tesco or similar supermarket, other shops selling foods do exist. They are usually smaller, often have specialised foods or may simply be in convenient locations. As the supermarkets have expanded, so the business at the corner stores has decreased as it cannot offer the same discounts, training and facilities as the bigger stores. The general public has grown to like the convenience of the larger supermarket, where everything is available.

A similar phenomenon has occurred in the travel industry in the past 20 years. Most travel agencies on your high street will be one of a chain, with multiple outlets. These 'multiples' now dominate the high streets. Lunn Poly, Going Places and Thomas Cook are the major multiples (all are Public Limited Companies and are in fact linked to tour operators). The corner shop equivalent, is the independent travel agency owned and run by one person (or a few people only). They may have one or two travel agencies and many are out of town, some specialising in particular products, for example cruising or skiing. These independent agencies do not have the purchasing power of the multiples and may not be able to offer the same additional services, such as currency exchange.

Independent travel agents may, however, be able to offer more choice. We will discuss this more in the section on vertical and horizontal integration, but in basic terms, an independent operator may offer you a greater choice of holiday products because they are not owned by a tour operator.

The multiple travel agency chains now dominate the high streets (see Figure 1.17).

Business travel agents

In addition to leisure travel agencies that you see on the high street that are providing for the leisure traveller, there are also agencies that cater for the business traveller. Many business travel agents are based in office blocks – their location being unimportant as they do not deal with their clients face to face, but rather by telephone, fax, or E-mail.

DID YOU KNOW?

The Association of British Travel Agents (ABTA) was founded in 1950 and its members now account for the sale of 90% of all UK package holidays. Both travel agents and tour operators can join ABTA. More information is available from information@abta.co.uk.

Some large companies, however, choose to have their own business travel agents in-house. Known as 'implants', these agencies are usually one of a chain of large business agents, that set up office within the company and deal exclusively with that particular company's travel arrangements. In this case some of the business may be face to face, and the executive who wishes to go to Zurich in the morning may simply walk down the corridor to pick up their tickets. The Guild of Business Travel Agents (GBTA) is the professional body representing these agencies. Members include American Express, Carlson Wagonlit and Hogg Robinson.

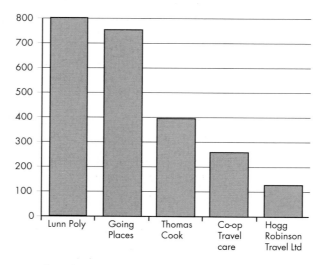

Figure 1.17 *Numbers of multiple travel agency outlets in the UK (1999)*

Source: ARTA, September 1999

CASE STUDY *Agent of the future*

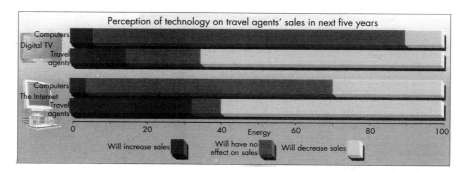

- Research commissioned by Amadeus and sponsored by ABTA, The Agent Of The Future study, found that 58 per cent of consumers have no preference for a particular agent and 13 per cent use no agent at all.

- Consumers have a high opinion of the service from agencies – 72 per cent say agents are great or good value, compared with 17.4 per cent who think they are poor value.

- Almost 90 per cent of counter staff predict demand for tailor-made itineraries will increase in the next five years.
- Approximately half of agencies now charge booking fees because of lower airline ticket commission rates and heavily discounted holiday prices.
- Counter staff are concerned that booking fees are unpopular. They say 44 per cent of customers make bookings reluctantly when booking fees are involved, eight per cent decline to make a booking at all and only 29 per cent accept that the fees are reasonable.
- Two-thirds of counter staff predict that public acceptance of booking fees will increase in the next five years.
- Nearly 69 per cent of agents predict agency sales will decline in the next five years as a result of direct bookings made over the Internet and on digital TV. Fewer consumers say their use of agents will be unaffected.
- The replacement of viewdata technology will affect the use of global distribution systems in the next five years. Business agents predict their GDS use will increase by 26 per cent, compared with 17 per cent for leisure agents.
- Source: Agent Of The Future 1999. For more details go to www.global.amadeus.net

Source: Travel Trade Gazette, *29 November 1999*

A package holiday

Transport

$+$

Accommodation

$+$

Transfers

$+$

Ancillary services

Note: This 'package' of goods services is sold to the customer at a price, either directly or indirectly, through a travel agency.

Figure 1.18 *Producing a package holiday*

ACTIVITY

Travel agents now have to compete with new technology that allows clients to book directly with the principals. The research, outlined in the Agent of the Future Case Study, suggests that travel agents can do several things to ensure that they stay in business.

You are the Trainee Manager at a local branch of one of the multiple travel agencies. You know that your staff are worried about their jobs. You are keen that none of them leave, as it is their experience that will help your agency remain successful. Write a memo to all staff, outlining how your branch is going to compete against the new technology.

Tour operators

A tour operator is an organisation that produces package holidays. It combines the separate components of accommodation, transport, transfers and any ancillary services, for example, services of a resort representative, excursions or meals. This package is then sold at an inclusive price, either directly to the public (direct sell) or via a travel agency.

It is estimated that there are approximately 700 tour operators in the UK at the start of the twenty first century. As with supermarkets and travel agents, the tour operators also vary in size and the products offered. We will examine the following types of operators and their products:

- Outbound – specialist and mass-market.
- Domestic – operating holidays within the UK for UK residents.
- Inbound – operating within the UK for overseas residents.

Outbound tour operators

The **mass-market** operators of Thomson Holidays, Airtours and First Choice dominate the package holiday market. Although it is difficult to estimate, due to constant changes, recent research by Thomson suggests that these three operators account for approximately 37% of all the overseas package holidays sold in the UK.

	DEC '98	DEC '97	%DIFF
1 Thomson Group	5,079,848	4,440,427	14
2 Airtours Group	3,841,046	3,082,886	25
3 First Choice Group	3,163,784	1,916,651	65
4 Thomas Cook Group	2,710,924	1,462,558	85
5 Carlson Leisure Group	1,213,295	880,480	38
6 Cosmos	1,110,513	1,049,317	6
7 Trailfinders	523,654	538,183	−3
8 Virgin Travel Group	409,063	274,001	49
9 Gold Medal Travel Group	393,520	371,170	6
10 British Airways Holidays Group	375,987	395,110	−5

Table 1.5 *Licensed capacity of the top ten mass-market operators*

Source: TTG, *27 January 1999*

Table 1.5 shows the top ten tour operating groups and the number of passengers they are permitted to carry.

KEY TERMS

Mass market: tour operators catering for the majority of the customers.

Specialist: a company that deals in one or more niche markets.

Direct sell: a tour operator that sells directly to the public, not through a travel agent.

Integration: the purchasing of one company by another.

ACTIVITY

The Thomson Holidays website (www.thomson-holidays.com) has a hot link to statistics on the holiday market. Use this site to establish the market share of each major tour operator.

Write a summary of the major trends revealed thorough the statistics on this website.

As we have already established, customers today are more demanding than they were 50 years ago. Two things have happened within tour operating to cater for our increased needs:

1 Mass-market operators have produced individual brochures/products to cater for specific customer needs.
2 Specialist operators have developed to cater for niche markets.

The mass-market operators have produced a multitude of brochures, covering most possible holiday choices, such as:

- summer sun
- winter sun
- winter ski
- sport
- activity/adventure
- domestic
- self-catering (holiday cottages)
- fly/drive
- fly/cruise
- coach tours
- short/city breaks/day trips
- lakes and mountains
- holidays for young people
- holidays for the over 50s
- singles holidays

Simultaneously, specialist operators have developed to cater for groups of holiday makers with similar needs. Many of these tour operators are direct sell (i.e. they only sell directly to the public and so their brochures cannot be found in the travel agencies). Others do sell some holidays through travel agents. The reasons for their small number of sales from the travel agents could be due to limited space in the travel

COMPANY NAME	SPECIALIST MARKET	DIRECT SELL OR THROUGH AGENTS
Saga Holidays	UK and worldwide holidays for the over 55s.	Direct sell
The Villa Agency	Specialises in holidays to Portugal and Florida, using self catering villas, most of which have pools.	Both
Explore Holidays	Small group exploratory holidays for active people.	Direct sell
Regal Holidays	Diving holidays throughout the world, plus a few classical tours in Jordan and Syria.	Both

Table 1.6 *Examples of specialist holidays*

agency or simply limited demand for the specialist products. Alternatively, it could be because some travel agencies prefer to market particular tour operators.

Such specialist operators may specialise in particular age groups (see Case Study of Saga on page 12), destinations, types of transportation or activities available.

PROFILE *Association of Independent Tour Operators (AITO)*

AITO was formed in 1976. It now represents 150 smaller specialised companies 'dedicated to providing a quality product, personal service and choice to members'. In recent years AITO has come to be recognised, increasingly, as the official voice of the smaller or specialist tour operator.

The significant difference between AITO members and the largest tour operators is that, while AITO members cannot expect to compete on equal financial terms with the giants of the industry, they are in a class of their own when it comes to the innovative flair of the specialist. Invariably, the specialists are the pioneers of every new holiday concept – followed, at a later stage, by the large companies.

The majority of AITO members are small and owner-managed. They therefore score highly when compared to their mass-market competitors in the areas of product knowledge and personal service. Selling the right holiday to each client and gaining maximum customer satisfaction are amongst the main aims of each AITO member.

AITO currently has 150 members. Some operators only carry a few hundred passengers per year; others carry 200,000 passengers per annum. For more information AITO has a website: www.aito.co.uk.

Source: An Introduction to AITO

ACTIVITY

Research one mass-market tour operator. Write a synopsis of its history and development. It may have purchased many companies – make a note of these. Establish how many brochures it now produces and the types of holidays on offer.

Research one specialist tour operator. Write a profile of what they do and how they are run. What product do they produce and who is their typical client?

Domestic tour operators

These operate in the UK and sell to UK residents. Although many domestic tour operators' brochures exist on the travel agencies' shelves, some may also sell directly. They may also be operated by a local coach company who place advertisements in your local newspaper. Similar to the outbound market, domestic tour operators also offer beach, city, touring and special interest holidays.

ACTIVITY

Research five domestic tour operators. You will need to get their brochures. Ensure that you have at least one 'direct sell' operator's brochure.

Profile the type of holiday offered. Who is this holiday aimed at? Describe a typical client for each holiday (this will be studied in more detail in Chapter 4). Write up your findings in a table, as shown below.

NAME OF DOMESTIC OPERATOR	DESCRIPTION OF HOLIDAY	CLIENT PROFILE
Shearings	Coach holidays throughout UK. Local pick-up points. Good off-season prices and mid-week breaks.	Couples or single people over 60 years old who are retired and have limited incomes.

Inbound tour operators

These cater for the needs of overseas visitors to the UK. They are represented by the British Incoming Tour Operators Association (BITOA). Some incoming tour operators offer complete packages based on themes, cities or activities. Other organisations, known as 'handling services', simply assist with parts of a tour, for example, transfers or excursions.

Horizontal and vertical integration

Since the 1980s, the large tour operators have tried to dominate the market by integrating with other travel companies. Thus, tour operators have bought airlines, hotels, other tour operations and retail travel agencies. In doing so, they own all components of the package holiday and the agencies that sell them to the public. They claim that because of this (economies of scale) they are able to offer customers better prices. However, some people within the travel trade are concerned that these operators may also be able to dominate the market and force other operators out of business. It was this fear that led the Monopolies and Mergers Commission to investigate the travel trade in 1996.

Integration takes two forms. If a tour operator buys another tour operating business or similar company operating at the same level in the

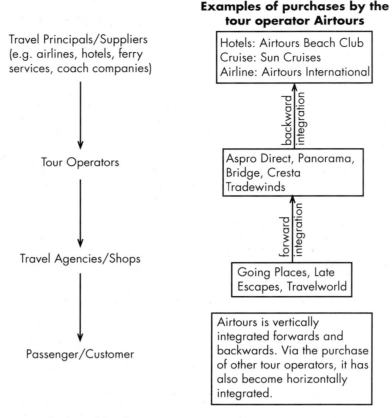

Figure 1.19 *The chain of distribution*

chain of distribution (see Figure 1.19) this is known as horizontal integration. Examples of horizontal integration occurred in February 1999, when Thomson Holidays purchased two independent tour operators: Head Water and Simply Travel, having already purchased Magic Travel Group in the previous year. Airtours also purchased Panorama Holidays in 1988.

Vertical integration occurs when two companies at different levels in the chain of distribution merge. This may either be backward integration (i.e. the tour operator buys companies that provide the components of the package holiday) or forward integration (the tour operator purchases the retail travel agency).

Each of the three major tour operators in the UK are vertically and horizontally integrated. The largest tour operator in the UK, Thomson Holidays, also owns the number one travel agency chain, Lunn Poly. The number two tour operator, Airtours, owns its own travel agency, Going Places (forward integration). Both own their own charter airline and hotels (backward integration). The tour operator First Choice has a business alliance with Thomas Cook. All three operators have continuously horizontally integrated in recent years, and through this have increased their product ranges. For example, the purchase of Holiday Cottages (the largest UK holiday cottage company) by Thomson gave

Travel agents 'dupe clients' with advice

HOLIDAYMAKERS are being ''hoodwinked'' because Britain's biggest tour companies are indulging in anti-competitive practices, an official inquiry has found.

Companies including Thomson, Thomas Cook and Airtours have been accused by the Monopolies and Mergers Commission of misleading consumers. The year-long inquiry has found that holidaymakers think they are receiving impartial advice from ''independent'' travel agents when in fact they are being encouraged to buy ''in-house'' holidays from agents owned by the parent companies.

The commission wrote earlier this month to associations representing the travel industry to tell them that the package holiday market was being unfairly dominated by a handful of conglomerates. It said it had previously concluded that a ''complex monopoly'' existed in the market.

The practices of companies including Thomson Travel Group, the Thomas Cook Group, Airtours, First Choice Holidays and Inspirations ''appear to prevent, restrict or distort competition'', it said.

Last week The Sunday Times sent reporters to travel agents owned by the four big holiday companies to test the advice given. They asked the agents to recommend a two-week European holiday in November which would be suitable for a honeymoon.

In all but one case, the agents picked holidays offered by their parent companies without making their link to those firms clear. In addition, all the agents offered a 10% discount on their holidays but made the offer subject to the customer taking out a costly travel insurance policy with the firm.

At Thomas Cook travel agents, in High Holborn, London, Tracy Jones, a saleswoman immediately called up details of holidays in the Canary Islands offered by Sunworld on her computer. She did not volunteer any information about the ownership of Sunworld until she was challenged. Only then did Jones admit that it was owned by the Thomas Cook Group. ''No travel agent is allowed to promote any tour operator ahead of others,'' she added.

It was the same story a few yards down the road at a branch of Going Places, the chain of travel agents owned by Airtours. When asked to recommend a holiday, the sales assistant supplied three quotes for destinations in the Canaries – all offered by Airtours. She did not make clear the link between the travel agent and the tour operator until asked. She then admitted that by selling Airtours holidays she made more commission.

At Lunn Poly, which is owned by Thomson, it was Thomson holidays that were offered. Only at the East Sheen branch of AT Mays, which is owned by Inspirations, did the agent initially recommend a tour operator that was not linked to his company.

The Association of Independent Tour Operators welcomed the MMC's findings. A spokesman said that its members were being unfairly squeezed by the big groups and that many found it impossible to get their holiday packages advertised on travel agents' shelves.

The big four tour operators and their travel agents denied they were using anti-competitive practices last week. Airtours said notices were hung on the walls of Going Places which made it clear that the companies were linked.

Thomas Cook said it had a ''clear and transparent'' sales policy which meant that customers would not be confused by its corporate links.

Lunn Poly, Britain's largest chain of travel agents, said its links with Thomson did not affect the service it provided. Of the 3.2 m holidays it sold last year, only 1.1 m were with Thomson.

Figure 1.20 *Sunday Times article on integration*

Source: Sunday Times, *17 August 1997*

ACTIVITY

What are the advantages and disadvantages of integration to:

1 the customers
2 the independent travel agents and independent tour operators
3 the integrated organisations themselves

	ADVANTAGES	DISADVANTAGES
Customers/general public		
Competitors (specialist tour operators and independent travel agents)		
Integrated companies		

them domination in yet another holiday product area. Also, when Airtours purchased Tradewinds they gained access to the long haul section of the UK market. Integration may result in cheaper prices, but the fact that there is a business relationship between the three major UK tour operators and the three major UK travel agents led to an inquiry by the Monopolies and Mergers Commission in 1996. There has been much concern from independent tour operators and some consumers that consumer choice is being restricted.

Private sector ownership

 ACTIVITY

Draw a chart similar to the following. Give three examples of organisations providing the services in each component category.

COMPONENTS	EXAMPLES OF ORGANISATIONS
Tourist attractions • natural • built	
Accommodation • serviced • non-serviced	
Catering	
Tourism development and promotion	
Transportation • air • land • sea	
Travel agents • multiples • independents	
Tour operators • mass-market • specialist • inbound • domestic	

Using different colours or highlighter pens, indicate all those organisations in the chart above that are in the private sector, voluntary or public sector, calculate the percentage of organisations in each sector.

Features of the travel and tourism industry

The key feature about this industry is that it is constantly changing. While studying for your Vocational A Level, the major tour operators will all have purchased other specialist companies, some organisations will have ceased trading and some resorts will have gone out of fashion while others have emerged. This makes it a very exciting industry to be involved in. In this section we will summarise the key features of the industry, some of which will already have been discussed in previous sections.

Through study of the components of the travel and tourism industry you will learn that this industry is highly fragmented. It is in fact made up of parts of lots of separate industries, for example, the hotel industry, transportation industry, catering industry and entertainment industry, to name but a few (some academics even argue that travel and tourism is not an industry at all but simply a collection of fragmented parts). The majority of the businesses that deal with tourists, tourism and the industry as a whole, are small or medium sized. They are also predominantly privately owned.

Small and medium-sized enterprises

Although you may be familiar with the larger travel and tourism organisations because they are in the press and/or have more publicity, the majority of organisations within the industry would officially be described as small or medium sized. A good example of this is the tour operating business. On page 45 we stated that there were over 700 tour operators in the UK in 1998. However, the top seven companies had 57% of the market in 1998:

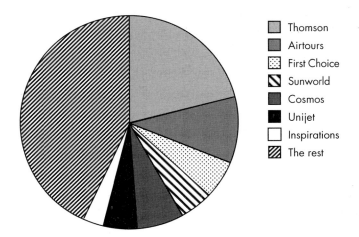

Figure 1.21 *Market share of the tour operator market*

Figure 1.21 shows that approximately 693 tour operators have just 43% of the market. Thus, while we may hear a lot about the top three companies, there are many others to consider. How many of them can you name?

❛ Tourism is ... made up of 120,000 businesses as well as a huge number of government departments and agencies, local authorities and national bodies covering everything from transport to heritage, all with an interest in tourism ❜

Source: Mr Alan Britten at the launch of the ETC in July 1999

Impact of new technology on travel and tourism

As discussed in the section on the development of travel and tourism, the development of new technologies is having a tremendous impact on the industry. On page 17, we discussed the impact that the Internet may have on the travel agency network. Few travel and tourism organisations exist today that are not dependent on technology for their communication, finance and administration systems. Most also depend on technology for health and safety issues (for example, fire detection and security). Technology is affecting all industries and this one is no exception.

ACTIVITY

In small groups, identify the uses of technology in one major travel and tourism organisation with which you are familiar.

How much of this technology would have been in use just ten years ago?

HOLIDAYMAKERS' plans have been thrown into chaos by one of the worst Caribbean hurricane seasons for more than 120 years. All bookings to Antigua have been cancelled until at least November, dozens of cruise ships are being diverted and flights between many small islands have been halted.

Now the islands are racing to repair the widespread damage before the high season starts in early December. A Caribbean Tourism Organisation official in London said: "Antigua is gradually recovering and some hotels should be operating again in time for the main Christmas season. One hotel will not open until late 1996, because its bungalows have been swept into the sea." The islands of St Kitts-Nevis were damaged only lightly.

Figure 1.22(a) External Pressures

Source: Times, 21 September 1995

Israel, Egypt and Jordan specialist Destination Red Sea has ceased trading after the Gulf crisis caused a dramatic slump in bookings.

Managing director and owner Philip Breckner took the unprecedented step on Friday of walking into the Civil Aviation Authority's London offices and asking it to call the company's £600,000 bond.

Breckner said a lack of bookings had led to a cash-flow problem. Destination Red Sea already owed money to overseas hoteliers, but Breckner decided to cease trading before debts spiralled out of control. He estimated he could have lost another £100,000 in January if he had continued trading.

"I could have kept going, fobbing off hotels about payments, but that's not the decent thing to do," he said.

In an exclusive interview with *Travel Weekly*, an emotional Breckner told how he informed his 25 staff at the Barnet offices they were being made redundant and the company was finished.

Breckner formed Destination Red Sea from the ashes of collapsed Twickers World in 1995. The company was licensed to carry 14,000 passengers.

Breckner said the first crisis was the Luxor massacre in November 1997.

"It hurt me commercially," he said. "I spent around £50,000 in the next 12 months just promoting Egypt."

The minor Gulf conflict in February 1998 also had an impact, but it was the West's two clashes with Iraq on November 15 and December 20 which sealed Destination Red Sea's fate.

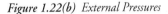

Figure 1.22(b) External Pressures

Source: Travel Weekly, *13 January 1995*

The health scare in the Dominican Republic last summer saw UK arrivals fall 33 per cent below forecasts, costing the island's tourism industry more than £600,000.

This followed a 78 per cent rise in UK visitors in 1997.

But Rafael Blanco Canto, president of the Dominican National Hotel and Restaurant Association, claimed the crisis was now over.

"The problem was only in the UK market," he said.

"We retained a UK company to supervise health measures in 80 hotels and employed a UK public relations company."

He said he hoped UK arrivals this year would reach the 1997 total of 216,000.

Figure 1.22(c) External Pressures

Source: TTG, *27 January 1995*

External pressures

Some of the changes that occur in tourism may be completely outside the influence of the industry itself, i.e. they may be vulnerable to external events. There are many examples in recent years of the industry being affected by external pressures. Examples include: hurricanes, tornadoes, diseases in destination countries, outbreaks of war, political unrest, crime and terrorism. Changes in UK government legislation and changes in currency rates also can have an impact.

Fashion also influences changes in the travel and tourism industry. The demise in the popularity of Benidorm in the 1980s was simply due to a result in changes in fashion. In contrast, Prague has become more fashionable – this change in fashion and increase in tourists numbers to Prague is predominantly due to its changing politics. However, it has also been aided by the tour operators who have facilitated growth by providing the package holidays.

ACTIVITY

Study the extracts from the national and trade press in Figure 1.22. Each of these events required emergency action from the tour operators concerned. Foreign Office officials and trade organisations were required to offer advice to clients.

In small groups discuss:

- The immediate impact of each event.
- The medium to long-term impacts of each.

Identify the most recent 'external events' that have had an impact on the travel and tourism industry.

Impacts on host communities

The key word of the travel industry at the beginning of the twenty first century is sustainability. We are increasingly made aware of the impacts of the travel and tourism industry and the tourists on destinations. While it is recognised that some of these impacts are undoubtedly positive, many destinations are still suffering because of the tourist trade – this subject is covered in detail in Chapter 2: Tourism Development. Table 1.7 provides a summary of the impacts of travel and tourism.

CASE STUDY *Tourism in the Peak National Park*

In 1951 the Peak National Park became the first National Park in Britain. It covers 542 square miles (1404 sq km) of

TYPE OF IMPACT	POSITIVE IMPACTS	NEGATIVE IMPACTS
Economic	<ul><li>jobs are created</li><li>income is brought into an area</li><li>increased wealth</li><li>investment may be attracted</li><li>prosperity</li></ul>	<ul><li>loss of jobs in other areas of the local economy</li><li>seasonal nature of tourism jobs</li><li>may cause inflation in housing market</li></ul>
Social/cultural	<ul><li>jobs created</li><li>feeling of wellbeing</li><li>local people proud of their community</li><li>people working together to cater for visitors</li><li>promotes local crafts and customs</li></ul>	<ul><li>tensions between visitors and local population</li><li>tourists exploited by local people for quick profit</li><li>envy</li><li>crime</li></ul>
Environmental	<ul><li>conservation and preservation occurs to encourage tourism</li><li>restoration of buildings</li><li>new amenities from which local population can benefit</li></ul>	<ul><li>overcrowding</li><li>wear and tear on footpaths and buildings</li><li>litter</li><li>noise, air and water pollution</li><li>traffic congestion</li><li>parking problems</li></ul>

Table 1.7 *Summary: positive and negative impacts of travel and tourism*

beautiful and often wild countryside from the high (636 m) moorlands in the north to the green farmland in the south. The great majority of the National Park is still in private ownership and most of it is farmed.

What are the benefits of tourism?

Tourism is one of the world's most rapidly growing industries. Of the 12,000 jobs in the Peak Park, 15% are in the Tourism and Leisure areas and a further 38%, in the service industries, are often directly affected by Tourism.

Tourism provides the income to keep many of the great houses in good hands. Chatsworth, home of the Duke of Devonshire, is one example. Here, paying visitors to the house and gardens are supplemented by a popular Farm yard and Adventure Playground as well as "Fairs" and other events in the grounds.

Tourism can encourage the preservation of historic buildings and sites. Former mills such as Caudwells Mill have been restored in anticipation of the number of visits by tourists who are interested in such places. Other industrial sites such as Magpie Mine have also been preserved. Redundant farm buildings have found new uses as holiday accommodation, camping barns etc.

Continuation of traditional crafts is also encouraged. Thousands of visitors admire the well dressings in Peak Park villages and money is raised for local causes.

Tourism provides an income and a livelihood for many local people. Visitors bring in an income to farmers with caravan and camping sites in their fields, to local villagers offering Bed & Breakfast in their homes and also to hotels and those renting out self catering cottages. Farming in the bleak upland areas of the Peak Park is not a profitable occupation and many farmers can only continue to farm because of the additional income from visitors.

What problems does tourism bring?

90% of visits to the Park are made by car. Some of the most popular "honeypot" areas attract large numbers of visitors, resulting in overcrowded car parks, blocked roads, and overstretched local facilities – particularly on Summer Sundays. The Upper Derwent became so congested that a special Joint Management Scheme was developed by the National Park Authority, local landowners and other bodies. An Information Centre, cycle hire, refreshments and toilets were opened and parking was reorganised. Motor access was restricted, so creating closed roads for walking, cycling etc. A full time Ranger service was established and bus services from towns and cities were encouraged. This partnership approach now extends to 10 area Management Schemes in the Peak Park.

There are 3,510 footpaths in the Peak Park and heavy use of the most popular paths has led to considerable erosion. Particularly heavy wear is caused by sponsored walks and by horse riding on unsurfaced bridleways. The Pennine Way, the most popular long distance path and that with the greatest problems, has had 27 erosion "black spots" identified in the most heavily used stretch between Edale and the moors above Oldham. Many of these are on peat which is easily eroded under heavy pressure. The average width of the path in 1987 was 14.28 metres, 3 times its width in 1971. A project has been set up and a variety of hard surfaces are being tried. Dovedale is a honeypot area where the footpath through the dale can be used by up to 1,000 people an hour. A new path has now been constructed to cope with this heavy pressure.

Source: Peak National Environmental Education Service

ACTIVITY

Using the table below as a guide, identify the different impacts that tourism has had on the Peak National Park.

TYPE OF IMPACT	POSITIVE IMPACTS	NEGATIVE IMPACTS
Economic		
Social/cultural		
Environmental		

Scale of the UK travel and tourism industry

It is often claimed that the travel and tourism industry is the biggest and fastest growing industry, but how big is it and how fast is it growing? In this section we will look at key industry statistics to assess the scale of the industry and how it contributes to the UK economy.

At the simplest level, travel and tourism contributes to the UK economy by:

- providing jobs
- providing income (inbound and domestic tourists spending their money on goods and services in the UK)

We must also, however, be aware that when we go abroad and spend money, we are effectively taking money out of the UK economy, and therefore, reducing the benefits that the inbound and domestic tourists are having on the British economy.

To investigate all aspects of the scale of the UK industry, a variety of statistical sources will be used. The main ones are published by:

- British Tourist Authority (BTA)
- Her Majesty's Stationery Office (HMSO)
- Office for National Statistics (ONS)
- World Travel and Tourism Council (WTTC)
- World Tourism Organisation (WTO)

DID YOU KNOW?

The BTA has a website with statistics and research data (www.star.uk.com)

ACTIVITY

Find the web sites for the organisations listed previously. Establish what else they do, aside from publishing statistics.

KEY TERMS

Balance of Payments: the difference in the nation's economy between the income from exports and the cost of imports.

Invisible export: income received by a country through selling services rather than goods. Inbound tourism is an invisible export.

Invisible import: costs paid for receiving a service from overseas. Outbound tourism is an invisible import.

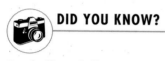

DID YOU KNOW?

One in five of all new jobs created in the UK is in the tourist industry.

We will use statistics to assess the scale of the industry, on the basis of the following criteria:

● Number of people employed in travel and tourism in the UK.

● Number of tourists coming into the UK (inbound tourism) and their expenditure.

● Number of UK residents taking holidays in the UK (domestic tourism) and their expenditure.

● Number of UK residents taking holidays overseas (outbound tourism) and their expenditure.

● Net amount of money generated for the UK economy and contribution to the Balance of Payments.

Travel and tourism as an employer

The Office for National Statistics (ONS) states that in 1998 the industry supported around 1.7 million jobs within the UK. ONS breaks down this figure into discrete sectors, as can be seen in Table 1.8 below. The industry was, therefore, a major provider of employment opportunities in the UK in that year. More people are now employed in tourism than the health service or the construction industries.

(All figures in 000s)	DECEMBER 1994	DECEMBER 1995	DECEMBER 1996	DECEMBER 1997	DECEMBER 1998
Hotels and other tourist accommodation	336.4	327.3	331.4	317.9	313.5
Restaurants, cafes, etc.	374.3	391.2	390.8	414.9	407.5
Bars, public houses and nightclubs	414.2	427.4	463.6	495.9	455.2
Travel agencies/tour operators	81.7	88.5	98	101.3	116.1
Libraries, museums and other cultural activities	76.0	74.6	77.4	78.9	82.1
Sport and other recreational activities	346.2	349.8	364.9	367.8	355.6
Total	**1,628.8**	**1,658.8**	**1,726.2**	**1,776.7**	**1,730.0**

Table 1.8 *Employment in tourism-related industries in Great Britain*

Source: ONS

ACTIVITY

Analyse the statistics on tourism employment in Table 1.8 to identify the sectors within the industry that employ the most people.

Identify which sectors of the industry are missing from the table.

Use alternative sources to establish their contribution to the employment statistics.

Due to the fact that travel and tourism consists of so many diverse sectors and components, it is difficult to estimate how many people are employed within the industry. Furthermore, many sectors serve both tourists and local residents: Is the waitress serving a tourist in a restaurant, part of the tourism economy, despite the fact that most of her day is spent serving local business people?

People can be employed directly in tourism or indirectly: for example, the rides attendant at Alton Towers is clearly employed directly in tourism, but those printing the entrance tickets and manufacturing the rides are also involved in tourism, albeit indirectly.

Published figures, therefore, can only be used as guidelines and for comparative purposes. Statistics should also be interpreted with caution and their significance checked carefully.

Tourism creates jobs in:

- travel agencies
- tour operators
- transport companies
- restaurants
- hotels

- organising conferences
- tourist attractions
- tourist information
- tourist boards

Tourism helps to create jobs in:

- arts and crafts
- retailing
- leisure facilities
- information technology
- agriculture

- manufacturing
- wholesale
- construction
- financial services

Travel and tourism as an income generator

Changing socio-economic conditions and the rise in expectations (a holiday is now considered to be a necessity by many people) have resulted in the travel and tourism industry becoming a major income generator for the UK economy. This income arises from domestic and inbound tourists spending on goods and services within the UK (see Table 1.9).

DID YOU KNOW?

In 1999 over 8% of all jobs in the world depended on travel and tourism. It has been predicted that 5.5 million new jobs will be created each year in travel and tourism, until 2010.

(all figures in millions)	TRIPS	NIGHTS	SPENDING
UK residents	133.6	474	£15,075
Overseas visitors	25.5	223	£12,244
Total	**159.1**	**697**	**£27,319**

Note: Trips: at least one night away from home. Nights: estimated number of nights spent away from home. Spending: estimated expenditure on all trips, whether paid by self or employer (if business travel).

Table 1.9 *Volume of spending of tourists in the UK (1997)*

DID YOU KNOW?

The BTA estimate that tourism contributed £52,524 million to the UK economy in 1997.

In addition to the data in Table 1.9, approximately £3,200 million comes into the economy as fares paid to UK carriers (for example, airfares to UK airlines).

£52,524 million

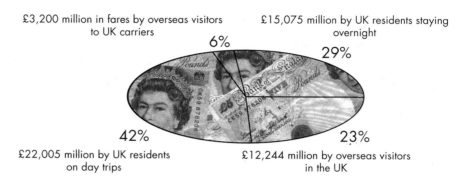

£3,200 million in fares by overseas visitors to UK carriers

£15,075 million by UK residents staying overnight

6%

29%

42%

23%

£22,005 million by UK residents on day trips

£12,244 million by overseas visitors in the UK

Figure 1.23 Value of tourism in the UK (1997)

Source: Adapted from chart at BTA Leisure

With minor exceptions, the value of domestic and inbound tourism have risen consistently during the past two decades (see Figure 1.28: value of tourism spending, 1977–1997).

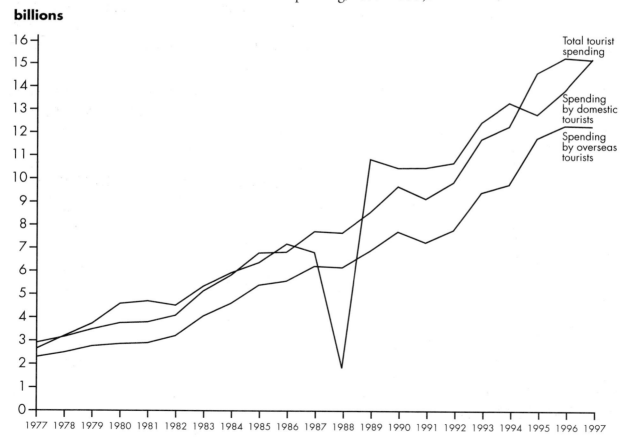

Figure 1.24 Value of tourism and consumer spending (1977–1997)

Source: Tourism Intelligence Quarterly

DID YOU KNOW?

Spending on tourism represents 10.5% of all consumer spending.

YEAR	VISITS TOTAL '000	EXPENDITURE* £M
1964	3,257	190
1965	3,597	193
1966	3,967	219
1967	4,289	236
1968	4,828	282
1969	5,821	359
1970	6,692	432
1971	7,131	500
1972	7,459	576
1973	8,167	726
1974	8,543	898
1975	9,490	1,218
1976	10,808	1,768
1977	12,281	2,352
1978	12,646	2,507
1979	12,486	2,797
1980	12,421	2,961
1981	11,452	2,970
1982	11,636	3,188
1983	12,464	4,003
1984	13,644	4,614
1985	14,449	5,442
1986	13,897	5,553
1987	15,566	6,260
1988	15,799	6,184
1989	17,338	6,945
1990	18,013	7,748
1991	17,125	7,386
1992	18,535	7,891
1993	19,863	9,487
1994	20,794	9,786
1995	23,537	11,763
1996	25,163	12,290
1997	25,515	12,244

*Figures from 1975 onward include the Channel Islands. Estimates for earlier years are not available.

Table 1.10 *Overseas visitors to the UK – visits and expenditure, 1964 to 1997*

ACTIVITY

Examine Figure 1.24. In which years was there a decrease in the value of either domestic or international tourism? Discuss why this occurred.

Consumer spending

The BTA estimate that domestic and overseas tourists spent a total of £27,319 million in 1997. Not surprisingly, accommodation and catering account for a total of 60% of all spending. This explains why many destinations particularly want overnight visitors, as it vastly increases the income into their area.

Spending on inbound tourism

Inbound tourism generates money for the UK economy and is, therefore, encouraged by the UK government via the British Tourist Authority (BTA) and Regional Tourist Boards. Money flows into the UK, just as it would if we were selling products abroad – inbound tourism is therefore an export. It is described as being 'invisible' as it is a service rather than a physical product.

Inbound tourism has risen consistently, with a few minor blips. In 1997 there were 25 million visitors to the UK. This is twice as many as 20 years ago, however, their total expenditure has more than quadrupled in the same period.

Most of the overseas visitors to the UK are Western Europeans (64%), of which the French visit the most (the Germans, however spend more money!). The Americans are the highest spenders of all overseas visitors.

	COUNTRY	VISIT THOUSANDS	SPENDING £M
1	France	3,586	649
2	USA	3,432	2,164
3	Germany	2,911	1,071
4	Irish Republic	2,232	856
5	Netherlands	1,653	409
6	Belgium	1,345	217
7	Italy	990	471
8	Spain	825	380
9	Australia	684	525
10	Sweden	616	263

Table 1.11 *Countries of origin*

Once in the UK, the spread of tourism varies greatly. Not surprisingly, of all regions within the UK, London is the most popular destination

(All figures in millions)	UK RESIDENTS		OVERSEAS VISITORS	
	TRIPS	**SPENDING**	**TRIPS**	**SPENDING**
Cumbria	3.1	£405	0.31	£63
Northumbria	3.8	£380	0.51	£205
North West	9.7	£1,000	1.26	£490
Yorkshire	10.1	£965	1.04	£327
Heart of England	17.0	£1,300	2.18	£689
East of England	14.8	£1,565	1.65	£571
London	14.6	£1,040	13.46	£6,449
West Country	16.7	£2,755	1.66	£513
Southern	11.9	£1,250	2.11	£755
South East	11.6	£1,000	2.44	£712
England	111.5	£11,665	21.49	£10,788
N. Ireland	1.1	£290	0.14	£55
Scotland	11.1	£1,690	2.09	£860
Wales	10.0	£1,125	0.92	£226
UK*	**133.6**	**£15,075**	**25.5**	**£12,244**

*UK includes Channel Islands and the Isle of Man.

Table 1.12 *Distribution of tourism within Great Britain in 1997*

for overseas visitors. There are many reasons for this. Not only is London our capital city and cultural centre, it is also the major gateway into Great Britain with five international airports serving the city.

Spending on domestic tourism

Domestic tourism, like inbound tourism, generates income for the UK economy and so is promoted through the Tourist Boards. However, the number of domestic holidays taken is currently decreasing in favour of overseas tourism.

Despite this, domestic tourism currently generates more expenditure than overseas tourism (see Figure 1.24: Value of tourism and consumer spending (1977–1997). Spending patterns and destinations are also very different for domestic tourists when compared to inbound tourists.

ACTIVITY

Use Table 1.12: Distribution of tourism within Great Britain in 1997, to analyse the variations in domestic and overseas tourists' destination choices.

Select those destinations that attract the most and least expenditure for both domestic and overseas tourists. Explain your findings.

Spending on outbound tourism

Outbound tourists spend money outside the UK economy (an invisible import). British tourists benefit the Spanish or French economy when they are buying hotel accommodation, drinking wine and other goods and services to enjoy their stay in those countries.

Outbound tourism continues to grow. The result is that British tourists now spend more money abroad than is spent by overseas tourists in the UK. We, therefore, have a balance of payments deficit on the travel account. This is a matter of concern for the British economy and the government is trying to resolve it by encouraging more overseas visitors to Britain. The alternative is that British tourists could be encouraged to stay within the UK but the lure of the sun is too attractive for most UK residents.

Millions

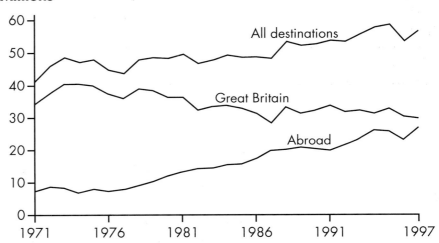

Figure 1.25 *Holidays taken by Great Britain residents: by destination*

Source: ONS

ACTIVITY

Investigate the economic importance of tourism to either your local area or the nearest significant tourist town.

You will need to gather statistics from either the regional or national Tourist Board, the TIC or local council. Alternatively, you may find the information in your college Learning Resource Centre or the public library. Some councils also now have websites.

Working in the travel and tourism industry

We have established that the travel industry is large, diverse and growing rapidly. These three things make it an ideal sector in which to be looking for work: there are lots of different types of employment

KEY TERMS

Curriculum vitae (CV): a word processed document that lists information about you.

Seasonal job: a job that is only available at certain times of the year.

Speculative application: applying to an organisation for work, although they have not advertised any positions.

DID YOU KNOW?

It is estimated that in the peak summer season up to 5,000 overseas resort representatives are employed by the major tour operators.

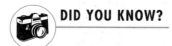

DID YOU KNOW?

Alton Towers employs up to 1,300 staff on a seasonal basis but has just 350 permanent employees.

opportunities in a variety of areas and the number of opportunities increases with the growth of the industry. It is important, however, to be realistic about the opportunities available and the types of work involved. The fact that the industry predominantly deals with 'holidays', plus the mass of travel programmes, including 'soaps' now on TV, make it easy to glamorise this industry. The reality can be quite different, as you will discover through exploring job opportunities.

Range of employment opportunities

Due to the fragmented nature of the industry, there are endless types of jobs available. Refer back to the table you completed on page 52. You named three organisations in each sector of the travel and tourism industry in the UK, and every sector is a potential employer. In addition to these opportunities in the UK, there are overseas jobs, for example, many Vocational A Level students wish to become a 'rep'. Within all of these sectors you should also consider the different functions within organisations – from administration, reservations and operations to marketing, customer care and guiding.

The nature of employment in the travel and tourism industry

The nature of the jobs varies from sector to sector and also within each sector. Many of the jobs in the UK are permanent, for example, working as a travel consultant in a travel agency can be full-time or part-time and is usually permanent. However, the nature of the industry means that many companies require extra staff in the period between May and October. These are known as seasonal staff, simply because they are temporary staff employed for the period of the summer season.

If you are involved in a part of the business that deals with clients you have to be available when the client is most likely to need you. This may involve working shifts, and some unsociable working hours will be required in many sectors. You will in fact have to work according to the customers' needs. Hotel staff, 'reps' and ride attendants at Alton Towers do not work from Monday to Friday, from 9 to 5 pm! In fact, the busiest times tend to be weekends and evenings (part-time jobs are sometimes available to fill these busy periods that fall outside the normal 9 to 5 day). However this need not always be the case. For example, those involved in brochure production for a tour operator are not dealing with clients and therefore work more regular hours.

SIMPLY TRAVEL

This leading specialist Tour Operator requires dynamic, customer-focused individuals to care for its clients in Turkey, Greece, Spain, Portugal, Corsica & Italy.

AREA MANAGER: GREECE

With overall responsibility for suppliers, staff and guests overseas, the successful applicant will be an excellent manager and motivator, ideally with some overseas experience. Applicants must be 27+, hold a clean driving licence and be fluent in the local language. The position is offered on a permanent 12 month basis, with around one third of the year spent in our London office.

ADMINISTRATORS: ALL PROGRAMMES

Offering admin. support & backup to the Area Manager, applicants should have detailed office and book-keeping skills, knowledge of the local language (not essential in Greece & Turkey) and computer literacy.

REPRESENTATIVES: ALL PROGRAMMES

Our Representatives are a vital link in our chain of customer service. Key requirements are fluency in the local language (not essential in Greece and Turkey), and a good knowledge of the area. A clean driving licence and experience in customer care is essential.

VILLA MAIDS: CORSICA ONLY

To clean holiday cottages, mid-April to July or July to October. Must be hard-working, flexible & sociable.

WATERSPORTS INSTRUCTORS: TURKEY & CORSICA

Must have RYA qualifications in windsurfing & sailing, a conscientious approach to safety & an outgoing manner.

NANNIES: CORSICA & GREECE

Must have childcare qualifications (e.g. NNEB, BTEC, RGN) and relevant work experience.

Enthusiasm, stamina and common sense are essential for all positions.

Please telephone for an application form

OVERSEAS WORK - SUMMER 1999

Figure 1.26 Example of an advert for seasonal work

Source: Travel Weekly, *6 January 1999*

DID YOU KNOW?

The software Odyssey provides comprehensive details on jobs available within travel and tourism. Check to see if it is available in your careers centre.

Skills and qualities required

Employees working with clients require exceptional customer service skills. The industry is often referred to as a people business, and you will certainly need to be able to deal with people effectively if you are going to be working with the general public. If this is not one of your strengths you may wish to consider a more 'back-office' role in administration, ticketing, or marketing.

All employers, however, tend to prefer 'people people', i.e. they will be looking for your interpersonal skills at interview. Even if you are not dealing with clients, you will need to get on with your colleagues. In addition to your personal qualities, employers will also look for your technical skills and experience.

ACTIVITY

Do you:

- enjoy meeting people?
- get on with all types of people?
- like working as part of a team?
- stay calm when under pressure?
- meet deadlines?
- have good customer care skills?
- communicate easily with new people?
- like using the telephone?

If you have answered yes to all eight questions above, then you could be highly employable within the travel industry!

Work in pairs. Role-play an interview situation where you are asked the above questions. Answer positively and give examples to prove your interpersonal skills in each of the areas.

ACTIVITY

A few technical skills and experience that employers require are indicated below. Comment on your own abilities in these areas.

1 Computer literacy: word processing, spreadsheets, databases
2 First Aid qualifications (useful for airline cabin crew and overseas resort reps)
3 Experience of Galileo (for travel agents and airlines)
4 Experience of dealing with customers
5 Experience of dealing with difficult customers
6 Experience of working under pressure
7 Ability to meet deadlines

Are there any other skills or qualities that you think employers will look for?

Travel and tourism employers will certainly look at your qualifications. However, you will have a Vocational A Level when going for an interview. You may also be considering going on to higher education. Many employers may in fact focus more on your interpersonal skills and customer care experience. They may not require any particular experience in travel work. In fact, they may offer their own internal training programme to give you the right levels of experience and training to meet their specific requirements. Before they offer a job though, they will assess your abilities to get on with people. This is where your part-time job working in the evenings in a restaurant or weekend job in a shop could prove extremely relevant, as many part-time jobs that students undertake are in roles that deal with customers. Remember that customer care skills are what most employers are looking for.

If you do not have a part-time job at the moment, you may wish to consider getting one. Although any customer service role will eventually help you get a job in travel, you could try to get work directly in travel now. Agencies often need Saturday staff and the TIC will need summer staff. Even if they do not have a vacancy now, they may have one in the future.

How to find a job

DID YOU KNOW?

There is an increasing number of jobs advertised on the Internet. Try www.datalake.com or www.careercompass.co.uk

First you should check your local newspapers. You may have a regional paper to look in too. You could also look in the national newspapers to see what is available away from your home environment. Travel trade publications will also give you an idea of opportunities. Although some may require experience, reading these publications may help you find your ideal job (although it may not be appropriate to apply now, this will give you something to work towards).

Examples of trade press include:

- *Travel Weekly*
- *Travel Trade Gazette*
- *Flight International*
- *The Stage and Television Today*

You may also like to find out about all the relevant books that are published, to assist in your job hunting. Use the Internet and software at your careers centre (for example, Odyssey), and finally, investigate recruitment agencies, as these are another method used by employers to find staff.

ACTIVITY

Find out on which days jobs are advertised in your local and regional press. Establish which travel trade publications are available in both your college and local library.

Use all publications to familiarise yourself with the types of jobs available. Photocopy advertisements of jobs in which you are interested. Do this over an extended period of time. From the advertisements that you have collected, select ten jobs that appeal to you.

Analyse each job. What skills, qualifications and experience do you need for each of for these jobs. Create a chart, using the headings: job title, skills required, qualifications required, experience required, and 'Do I possess all of these skills?'.

Of the jobs that are not available to you now, analyse what experience training or education you will need in order to be able to apply for these positions.

Speculative applications

Although the formal way of getting jobs in the travel and tourism industry may be through applying for advertised positions, you should also be aware of the informal method.

We have already established that many companies are small, privately owned organisations. They may not have a separate Human Resources Manager who plans and organises recruitment; it may simply be done by the overall manager – and if he or she is busy, the organisation may in fact be understaffed. This is very common in the travel industry. It can, therefore, be highly beneficial to visit or telephone employers asking if they have vacancies, or simply send in a speculative CV. This also demonstrates that you are enterprising and confident, both of which are attractive qualities to employers in this people business!

PROFILE *Travel consultancy*

The nature of the job:

Working in a travel agency involves dealing with customers throughout the day. You will issue brochures, help plan holidays, advise clients, research availability and destinations, sell extra services and make bookings.

Personal/technical skills/qualities required:

Computer skills (some agencies require knowledge of Galileo) are required. You will need to have good customer care skills and be able to work under pressure. Some customer experience is usually preferred. Good personal presentation and communication skills are essential.

How to find a job:

Keep an eye on your local press, however, many vacancies are not advertised. A speculative CV to the travel agencies in your area is a good idea, or call in and give your CV to their Manager.

PROFILE *Cabin crew*

The nature of the job:

This much sought after role is generally perceived as being very glamorous. The role involves looking after all passenger needs: serving food and drinks, answering queries and administering first aid. As cabin crew you are the face of the company so smart/professional appearance and manner are essential. Cabin crew work hard and have a responsible position – lives will depend on them should an emergency occur. Permanent jobs are often available but some airlines now only offer 6 month contracts.

Personal/technical skills/qualities required:

Personality, appearance, stamina and customer care skills are essential. Most scheduled airlines only recruit staff over 21 years of age, but the age limit is lower for some budget airlines and charter fleets. Full and rigorous training is given. Depending on the airline, no minimum qualification may be demanded, but languages are often desirable.

How to find a job:

Look in the national press and the regional press may also feature advertisements as some airlines have regional recruitment fairs when they add flights from local airports. Write directly to airlines for details of their recruitment campaigns and entry requirements.

PROFILE *Ride attendant*

The nature of the job:

Assisting with the running of rides, the on/off loading and safety of all guests and providing a high level of customer care and service.

Personal/technical skills/qualities required:

Previous service industry experience is preferred. Having the 'right attitude' is essential – friendly outgoing personality, good communication skills, smart appearance, good team skills and physically fit. You will be working on rides in the park five days out of seven, often in unfavourable conditions, so stamina is also required.

How to find a job:

Due to the fact that Alton Towers does not have accommodation facilities, these posts are only advertised in the local press in Stoke-on-Trent and Staffordshire.

PROFILE *Tour operations*

The nature of the job:

A tremendous variety of work. You could be involved in reservations, marketing, brochure production, destination research or liaison with overseas offices and resort reps. There are many opportunities within operations. Much of the work carried out at Head Office is by telephone with clients, suppliers and staff. Permanent, full-time and part-time posts are usually available in the UK, with seasonal jobs in resorts.

Personal/technical skills/qualities required for UK positions:

A good telephone manner is essential, as much business is still done by telephone. Team skills are important. Computer skills, communication and numeracy are required at various levels, dependent upon the position. Most tour operators train in-house. This is often the only way, as you need to learn about the products on offer.

How to find a job:

National press and trade publications. If there are tour operators in your local area, keep an eye on your local press, try to get work experience there or send in a speculative CV.

PROFILE *Overseas resort representative*

The nature of the job:

To the clients on holiday, you are the company. Your role is to ensure a trouble free stay for all holiday makers – a demanding job with customers in the 21st century! Duties include airport transfers, welcome meetings, sales of excursions, dealing with problems and emergencies. Very few full-time jobs exist. It is predominantly seasonal work (May to October) with fewer winter vacancies in ski resorts (December to April).

Personal/technical skills/qualities required:

Ability to work under pressure, stamina, faultless customer care skills and an outgoing personality are essential. Good administration skills help and a foreign language may be required.

How to find a job:

Tour operators generally recruit more than six months in advance. Write to tour operators to establish their requirements and recruitment schedule. Some will send you a recruitment pack. There is high demand for these jobs so advertisements tend to be rare and national. Your Careers Office may receive mail shots from tour operators' recruitment departments.

Questions to ask yourself

The range of jobs available and their diverse nature may make looking for a job seem daunting. It need not be, but you must be systematic. Ideally, you will be able to find work that you enjoy – it is common for people to enjoy those things that they are good at. Do the activities in this section thoroughly to help you establish your strengths and interests.

ACTIVITY

Think about all the things that you enjoy doing, that you are good at (i.e. your strengths) or that interest you. Do not limit yourself to college activities or subjects. Think also about your part-time jobs, roles outside college or sports interests, for example. You may like to consider some of the following questions to get you started:

- Do you hand in work on time (i.e. work to deadlines)?
- Do you get on well with your colleagues and staff?
- Have you any experience of dealing with customers?
- Do you enjoy dealing with customers?
- Are you organised?
- In group activities, do you tend to lead or follow?
- Are you confident?
- Do you like meeting new people?
- Are you sociable?
- Do you have a good sense of humour?
- Do you see things through to the end (i.e. are you committed)?
- Are you determined, or do you tend to give up easily?
- Do you take care with your appearance?
- Can you communicate well – both written and orally?

List all of your strengths. Now consider the things that you are not so good at and list these.

Others see us differently to how we view ourselves. Work in small groups of close friends and discuss each other's strengths. Amend/add these to your list as appropriate.

ACTIVITY

Examine your list of strengths created in the previous activity. Are these the skills and qualities being sought by the employers you selected in the Activity on page 69? Select three skills/qualities that you need to work on to improve your employability.

Pursuing your progression aims

In order to plan your career, it is important to know what is available to you and how to pursue it. You may not want to pursue a career immediately, in preference to further education or training. However, knowledge of employment opportunities may help you in your choice of courses.

Employment opportunities

We have already looked at some employment opportunities in the Activity on page 69. It is a good idea to read the local, regional and travel press on a regular basis in order to keep up-to-date with opportunities that become available. Even if you do not apply immediately, you can use the addresses and contact names that are in the advertisements to apply speculatively at a later date. It is also important that you make yourself fully aware of the information and advice services available to you (free of charge) at your local job centre and the Careers Centre at your college.

ACTIVITY

Visit your college Careers Centre and establish what information and guidance they have for both people seeking employment and for those going on to higher education. If you are considering going to University establish the following:

- What types of course are available?
- How difficult is it to get a place?
- Where can you study?
- Can you afford it?
- What about accommodation and social life?
- How do you apply?
- What should you expect when you get there?
- What if you want to take a year out?

If you plan to go into employment, establish the following:

- What software do the Career Centre have?
- Do they help with CVs?
- Where is the vacancy bulletin board?
- Do they have a travel and tourism file?

KEY TERMS

'**Education** provides students with abilities to interpret and analyse new knowledge. It develops the critical abilities of a student.

Training is a much more specific activity, often concerned with practical skills.' (Adapted from WTO)

Training, education or employment?

Using information gained thus far from the activities in this section your first decision may be whether to go on to higher education or to job hunt. You may, however, have had enough of full-time study and want to put into practice your travel and tourism knowledge and earn some money! If so, consider whether you want to stay in your local area or are prepared to move away?

You will need to be aware of any training opportunities that are available. Although some employers will offer these, you could also gain such qualifications at your local college or through the Travel Training Company (the training company part of ABTA). Examples of courses include:

- Air Fares and Ticketing
- ABTA Travel Agents Certificate (ABTAC)
- ABTA Tour Operators Certificate (ABTOC)
- National Vocational Qualifications (NVQs)

In addition, there are BTEC Awards offering qualifications in Overseas Resort Operations, Tour Operating and Guiding, amongst others.

Applying for a job

The Curriculum Vitae (CV)

Whether job hunting or not, it is important that you have a CV. Once created, this record of your personal details, employment and education history can easily be updated whenever your circumstances change.

Your CV (and accompanying covering letter) are your opportunity to convince the employer that you are the right person for the job. Both the content and the presentation of the CV are, therefore, important. You must allocate plenty of time to produce a good CV.

Presentation of your CV

Although there are no rules about the presentation of your CV, you must ensure that it is neat, pleasing to the eye and that it gives the employer a clear indication of your experience and qualifications. At this stage in your career you may be able to fit this information on one page – you should certainly not use more than two pages. CVs have changed over the past few years, from the traditional type ('telling'/information based), to a more modern skills based 'selling' type of CV. The information is just the same; it is simply presented in a different way. You must choose the format that you are most happy with.

ACTIVITY

You may already be familiar with a traditional CV. Consider the more modern CV shown in Figure 1.27 and decide which you prefer.

Using the headings on the examples of CVs, produce your own draft CV. Word process this and get someone to check it. Redraft this until you have a perfect CV.

Remember that the purpose of the CV is to get the employer sufficiently interested in you to offer you an interview. It is, therefore, worthwhile spending as much time as possible in perfecting your CV. You may also wish to tailor it for each individual application, to highlight your own skills against specific employers' requirements. It is, however, sometimes sufficient to do this in your covering letter alone.

The covering letter

The covering letter is just as important as the CV in terms of selling yourself to your potential employer. Although it can be handwritten or word processed, it must always be neat, logical and without errors. Remember to read the advertisement carefully, pick out the key qualities and skills that the employer is looking for and highlight these in your letter. Remember also to tell the employer if you are replying to an advertisement or if it is a speculative application.

Rachel Evans
47 Eagle Street
WESTHAMPTON
W13 7PZ
(0538) 456986
Date of Birth: 19 September 1978

Enthusiastic, creative college leaver seeks varied and challenging opportunity within the travel industry.

Skills and Capabilities

*   I have excellent customer service skills, and experience of serving the public in a variety of situations.

*   I can communicate in French and Spanish, and I have a good knowledge of the Travel and Tourism industry.

*   My work experience reports have commented on my confident nature, energetic approach, and my outgoing personality. I also function well under pressure.

*   Juggling a full-time course with a part-time job has highlighted my flexibility, my organisational skills and my determination to succeed.

Education and Qualifications

Westhampton Regional College
2000–present
(Results due June 2002)

Hartford Secondary School
1995–2000

Vocational A Level Advanced Travel and Tourism
Units studies include: Marketing, Customer Service, Tourism Development, Health, Safety and Security, Finance, Worldwide Travel Destinations, and Spanish.

Air Fares and Ticketing

GCSEs

English Language	(B)
English Literature	(C)
Geography	(C)
French	(C)
Drama	(C)
Mathematics	(D)
Science	(DD)

Work Experience

Tesco, Milton, Westhampton
1998 – present

Sales Assistant (part-time)
Duties include using the till, dealing with customer enquiries, cashing up, and re-stocking shelves.

Tramway Travel Services
2 weeks – June 1997

Travel Agency Clerk (work experience)
Duties included, filing, typing, dealing with customer enquiries, and assisting with foreign currency exchange.

Grange Residential Home
2 weeks – November 1996

Care Assistant (work experience)
Duties included caring for elderly residents, feeding, bathing, keeping them company, and general cleaning tasks.

Additional Information

I have a clean Driving Licence and my own transport.

I am computer literate, and have used the Viewdata Reservation System, and the Galileo booking system.

My hobbies include amateur dramatics (I am involved in acting, and front of house activities), and I also enjoy swimming and aerobics, and I play netball in the College Team.

References

Mrs J Hill
(Course Tutor)
Westhampton Regional College
Kings Hedges Road
WESTHAMPTON
W4 3ZZ
Tel: (0538) 418200

Mr B Jones
(Personnel Manager)
Tesco Stores
Milton
WESTHAMPTON
W3 7ZY
Tel:(0538) 678000

Figure 1.27 Example of CV

ACTIVITY

Write a covering letter to accompany your CV. This can be either a speculative application to a company that you would like to work for or in response to one of the advertised positions you have already researched. Remember to keep both your covering letter and CV on disk so that you can easily amend each to match the positions you are applying for.

The application form

Some employers may wish you to complete an application form, rather than sending in a CV. If an employer asks you to complete an application form *do not* send in a CV.

Photocopy the application form first so that it does not matter if you make mistakes. Complete it using black ink so that it can be photo-copied. Remember that all your information is now on your CV, there-fore it should be easy to transfer onto the form. There is also often a large space asking you what you have to offer the organisation or why you would be good at the job. Consider this carefully, draft it several times and get help from your tutor. Finally, make sure you fill in all the space available – this is your opportunity to 'sell' yourself.

Whichever method you have used to apply for a position, it is always a good idea to keep a copy of all your correspondence, so that you can refer to it prior to going for an interview

Interview preparation

Let us presume that your application has been successful and that you have been invited for an interview. Your CV and covering letter, or your application form, will have been evaluated, both in terms of their content and presentation. Similarly, at interview, you will be assessed on how you present yourself and what you say.

The key to success at interview is good preparation. As soon as you are invited to interview, begin to prepare. Consider the following questions:

● How you are going to get there?
● What will you wear?
● What research you need to do on the company?

Think about what the employer will be looking for and the types of questions they may ask. Many interviewers ask standard questions and these may include:

● What skills and qualities do you feel you have to offer our organisa-tion?

- Describe a situation where you have had to work under pressure? How did you cope?
- What experience do you have in dealing with customers?
- What do you hope to be doing in five years time?

Practise your answers to the questions above. Memorise them – this will increase your confidence.

Research the company before you go for an interview. You may be able to do this at your local library, on the Internet or you may have to call them and ask if they can send you details. Either way, your research into the company will demonstrate to your employer that you are committed. It will also boost your own confidence.

Use the information you gain from your research to prepare some questions to ask them at the end of the interview. It is a good idea to have a few questions prepared, but do make sure that the information has not

Help yourself to create a good impression

Remember – at interview you may be entering a traditional environment. A conservative dress code is advised. Suggested Guidelines:

MALE	FEMALE
Suit or jacket	Smart trousers or skirts
Trousers not jeans	Jacket
Shoes not trainers	Ironed shirt or jumper
Dark socks	"Sensible" shoes
Shirt-ironed!	Minimal visible bodily piercing (i.e. one earring in each ear)
Clean shaven	
No body piercing	

Although dress code for women is less restrictive, you must remember that the clothes you wear when socialising may not be suitable. Be well groomed – clean hair and nails. Polish your shoes and iron everything.

Figure 1.28 *Help yourself to create a good impression at interview*

been covered in anything sent out to you or discussed during the interview. Positive questions about training opportunities, expansion plans or anything that you are confused about create a better impression than simply asking about pay and holidays.

Body language is an important element of how you communicate at interview. Although you will be nervous, make sure you smile, greet people warmly and appear positive.

Finally, before you go to the interview:

- Reread all the correspondence you have received.
- Make sure you are familiar with the skills and qualities the employer is looking for.
- Prepare some questions.

ASSESSMENT

A group of business leaders from one of the Eastern European countries will be visiting your college in the near future. Their countries have all experienced a vast increase in tourism in the past ten years. This has brought with it many economic benefits, but also presented some problems. The delegates are interested in comparing their own experiences with those of the UK. They wish to see how tourism has developed in the UK, what the industry is like at the beginning of the 21st century and what sort of opportunities it offers to young people.

You have been asked to prepare material to present to them. This will consist of two parts: a written report and a display.

Write a report on the UK travel and tourism industry and its development. This should detail the following points:

- The development of the travel and tourism industry and the reasons for its rapid development since the end of the Second World War. You may also wish to predict future developments.
- The size of the UK industry, in terms of both income and employment; and its importance to the UK economy. Use charts and graphs to display your data. Make sure you have checked the validity of the data that you are using.
- How the industry is structured and the features that make it so unique. Make sure you give examples of all the key components and show how they interact with each other. Support your information with a diagram.
- Different types of organisations (commercial and non-commercial) and how they interact with each other. Give examples. You may also wish to investigate two organisations that work together in your local area and present this information as a Case Study. Ensure the organisations are from different sectors and then show how funding and business objectives are different for commercial and non-commercial organisations.

In order to show the delegates the employment opportunities that travel and tourism offers, you have also been asked to produce a display. This must show a full range of possible jobs available to you and then focus on one that particularly interests you. Ensure you include the following:

- An outline of the range of employment opportunities available to you. To do this you should collect advertisements from local, national and regional newspapers, as well as from the trade press. You should also establish what other information sources (including software) are available in your Careers Centre. You could work in small groups to interview local travel and tourism employers, establish opportunities within their company and share information.

- Identify one job that interests you and describe the personal and technical skills required to do that job. Evaluate and explain why you think this is the job for you.
- Display your own CV – as an example of good practice! This should be tailored for the job that interests you and should be accompanied by a covering letter.

Ensure that the display is professionally produced and pleasing to the eye. Your audience is Eastern European business leaders. Remember that it will be assessed in terms both of content and presentation.

Key skills

In completing the assessment for this unit, you can achieve the following key skills. These will be accredited at the discretion of your tutor on the basis of the quality of the work you submit.

C3.2 Read and synthesise information from two extended documents about a complex subject. One of these documents should include at least one image.

C3.3 Write two different types of documents about complex subjects. One piece of writing should be an extended document and include at least one image.

2

Tourism development

Aims and objectives

At the end of this chapter you will:

- **know the types of organisations involved in tourism development**
- **understand the different reasons why different organisations become involved**
- **know why tourism development occurs both in developed and developing countries**
- **have an understanding of the positive impacts of tourism and how these can be maximised**
- **have an understanding of the negative impacts of tourism and how these can be minimised**

Introduction

We established in Chapter 1 that tourism is considered to be the world's largest industry, involving many types of organisations with differing objectives. This chapter examines the development of the tourism industry, both in the UK and overseas, in greater detail.

The chapter begins by investigating why organisations aim to develop, or contribute to developing tourism. We will first examine the many and diverse profit-driven private sector enterprises who dominate the tourism industry (see Chapter 1).

Public sector bodies also have a role in tourism development. These include the national and regional government and tourist boards, as well as such organisations as the Rural Development Agencies, the Council for Protection of Rural England and the National Parks Authorities. Voluntary organisations, in particular, pressure groups, are also an agent of tourism development and, as such, their important role will also be examined.

Each of the different sectors has different reasons for becoming involved in tourism development. You will gain an understanding of the economic, environmental, socio-cultural and political reasons that motivate organisations to become involved.

Much of the motivation for organisations wanting to develop tourism is to make money. This can greatly benefit the wealth of an area, or even a country and it also creates jobs. Other positive impacts may include the restoration of buildings, regeneration of disused facilities, an increase in local pride or sense of community and other facilities being developed in the area (which may benefit local residents). However, development in some areas can also have negative impacts. Although there may be more wealth within a community as a result of increased tourism, the cost of living (in particular, house prices) may increase. Increased traffic, litter and noise are just some of the negative environmental impacts. Finally, communities may become outnumbered by tourists and feel resentful; crime may increase.

All of the impacts of tourism, both positive and negative, will be investigated. Although these are numerous, it is increasingly recognised that they must be managed. Those involved in tourism must work towards maximising the positive impacts of tourism and minimising the negative impacts. The many ways in which tourism can be managed will be examined. These include: marketing techniques (e.g. encouraging overnight stays), planning systems, park and ride schemes, training and community education.

What is tourism development?

KEY TERM

Development: the change of an area. This is usually seen as an improvement to the destination (and it may involve the establishment of roads, electricity and running water).

Before we start the chapter, we must first consider exactly what we mean by the term 'tourism development'. It is a term that is often used, but which has rarely been defined. It can be used to describe the way in which a region or country has developed through the process of tourism. For example, The Gambia has developed due to its emergence as a tourist destination. The Kenyan coast, Dominican Republic and, closer to home, Bradford provide similar examples of destinations that have developed as a direct result of tourism.

Tourism development, however, may also refer to the construction of a particular facility, for example, a hotel, attraction or resort complex. Thus, Disneyland Paris is a tourism development in itself.

The agents of tourism development

Three sectors are involved in the process of tourism development:

- private sector enterprises
- public sector organisations
- voluntary sector bodies

Partnership: two or more sectors working together.

Sustainability: ensuring that our environment is not damaged for the next generation.

Each of the public, private and voluntary sectors have contrasting objectives (see Table 2.1). This section will examine each of the three sectors and their reasons (i.e. objectives) for becoming involved in tourism development.

Public sector organisations	Provide services and facilities. They often provide the infrastructure that enables development to take place. Their motive is often to create jobs and more income for an area.
Private sector organisations	Aim to make a profit.
Voluntary sector organisations	Often contribute towards the conservation and preservation of environmental and cultural heritage.

Table 2.1 *Tourism development sector objectives*

It is important, however, to recognise that by the end of the twentieth century, all sectors had seen the need to work together. Partnership and sustainability are the two key words now used in tourism development.

Private sector enterprises

Throughout the world the tourism industry is dominated by private sector organisations. The greatest proportion of facilities for tourism are provided by this sector, including accommodation, attractions, transportation, catering and entertainment. They are often supplied to the general public by other private sector organisations, such as travel agencies and tour operators. The primary aim of them all is to make a profit.

Multinational: a large business operating in many countries.

Infrastructure: the basic necessities needed (e.g. sewage, roads, transportation, running water and other services).

Sustainable tourism: tourism that does not damage the physical, social or cultural environment.

Regeneration: improving an area, normally old industrial sites.

Imagine you are a tourist visiting your home town on a three day break. List all the organisations you would come into contact with (include accommodation, transportation, entertainment facilities, etc.). How many of these do **not** belong to the private sector?

Though organisations may state many objectives, we must recognise that profit is essential to them all. For example, British Airways is aware that in order to secure profits, important customer safety requirements must be observed. Many organisations also refer to customer service and taking care of the environment as part of their goals.

Profit maximisation

Profit maximisation, whether stated as the primary objective or not, is essential for all private organisations. Without it they will go out of

KEY TERM

Profit maximisation: the wish to increase profits to as high a level as possible.

business if they are small organisations. Alternatively, if they are Public Limited Companies, in which the general public have invested with the hope of a return on the profits generated, the shareholders will look to invest elsewhere.

DID YOU KNOW?

A recent EU survey showed that in the hotel and restaurant sector, 80% of hotel beds available throughout the EU were provided by independent hotels: 'Micro-enterprises' (0–9 employees) made up 96% of the businesses. In the UK, 70% of hotels and guest houses have ten or fewer bedrooms.

KEY TERM

Development agencies: organisations whose aim is to develop the economic potential of an area (i.e. to help create jobs and income).

ACTIVITY

Research five private sector organisations and identify their goals.

In addition to the organisations providing directly for tourist needs (e.g. accommodation, transportation), there are other private organisations that are specifically involved in the process of developing tourism.

Development agencies

These exist to develop and/or market the tourism potential of an area. Their role and funding varies. In the UK some development agencies are funded by both the public and private sector, for example, Norwich Area Tourism Agency receives some funding from four local authorities, but the majority comes from private organisations who pay a membership fee.

Marketing Manchester is an example of a company that is aiming to develop tourism through increased marketing (Destination Marketing Company). Although it describes itself as a private company (limited by guarantee), it is funded by the public sector.

PROFILE *Marketing Manchester*

Marketing Manchester (a private company limited by guarantee) is a 'not for profit organisation' that is funded by ten local authorities, one of which is greater Manchester. Their aim is to promote Manchester internationally as an exciting and attractive destination for business and leisure and as a gateway to the north of Britain.

Landowners

These may choose to develop attractions, hotels or similar, on their land and so contribute to the process of tourism development. Examples include:

- Lord Spencer has used his land to develop a museum to commemorate the life of Princess Diana at Althorp Hall.

- The purchase of land in Thetford, Longleat and Sherwood Forest has allowed Center Parcs to become a successful all year round tourist development within the UK.

PROFILE *Phuket*

The sale of large areas of the island of Phuket in Thailand by the Thai government to property developers means that it is now a mass tourism destination, providing an airport, hotels and golf courses for the western tourist.

There has been much criticism of the sale of these parcels of land. Local campaigners claim that the land was the historical home of the local people and does not belong to the Thai government to sell.

DID YOU KNOW?

In Zanzibar, local people are fighting against several UK development companies who are trying to build a $14 billion tourism development, to include 14 luxury hotels, several hundred villas, a cruise ship harbour, three championship golf courses and a world trade centre.

In contrast to Phuket, Richard Branson has ensured that Necker Island does not become a mass tourism destination (by charging from $1,300 per person per day!). However, it is certainly a site developed for tourism purposes.

Necker Island, the British Virgin Island

"The Ultimate Caribbean Escape"

We invite you to discover and enjoy Richard Branson's private Caribbean retreat – NECKER ISLAND, the tiny piece of paradise found in the British Virgin Islands. This Island gem is available for you exclusively! Just 74 acres of sheer pleasure offering the ultimate in comfort, magnificent cuisine and a superb range of activities.

Offered to you on a truly ALL-INCLUSIVE basis. Your private Island will provide you with all your food, drinks of every kind (from a magnificent cellar), leisure activities (water sports feature heavily) and perfect, unobtrusive service and attention from the Island's staff.

The History of Necker

Named after a Danish Admiral (the Danes were big around these parts once), not much happened to Necker over the years until Richard bought it in 1978. He set about creating the most exclusive and beautiful Island in the Caribbean! On top of the hill, the "Great House" with its 10 bedrooms was built. In addition, two smaller houses were created called "Bali Hi" and "Bali Lo"! They each take an additional couple and afford even greater privacy and intimacy.

Construction materials included York Stone, Timbers from Brazil, Furniture and Fabrics from Bali and a Snooker table from the East End! All the Bedrooms have en-suite facilities and Terraces with the most amazing views across the ocean.

To keep you entertained, you will find two Tennis Courts (floodlit), two Swimming Pools, Plunge Pool, Water Skiing, Snorkelling, Sailing, Wind Surfing and fabulous Beaches!

Anything goes in this little paradise and the attentive Staff will always be there to ensure your every comfort. The Private Virgin Island. Where Dreams really come true . . .

Figure 2.1 Necker Island

Source: Virgin Territory 1999

Development companies

These vary in their size and services and are often construction companies who have purchased land and financed some sort of development, be it housing, timeshare, shopping malls or attractions. Such development may be small, for example, an individual who purchases a barn and makes it into a holiday cottage is essentially a developer.

Large multinational companies, however, are more often associated with the term 'development companies'. They may be responsible for the development of airports, infrastructure and bridges, as well as entire resorts.

DID YOU KNOW?

The developers of the Bluewater shopping centre near Dartford are the Australian Land Lease Company. They have included in this mega-mall a 12 screen cinema and a man-made lake where shoppers can hire boats, ice-skate and cycle.

KEY TERM

Development companies: profit-making organisations involved in developing areas, e.g. building hotels or houses. They may build something from scratch, or convert existing facilities, e.g. dockland areas.

PROFILE *Laing*

Often seen throughout the UK on large building projects, Laing are also responsible for the construction of the Millennium Dome, the Severn Crossing, the Heathrow Express and the Hong Kong Convention centre.

'Laing provides complete solutions to a wide range of accommodation and infrastructure needs across the world. We provide project development, finance, construction and design services in the UK and overseas, as well as property development ... in the UK.'

Source: extract from Laing web site

CASE STUDY *Redevelopment of Spitalfields market*

The market at Spitalfields opened in 1683 selling 'flesh, fowl and roots'. By 1991 this consisted of over 100 small businesses selling fruit and vegetables. They all existed within a four acre site of Victorian ironwork buildings under glass. Its success had resulted in congestion and so a new market was developed to the east of London, leaving the Spitalfields site empty.

Close to London's financial centre and only a few minutes walk from Liverpool Street station, this site was first bought by a consortium of developers (Spitalfields Development Group), to build offices. When recession struck, this type of speculative development was no longer attractive and so Urban Space Management created a joint venture with the Spitalfields Development Group. They decided to develop the site for retail use, and maintain the market atmosphere. It was important that the project had the support of the local community and did not compete with the local traders, who were predominantly Bangladeshi shop owners selling clothes. Flyers were sent to local households inviting them to open days.

Spitalfields is now a thriving market area catering for city workers. It consists of wholesale fruit and vegetable units, art and craft stalls, bars and restaurants and some sporting facilities. A town centre manager has been employed and many Georgian buildings in the area have been renovated. Publicity in guide books and by word-of-mouth means that the market has now also become popular with overseas visitors. It is estimated that the regeneration of this area has created over 1,000 jobs.

Source: Adapted from Insights, *November 1998, ETB/BTA*

ACTIVITY

Referring to the Case Study name the organisations involved in the redevelopment of Spitalfields project.

What were their objectives? Give five possibilities.

What did they do to ensure these were met?

How has the local community benefited?

Consultancies

Consultancies: private companies who give specialist advice.

Consultancies are essentially companies or individuals who give specialist advice. They may offer guidance on the design of a new theme park, the staff training needs of a company, how a product needs to be changed to attract more tourists or where a new hotel should be built. Many consultancies work in developing countries (now called emerging markets) advising on how to develop their tourism business, market the country or develop the product. Deloitte & Touche is a consultancy that deals with such projects (see Figure 2.2).

Deloitte & Touche Hospitality and Leisure Consulting

The rapid growth of the travel industry creates opportunities and challenges in equal measure.

Opportunities are there for tourism destinations to increase their market share, to raise visitor spending and to improve foreign exchange earnings and employment. Opportunities are there for travel businesses to expand their product portfolio, to make carefully chosen acquisitions and to improve shareholder value.

We have highly practical experience in:

- tourism planning at regional, national and local levels;
- destination marketing;
- business planning and fundraising;
- market research and statistics;
- transaction support and commercial due diligence;
- human resource development and training;
- operational reviews, benchmarking and competitor analysis;

- privatisation;
- forensic support; and
- tourism taxation.

Examples of the diversity of our work include:

Fiji – as a tourism destination, we researched the market opportunities, identified the improvements required to its product and showed how they could be achieved. The plans were worked out with government and the industry, and following their adoption as government policy, we have been helping to bring them to fruition.

Eurotunnel – we devised a strategy and action plan for the distribution of car shuttle tickets.

Ministry of Environment and Tourism of Namibia – we devised and implemented training and train the trainer programmes in customr care.

Kenya – we reviewed all the government owned tourism businesses and showed how their performance could be improved. Our work there led directly to the establishment of a new tourism board.

Source: extract from Hospitality and Leisure Consulting

Figure 2.2 Deloitte & Touche Consulting

Source: Deloitte & Touche Hospitality and Leisure Consulting

Leisure and entertainment organisations

These cover a multitude of companies, from a local multiscreen cinema development to Center Parcs, from Disneyland Paris to Bluewater. Such organisations often locate their new development to benefit from tourism. They may be the main attraction themselves (for example, Disneyland Paris), or simply add to a destination's products to make it more attractive.

ACTIVITY

Name five leisure or entertainment organisations that are the main attractions of an area (i.e. flagship attractions).

Name five other leisure or entertainment organisations that contribute to the attractiveness of an area to tourists.

CASE STUDY *Designer outlets as tourist destinations*

Outlet shopping, which has taken the UK retail market by storm in recent years, has become a significant factor in the tourism industry. The group travel business, for example, cites outlet shopping programmes as one of its fastest growing sectors, as outlet retailing continues to revolutionise consumer attitudes towards shopping, leisure and tourism.

The growing tourism potential of outlet centres was clearly demonstrated recently when McArthurGlen Designer Outlet Great Western at Swindon was chosen as joint Southern Tourist Board regional winner of the English Tourist Board's England for Excellence Award. The centre won the award in the Visitor Attraction of the Year category for sites attracting over 50,000 visitors a year.

For outlet centre developers such as BAA McArthurGlen, site preference is now as much a matter of tourism potential as it is of local population catchment. As a result, McArthurGlen Designer Outlets act as tourist destinations in their own right, attracting visitors by the millions from throughout the UK and overseas, and encouraging those visitors to seek out other nearby attractions and activities as well as its own designer outlets.

To further promote designer outlets as a major force in the tourism business, BAA McArthurGlen works continually to forge close working partnerships with national, regional and local tourist boards and organisations, as well as heritage associations, local attractions and hotel groups to encourage as many visitors and tourists as possible to visit the regions in which its designer outlets operate.

Source: English Tourist Board 1999

ACTIVITY

Why do local and regional tourist boards work in partnership with the developer in the Designer outlet Case Study?

What are the benefits to hotels and local attractions within ten miles of a Designer Outlet?

Why might the local Chamber of Commerce object to or encourage such a development?

KEY TERM

Multinational companies: large organisations who are operating in many countries, e.g. MacDonalds and Coca Cola; Holiday Inn and Hyatt.

Private and public sectors in developed or developing countries

The public and private sectors have slightly differing roles, depending on whether a country is developed or developing. The private sector is dominant in developed countries – multinational companies exist, finance is available from both public and private sources and the infrastructure is already in place. However, in developing countries the government may have to take a central and more influential role. The private sector may not want to build hotels and attractions until it is established that the destination will create profits for them (i.e. there is too high a risk). Therefore, some of the initial investments may need to be taken by the government.

KEY TERMS

Superstructure: all the facilities and amenities within a destination, usually provided by the private sector (e.g. hotels, golf courses).

Gross Domestic Product (GDP): total value of all goods and services produced in a country, minus the income the country earns from investment abroad.

Public sector organisations

Within the UK, local governments (also known as local authorities) have been involved in tourism since the late nineteenth century, when they provided attractive promenades, piers, parks and gardens in order to make towns attractive. Local pride and competition with other towns were the main motivations behind this development.

It was much later that the British government realised that tourism was potentially an important part of the country's economy as it could provide both jobs and income. It is for this reason that the UK government and many other national governments initially became involved in tourism. In the UK the Development of Tourism Act in 1969 established the tourist boards through which tourism could officially be promoted. More recently, the government has also recognised the need to manage the industry, in particular its social and environmental impacts. Sustainability is now a key motivation.

DID YOU KNOW?

Tourism contribution to GDP reflects the importance of tourism to a country's economy. This varies from approximately 5% in the UK, to around 10% in Spain and 11% in Kenya.

In the UK, tourism's interests are now represented by the Department of Culture, Media and Sport (DCMS). Although this department has a dedicated minister, the fact that tourism is only a small part of this department's overall responsibilities means that there is an under-secretary responsible for tourism. By way of contrast, in countries that are more dependent on tourism, the government is more likely to become involved. Spain's tourism industry is represented by the Ministry of Tourism, Transport and Communications and in Kenya the importance of tourism is reflected in the fact that there is a Ministry of Tourism and Wildlife.

ACTIVITY

Use the Internet (try www.odci.gov/cia/publications) or alternative sources to establish the current contribution that tourism makes to GDP in:

Three European countries.

Three long haul destinations with developed economies.

Three long haul countries with developing economies.

Compare your findings and discuss reasons for any differences.

National government's role in tourism development

This section will look at the differing reasons for national government involvement in UK tourism, before examining how they have allocated responsibilities to local governments and the tourist boards.

National government's reasons for involvement are numerous and are summarised below (adapted from *Tourism Principles and Practice*, Cooper, Fletcher, Gilbert and Wanhill, Pitman, 1993):

- It earns foreign exchange and is important to the balance of payments.

- It creates jobs – and the government, therefore, needs to provide education and training.

- As the industry is large and fragmented, it needs someone (the government) to co-ordinate its development and marketing.

- The positive impacts to the host community (the local residents) must be maximised to spread the benefits and the costs fairly.

- To build the image of the country as an attractive destination (marketing).

- To protect customers and prevent unfair competition (legislation).

- To provide public goods and infrastructure (roads, rail, services such as electricity and water supply).

- To protect the environment and other tourism resources (e.g. Stonehenge).

- To regulate certain activities (e.g. gambling).

- To conduct surveys.

DID YOU KNOW?

1.5 million people are employed in tourism in the UK. However, if we include those employed indirectly, this figure rises to 3 million (i.e. one of every nine jobs available is in tourism).

DID YOU KNOW?

The BTA tries to 'spread the benefits of tourism' by spreading visitors more across the regions of the UK and also across the months of the year, with the aim of avoiding congestion.

KEY TERM

Infrastructure: the basic necessities needed to operate within a country or town (i.e. sewers, running water, lighting, roads and transportation).

If tourism is important to a country's income and job market, the government will need to produce plans and policies. These will ensure that tourism develops as the country wishes it to with foreign exchange earnings and jobs opportunities being maximised. This may involve funding some aspects of the industry, in particular its marketing.

In the UK, the government first gave money to tourism in 1929 when £5,000 was given to the Travel Association of Great Britain. Since then substantial amounts have been given as grant in aid to the BTA. The amounts have, however, reduced since the early 1990s as the government now wants the private sector to take on the role of developing tourism.

The BTA and other tourist boards serve many functions, however, marketing and co-ordination of the development process are key roles that the government has assigned them. Through national marketing, some areas of the country can be promoted and others not. This can support government objectives regarding employment and regeneration.

National governments wish to **spread the benefits of tourism** across the whole country. While it may not be possible to get tourists to visit all areas of a country, marketing can help. The German government, for example, does this by rotating the holiday periods throughout the country's regions in order to avoid the rush on school holidays. The dominance of coastal tourism in Spain has been tackled by the Spanish government by funding a campaign that promotes rural Spain.

Tourists traditionally have either **positive or negative images of holiday destinations**. Governments may wish to promote a positive image in order to encourage tourism. In the Caribbean, for example, campaigns have been needed to remove some of the local people's resentment of the tourists' wealth.

Consumer protection is an integral role for governments. The transport industry must be regulated in order to ensure that passengers are safe. In the UK all airlines must be licenced by the Civil Aviation Authority, tour operators need an Air Travel Operators Licence (ATOL) and the Air Travel Trust Fund was introduced by the government to protect consumers in the event of tour operators collapsing. In some countries, tour guides and travel agencies also require licences to operate.

Further consumer protection is offered in the UK by such legislation as The Trade Descriptions Act or the Data Protection Act. These are not exclusive to tourism, but are highly relevant. Finally, the Monopolies and Mergers Commission is a government body that prevents unfair practice. This has been particularly relevant to the travel industry in recent years, within the tour operating sector.

All countries need **infrastructure** in order for tourism to develop. Without roads, electricity and water supplies, private investors cannot be persuaded to build hotels and attractions (i.e. the superstructure). In less developed countries the government may also have to provide the initial superstructure in order to encourage further investment.

National governments are in a position to finance some projects that may be unprofitable and, therefore, unattractive to the private sector. The resort developments of Cancun in Mexico and Languedoc Roussillon in France are both examples of massive government investment to encourage private sector investment. In Languedoc Roussillon the public sector provided the money necessary to buy the land and set up the infrastructure. The private sector was then able to develop the superstructure.

PROFILE *Vietnam*

Vietnam is an attractive destination for the adventurous tourist and for backpackers. However, it is the mass tourist packages that are attractive to the Vietnamese government, as these will provide significant revenue. Vietnam's lack of a basic infrastructure – including paved roads, drinking water and electricity – is, however, a constraint for the tourism industry. Tourist facilities outside the main towns are virtually non-existent.

There is also a shortage of hotel accommodation. Despite interest from over 100 foreign-funded tourist projects, none have yet been started, mainly due to bureaucracy. Unfortunately, such investments by foreign investors could benefit the foreign investors more than the Vietnamese economy. The investors of course need a return on their capital.

Despite this, the Vietnam government welcomes foreign investment in tourism – they need the capital from the foreign investors. They need help from the overseas developers to learn about the tourism industry.

Source: Adapted from Financial Times, *8 December 1994*

KEY TERM

Tourism resources: the things that tourism needs, in order to take place. This includes hotels, roads and water. It also includes natural resources (e.g. beaches, woodlands and open spaces). Historic sites are also a key resource.

Many **tourism resources** are irreplaceable, and, therefore, need the highest level of protection. Tourism resources include beaches, landscapes, flora and fauna, woodlands, historic monuments and buildings and archaeological sites. Many organisations have been set up, or are supported by, the UK government to ensure that our tourism resources are protected. These include English Heritage (Cadw in Wales, or Heritage in Scotland), the National Parks Authority, the Forestry Commission, the Countryside Commission, the Council for the Protection of Rural England and the Society for the Protection of Ancient Buildings.

In Kenya the importance of protecting their main tourism resource (the wildlife) is clearly reflected in the title 'Ministry of Tourism and Wildlife'.

ACTIVITY

Investigate one of the UK public sector bodies named previously. Find out how much money it receives from the government and whether it has alternative sources of income.

What are its aims and objectives? Give two examples of specific activities in which it is currently involved.

Governments can play a role in **controlling and overseeing tourism** and can also make sure projects happen. They can prevent tourism occurring in certain areas and encourage it in others, encouraging quality and protecting consumers (this may be done by the government and/or local authorities).

Some control can occur through planning permission and infrastructure development. Put simply, if planning permission is granted for a four star hotel near a beach and for the infrastructure to be set up, then it is possible that the area may develop as a tourism resort. Alternatively, if a government refuses planning permission and does not develop the infrastructure, development is unlikely. The planning system may also be used to encourage different types of tourism (for example, in Cornwall planning permission for caravan parks has been restricted since 1954).

Local authorities' role in tourism development

In the UK, the role of local authorities is important to the operation and development of tourism on a local basis. Not only do they market their areas (usually in conjunction with the Regional Tourist Boards), but they also provide much of the basic infrastructure needed for tourism to take place (for example, parks and gardens, theatres, arts centres, golf courses, leisure facilities, caravan sites, car parking facilities, transport and museums). Even refuse collection, building maintenance and planning controls contribute to an area's tourism industry.

Some local authorities are directly involved in running tourism businesses or organisations, for example a local museum or heritage centre. In some towns, libraries exhibit historical features. In Horncastle in Lincolnshire, the local library was built to incorporate part of the Roman Wall to ensure it was accessible to both tourists and the local population.

The Local Government Act of 1948 and Local Government Act of 1972 gave local authorities the powers to set up information and publicity services for tourists and to provide for visitors. They now run the Tourist Information Centres (TICs), usually in conjunction with the Regional Tourist Board (RTB).

The extent to which local authorities pursue tourism varies tremendously throughout the UK. While some local authorities may have a Director of Tourism and a separate tourism department, within many authorities the responsiblity for tourism often falls to a department with many other responsibilities, for example planning, leisure or economic development. So while some local authorities produce tourism strategies plans and policies in great detail, it is estimated that 50% of local authorities still make no mention of tourism in their planning.

ACTIVITY

Establish where the responsibility for tourism lies within your own local authority.

Visit your public library to look at the plans for your local area. Does your area mention tourism in its Local Structure Plan? If so, what are its main objectives for tourism?

With respect to tourism, the main responsibilities of local authorities are as follows (adapted from *The Business of Tourism*, J.C. Holloway, Longman, 1998):

- Providing leisure facilities for tourists (e.g. conference centres) and for residents (e.g. theatres, parks, sports centres, museums).

- Planning for tourism.

- Development control over land use.

- Provision of visitor services (usually in conjunction with tourist bodies).

- Parking for coaches and cars.

- Provision of caravan sites.

- Production of statistics on tourism.

- Marketing the area.

- Upkeep of historic buildings.

- Public health and safety issues.

CASE STUDY *Farmers' markets come to town*

Although farmers' markets are often started by local authorities, once established the organisation is usually handed over to the farmers themselves. Many put on entertainment to create a social and festive atmosphere, and some have cookery demonstrations, where local chefs are invited to make a meal using market produce.

Boosting tourism

Flourishing farmers' markets bring a number of benefits to visitors and those involved in tourism development. They broaden the range of attractions on offer to the visitor and provide a richer experience, and can bring people into an area of the town which they might not otherwise have visited. These showcases for local produce can be linked with special events, eg Cheese Day and Apple Day in Bristol, so strengthening regional identity. They also offer an opportunity to promote other commercial activities linked to farms, such as B&B or self-catering accommodation.

Council backing

Councils are welcoming farmers' markets. Waverley Borough Council, for example, offered financial support to start up a South West Surrey farmers' market. As the plans progressed the council tourism and economic development departments also became involved, as well as external parties such as Surrey County Council who provided additional support. The first market was a great success, attracting an estimated 8,000 visitors.

Source: News ETC, *October 1999*

ACTIVITY

What is the appeal of farmers markets to: the farmers, the local authorities, local businesses and the visitors?

National tourist boards' role in tourism development

National tourist boards (NTBs) aim to maximise the economic benefits to their country by encouraging the development and marketing of tourism. They do not manage tourism venues on a day-to-day basis. Rather, they provide a framework of policies within which both the private sector and public sector can work. How they do this varies from country to country. Most NTBs, however, will need overseas offices in the countries from which they attract the most tourists.

As established in Chapter 1, the BTA is essentially responsible for overseas promotion with a structure of National and Regional Tourist Boards promoting domestic tourism. Although this has slightly changed with the introduction of the English Tourism Council*, many of the roles remain the same. When established in 1969, the aims of the National Tourist Boards were as follows:

- Encouraging residents of the UK to travel within their own country.

- Encouraging the provision and improvement of attractions and facilities for tourists in Britain.

- Administering the section four grants.

- Advising the government on matters relating to their country.

Section four grants were essentially financial aid distributed by the Tourist Boards to the hotel industry to improve the number and quality of hotel rooms. These no longer exist in England, but in Wales and Scotland they are still available. Although still intended for hotel development, they are used for wider purposes such as developing farmhouse accommodation and supporting local attractions.

The primary roles of the National Tourist Boards are tourism development within their own regions and marketing of their territories. In order to do this they conduct research, publish promotional material and develop marketing ideas.

ACTIVITY

The Internet has many sites established by various countries' National Tourist Boards.

Select one European and one non-European country. Research Internet sites for the national tourist boards. What do they promote nationally? Name the main tourism resources, both man-made and natural, that are being promoted by the NTB.

For each country select one of its regions and see how it is promoted through the RTB. Discuss any differences.

The Regional Tourist Boards (RTBs) essentially operate in a similar way in Wales and Scotland. In England their roles are larger, as they must also cover a national role, formerly performed by the English Tourist Board (ETB).

They receive funds from the DCMS and local authorities and are, therefore, considered to be public organisations. However, we must be

* Since the time of writing the English Tourism Board has been replaced by the English Tourism Council. The aims above now only apply to the Scottish, Welsh and Northern Ireland Tourist Boards. The Regional Tourist Boards (RTBs) in England have jointly taken on these responsibilities.

The Minister's message

The following is an edited message from the Minister of Foreign Affairs, Tourism and International Transport, Miss Billie A. Miller, on the 40th Anniversary of the Barbados Tourism Authority.

In 1958 the Government of Barbados made a visionary move when it established the Barbados Tourist Board. Faced with the declining fortunes of agriculture which was at the time the major industry and economic activity, tourism was seen to be a potentially viable option.

Today, exactly 40 years later tourism has proved itself not only to be a viable option but has firmly established itself as the mainstay of the Barbadian economy accounting in 1997 for 70 per cent of foreign exchange receipts, 15 per cent of Gross Domestic Product (GDP) and employing some 20,000 persons.

From a fledgling industry with modest beginnings and registered visitor arrival statistics of 37,090 in 1958, the tourism industry has certainly taken full flight with visitor arrivals in 1997 soaring to a record 990,178.

Demand for tourism across the globe is phenomenal. Barbados cannot ignore the increasing competition from the East Asia/Pacific countries and the traditional US tourist generating regions where domestic tourism is growing in popularity.

The Barbados Tourism Authority continues to be proactive in its marketing strategy as it seeks to surpass the competition. It is poised to meet the turn of the century with its predictable expectations and its unpredictable eventualities.

Operating at times under constraints of staff shortages and modest budgets, the Authority has been able to record major successes. Arrivals for 1997 easily make the year a landmark year in the history of the Authority's operations with the 1989 record being eclipsed by a 24 per cent increase in arrivals.

Great success is not always given public acclaim but I would like to congratulate the Barbados Tourism Authority for having captured three prestigious tourism awards during 1997.

The World Travel Association named the Barbados Tourism Authority the Top Caribbean Tourist and Convention Bureau.

The World Travel Market named Barbados Tourism Authority as one of their Best Stand Award winners and Bride's Magazine presented the Barbados Tourism Authority with a plaque congratulating Barbados on being voted one of the world's outstanding honeymoon destinations by the All-Stars Readers honeymoon poll.

Figure 2.3 The Barbados Tourism Authority

Source: Extract from The Sunseeker, *8 October 1998*

aware that the UK Regional Tourist Boards have become commercial organisations which now provide a range of services for their members. These members come from both the public and private sectors and will typically include hoteliers, restaurateurs, attractions, local councils, educational establishments and guest houses.

The original role of the Regional Tourist Boards was:

- To produce a co-ordinated strategy for tourism within their region in association with the local authority.

- To represent the interests of the region at national level and the interests of the tourism industry within the region.

- To encourage the development of facilities that meet the changing needs of the market.

- To market the region by providing reception and information services (in conjunction with the NTB), producing and supplying suitable literature and undertaking miscellaneous promotional activities.

These remain their aims in 2000. Today, however, instead of receiving money predominantly from public funds, they gain an income from their commercial activities. These include selling publications, inspecting accommodation, running training programmes and conducting research.

PROFILE *Welcome family programme*

The Regional Tourist Boards in England run a series of customer service training programmes aimed at all businesses within the travel industry. One day programmes at competitive prices, these courses are part of the RTBs strategy for ensuring tourists enjoy their stay and so wish to return. The five different courses have a variety of aims, including customer care, understanding disability and special needs issues, telephone techniques, basic proficiency in foreign language skills and staff motivation.

PROFILE *Practical help from the East of England Tourist Board*

The East of England Tourist Board has a department of nine people working to support and develop tourism business in this region. They offer services such as:

- **helping organisations develop economic strategies**

- **advice on funding/grants available (especially from the European Union)**

- **suitability of particular sites for tourism businesses (e.g. is there sufficient demand for this business?)**

- **advice on how to be environmentally friendly**

- **how to ensure visitors know that your attraction/facility exists.**

In addition the RTB carries out research. This helps business assess trends.

KEY TERM

Regional Development Agencies: public sector bodies, set up to increase the economic wealth of their area.

KEY TERM

Partnership: two or more sectors working together.

As part of the government's drive to decentralise power, **Regional Development Agencies** were created in 1999. Their role is in business development, economic support, skills, employment and sustainable development. They must work closely with the RTBs, include tourism in their own regional economic development strategy and include representatives from local authorities and businesses on their board. From April 2000 the boundaries of the RTBs and RDAs were matched so that the RDAs can support the tourist boards and ensure that policies complement each other. Although they have been allocated only small amounts of money from the government, they do have funds to allocate to some projects.

Partnerships

Until the 1990s there was quite a clear distinction between the roles of the public and private sectors. The public sector provided services and the private sector tried to make a profit. However, it is now recognised that partnerships between the sectors are the way forward.

Private sector money is needed to develop an area's resources, but the road and infrastructure requirements need public sector consent. Thus, a local authority wishing to develop a run down area of its city is likely to seek a private investor to provide funds for the necessary hotel developments and visitor attractions. Partnerships, especially between private companies and local authorities, are now fundamental to many regeneration schemes (see Case Study on Tourism Development Action Programmes on page 108). Partnerships between governments and private developers are also often necessary to develop a country's tourism potential (e.g. Vietnam – see profile on page 92).

Furthermore, although some city councils may now employ 'City Managers' to aid the smooth running of all the services and facilities, the success is dependent upon a partnership approach.

PROFILE *Lincoln City Centre Management*

Lincoln City Centre Management is a partnership of Lincoln City Council, city centre retailers, Lincolnshire Training and Enterprise Council, Lincoln Chamber of Commerce and Lincoln City Forum. Their aims are to improve the vitality and viability of Lincoln city centre. They are involved in a project that has resulted in: 100 hanging baskets in the city centre, publicity to promote 'Summer in the City', a student guide and the licensing of the city's pavement cafés. The project has also introduced CCTV to the city, which has resulted in reduced vandalism to local traders and improved safety for all.

CASE STUDY *Languedoc Roussillon*

In France the recognition of differing public and private roles in tourism development led to a detailed plan for the development of the Languedoc Roussillon coastline in the 1960s. 180 kilometres of Mediterranean coastline were developed over several years through a partnership agreement between the state, local and regional authorities and the private sector.

The French government was in a position to plan the project, buy the land and finance some of the necessary infrastructure for the development to take place (roads, ports, water supply and mosquito eradication). The land was divided into resorts and then water, electricity, roads, parking and telephones were installed by the local authorities. Only at this stage did the private sector enter the development process, in order to construct the hotels, villas, apartments, shops, entertainment facilities and other tourist enterprises.

Voluntary sector bodies

Although the development process may essentially be instigated and then developed by either the public or the private sector, their plans are sometimes thwarted by community or pressure groups. These voluntary sector organisations have exerted an increasing amount of influence in recent years, through generation of public opposition. This can stop or change developments in tourism.

Pressure groups

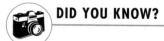

ACTIVITY

Go through back copies of your local newspaper and investigate recent developments in your home town (these may be shopping centres, leisure developments or new infrastructure). Was there public opposition? Did the opposers form community groups and give themselves a name? What impact did they have?

The pressure group Tourism Concern was set up in 1989 to raise awareness of global tourism issues. The founder members recognised the power of the tourism industry and the fact that tourism's impacts on the people in less developed countries are very often negative.

Now an educational charity with over 1,000 members, Tourism Concern publishes regularly, provides educational resources and campaigns vigorously.

KEY TERM

NIMBYism (Not In My Back Yard): is the term that has been given to well organised community groups who prevent developments in their commuter villages or local conservation areas.

DID YOU KNOW?

A man called Swampy lived in tunnels under the proposed Newbury by-pass in order to prevent its construction.

DID YOU KNOW?

Tourism Concern provides some free educational materials to non-members and extensive resources to members, including access to their library.

Why Join *Tourism Concern*?

Thank you for your interest in our organisation. *Tourism Concern* was set up in 1989, to campaign for change in the world's largest industry. We are a membership organisation and registered charity, based in the UK, but also part of a global network. *Tourism Concern* advocates tourism that is just, participatory and sustainable and campaigns for tourism to take into account the rights and interests of the communities affected.

Tourism is big business affecting the lives of millions of people worldwide. As a result it is very powerful. There are times when it seems that absolutely nothing can stand in its way.

Almost all of us have been a **tourist** at some point in our lives and have seen the negative impacts of tourism. All too often the host community benefits little from the tourist trade but bears most of the environmental and economic costs.

Our Holidays, Their Homes

◆ Luxurious hotels are built on beautiful beach front property, and can displace local villagers and make it difficult for local fishermen to use the beaches.

◆ Local villagers in Goa suffer water shortages, while luxury hotels fill their swimming pools and provide their hotel guests with hot showers around the clock.

◆ Safari parks are created to protect wildlife and to attract ecotourists, but often at the expense of local inhabitants who are evicted and told they may no longer graze their livestock there. In East Africa the Maasai and Samburu peoples have lost much of their ancestral lands in this way.

◆ In Burma, thousands of people have been displaced at the military junta's behest to 'clean up' areas that are to be visited by tourists. In Pagan the local people were given two weeks to leave their homes around ancient pagodas. They were moved a few miles away to New Pagan, to a site of bare parched earth with little shelter.

Tourism is a Human Rights issue

Tourism Concern is campaigning on behalf of people who suffer as a result of tourism but also works to encourage best practice within the industry. Tourism is a Fair Trade issue.

For example, in many cases in less industrialised countries, less than 20% of the money spent by tourists on a holiday stays in the host community. Most of it goes to companies based in the North, who own, operate and supply most of the airlines, hotels and fittings in tourist resorts.

Surely the communities we visit should benefit fairly and squarely from our holidays.

Figure 2.4 Why join Tourism Concern?

Source: Tourism Concern membership flyer

ACTIVITY

Visit the Tourism Concern website at www.tourismconcern.com. Establish what campaigns they are currently involved in.

Tourism development and the European Union

One of the aims of the European Union is 'economic and social cohesion', and yet, at the end of the 1980s it was established that the average income of countries such as Greece and Portugal amounted to less than a third of the most affluent areas.

Funds, therefore, exist to assist the most disadvantaged regions within the EU:

● European Regional Development Fund – finances infrastructure in disadvantaged regions.

● European Agricultural Guidance and Guarantee Fund – helps develop rural areas.

Through these funds, marinas, airports and conference centres have been built, and transport for the environment and telecommunications have been improved. In the UK, Northern Ireland, the Scottish Highlands, Merseyside and Northumbria have been the main beneficiaries. Within Europe, Greece, Spain, France and Ireland have received the most funding.

Figure 2.5 *Example of a former tourism grant scheme (note: this is a purely historical example, as such a scheme is no longer in operation)*

Source: East of England Tourist Board

PROFILE *EU assistance in Northumbria*

Northumbria has, in recent years, suffered from the decline of its traditional industries. The Northumbria Tourism Board was successful in attracting EU funds in order to promote their area for tourism purposes. An initiative, known as Venue Points North, was set up in partnership with the RTB and successfully attracted £43,000 in EU grant money in 1993.

ACTIVITY

Investigate the grant schemes available within your local area for tourism businesses (these schemes are administered by the RTB).

DID YOU KNOW?

The WTO carried out development activities worth US $4.4 million in 42 different countries in 1996/7

KEY TERM

Global: covering the whole world.

Tourism development and the World Tourism Organisation (WTO)

The World Tourism Organisation (WTO) is involved in tourism development on a global basis. National governments can use the WTO for advice, to seek funding and to find experts to carry out the projects. The projects that they are involved in often cover the whole of the tourism industry in a country. These long-term projects involve national strategies and plans, examples of which include:

- tourism master plan in Ghana
- reconstruction and development plan in the Lebanon
- action for sustainable development in Uzbekistan

Shorter projects that they have been involved in include:

- hotel classification scheme in Ecuador
- new tourism laws for Nicaragua
- resort management in the Maldives
- resort marketing in China

The objectives of tourism development (the positive impacts of tourism)

The objectives of any tourism development will vary according to who is involved. While the private sector will essentially have a profit motive for involvement, other agencies' objectives may be seen in terms of economical, environmental, socio-cultural or political benefits.

Regional Promotional Projects

WTO is in a unique position to carry out special projects that promote tourism to a group of member countries. The Silk Road and the Slave Route are two of these projects, being implemented in cooperation with the United Nations Scientific and Cultural Organization (UNESCO).

The Silk Road: Launched in 1994, WTO's Silk Road project aims to revitalize through tourism the ancient highways used by Marco Polo and the caravan traders who came after him. The Silk Road stretches 12,000 km from Asia to Europe. Sixteen Silk Road countries have joined forces for this project: Japan, Republic of Korea, DPR Korea, China, Kazakstan, Kyrgyzstan, Pakistan, Uzbekistan, Tajikistan, Turkmenistan, Iran, Azerbaijan, Turkey, Georgia, Greece and Egypt. Joint promotional activities include a brochure and video, familiarization trips and special events at major tourism trade fairs.

The Slave Route: Initiated in 1995 as part of the United Nations' International Year of Tolerance, the Slave Route aims to boost cultural tourism to western African nations. Its immediate goals are to restore monuments, enhance history museums and launch joint promotional campaigns in selected tourism generating markets, which will motivate foreign visitors to learn about the history of these countries and to discover their roots. The project is expected to be expanded in the future to include other nations in southern and eastern Africa, as well as countries in the Caribbean.

Figure 2.6 *Regional Promotional Projects of the WTO*

Source: WTO website, 1999

KEY TERMS

Economic benefits: jobs and income.

Sustainable tourism: tourism that does not destroy the resources on which it depends.

In the past, tourism has predominantly been seen by the public sector in terms of its economic benefits. The fact that this industry created jobs and brought wealth to a destination made it attractive to governments, regional agencies and local authorities who were trying to increase their area's prosperity. While these remain the primary objectives of many tourism developments, all sectors are becoming increasingly aware of the need to protect the environment and communities from the negative impacts of tourism. The concept of sustainable tourism has, therefore, been an essential part of all tourism developments since the early 1990s and will be examined later in this chapter.

Naturally, there are similarities between an organisation's objectives and the positive impacts of tourism. All developments *aim* to bring positive impacts, even though they may not be successful. The objectives of tourism development and the positive impacts of tourism will, therefore, be examined together.

Economic objectives

The most powerful argument used by those wishing to develop tourism in a destination is its economic benefits. These include:

- employment opportunities
- increased income
- the effects of the multiplier
- development of the region

In addition, international tourism may well also bring foreign exchange which may create a healthier balance of payments.

Employment opportunities

 **DID YOU KNOW?**

Research shows that job creation in tourism is growing 1.5 times faster than any other industry sector.

An increase in the number of tourists in an area will mean that a greater number of employment opportunities are created as more staff will be required in all facilities used by tourists. Hotels, airlines, information centres, shops and restaurants will all need extra staff for existing businesses and may even need to expand their businesses to cope with demand. Tourism is a service industry and so is labour intensive. As a result, the growth in the tourism industry continues to create jobs.

It was estimated in 1999, by the World Travel & Tourism Council, that in the EU tourism accounts for 22.1 million jobs, that is, approximately 14.5% of the total (see Table 2.2). They also estimated that in the UK 3.4 million jobs were created (12.6% of the total).

You may remember from Chapter 1, that it was claimed by the BTA that tourism accounts for 1.5 million jobs here in the UK, approximately 6% of the workforce. The difference between these figures and those shown in Table 2.2 simply reflects different types of employment being included, or not, in each category. These include:

- Direct employees: those people who work in tourism organisations, such as hotels, travel agencies, tour operators or tourist shops.

- Indirect employees: those people who work for organisations that supply tourism organisations. This includes people working in agriculture and manufacturing (e.g. suppliers of hotel equipment, food packaging and ticket printing companies).

- Induced employment: the direct and indirect employers of travel and tourism spend money, which in turn creates extra jobs.

- Construction employment: those employed to build tourist facilities and infrastructure.

1999 ESTIMATES	GROSS DOMESTIC PRODUCT		EMPLOYMENT		
	% OF TOTAL	GROWTH*	JOBS (M)	% OF TOTAL	GROWTH*
European Union	14.1	2.3	22.1	14.5	0.5
Austria	17.6	3.1	0.6	17.2	1.0
Belgium	13.8	1.9	0.6	14.2	0.2
Denmark	15.1	3.3	0.4	15.3	1.4
Finland	15.5	2.6	0.3	15.2	1.1
France	14.8	2.4	3.6	14.7	0.7
Germany	10.8	2.4	3.0	8.9	0.5
Greece	18.3	2.7	0.6	16.3	0.0
Ireland	16.5	5.8	0.3	18.8	2.3
Italy	16.1	1.9	3.7	18.4	0.3
Luxembourg	10.4	2.1	0.0	10.4	0.4
Netherlands	13.2	2.8	0.9	12.7	1.1
Portugal	19.4	2.8	0.9	19.5	0.8
Spain	22.7	2.1	3.3	24.3	0.6
Sweden	11.7	2.1	0.5	12.0	0.3
United Kingdom	12.3	2.0	3.4	12.6	0.0

* 1999–2010 Annualised Real Growth Adjusted for Inflation (%)

Table 2.2   *1999 GDP and employment estimates*

Source: World Travel & Tourism Council

Income from tourism

Tourism creates an income for employees, businesses and the government. Tourists spending money in a destination create the income for those employed in the industry; their wages and salaries come originally from the tourists. Business income is also created by the tourists who buy services, such as overnight accommodation, guided tours and meals. Finally, the government also receives an income from the tourists via the tax system. In the UK this may be the VAT on the goods purchased or the departure tax of £10. Some countries also impose a tourist tax. In France this is known as the taxe de sejour.

The effects of the multiplier

Just as employment can be direct, indirect or induced, so can the income of a region. The income spent in a region by the tourist is re-

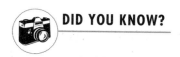

DID YOU KNOW?

The multiplier effect varies from country to country as well as within countries. It is generally higher in developed countries or regions.

YEAR	DIRECT TOURISM JOBS	INDIRECT TOURISM JOBS	TOTAL TOURISM JOBS	GROWTH IN TOTAL TOURISM JOBS	TOURISM JOBS AS % OF TOTAL EMPLOYMENT
1988	233,572	277,857	511,429		5.26%
1989	233,805	286,388	520,193	1.7%	5.25%
1990	223,539	277,745	501,284	−3.6%	5.02%
1991	220,356	290,447	510,803	1.9%	5.17%
1992	205,260	260,682	465,942	−8.8%	4.71%
1993	204,825	258,368	463,193	−0.6%	4.69%
1994	206,306	256,504	462,810	−0.1%	4.65%
1995	248,448	302,004	550,451	18.9%	5.42%
1996	289,763	338,149	627,912	14.1%	6.16%
1997	309,499	363,360	672,860	7.2%	6.54%
1998	341,932	395,685	737,617	9.6%	7.02%

Table 2.3 *South African employment in the travel and tourism economy*

Source: World Travel & Tourism Council website

ACTIVITY

What are the reasons for the substantial growth in tourism jobs in South Africa?

Give examples of ten 'direct tourism' jobs.

Give examples of ten 'indirect tourism' jobs.

DID YOU KNOW?

The UK supports an internationally agreed target to halve the number of people living in poverty by 2015.

circulated in the economy by those who receive it. For example, if you work in the Tourist Information Centre for the summer, some of the money you earn may be spent on items such as clothes, CDs or social life. You will spend the money on things that you would not have been able to buy without the job, i.e. the money you have earned is going back into the economy.

The fact that some of the money earned from tourism is re-spent locally is known as the **multiplier effect**. There are many different methods for calculating the impact of the multiplier, but at this stage it is sufficient to know that a certain amount of money initially spent in an area will be re-spent, creating an income that is greater than the initial input. The multiplier rate from tourism varies from area to area, but in the UK is generally calculated at 1.7. Thus if a tourist spends £100 when on holiday in your town, the net benefit in terms of increased income is estimated to be £170.

Tourism development and economic development

Tourism development is often used by governments for economic development, specifically to regenerate areas. Inequalities in standards of living within countries can be tackled by encouraging tourism to specific areas. To achieve this governments may build resort complexes (for example Nusa Dua in Bali and Languedoc Roussillon in France) or alternatively develop local programmes.

PROFILE *Tourism Development Action Programme (TDAP) in Lancaster*

Developed by the ETB in the 1980s, the TDAPs were partnership agreements aimed to alleviate some of the employment problems in specific areas of the country that had suffered from the decline of traditional industries.

Lancaster suffered due to the demise of its manufacturing industry. Although the nearby towns of Blackpool and Morecambe, as well as the Lake District, had successfully attracted tourists, Lancaster failed to do so. The TDAP was a three year project aimed to strengthen the local economy through tourism, by generating jobs, income and support for local facilities. It was hoped that the area's image could be enhanced, thus attracting other investment.

A partnership was set up including:

- **Lancaster City Council**
- **Lancaster County Council**
- **Lancaster Chamber of Commerce, Trade and Industry**
- **Lancaster Enterprises Ltd.**
- **Lancaster Restaurateurs Association**
- **ETB**
- **North West Tourist Board**

The City Council, County Council and ETB all contributed finances towards the TDAP projects. Examples of projects carried out included:

- **marketing of Lancaster as a heritage destination**
- **participation at the World Travel Market**
- **organising historical events (e.g. an Elizabethan Fair and Maritime Festival)**

- **a consortium of attractions was established which co-ordinated their own marketing activities and opening times**
- **trail leaflets**
- **a feasibility study for a conference centre**
- **development of a short break package**
- **coach park**
- **Tourist Information Points**
- **cast iron pedestrian signs**

The success of these projects is indicated by the fact that the City of Lancaster won the England for Excellence Tourism Destination Award in 1989.

 **DID YOU KNOW?**

Overseas tourists spent over £12 billion in the UK at the end of the twentieth century. The BTA estimate that this will rise by around 47% by 2003.

Contribution to the Balance of Payments

Perhaps the major motivation of a government to attempt to increase inbound tourism is that it will create an increased amount of **foreign currency earnings**. This contributes to a country's balance of payments. Governments prefer that the income from inbound tourism is greater than that spent by residents going abroad, i.e. their tourism balance of payments is positive. As seen in Chapter 1, this is not the case in the UK and has not been so since 1980.

In most developing countries, however, local residents cannot afford to travel, the result of which, is that the travel balance is positive. Indeed the balance of payments may be dependent on tourism in some countries. Although the governments may view the income from tourism positively, their dependence on tourism makes them vulnerable. Natural disasters, political change or fashion may reduce tourist numbers with dramatic results for those economies that are dependent on tourism revenue.

 ACTIVITY

Refer to Table 2.4. Which continent is most dependent on tourism? Within each continent, which areas are most dependent on tourism? Name three of the most popular tourism destinations within each area.

List the five EU countries where tourism accounts for the highest percentage of GDP. Explain why this is the case (see Table 2.2 on page 106).

1999 ESTIMATES	GROSS DOMESTIC PRODUCT % OF TOTAL
World	11.7
Africa	8.8
North Africa	6.8
Sub-Saharan Africa	11.2
Americas	11.1
North America	11.8
Latin America	5.6
Caribbean	20.6
Asia/Pacific	10.0
Oceania	14.7
Northeast Asia	10.0
Southeast Asia	10.6
South Asia	5.3
Europe	14.0
European Union	14.1
Other Western Europe	15.4
Central and Eastern Europe	11.1
Middle East	7.3

Table 2.4 *Chart of European GDP percentages*

Source: *WTTC, March 1999*

DID YOU KNOW?

According to the WTO, international and domestic tourism combined generate up to 10% of the world's GDP and a considerably higher share in many small nations and developing countries.

PROFILE *Kenya*

Historically, Kenya was a major exporter of tea and coffee. These two cash crops were the basis of its foreign exchange earnings. However, tourism has steadily become increasingly important in the Kenyan economy with the result that it now creates as much foreign exchange earnings as the two crops combined. Tourism is now the single most important product to the Kenyan economy in terms of foreign export earnings, contributing almost 35%. It accounts for approximately 11% of GNP (1994 figures).

The importance of tourism to the Kenyan economy is demonstrated through the establishment of high profile tourism agencies – the Ministry for Tourism and Wildlife as well as the Kenya Tourist Board. Tourism also forms part of the National Development Plan and Economic Reforms Policy.

Infrastructure development

A knock-on benefit of tourism development in an area is that infrastructure will develop. As discussed earlier, governments need to provide infrastructure before tourism can begin to develop. This may include airports, roads, marinas, sewage systems and water treatment plants. These developments benefit the local community, as well as tourists.

PROFILE *India*

The Indian government promotes investment opportunities on their website. Claiming that India now represents the 'business opportunity of a lifetime', the Department of Tourism seeks investors in 'hotels, amenities, golf courses, domestic airports, etc.' They are offering loans and the government itself will act as a 'facilitator in getting project clearances and permits'. Investors who are not Indian are allowed to hold up to 51% equity in any project.

Source: Adapted from the Explore India website

PROFILE *Tourism in South Africa*

In the mid-1990s, tourism is the fourth largest earner of foreign exchange in South Africa. It was estimated to have contributed 4% to GDP in 1995. When compared with the world average of 11.6%, it can be seen that its tremendous natural resources (wildlife, coast and wilderness areas) offer a vast potential for growth.

The South African government wants to reap the economic advantages of tourism. Furthermore, it is looking to tourism to boost the South African economy, i.e. to generate demand and production in other sectors. The White Paper on 'The development and promotion of tourism', published in 1996 by the Government of South Africa outlines eight specific targets:

- To increase the contribution of tourism to GDP to 10% by 2005.

- To sustain a 15% increase in visitor arrivals over the next ten years.

- To create one million additional jobs in tourism by 2005.

- To increase foreign exchange earnings of tourism to R40 billion per annum by 2005.

- To welcome two million overseas visitors and four million visitors from the rest of Africa by 2000.

- To develop a tourism action plan to implement the strategies, objectives and targets of the tourism policy.

- To identify and execute at least five national priority tourist projects.

- To establish tourism as a subject on the school curriculum.

ACTIVITY

Environmental objectives

It is important to be aware that tourism can have some positive impacts on the environment, and indeed, the objectives of some tourism developments concern the protection of the environment (it is debatable whether some of these would be necessary if there were not so many tourists!).

The responsibility of protecting the environment usually lies with the public sector. However, an increasing concern throughout the world for the environment led to the Earth Summit in Rio de Janeiro in 1992. The result has been the placing of pressure on the private sector to 'clean up after themselves'. It is now generally unacceptable for profits to be made at the expense of the environment or a culture. This will be explored in more detail in the section on sustainable tourism.

DID YOU KNOW?

In the USA national parks are owned by the state, who have total control over running them.

National parks

Protecting tourism sites started in the USA in 1872, with Yellowstone National Park. In the UK, ten National Parks were established under the National Parks and Access to the Countryside Act of 1949. Since then the Norfolk Broads and the New Forest have achieved a similar status to a National Park.

In Scotland it is expected that national parks will be formed as a result of devolution. Loch Lomond and the Cairngorms have already been named as sites in need of protection and other sites are expected to follow.

ACTIVITY

National Parks are run by the National Parks Authority. Investigate its role and what powers it has to either encourage or prevent developments.

It could be argued that while National Parks are tourism developments that do protect the environment, the very fact that they cater so well for the tourists encourages more tourism.

In Kenya the 13 National Parks and 24 National Reserves now cover 7.5% of the country and provide the western tourist with wonderful game viewing. They were established in the 1940s, originally to ensure the survival of the game that had been over-hunted by the white settlers.

ACTIVITY

The ten National Parks of England and Wales are: Northumberland, the Lake District, Yorkshire Dales, North York Moors, Peak District, Exmoor, Dartmoor, Snowdonia, Brecon Beacons and the Pembrokeshire Coast. In addition, the Norfolk Broads and the New Forest now have similar status. Place these on the map below.

Investigate which National Parks have been established in Scotland.

DID YOU KNOW?

Mount Fuji in Japan is the world's most visited National Park. The Peak District claims to be the second most visited in the world, with 22 million visitors per year.

They now provide protected areas for the country's wildlife – the reason why most people visit Kenya and, therefore, the country's main tourism resource.

The creation of National Parks is not always perceived to be positive. The fact that local people have been moved to create these parks and are not allowed within them, except as paying tourists, has caused resentment.

Areas of Outstanding Natural Beauty (AONBs) were also established as a result of the National Parks Act. There are currently 37 designated areas in England and Wales (approximately 8% of the land surface). Examples include the Lincolnshire Wolds, Cotswolds, North Pennines and the Surrey Hills.

CASE STUDY *National Trust*

The National Trust – an introduction

1 Introduction

The National Trust for Places of Historic Interest or Natural Beauty is a charity which holds countryside and buildings in England, Wales and Northern Ireland for the benefit of everyone. The Trust is independent of Government: it depends on the generosity of those who give it properties and the money to maintain them, on more than 2.5 million subscribing members and on its friends and supporters everywhere. The Trust accepts grants from statutory bodies in the same way that other owners of historic properties and other charities may accept them when eligible. It is 'national' in the sense that it works on behalf of the nation. There is an independent National Trust for Scotland.

2 Founders

The Trust was founded in 1895. Three imaginative people foresaw an increasing threat to the countryside and historic buildings: Miss Octavia Hill, a social worker of vision known also for her pioneering work in housing reform; Sir Robert Hunter, a solicitor whose special concern was for the open countryside in Surrey; and Canon Hardwicke Rawnsley, a parson who lived in and loved the Lake District. They formed the National Trust as a public company not trading for profit, with powers to acquire and preserve beautiful and historic places. The Trust's first property was the gift of $4\frac{1}{2}$ acres (1.82 hectares) of cliff land in North Wales; its second the purchase – for a mere £10 – of the 14th-century timber-framed Clergy House at Alfriston (East Sussex).

3 Growth

In 1907 the Trust was incorporated by an Act of Parliament with a mandate to promote *'the permanent preservation for the benefit of the nation of lands and tenements (including buildings) of beauty or historic interest'*. The Act granted the Trust its unique power to declare its property 'inalienable'. Nearly all its properties are inalienable which means that they can never be sold or mortgaged. If the Trust so wishes, and with the approval of the Charity Commission, inalienable land can however be leased.

For forty years the Trust grew steadily. Money from legacies, gifts and public subscription enabled it to secure considerable stretches of coast and country and a number of ancient buildings. In 1937 a further Act of Parliament enabled the Trust to hold country houses and their contents as well as land and ancient buildings, as many were threatened by heavy taxation. Blickling Hall in Norfolk was the first country house to be left to the Trust.

Under the Trust's 'Country Houses Scheme' a house – with or without its contents – may be presented to the Trust with a financial endowment to maintain it in perpetuity. In return, the donor and his/her family may go on living in the house, subject to public access and measures to retain the essential character of the property.

The Acquisition of Land (Authorisation Procedure) Act of 1946 gave the Trust the ultimate right (granted to no other private landowner) of appeal to a joint committee of both Houses of Parliament if a public authority proposed to take its inalienable land by the use of compulsory powers.

In 1965, when it already protected 187 miles of coastline, the Trust launched its Enterprise Neptune appeal. This was a special conservation measure to extend the Trust's protection over as much as possible of the remaining 700 miles or so of our finest, unspoilt coastline. Some £25 m has been raised through Neptune and 575 miles of unspoilt coast are now both safe from damaging development and permanently available to the public.

© 1998 The National Trust

Source: The National Trust Education: Notes for Students, 1998

ACTIVITY

The National Trust provides and protects many 'visitor attractions' inclusive of historic buildings, countryside and coastline.

Investigate the three National Trust sites closest to your home. If you can, visit one of them or speak to a National Trust Education Officer. Alternatively, use the National Trust website at www.nt-education.org.

How do these visitor attractions protect the environment?

What economic advantages does the National Trust bring to your local area?

Environmental education for the local community

On a smaller scale, **tourist information points** can educate the local population as well as the tourists on the local environment. This may include aspects of the architecture or the natural environment. Usually provided by the local authorities, these are often found at the start of rural walks or outside historic buildings. Leaflets and the information provided by the TIC, although aimed at tourists, may all benefit the residents.

Improving the local environment

Tourism developments may also stimulate environmental improvements, which may benefit local people and tourists. We all prefer an attractive environment and so destinations may be encouraged to 'clean up' a river front or building in order to enhance the environment. Many waterside areas that had been derelict since the beginning of the nineteenth century have been given a face-lift.

In the UK, Liverpool, Leeds and Manchester have all benefited from the development of riverside and canal areas. One of the benefits may be attracting tourism, but the local residents also notice an improved environment. In Sydney, Australia, these areas have become the focus for new restaurants, expensive bars, tourists trails and other private sector amenities.

Figure 2.7 Sydney harbour

PROFILE *Kings College Cambridge*

Cambridge is an historic city attracting approximately 3.4 million visitors per year. The city is known throughout the world for its University and colleges. These colleges are the main tourist attraction. Kings College chapel is the most visited attraction within the city, with 84% of all visitors going there.

Problems arise due to the volume of visitors within the colleges. Some of the negative impacts of having too many visitors to the colleges were partially reduced in 1995 by charging an entry to some of the colleges (prior to this visitors had been free to wander around). Two immediate benefits emerged from this charging scheme:

- First, visitor numbers decreased, thus reducing congestion, wear and tear on the buildings and disturbance to the students. In some colleges visitor numbers halved.

- Second, the income generated has been used for maintenance. The income from tourism at Kings College has contributed towards a new roof and now funds maintenance of the chapel each year.

KEY TERMS

Socio-cultural impacts: those impacts that affect the society or their culture (e.g. how leisure time is spent, local events, arts and family structures).

Culture: ideas, beliefs and values.

DID YOU KNOW?

40% of West End theatre tickets in London are purchased by tourists.

KEY TERM

Community facilities: those facilities provided for the benefit of everyone.

The monies generated from tourism development can be re-circulated to maintain and even further improve the environment. Historic houses need an income in order to maintain them. Although some of this may be managed through such organisations as English Heritage and the National Trust, some homes (for example, Chatsworth House) can remain in private hands as a result of tourism income.

Socio-cultural objectives

Socio-cultural objectives are those that aim to benefit society and/or culture. Tourists are often from a different culture to the people they are visiting, and so they bring with them different ways, religions, customs and values to those of the host community. This is particularly the case when western tourists visit developing countries. The contrast between the host and guest can be huge. While this can bring with it many negative impacts (see page 130), the positive impacts on cultures are also objectives for development.

Positive impact of tourism development on culture

It is often stated that tourism can bring **a greater understanding of cultures**. Through our travels, we become educated about different peoples, their customs and cultures. Conversely, the host community are exposed to western habits. This may aid understanding and some claim that it may contribute to world peace.

Not only will tourism educate the visitors, but local people may find that they become more knowledgeable about their own culture. The fact that visitors are interested in and appreciate the local culture may result in **a sense of pride**. Traditions, festivals and some religious ceremonies may be revived as a result of the tourist interest. It is claimed that the revival of morris dancing, for example, is a direct result of modern tourism, as customs such as traditional dances and local ceremonies become an attraction themselves.

Scotland has now firmly established itself as the place to spend the New Year. By launching an annual Hogmanay Festival, Edinburgh has become well-known as the host of Britain's biggest street party. By doing so it has ensured the continuation of the traditions of Hogmanay, and created much income for the city's hotels and bars every New Year!

This revival of traditional activities will reinforce local pride and ensure the continuation of local events which may otherwise disappear.

Community facilities are often enhanced by local authorities or private companies who develop leisure attractions, knowing that both the tourists and the local population will be customers. Museums, sports facilities and cinemas will only be built by the private sector if there are

A night to remember in the home of Hogmanay

Edinburgh

180,000 join 'world's largest street party'

Gerard Seenan

For years, Edinburgh, the city which perhaps more than any other is associated with new year revelry, had been preparing for its millennium celebrations.

Many of the 180,000 fortunate enough to get tickets for what was billed as the world's largest organised street party, queued for days to be there. They all appeared to believe it was worth the wait.

By mid-morning, police had sealed off the city centre. Shops closed, truck after truck arrived bearing equipment for the concerts and carnival the city had organised. Even the Scottish weather managed to curtail its worst excesses.

Throughout the day hundreds skated on the Winter Wonderland ice rink, built in the shadow of the castle. Nearby, families queued to enter a giant inflatable sculpture. In Waterloo Place, even more joined the fairground rides of the Hogmanay carnival.

In theatres and comedy clubs, the millennium was marked with sketches and plays. Pubs were packed. It was, said Pete Irvine, the event's organiser, the biggest and most diverse party the city could host.

Figure 2.7 Edinburgh's annual Hogmanay Festival

Source: The Guardian, *1 January 2000*

sufficient customers to visit them. In this respect, tourists can contribute to encouraging the provision of such services and then help to maintain them through using them. This is particularly the case in rural areas where local shops, cafés and bars continue to make a profit through the tourist trade. Local bus services, which may otherwise have been unprofitable, can often be maintained through tourist use. The local population also benefit, therefore.

The maintenance of such services can improve the **quality of life** for rural populations. In urban environments increased leisure facilities can also be seen as advantageous to the community. Quality of life may be more dramatically improved within some communities by the fact that tourism provides jobs for local people and so the income from the tourists is creating additional wealth. Add to this the fact that environmental improvements that have occurred as a result of tourist developments may encourage local pride and a feeling of wellbeing, and it becomes clear that tourism could sometimes be seen as a solution to local problems.

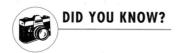

DID YOU KNOW?

Britain's most scenic railway – the Settle to Carlisle line – would have been closed had it not been recognised that increases in tourist revenue could make it profitable.

Political objectives

Like any other industry, tourism developments are subject to political considerations. The level of tourism development carried out, by the government for example, will vary from country to country, depending on the ideology of the government in question. At a simple level, government involvement in tourism development is more likely to be influential in such state planned economies as China, Cuba or developing countries, than in the European states led by a democracy.

The political motives for government involvement include enhancing an area. It may also wish to use tourism to boost national morale or pride, and consequently gain a political advantage. In Israel, the development of tourism is thought to have helped national pride and to have created sympathy for some of the political problems (national pride is also generated by encouraging domestic tourism). The increased foreign exchange earnings generated through tourism and the resulting improved balance of payments may benefit a government's political position. It is also claimed that international understanding is gained through tourism (it is impossible, however, to be certain whether this is really the case).

The negative impacts of tourism development

We have established that an increased number of tourists can bring considerable benefits to economies, societies, their cultures and the environment. This is in fact why government organisations and private companies develop tourist attractions, amenities and facilities. Their objectives are the very factors that make tourism a positive impact upon a destination. To obtain a balanced view, however, we must also investigate the negative impacts of tourism on the destination and its host community.

Economic impacts

Tourism can have substantial economic benefits. It can create employment, generate income and earn foreign exchange. It is for this reason that many governments of developing countries focus on tourism, in the hope that tourism will help the economic development of their country.

Tourism also generates costs for a country. A national government must develop the infrastructure and establish a national tourism organisation (such as the BTA) to promote the country. Local authorities may also need more facilities for the tourists, such as car and coach parks, public toilets and information points; services such as litter collection and police patrols may need to be increased. The negative economic effects are summarised in Table 2.5.

KEY TERMS

Stakeholders: everyone with a commitment to the organisation or project.

Host: the residents of the destination.

Guests: visitors.

KEY TERMS

Foreign exchange: currency used by other countries.

Service industry: industries which sell services rather than tangible products.

Departure tax: tax charged by UK government on tourists and residents leaving the UK.

NEGATIVE ECONOMIC IMPACT	EXAMPLE
employment	• types of jobs available • loss of traditional skills
cost of living	• rise in price of local goods (inflation) • rise in house prices
leakages	• imports to cater for tourists' demands • imports of building materials to build facilities for tourists • imported services (e.g. consultants, architects, hotel managers) • repatriation of profits and wages • marketing costs • infrastructure costs

Table 2.5 *Negative economic effects*

Employment

Although there is no doubt that employment is created through tourism, much criticism exists regarding the types of jobs offered. Many of the positions are seasonal and unskilled, they are not well paid, they may involve unsociable hours and do not offer good levels of security. In addition it is claimed that little or no training is given.

Some of these criticisms of tourism employers may be valid, but it is not universally true of all jobs in the industry. These criticisms are, however, more likely to be the case in developing countries where multinational companies, earning substantial profits, pay local wage rates to local staff (this may be as little as £1 per day in countries such as The Gambia). Further imbalances occur when overseas companies employ their own overseas staff to manage the operation. These staff will naturally be paid wage levels similar to their earnings at home. The differences between the incomes of the local and overseas staff, therefore, can cause resentment.

In developing countries employment impacts also include the **loss of traditional skills**. These occur as people move from agriculture and fishing to work in tourism. In Thailand the growth in the development of golf courses means that instead of farming their own land independently, some local families are working as caddies and waiting on tourists in the many newly developed golf complexes. Not only do they lose their traditional skills, but they also become dependent on the tourist.

 **DID YOU KNOW?**

In the most popular historic towns in the UK it is estimated that local taxes are increased by approximately £2 per resident to cover extra costs incurred through tourism.

KEY TERM

Leakages: the costs of tourism to a country, e.g. imported goods.

KEY TERM

Infrastructure: the basic necessities needed to operate within a country, or town (i.e. sewers, running water, lighting, roads and transportation).

Cost of living

Tourism can increase the cost of living for the local population – local goods increase in cost due to there being more demand. In addition, the local residents, through the local tax system, have to pay for the increased litter collections, police services or car parks, for example, that are needed by the tourist.

Property prices may rise as a result of tourism. If properties are bought as second homes, house prices may rise, with the result that local people can no longer afford to buy them. This may cause resentment in the local community and the population structure will also change if young people have to move away to affordable housing.

Leakages

Although tourism contributes to the balance of payments, the costs incurred attracting and then providing for international tourists can be substantial. These costs (known as leakages) must be deducted from the money generated by tourism in order to calculate the net impact on the balance of payments. To give an example, an African economy success-fully attracting British tourists may have the following costs:

- imported goods for the tourists (e.g. American burgers, French wines)

- imported services (e.g. consultants, specialised staff, hotel managers)

- profits made by the international companies will be 'repatriated' (i.e. returned to the parent company, often in the USA)

- overseas workers will take some of their wages home

- payment must be made on loans

- the costs of promoting overseas to attract relatively rich tourists

- the development of infrastructure

Such leakages are not large in the UK and other developed countries (see Figure 2.8). Here we have a well developed national economy, which can provide the goods required by the tourists. In a less developed country, the result of such leakages can mean that as much as 90% of the foreign exchange leaks out of the country. This money is usually paying for food, labour and imports to build infrastruc-ture. Thus, the net benefit to countries can be far less than originally imagined.

Environmental impacts

As with all other impacts, environmental impacts can be both positive and negative. As discussed on page 117 the positive impacts on the

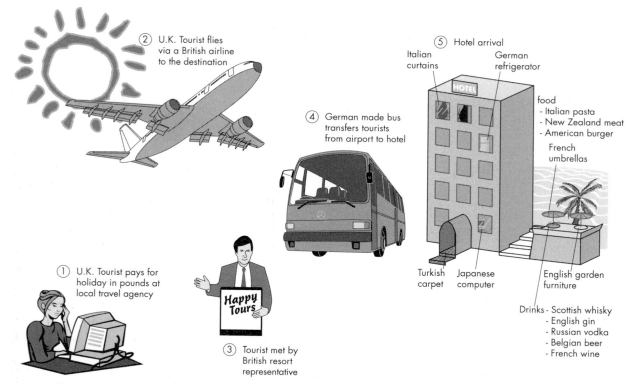

Figure 2.8 *Five Steps to Heaven? An example of possible leakages from a destination's economy*

Source: Dianne P. Laws (1996)

DID YOU KNOW?

In the Caribbean 75% of the airlines flying to the islands are not owned by Caribbean countries; the tour operators are based in Europe and New York. The hotels are also 60% owned by foreign investors.

KEY TERMS

The Earth Summit: a meeting held in Rio de Janeiro in 1992, at which heads of governments discussed the world's environment and how to take better care of it.

Sustainable: not 'using up' the resources

environment include:

- the creation of protected areas
- increased environmental awareness
- physical improvements to the landscape.

In both developed and developing countries tourism can create an awareness of the natural and built environment, its importance and the need for care.

It cannot be ignored that throughout the world tourism has been and continues to be developed with little regard for the environment. The very features that attract tourists in the first place are often destroyed or damaged. Many examples exist where both governments and developers have increased profits at the expense of both the physical and cultural environment.

In recent years there has been a growing awareness of the need to look after the earth's resources. All tourism organisations now recognise the need for **sustainable development**, i.e. we must not damage or destroy the resources on which tourism depends, be it the landscapes of the Lake District, the cultural practices of African tribes, the flora and fauna of the Alps or the sheer remoteness of the Highlands of Scotland. The negative impacts of tourism on the environment are numerous. They include: pollution (air, water and noise), visual pollution (unsightly landscapes), erosion (in both the natural landscape and man-made

ACTIVITY

How to travel with a conscience

ACCORDING to the World Bank, only 10p in every pound spent on a holiday ends up in the host country.

The local holiday representative probably will not be a native. The food may well be imported. And many tourists staying in an all-inclusive resort will never venture outside, let alone buy a meal or a beer locally.

Meanwhile, they are using local resources, such as water, which is then in short supply for local people and prices are driven up.

Are you sitting comfortably?

Two years ago, Voluntary Service Overseas (VSO) launched its World-Wise Tourism Campaign, precisely to help increase awareness of the problems and benefits of tourism for the host countries.

VSO does not preach against mass tourism – but it does want to educate travellers on how they can play a part in responsible tourism. And it wants the holiday companies to play their part as well.

In February, VSO published a survey, *Travelling in the Dark*, which rated 50 long-haul tour operators on the level of advice they gave to tourists about respecting and understanding local people and their customs.

It found that two-thirds of the companies do not give adequate advice to tourists about the developing countries they are visiting. Only Himalayan Kingdoms and World Expeditions scored five stars: five firms scored no stars at all. Dan Rees, VSO's head of global education, said: "Many of the countries we work in are very poor indeed but tourism is an economic lifeline. It must be managed properly.

"We must ask questions such as: can local produce be consumed by tourists instead of being imported? We may then see local handicrafts flourishing, local agriculture diversifying and selling to the market which is sitting on their doorstep, rather than trying to compete in the international markets."

Source: The Times Weekend, 23 October 1999

A tour operator 'with a conscience' has read this article and wants to minimise the negative impacts he has on the country in which he operates. Produce a set of guidelines for him. Remember to include information on the staff he employs, the suppliers he uses, and the hotels. Your aim is to minimise leakages from the host country.

attractions), congestion, damage (to flora and fauna), disturbance (of wildlife or sensitive environments).

DID YOU KNOW?

It is claimed that civilian aircraft account for 3% of all carbon dioxide emissions created by man.

Air pollution

Tourism requires transportation and transportation creates air pollution. Emissions from aircraft and cars and increased noise levels from vehicles make some of the world's cities unpleasant. On beaches, the noise of jetbikes causes a disturbance and pollutes the water. Tourists themselves can be rowdy and the non-stop clubbing scene in some resorts disturbs the local residents.

Cars are banned from the streets of Milan

THE STREETS of Italy's chaotic business and fashion capital were eerily quiet yesterday after alarming pollution levels forced the regional government to ban all private vehicles.

Thousands of residents joined bewildered tourists strolling around the centre of Milan and people on bicycles and in-line skates, and even in horse-drawn carriages, were able to move freely through the normally congested streets.

Public transport services were doubled and a 50p ticket was valid for the entire day.

Around 60,000 football supporters were forced to use public transport to reach the San Siro stadium for the match between Inter Milan and Cagliari. Six hundred traffic police were deployed to ensure that the 12-hour ban, which began at 8 am, was respected. There was a £40 fine for transgressors but taxi drivers, doctors, journalists and other people carrying out "socially useful" jobs were allowed to use their cars.

Milan's car-less Sunday and similar restrictions in the lakeside town of Como come after a week of alarmingly high pollution levels. Cars without catalytic converters have been banned from Milan for the past four days but the smog levels still had not fallen, prompting city administrators to take draconian measures.

From 6 February, 30 other Italian cities will also ban private cars and scooters from their centres on Sundays. Rome, Milan, Turin, Genoa, Florence and Naples are all taking part.

Figure 2.9 *Extract on air pollution in Milan*

Source: The Independent, *17 January 2000*

 DID YOU KNOW?

Due to the fact that the Mediterranean sea can only replenish itself via the narrow Straits of Gibraltar, it takes 75 years for the whole of the waters of the Mediterranean to be replaced by fresh waters from the Atlantic Ocean.

Water pollution

Water pollution is a problem here in the UK where the EU monitors the quality of bathing water. At the beginning of the 21st century, despite numerous warnings from the EU, Blackpool still did not meet the conditions of the EU Bathing Water Directive of 1976.

The Mediterranean sea, being an 'enclosed sea', suffers from the fact that pollution entering it is not dispersed by the waves and swell of an ocean. The main tourist resorts of the world are concentrated around the coasts on the Mediterranean. The tourists certainly contribute towards the 100 billion tons of sewage, much of it raw, that flows into it each year. Add to this the 170 oil refineries, terminal and power stations on its shores, the waste and the spillage from tankers supplying them, and the state of the Mediterranean should give cause for concern.

Visual pollution

Visual pollution may include solid debris washed up on the coastline, graffiti on heritage sites, litter in our urban environment or unsightly buildings. We are all familiar with the brochure pictures of high rise hotels on the Spanish Costas. A feature of the 1960s and 1970s, local authorities now try to protect their environments from such visual pollution through planning restrictions.

ACTIVITY

Ulixes 21 is an international campaign aimed at tourists visiting the Mediterranean. Research the website at www.medforum.org/ulixes21.

What is the campaign trying to achieve? Are you the tourist of the future (complete the questionnaire)?

On the Kenyan coast, the local authorities have learnt from the experiences of the environmental impacts in Mombassa. In the resort of Lamu they do not allow buildings to be any higher than palm trees. The Maltese government has legislation to prevent anything being built over four stories high and in Bermuda no building is allowed to be taller than the cathedral.

Erosion

Erosion occurs both in landscapes and buildings. Well-trodden paths become compacted and spread across the hillsides. River banks and shorelines are eroded through water sports. In Kenya the sea coral is often destroyed or even removed by the coastal tourists who are unaware that it is a living organism. This destroys the marine environment and the beaches, which if unprotected by the coral, are damaged.

Historic cities suffer from erosion due to overcrowding. Their pavements and buildings become worn by our feet; monuments are damaged due to the simple fact that we breath out carbon dioxide and touch the stone.

In the following Case Study on the impacts of tourism on our heritage historical and cultural sites in the world, Brian Sewell argues that most tourists are happier on the beach or at Disneyland (see page 126). The reality is that it is the tour operators who encourage them to get off their sunbeds and go on excursions into the mountains, cathedrals, Greek ruins and Italian museums. The operators' motive is to make a profit from these excursions. Although the International Council on Monuments and Sites (ICOMS) states that world culture sites are not just for a privileged few, Brian Sewell questions the wisdom of this.

DID YOU KNOW?

Due to environmental damage, Stonehenge has been described as a 'national disgrace'.

DID YOU KNOW?

Carbon dioxide damages.

Moor's code [8]

1. **Park only in designated parking places.**
2. **Follow guidelines established for your activity.**
3. **Stick to the line of a path. Single file if necessary.**
4. **In wet weather stick to hard surface tracks where possible.**
5. **Do not climb stone walls. Use gate or stile.**
6. **Take care with matches and cigarettes.**
7. **Do not disturb stones and rocks – you may damage archeological features.**
8. **Follow signs where repair work is in progress.**
9. **Leave your car behind – consider using bus services.**
10. **Spread the word – buy a sticker.**

Figure 2.10 The Moor's Code
Source: The Guardian,
27 March 1997

CASE STUDY *Tourism destroys tourism*

❝ We are at the point where tourists in their numbers and their ignorance destroy the very things and places that they are urged to see, mostly through wear and tear of being there.

Cappadocian stone (in Turkey) is a soft volcanic deposit that erodes to the finger's touch – its architectural detail can be scratched away, its ancient paintings worn from it by every passing bum and shoulder. A heritage that reaches back to the Acts of the Apostles and the monastic rule of St Basil in the 4th century is being destroyed by tourists who see it only as Disneyland.

The destruction of Westminster Abbey and St Paul's will take a little longer, for the stone is tougher and more resistant to the exhalations of carbon dioxide that must be measured in multiples of 10,000 gallons every day, the tons of sweaty vapour and the countless calories of body heat as the mobs scramble from coaches that poison the air with noise and fumes, but inexorably the scrape of feet and pry of fingers do the same irreversible damage. Tourists wear away the houses treasured by the National Trust, and erode the earth on which stand Hadrian's Wall and Stonehenge. ❞

Source: Tourism Concern In Focus Magazine, *Winter 1996/7*

ACTIVITY

Should tourists be excluded from ancient or sensitive sites. Prepare notes to debate the issue with a colleague.

Overcrowding

The sheer number of tourists can cause both environmental and socio-cultural problems. Overcrowding in historic cities causes congestion and resentment amongst the local communities who cannot go about their daily business. Historic city centres tend to be small and compact with narrow streets, which only allow limited space for traffic and people. Pavements become overcrowded, traffic is congested, buses are too busy and queues in the shops are inevitable.

ACTIVITY

The historic city of Florence is becoming 'endangered'. Despite this tourists continue to visit.

What are the negative impacts of tourism on Florence?

Why are the local authorities, residents and national government concerned?

What measures are being taken to deal with the problems? Others are being considered – do you think they would be successful? Justify your answers.

CASE STUDY *Florence*

Italians go on offensive

CHRIS ENDEAN

AS A WAITER in Florence's Piazza della Signoria, Marco Trevisan is something of a student of mass tourism.

From Germans taking impromptu showers in the square's fountain to English backpackers bedding down in the shadow of Michelangelo's *David*, Marco thought he had seen everything – until the day, less than a month ago, when a tourist walked calmly across the square to hack a leg off the bronze horse at the base of the fountain of Neptune.

"In broad daylight," said Marco. "I watched him every step of the way. He didn't blink an eyelid. He made a heinous crime against our city look like the most natural thing in the world."

The blow broke more than the horse's hoof. It also snapped the local council's patience. As if admitting that their city has capitulated to the seven million tourists who invade Florence every year, councillors are drawing up a code of conduct. The grandly named *Carta dei Diritti* is, in effect, a list of "Do's and Don'ts", to be handed out in restaurants, hotels and railway stations in the autumn.

"Visitors must learn to treat Florence like a vast museum," said Annamarie Petrioli Tofani, director of the Uffizi museum, the world's oldest. "Only when tourists behave like curators will the city be safe."

The Uffizi is nearly 450 years old and its narrow corridors make it imperative for tourists to obey the first rule written in the entrance hall: "Don't touch." But the days when the city was a magnet for the culturally-aware tourist disappeared with the advent of package holidays.

"For instance, how many people realise that even our hands carry pollution," said Petrioli. "Do they know that if you brush your hand across the surface of a statue, you leave behind a layer of acidity that eats into the marble or stone?"

When she first arrived at the Uffizi in 1987, 11,000 tourists would file through the museum's corridors in a day. Today that figure is limited to 5,000, with no more than a few hundred allowed in the museum at any one time.

The four-page brochure will outlaw picnics on the steps of museums and churches, sunbathing in parks and piazzas, and feeding the pigeons. Any failure to comply will mean a L400,000 fine ($235). Despite the summer weather, holidaymakers are even forbidden from wearing undershirts inside museums and churches.

"It's 33 degrees out here. What else are we supposed to wear?" asked 16-year-old Dutch schoolgirl Anneflor De Kock after a porter judged her hotpants too short for the Duomo.

There is even talk of erecting signposts along the 400-metre pedestrian zone that joins Piazza della Signoria to the Duomo – Florence's cathedral. Guido Clemente, arts councillor and the man holding the keys, said: "We cannot and do not want to militarise the city, but here too many people do things that they would never dream of doing at home."

Amelio Fara, a professor at Florence University's Institute of Art History, likes nothing more than an early morning stroll across his beloved Piazza della Signoria.

The square is a short walk from the Duomo, but often there is hardly a soul to be seen. Fara said: "Most visitors to Florence are not interested in the spirit of the city. They just want to say they've seen something."

Fara insists that protection should go hand in hand with conservation. Throughout the city there is growing evidence of neglect. The damage is less visible than the chewing-gum littering the colonnade outside the Uffizi, but its consequences are irreparable.

Take the entrance to the Church of SS Annunziata. It is 400 years old, and Florentines use this rare surviving example of marble walkways as a pavement. Where it has chipped away over the ages, workmen have filled in the gaps with cement.

"I'm sure that if this was covered in glass and a sign was put up warning tourists not to walk across a 400-year-old marble floor, people would avoid stepping on it," said Fara.

In most European cities, the greatest threat to art comes from exhaust fumes, acid rain and other pollution. In Florence, where even the paving-stones are period pieces, the danger is the tourist. Three years ago, Tuscany's regional government discussed a proposal to build turnstiles at the gateways of medieval towns such as Siena to control the number of tourists who enter. The plan has not been adopted – yet.

Source: The European, *14–20 August 1997*

CASE STUDY *The Lake District*

Beside the lake, beneath the trees, a host of trippers ill at ease

TRIPPERS will flock to the country's most treasured sites this weekend, bringing congestion and litter, but also spending their money in areas that increasingly depend on sightseers for their income. Many of them will make the slow journey along the M6 to the Lake District.

Nowhere else in the Lake District are the commercial pressures more apparent than around Windermere, a small village that has been transformed in turn by the railways, the romantic poets Wordsworth and Coleridge and finally by tourism.

Visitors will pack the tea-shops, scatter litter through the streets, jam the winding roads and trample the worn hillsides with hikers' boots. But they will also leave behind their money.

Last year 15 million visitors to Cumbria spent £446 million and kept one in six people employed. But this success has heightened concern about damage to the Cumbrian wilderness.

The National Park authority has highlighted 90 areas of track and hillside that need urgent repair, including 2,000 miles of eroded pathways. The walk up to the 3,113 ft summit of Helvellyn

exemplifies the conservationists' concerns. Helvellyn's popularity has been its downfall. Ten years ago the pathway to the summit was just a few feet wide; today it has expanded to 30 feet. Repair work, as on many other popular routes, is regular and rangers try to encourage walkers to take different routes. The Lake District Tourism and Conservation Partnership was established a year ago to promote such repair projects and to educate the tourist industry on how to preserve the environment.

It was the first time the English Tourist Board, the Lake District National Park, the Rural Development Commission, the National Trust and Cumbria Tourist Board had acted in concert. Haydn Morris, of the Cumbria Tourist Board and chairman of the partnership steering committee, said: "In the past, conservation and tourism interests have been polarised and there has been conflict.

"By working together the two sides can achieve a lot more in terms of conservation and developing the economy of the area. People come to the Lakes purely

for the landscape; we have to keep that intact at all costs."

Recent research showed Cumbrian business people were beginning to realise they had to put something back into the land from which they were making money.

Claire Owen manages the partnership scheme and is attempting to harness this growing concern. She is also trying to extend the tourist season to diversify traffic levels and encourage people to avoid "honeypot" areas.

Threats to restrict visitor numbers, to charge for entry to the National Park or to ban cars have been the subject of speculation for most of the century.

But those involved in the running of the park have avoided imposing restrictions in the belief that everyone should have access to the countryside and that attempts at preservation should be voluntary. Bob Cartwright, head of park management, believes bans and restrictions are a simplistic solution but accepts they could have a limited role. This summer a number of new traffic management schemes will be in place.

Source: The Times, *15 April 1995*

ACTIVITY

What are the positive impacts of tourism on the Cumbrian economy (refer to Lake District case study)? List the negative impacts on this sensitive environment.

What measures have been taken so far to limit the damage caused by tourists? What other measures have been proposed? What are the arguments against these options?

Damaging wildlife

Disturbance to wildlife occurs when tourist routines do not take account of the natural environment. The loggerhead sea turtle's survival as a species, for example, has been threatened by tourism around the Mediterranean Sea. The beaches on which they have traditionally nested have been developed or are polluted. In addition, tractors driving over their nesting sites (delivering building materials) and tourists visiting beaches in the evenings have disturbed their breeding routines.

In Kenya, game viewing is usually carried out in minibuses and sometimes in a hot air balloon. Both are thought to disturb the game, the regions most important resource.

Sensitive environments

Sensitive environments exist throughout the world. The Alps, for example, are considered to be the most threatened mountain system in the world. Other mountain systems, historic sites and buildings may also need special attention, as it is argued that once such environments are damaged, they are lost to us forever.

PROFILE *Environmental impacts in the Himalayas*

Trekking in the Annapurna Conservation Area in the Himalayas has upset the ecological balance. It is estimated that nearly 36,000 trekkers visit this region every year. Each trek requires as many porters as there are tourists. This tourism is concentrated in just a small area and in just four months of the year (October, November, March and April).

The trekkers need firewood as there are no other sources of fuel. As a result, deforestation has occurred. It is estimated that hundreds of hectares of forest are consumed every year to cater for the tourists and this has led to soil erosion, which in turn has caused land slides and floods.

The economical impacts do not compensate for these environmental consequences. It is estimated that only 20 cents of the three dollars (US) spent by each trekker each day stays within the local economy. The rest is spent on imported goods and services, either from other regional towns or overseas.

Host/guest conflict: local populations resentment towards tourists.

Human rights: reasonable expectations for all human beings.

Socio-cultural impacts

To recap, the positive impacts of tourism on communities include:

- aiding understanding
- reviving traditions, skills and ceremonies
- providing improved community facilities
- enhancing the quality of life.

The other side of the argument is that local people are negatively affected by tourism, which can cause:

- the loss or degradation of traditional cultures
- the changing of family structures
- the creation of social problems, such as gambling, prostitution, begging and drug trafficking.

There are many examples of conflicts between local residents and visitors (host/guest conflicts) arising as a result of these problems. The extent to which tourism has an impact on a culture is often said to be greatest when the social and cultural differences between the host and the guest are most significant. This is clearly the case when we, from the developed world, visit developing countries. For this reason, there is a lot of information available on the negative cultural impacts on the Maasai tribes of Kenya, the Hindu population of Bali and Muslims of Egypt and Turkey, for example. Such destinations are often considered by us to be exotic – it is the differences in culture that attract us to these destinations.

Socio-cultural impacts on tourism, however, also exist in Europe and within cities. How much areas are affected by tourism also depends on the number of tourists per resident (tourist:resident ratio). A few tourists in a town may have no negative impacts; coach loads of tourists in villages do.

ACTIVITY

The table below gives one method of measuring tourism's socio-cultural impact. The number of tourists per resident (tourist:resident ratio) is extremely high in many European historic cities.

CITY	YEAR	TOURISTS	RESIDENTS	RATIO
Bruges	1990	2,740,000	117,000	23:1
Florence	1991	4,000,000	408,000	10:1
Oxford	1991	1,500,000	130,000	12:1
Salzburg	1992	5,415,000	150,000	36:1
Canterbury	1993	2,250,000	41,000	55:1
Venice	1992	8,627,000	80,000	108:1

Source: BTA Insights, *July 1996*

Reread the case study on Florence on page 127. Note that Florence has the lowest number of tourists per resident of all the cities listed.

Imagine you ran a hotel in Florence. How do you think you would feel about:

1 the number of tourists
2 the damage they do
3 the measures taken to manage tourism?

Discuss your feelings with a colleague. What could you do to help the situation? What would be the advantages and disadvantages of establishing a second hotel in Venice?

KEY TERM

Enclave tourism: a self-contained tourist development surrounded by fencing, which caters for all tourist needs so that they do not need to venture outside its gates. Usually found in developing countries.

Crime is a problem that increases with tourism development. This may involve petty crime in major cities, tourists being overcharged for goods at major attractions, gangs of pickpockets operating on tourist trains abroad or at major social events or ticket touts selling forged or over-priced tickets to unsuspecting foreigners.

It can also be even more alarming – tourists have been the targets of serious crimes in some destinations. One example was when a Muslim group in Egypt put tourists on a death list in order to promote awareness of their cause. In Miami, Florida, tourists have also been the subject of violent attacks and in Jamaica the level of crime has encouraged the development of enclave tourism. Prostitution and gambling also appear to increase with the development of tourism.

The negative impacts on societies are often greater in exotic destinations that have a very 'different' culture. The increase in package holidays to long haul destinations has exposed cultures to the western tourists. There are numerous examples of local peoples in developing countries viewing the affluent western tourists with money in their money belt

KEY TERM

Human rights: the basic rights of all individuals to freedom, justice, etc.

and cameras around their neck, wearing sophisticated jewellery, and thinking that the western civilisation is somehow better. As a result, they may come to desire this lifestyle and become dissatisfied with their traditional customs and rebel against restrictive family structures.

Their culture may become commercialised. Instead of traditional dances or ceremonies taking place, they adapt to meet the fast itinerary of tourists who can only concentrate for a 45 minute show after dinner (because they have had an exhausting day and must get up at 7am for the next day's busy itinerary). Arts and crafts may be produced to meet tourist demand (and their pockets). This may result in lower quality goods produced to be sold as souvenirs, known as 'airport art'.

Some environmental developments can also affect the way of life of a population. In Sri Lanka, for example, a lake has been dammed so that tourists can windsurf on it. As a result the local population can no longer produce their rice crops. Golf developments in Goa have caused problems for the local community – they cannot get water from former sources. Furthermore, they now work as caddies and waiters. This can mean that the young people are earning more than their parents, causing changes within family structures. Another example is in Phuket, where hotels have been built on ancient burial grounds, restricting important access for the local community.

A consequence of such impacts can be resentment from the host population. They may envy the tourists' wealth, be angry at their loss of livelihood, be made to feel inferior, and object to being crowded by tourists, when they are simply trying to go about their daily business. This is known as a host/guest conflict.

Tourism Concern claims that fundamental human rights are contravened by the development of tourism. Following are some examples.

- The right to freedom of movement: The privatisation of beaches in Kenya means local women can no longer collect crabs, which are part of their natural diet. The creation of the National Marine Park in Mombassa means that the fishing communities cannot access the beach. In India, tourists are encouraged to use the Keiladeo Ghana sanctuary while tribal families are no longer allowed to graze their cattle.

- The right to land, water and natural resources: In Goa, the Taj Holiday Village and Fort Aguada complex has constant running water, while the residents of the local village (through which the piped water to the complex runs) have been refused their request for piped water.

- The right to health and wellbeing: It is estimated that 350 golf courses are built throughout the world each year. Their use of fertilisers, pesticides and herbicides are thought to have affected the lives of people living near the golf courses in Thailand.

- The right to respect and dignity: Throughout the developing world, local peoples are treated as a tourist commodity. They are moved for the benefit of the tourists, photographed doing their sacred dances and asked to perform for the tourist.

- The right of the child to protection: Tourism Concern estimate that between 13 and 19 million children are working in the tourism sector worldwide. Tourism lures children away from school and can encourage begging. Some destinations, especially in Asia and eastern Europe, have a reputation for being 'sex havens for tourists and paedophiles'.

Source: Adapted from Tourism Concern, Tourism and Human Rights.

CASE STUDY *Host/guest relationships on the Kenyan coast*

The Kenyan coast offers the tourist fine, sandy beaches, an attractive winter climate and an abundance of wildlife, both in the sea and inland. As the western tourists are increasingly seeking different holiday destinations, Kenya offers the glamorous combination of safari and enclave beach tourism. Growth of this area was aided by government involvement – tourism has been considered in the Kenyan National Development Plans to be of national importance. Thus, charter flights to Mombassa started in 1965 and the extension of the airport was completed in 1979, allowing wide-bodied jets to land.

Another reason for the popularity of this coastal strip is the superstructure. Many hotels are owned by foreign nationals, providing high quality tourist accommodation. Although the Kenyan government has officially encouraged local ownership (kenyanisation), some of the hotels are entirely foreign owned and 78% have direct foreign investment.

The Kenyan coast has a mixture of ethnic communities. The majority are Mijikendi people (1.2 million) and immigrants from the Kenyan interior. The Wasahili people comprise just 0.5% of the population. Their life, language and culture is Islamic. The Wasahili consider themselves to be civilised, urban, literate and Muslim.

The basic feeling of the Wasahili people towards tourism is one of antipathy. The overt alcohol consumption, emergence of prostitution, open affection in public and dress code of tourists has created resentment amongst Muslims. They therefore do not participate in the industry. Their refusal to accept typical tourist jobs, such as cleaners, waiters or boatmen, is based on their view of this as slavery and a reflection of earlier colonial rule. These jobs, and the better paid ones, are more often taken by the non-Swahili Kenyans.

Hence, tourism on the coast takes place without Wasahili involvement. Consequently, they do not receive the economic benefits that many accept as compensation for cultural or environmental degradation.

Beach wear, open affection, evidence of prostitution, and the consumption of drugs and alcohol are all part of the life of the tourist on the Kenyan coast. There also appears to be a lack of sensitivity by developers, resulting in discos being built next to mosques. Video rooms showing blue movies are visited by local teenage boys who absorb the western style of living.

A further issue concerns the fact that the establishment of marine parks and reserves means that the Wasahili cannot fish or swim in their local waters. They also cannot use the products of the local mangrove forests that have become protected. Local people see the tourist as benefiting from facilities that they have historically used, but from which they are now excluded.

The Swahili people are resentful, but they appear to have maintained their culture, albeit with some changes, despite being surrounded by the tourist industry. The impact of tourism may in fact have reinforced their community culture. The culture gap between the tourist and the Wasahili is so great that the 'demonstration effect' has not occurred, and the community has reacted by imposing stricter standards. There is concern, however, that a greater Islamic fervour is developing – it is thought that the community wish to prevent further tourism development.

For the tourist, the Wasahili people provide an exotic backdrop. While they lie on sunbeds, the local community go to mosques or about their daily lives in traditional attire.

ACTIVITY

List the negative economic, environmental and socio-cultural impacts on the Kenyan community. Discuss the reaction of the Wasahili people to the development of the tourism industry.

Produce an information sheet for tourists going to this area. Your objective is to inform them of the cultural differences and encourage them to behave responsibly.

There is no doubt that tourism can bring with it negative impacts on the environment and the socio-cultural aspects of a destination. It is important that these impacts are managed. If they are not, and the tourists find a destination spoilt, they will go elsewhere. Tourism planning and management are, therefore, essential. Methods of maximising the positive impacts of tourism and minimising the negative impacts must be explored.

CASE STUDY *The all-inclusive concept*

Why The Gambia has banned all-inclusives

ALL-inclusive resorts, where tourists pre-pay for all of their accommodation, food, drinks, entertainment and sports, present the most serious problem to developing countries eager to benefit from tourism and foreign currency.

Not only does precious little from the tourist's purse end up being spent locally (there is little incentive to spend outside the hotel when everything there is "free"), but operators tend to import their own supplies rather than buying them in the host country.

Many all-inclusive resorts in Jamaica, for example, which are heavily dependent on American tourists, import food from the US, brought in on the same planes as visitors. Most of the cost of the holiday remains in the USA.

And the all-inclusives are a huge industry. At Airtours, all-inclusives account for a staggering 70 per cent (excluding Florida) of its long-haul business. At Thomson it accounts for 65 per cent.

The Gambia became so concerned about the problem that, from November this year, hotels will no longer be able to offer all-inclusive holidays. Just how beneficial this move may prove for local people can be seen in a case cited by VSO. Mama Ceesay used to sell eggs in the market in Serekunda in The Gambia. Now that three local tourist hotels buy her eggs directly, she has 5,000 chickens and can afford to educate her three children.

Source: The Times Weekend, *23 October 1999*

ACTIVITY

The all-inclusive holiday is becoming more and more popular. Read the Case Study on the all-inclusive concept. Gather two long haul and two short haul all-inclusive brochures.

What is the appeal of the all-inclusive to:

1 the consumer?
2 the tour operator?

Create a chart similar to the one below, detailing the impacts of the all-inclusive holidays on the host country.

Would you like to go on an all-inclusive holiday? Has this activity changed your opinions?

	ECONOMIC	ENVIRONMENTAL	SOCIO-CULTURAL
Positive			
Negative			

DID YOU KNOW?

The first of the fifteen action points in the government's tourism strategy *Tourism for Tomorrow*, is to 'develop a blue print for the sustainable development of tourism to safeguard our countryside, heritage and culture for future generations'.

KEY TERM

A definition of sustainable tourism: 'Tourism growth that ensures the resources on which it depends are not degraded'.

Source: Making the Connection: a practical guide to tourism management in historic towns

KEY TERM

A more commonly used definition of sustainable tourism: 'Meeting the needs of the present without compromising the ability of future generations to meet their own needs.'

Source: World Commission on Environment and Development, Brutland Report, OUP, 1987

Tourism management

Sustainable tourism

Some confusion surrounds the concept of sustainable tourism. The term itself is often interchanged with 'green', 'rural', 'soft', 'eco-', 'responsible', 'alternative' and 'low impact' tourism. Although all these terms have slightly different meanings, the concept of minimising negative impacts is a common feature to them all.

Package tourism and sustainability

Package tourism first began with a few UK tourists visiting the coasts (which were then fishing villages) of France and Spain. Numbers were small and impacts were low. However, as destinations and tour operators came to recognise the economic benefits, tourism began to be seen in a positive light and was actively promoted. Tourism destinations focused on increased tourist numbers in order to increase their income.

This is what happened on the Spanish mainland coasts. People were attracted to visit them in the 1960s, by cheap flights and the sun. These areas had access to good beaches, rural Spain, the Spanish culture and a good lifestyle. Gradually, however, they became a mass tourism destination: the beaches were full, hotels served English food and the destination no longer felt Spanish. The tourists consequently moved on to other destinations.

By the 1980s the impact of increasing numbers of tourists had been too high. The negative results of rapid tourism development meant that these destinations were no longer attractive and the affluent tourist had moved on elsewhere.

It is no longer acceptable for tourists to exhaust the resources which attracted them (for example the wildlife, beautiful beaches, access to local cultures) and then move on when that area is no longer attractive. Tourists, tour operators and local communities, as well as local governments, must not exploit these resources.

Tourism destinations, just like any other product, have a life cycle. Resorts are, for example, discovered by the backpacker travellers and are then developed by tour operators, other private sector organisations and local authorities, to make money. If this is not done attractively or happens too fast the resort may soon become unpopular and tourist numbers decline.

ACTIVITY

Identify destinations that you believe have exhausted some of their resources.

KEY TERM

Visitor management: methods used to influence number and types of visitors, as well as what they do when visiting.

❶

USING RESOURCES SUSTAINABLY

The conservation and sustainable use of resources – natural, social and cultural – is crucial and makes long-term business sense.

❷

REDUCING OVER-CONSUMPTION AND WASTE

Reduction of over-consumption and waste avoids the costs of restoring long-term environmental damage and contributes to the quality of tourism.

❸

MAINTAINING DIVERSITY

Maintaining and promoting natural, social and cultural diversity is essential for long-term sustainable tourism, and creates a resilient base for the industry.

❹

INTEGRATING TOURISM INTO PLANNING

Tourism development which is integrated into a national and local strategic planning framework and which undertakes environmental impact assessments, increases the long-term viability of tourism.

❺

SUPPORTING LOCAL ECONOMIES

Tourism that supports a wide range of local economic activities and which takes environmental costs and values into account, both protects those economies and avoids environmental damage.

❻

INVOLVING LOCAL COMMUNITIES

The full involvement of local communities in the tourism sector not only benefits them and the environment in general but also improves the quality of the tourism experience.

❼

CONSULTING STAKEHOLDERS AND THE PUBLIC

Consultation between the tourism industry and local communities, organisations and institutions is essential if they are to work alongside each other and resolve potential conflicts of interest.

❽

TRAINING STAFF

Staff training which integrates sustainable tourism into work practices, along with recruitment of local personnel at all levels, improves the quality of the tourism product.

❾

MARKETING TOURISM RESPONSIBLY

Marketing that provides tourists with full and responsible information increases respect for the natural, social and cultural environments of destination areas and enhances customer satisfaction.

❿

UNDERTAKING RESEARCH

On-going research and monitoring by the industry using effective data collection and analysis is essential to help solve problems and to bring benefits to destinations, the industry and consumers.

Figure 2.11 Principles for sustainable tourism
Source: Beyond the Green Horizon, *Tourism Concern WWF, 1992*

Long-term: extending over a long time.

Long-term approach to sustainable tourism

Today, governments, local authorities, tour operators and the general public recognise the need for other goals to be met. These include:

- protection of natural and cultural resources

- integration into the existing social and economic life

- increased visitor satisfaction.

The above can be achieved through a long-term sustainable approach. It is now recognised that tourism development must protect the resources on which it is dependent. A long-term approach to a community and environment is required so that negative impacts are minimised, economic, social and environmental benefits are maximised (and continue into the future), while the visitor remains satisfied. To do this, tourism must be planned and managed, developments must be limited and the communities involved.

CASE STUDY *The impacts of allocation on arrival*

KEY TERM

Short-term: only concerned with the immediate future.

Tour operators are often criticised for their short-term approach:

> During the 1980s, the town of Neohorio had become popular with tourists on account of its beautiful hills and scenery, and because it was suitable for birdwatching. Because of these features, and because it was also some miles from the coast, Neohorio was compatible with a higher-spending, less numerous type of tourist who preferred quiet countryside to crowded beaches and resorts.
>
> However, due to a practice known as 'allocation on arrival', an increasing number of tour operators had begun to sell holidays cheaply on the basis that customers may not know where they are going until the last minute. This practice makes good sense to companies because it enables them to fill every last seat on charter flights, rather than having too much demand for one destination, and too little demand for another. Yet as a result of this practice, tourists interested only in beaches were sent to Neohorio, and ended up being bored. The local people, keen to profit from the tourists, built bars and restaurants of a type which were appealing to the recent wave of tourists, but which succeeded in repelling the higher-spending numbers who always chose Neohorio because of its quiet and natural scenery.
>
> As a result of this short-term policy by tour operators, a destination which could have attracted high-paying tourists sustainably into the future was spoilt because of a short-term desire for profits, and a lack of concern for either the impact on the destination, or the quality of the holiday for the tourists. Neohorio now has problems attracting hill walkers and birdwatchers. Yet it could never compete with beach resorts because it was always so far from the coast.

Source: In Focus, *Spring Issue No. 19, Tourism Concern, 1996*

Sustainable tourism's aims are to ensure that local communities do not suffer from tourism development. The tour operators do not need to lose out in this – it is not intended that their profits be reduced through sustainable tourism. It is simply hoped that, by improving quality at destinations, ensuring the developments are of a high quality and stopping them becoming over popular, visitors will continue to want to visit, rather than leave and go elsewhere once tourism has destroyed tourism.

 ACTIVITY

Why was the allocation on arrival detailed in the Case Study so popular with the tour operator and the tourist?

Who could have prevented this occurrence?

Why is this considered to be such a short-term policy?

Suggest alternative courses of action for tour operators in similar circumstances.

Sustainable tourism needs to have the support of all:

● governments

● local authorities

● inbound tour operators

● local communities

 DID YOU KNOW?

Green Globe 21 applies the Earth Summit's Agenda 21 for sustainable development.

In order to support and encourage the pursuit of sustainable tourism, the World Travel and Tourism Council has defined its own guidelines (see Figure 2.12) and established an organisation known as **Green Globe**.

Companies can pay a fee to join Green Globe on the basis that they are committed to the WTTC's Environmental Guidelines. After an initial period, during which the companies learn about sustainable tourism, they must demonstrate that they are meeting the guidelines. Certification can then be achieved and the company can use the Green Globe logo. Thus, membership demonstrates to the public that the company is environmentally, socially and culturally responsible.

Now called Green Globe 21, Green Globe has extended its scheme to communities. In order to achieve certification, communities must agree a plan to manage the environment, involve the community and set targets for themselves. This plan must then be carried out and targets met in order to receive certification. The advantage to the environmentally-aware consumer is that we can easily see which companies are working towards or have achieved certification.

WTTC
Environmental Guidelines

A clean, healthy environment is essential to future growth - it is the core of the Travel & Tourism product. The WTTC commends these guidelines to Travel & Tourism companies and to governments and asks that they be taken into account in policy formation.

- Travel & Tourism companies should state their commitment to environmentally compatible development.
- Targets for improvements should be established and monitored.
- Environmental commitment should be company-wide.
- Education and research into improved environmental programs should be encouraged.
- Travel & Tourism companies should seek to implement sound environmental principles through self-regulation, recognizing that national and international regulation may be inevitable and that preparation is vital.

Environmental improvement programs should be systematic and comprehensive. They should aim to:

- Identify and continue to reduce environmental impact, paying particular attention to new projects.
- Pay due regard to environmental concern in design, planning, construction and implementation.
- Be sensitive to conservation of environmentally protected or threatened areas, species and scenic aesthetics, achieving landscape enhancement where possible.
- Practice energy conservation.
- Reduce and recycle waste.
- Practice fresh-water management and control sewage disposal.
- Control and diminish air emissions and pollutants.
- Monitor, control and reduce noise levels.
- Control and reduce environmentally unfriendly products, such as asbestos, CFCs, pesticides and toxic, corrosive, infectious, explosive or flammable materials.
- Respect and support historic or religious objects and sites.
- Exercise due regard for the interests of local populations, including their history, traditions, culture and future development.
- Consider environmental issues as a key factor in the overall development of Travel & Tourism destinations.

 The World Travel & Tourism Council (WTTC) is a global coalition of 70 Chief Executive Officers from all sectors of the Travel & Tourism industry, including accommodation, catering, recreation, transportation and travel-related services. Its goals are to convince governments of the economic and strategic importance of Travel & Tourism, to promote environmentally compatible development and to eliminate barriers to growth of the industry.

These guidelines have been prepared taking into account the International Chamber of Commerce (ICC) Business Charter for Sustainable Development.

Figure 2.12 *WWTC Environmental Guidelines*

Source: WWTC

ACTIVITY

Visit the Green Globe 21 website at www.greenglobe21.com. Name five organisations and destinations which have achieved Green Globe 21 status.

The principles of sustainable tourism must be implemented if we are not to destroy the resources on which tourism depends. We must maximise the positive impacts of tourism and minimise the negative impacts. These will now be examined in terms of:

1 **Minimising leakages** (i.e. maximising retention of visitor spending).
2 **Community participation** (i.e. training and employment of local people).

3 **Social programmes** (i.e. investing tourism income into community projects).
4 **Educating consumers and tour operators** (i.e. tourism education).
5 **Destination management** (i.e. planning controls, visitor and traffic management, widening access, environmental impact assessments (EIA) and auditing).

The principles of sustainable tourism are integrated into all the above measures, which in themselves contribute to good practice.

Minimising leakages

ACTIVITY

Look back at the negative economic impacts of tourism and the section on leakages (see page 121). How could you prevent these from happening?

Most leakages occur through imports (for example food for tourists, construction materials for hotels and specialist services) or the fact that profits earned by the multinational companies and foreign employers go to their home country.

All leakages can be minimised by government restrictions. These could include legislation regarding foreign ownership of land or property, restricting imports or high levels of taxation on profits and expatriate salaries. Many governments, however, are reluctant to do this. An alternative way is simply to produce better and/or cheaper goods locally so that companies' hotels and restaurants do not want to import (especially agricultural products and construction materials). This can be difficult – see Case Study on The Gambia.

KEY TERM

Expatriate: someone who is living away from their home country.

PROFILE *Tourism in Kuna Yale*

One of an archipelago of 360 islands in the Caribbean, Kuna Yale strongly resists tourism. The Kuna General Congress (KGC) control tourism policy and have legislated that 'the right to entertain tourist activities in Kuna Yale is reserved to the Kuna only.'

While the Kuna's traditional culture is protected as a result, the islanders themselves do not benefit from the same tourism income that some of their neighbouring islands have exploited. This is causing some local resentment.

DID YOU KNOW?

In 1999 the Gambian Government banned all-inclusive holidays.

ACTIVITY

Negative impacts in Kuna are minimised by the legislation. What recommendations would you make to the KGC?

CASE STUDY *Leakages in The Gambia*

'Right now in The Gambia, there aren't many links between agricultural production and what the tourist eats and drinks in hotels. A lot of food and drink is imported – despite the fact that The Gambia is an agricultural economy. The hotels do this for two reasons, the first being that it's cheaper, and the second because of structural adjustment policies (SAPs). The Gambian government has been forced to sign up to SAPs by the International Monetary Fund and they have to let foreign food companies in and open the country up to cheap products. Even eggs are imported from Holland. I understand that salmonella and other health risks are a worry for hotels and as our country has no testing mechanism for quality, we can't supply them.

If you were to ask any Third World government they'd say that tourism is a major foreign exchange earner. But the sad thing is that they haven't appreciated how much money goes out in order to import food and luxury facilities. The hotels import jam for instance, yet we grow oranges, mangoes and all sorts of fruits. They import juices – but oranges and tomatoes are grown in local gardens and farms everywhere. They import canned vegetables such as carrots and beans, and beef and other meats, all of which we grow and eat. The reasoning hotels give is that The Gambia can't guarantee constant supply and quality. But this is

a Catch 22, because people don't have the incentive to expand their businesses if the market is not available. Also, because farmers have no means of preserving fruit and vegetables the prices drop at harvest time as all the produce hits the market at the same time and a lot goes to waste. There are a number of things that need to happen for this situation to be rectified. Technical production advice needs to be given to farmers and some co-ordination facilitated between what the hotels consume and what the farmers produce so that regular supplies can be guaranteed. We also need to establish canning and bottling factories. I believe this is for the Gambian government and the private sector to do together.

People ask why the private sector should do this sort of thing, but when you talk to most of the guests about whether they would prefer to eat imported food or fresh food, they definitely vote for fresh. I feel it is in the interest of the hotels. Let's take tomato juice – thousands, if not millions of cans of these are imported every season, but a 28 cl can of tomato juice costs around £1 to the tourist. And if all that was bought locally and tinned locally, a lot of money would be saved by the hotel and the tourist and the local farmers would also make a living.'

Source: Article by Adama Bah, Tourism Concern *In Focus Magazine, Summer 1999*

ACTIVITY

Why does The Gambia import so much food and drink? List the solutions that Adama Bah proposes?

What role does the government have in these solutions? Suggest others. What advice would you give to tourists and tour operators visiting The Gambia.

The development of the agricultural industry to support a local tourism industry is an essential part of reducing leakages. This does not always happen, due to the culture gap – local farmers simply do not know what the western tourist wants. This problem has been solved in St. Lucia by the 'adopt a farmer scheme'. Established by the Ministry of Agriculture and the St. Lucia Hotel Association, each hotel taking part 'adopted' one or two farmers with whom they worked closely. The

hotels' chefs explained the types, quality and quantity of foods required and the farmers aimed to meet the needs of their particular hotel.

In the first stage of the scheme the Hotel Association was heavily involved and the government provided loans for greenhouses, so that standardised products could be produced. Now the farmers have set up their own co-operative. It has 66 members and they co-ordinate their own production and marketing to ensure the hotels' food requirements are met by local produce.

The repatriation of profits and wages from a country will be high if hotels are owned by multinational companies and expatriate staff are employed. Leakages are less if hotels are locally owned and local staff are employed (community participation). Again, governments can use legal measures to restrict the foreign ownership of property and/or prevent the employment of expatriate staff. Tax measures can also be used by governments to prevent wages and profits leaving their country. Alternatively, they can aid the development of local hotels and assist in the education and training of the local population so that expatriate staff and foreign hotels are not necessary (community participation).

Community participation

It is now clear that unless the local population are involved in and benefit from tourism, resentment will occur. This will affect visitor satisfaction and the long-term benefits of tourism to communities. In many parts of the world there are examples of communities being involved. In St. Lucia the 'adopt a farmer scheme' has been successful. In Zimbabwe a 'CAMPFIRE' programme (Communal Areas Management Programme for Indigenous Resources) has resulted in local farmers becoming involved in game ranching. This is more profitable for the community and means that wildlife is protected.

PROFILE *Campfire programme*

Zimbabwean zeal

In Mahenye, Zimbabwe Sun, one of the country's biggest hotels chains, put up a Z$30 m lodge on communal lands. We have been working with CAMPFIRE and talking to Zimbabwe Sun about the effects of their actions. Now there is an agreement between the Regional District Council, Zimbabwe Sun, the Ministry of Local Government, and the community. This year, the community received five per cent of gross turnover – a payment of Z$500,000, which will, in time, increase to 15 per cent. That is a lot of money for them. The benefit to Zimbabwe Sun is that it gets the support of the community, who will not interfere with the land, poach game, chop trees or start fires. At last things are changing for the better.

Champion Chinhoyi, of the Zimbabwe Trust, an associate organisation to CAMPFIRE (Communal Areas Management Programme for Indigenous Resources), Zimbabwe.

Source: WorldWise

In St. Lucia, initiatives have also been taken to ensure that local people making handicrafts have opportunities to sell their goods. Legislation requires all large hotels over a certain size to have a regular vendors' market, where local people can buy and sell their crafts. Furthermore, as vendors selling on the beaches used to be seen as a form of harassment by tourists, vendor areas have been established by the local authorities. Vendors have their stalls in this area and tourists can visit to buy local handicrafts. This has ensured that the rights of the communities and desires of the tourists have both been maintained.

Community involvement also means direct employment. Some hotels and tour operators do not employ local staff on the basis that they do not have the skills required to deal with the tourists. Voluntary Services Overseas (VSO) have been instrumental in creating **training pro-grammes** to ensure community participation. They have established programmes both in the Caribbean and Himalayas to train local staff in customer service and hotel management. This reduces the need for tour operators to employ expatriate staff – responsible tour operators now only employ local staff.

ACTIVITY

List all the aspects of Tribes Travel (see page 245) that contributed to them winning the 'Most Responsible Tour Operator Award' in 1999.

Social programmes

There is an increasing number of projects set up by charities, local community groups and tour operators that use tourism income to benefit the local community. This income either comes directly from the tourist or via tour operator donations. Examples include:

- The tour operator Sunvil Holidays gives 5% of its net profits to environmental projects in its host destinations, Cyprus and Costa Rica.

- AITO have set up a project called the Visitor Payback Scheme (see Profile on page 146).

- Tribes Travel pay 7.5% of the tour price directly to local projects.

- A £10 visa charge was introduced in the Dominican Republic to tarmac the island's roads.

PROFILE *Tribes Travel*

Tribes Holidays

Whether you want to relax on a beach or trek up a mountain, if you want to be a part of sustainable tourism and travel in the knowledge that your presence isn't compromising the environment or exploiting the people, Tribes is for you. If you don't mind putting a bit of effort into your leisure, but realise you don't have to be a martyr when you travel – there's nothing wrong with comfort and style when it's available – Tribes is for you. If you enjoy doing something different, learning something new, experiencing a foreign culture and expanding your knowledge of the world you will love our trips.

Small Group Holidays

Choose from a range of exciting trips such as African safaris, wildlife cruises, mountain trekking, cultural discoveries, and many more. The average group size is six, and trips range from one to three weeks long.

Guides

Tribes uses local guides wherever it is practically possible. We believe that no-one is better equipped to show a visitor around than a local who knows the environment, the people, their customs and traditions. On many trips we also use indigenous guides when appropriate. Our guides have become experts in coordinating our travel arrangements, translating, introducing us to the local people and often providing that vital link between cultures.

Accommodation

The range of accommodation we offer includes luxury tented camps and safari lodges, comfortable yacht cabins, good hotels full of local character, and occasionally even some traditional tribal huts.

Fair Trade Travel

Tribes considers the environmental and cultural implications of all aspects of the company's operations.

- Tribes works in cooperation with local communities, and offers fairly-traded revenue.
  You will find you hosts to be welcoming and open in their invitations to show you their region and cultures.
- We use local guides, and locally owned and run services.
  Good local guides generally have an excellent knowledge of their area which foreign guides struggle to match.
- You are offered explanations of how each trip helps local people.
  An understanding of the difference you can make is important.
- Group sizes are kept to a maximum of about 12 to minimise the impact on the local people, wildlife and environment.
  Small groups tend to have much better dynamics, and allow you to get closer to the people, wildlife and places you are visiting.
- We promote respect for local communities and their environment.
  We give you good information about your destination and the cultures you will meet. Understanding helps you to feel more comfortable and enjoy your experiences all the more.
- The folder (hand-made and printed in Nepal) and information sheets are all made from environmentally friendly paper.
  This format of 'brochure' means that you get only the information you are interested in, and therefore there is less waste of paper.

Source: The Spirit of Tribes promotional leaflet

PROFILE *The Gambia Experience*

Set up in 1986 by Stephen and Sandra Wilde, The Gambia Experience was involved in educational projects helping The Gambia. They worked with the charitable organisation Schools for Progress, who guided them towards sustainable projects. These have included:

- **Buying building materials for schools, which have then been built by villagers.**

- **Asking clients to take pens and papers.**

- **Ensuring such gifts are not given directly to children (to avoid begging) but instead given publicly via the charity to schools (so avoiding them being resold).**

- **Encouraging donations from clients and then matching them.**

- **Close liaison with the Gambian government.**

PROFILE *The Visitor Payback Scheme*

Funded by the EU, this scheme set up voluntary systems whereby tourists could give money to assist the conservation of places they visit. How this was done varied between schemes. Donations, sponsorship schemes, membership, selling merchandise, additional voluntary charges or voluntary work were some of the methods used.

Examples such as those above are entirely voluntary schemes. There is, however, a growing interest in using other schemes to collect income from visitors and tourism business. These could be used to share the benefits of tourism equitably amongst a community. This is important in areas where only some businesses and their employees benefit from tourism, while congestion, inflation and other impacts affect everyone.

In addition to helping communities such schemes could be used to protect and conserve the environment. Perhaps tourists and the travel companies would not mind contributing more money to the environment that they are enjoying free of charge?

Examples of methods used to collect money from tourists include:

- local tourism taxes
- charging for tourist entry (lower or no rates for residents)
- car parking charges
- membership schemes
- donation boxes

DID YOU KNOW?

Tourists pay a very high price to visit some natural resources. In Botswana tourists to National Parks are charged £25 per person per day, while the Kingdom of Bhutan charges $200 per day at peak times (reducing to $165 off season!).

ACTIVITY

Select two schemes, such as those described previously. What are their potential problems?

Educating consumers and tour operators

The slogan 'take nothing but photographs, leave nothing but footprints' is now well-known. Since the initial Countryside Code was written, many other guidelines have been produced by public bodies and charities.

---

follow the code

a six-point guide to better practice abroad

- save natural resources – try not to waste water; switch off lights and air conditioning when you go out
- support local trade and craftspeople – buy locally made souvenirs wherever possible, but avoid those made from ivory, fur, skins or other wildlife
- ask before taking photos or videos of people – don't worry if you don't speak the language; a smile and a gesture will be understood and appreciated
- don't give money or sweets to children – it encourages begging and demeans the child; a donation to a recognised project, health centre or school is a more constructive way to help
- respect local etiquette – in many countries loose clothes are preferable to skimpy tops or revealing shorts; also kissing in public is often inappropriate
- learn about the country – knowing about its history and current affairs can help you appreciate many national indiosyncracies and prevent misunderstandings

code developed by Tourism Concern in consultation with local tourism groups

---

Figure 2.13 VSO guidelines for education of tourists

Source: VSO website, January 2000

ACTIVITY

Green Globe 21 encourages us to travel responsibly. Find out what this means, at www.greenglobe21.com.

Compare this with the advice given by the VSO at www.vso.org.uk.

Now look once again at the Moor's Code on page 125. Add another five guidelines to the list.

DID YOU KNOW?

According to Voluntary Services Overseas (VSO), two thirds of long haul operators do not give adequate advice to tourists about respecting and understanding the local people and their customs.

As we have already established, it is the tour operator as well as the consumer who must behave responsibly, in order for benefits to be maximised and negative impacts minimised. Many believe that it is the tour operator's responsibility to educate the tourist. As they are making the profits, it is thought that perhaps they should publish guidelines in their brochures about showing respect for local custom and cultures, as well as for the environment.

In 1999, VSO conducted a survey of 50 tour operators who operate in the developing countries of Kenya, Tanzania, The Gambia, India and Thailand. They assessed the advice each tour operator gave to their clients against the criteria shown in Figure 2.14 below, and found many to be lacking. Himalayan Kingdoms and World Expeditions were found to be exemplary.

respecting local people	• asking before taking photographs • respecting private property • learning a few words of the local language • differences in body language between destination and home countries
respecting local customs	• dressing so as not to cause offence • when physical contact between men and women can offend • behaviour in holy places • respecting national figures
interacting with the local economy	• opportunities to buy local food and use local services e.g. transport • opportunities to buy local crafts • awareness of a tipping culture • responding to poverty
respecting the local environment	• conserving local resources e.g. water, wood • not dropping litter/causing pollution • not touching coral, picking flowers or harming wildlife

Figure 2.14 Advice criteria

Source: VSO Worldwise Campaign Survey of Travel Advice

ACTIVITY

Collect five long haul tour operators' brochures. Compare the advice given by each tour operator to customers. Use the same criteria as VSO (see Figure 2.14).

The use of in-flight videos to educate tourists is now becoming increasingly popular. Tourists going to The Gambia are shown a film highlighting issues they should be aware of, including dress codes and the importance of spending money to aid the local economy. This has been funded by the EU, VSO, Joseph Rowntree Foundation and the Department for International Development.

PROFILE *Thai Airways*

Thai Airways shows a 15 minute film on all flights to Thailand. While Thais enjoy being hosts to tourists, they find the lack of knowledge regarding their own religion offensive. The film, therefore, addresses such issues as how to speak to a monk and what to wear in a temple.

KEY TERM

Destination management: managing a destination to ensure harmony exists between visitor, destination and residents.

Destination management

Destination management involves managing a destination in a way that promotes harmony between the visitor, the destination and the host community. This will normally be handled by local authorities and it includes visitor and traffic management, as well as ensuring the environment develops appropriately, through planning control. In its simplest form, in a UK city this may involve:

- ensuring developments conform to local and governmental plans
- providing for tourist and resident traffic (e.g. car parks)
- providing coach parks
- managing car parking facilities (and increasing them during peak seasons)
- developing park and ride facilities
- increasing litter collections during busy summer periods
- providing signage
- providing visitor services (e.g. toilets, guides)
- marketing methods
- providing information (TIC and information points at key sites)

A more sophisticated destination management plan would consider:

- using marketing techniques to increase or decrease visitor numbers
- how to enhance a visitor experience (e.g. cleanliness, information, good transport)
- encouraging overnight stays (e.g. range of accommodation, evening attractions, short breaks brochure, bed booking service)
- reducing seasonality (e.g. cheaper rates off season, special packages, special events)
- community consultation methods (e.g. public meetings, press information)
- environmental impact assessment
- environmental impact auditing.

Some destinations may wish to increase tourist numbers and so will need to make their facilities more accessible. This may involve infrastructure developments (e.g. park and ride, coach parks) as well as an increase in their marketing. Other cities have sufficient numbers of tourists and their objective is not to promote, but to manage, the tourists.

Planning and destination management

Within the UK planning is a complex system. In brief, all developments must submit plans to local authorities, who must ensure that they meet appropriate guidelines and local structural plans. Planning applications can restrict the development of facilities and, therefore, control how a city or town develops. For example, by allowing a four star hotel with conference facilities to be built, but preventing the conversion of a house into a Bed and Breakfast establishment, the local authorities will be encouraging the high spending business visitors. Planning officers must ensure that:

- the land available is used sensibly
- any developments 'fit' with the surroundings
- the environment is not damaged
- any developments are acceptable to the local community

Planning systems are generally less sophisticated in developing countries, and many are even considered to be corrupt. Governments and local authorities may be reluctant to impose too many planning restrictions simply because they want that tourist income to continue.

KEY TERMS

Park and ride: a car park on the edge of a town or city with a regular bus service to the centre.

Reduce seasonality: reduce the effects of peaks and troughs in visitor numbers.

ACTIVITY

Bermuda has taken several measures to limit tourism's impact on the environment and local community. Read the following extract and then list these measures.

Enjoying life in the slow lane

Bermuda sells itself unashamedly on its individualism and that has verged – equally unashamedly – on the quirky.

So how different from its nearest island neighbours, in the Caribbean, has Bermuda proved to be?

While a number of Caribbean destinations have openly courted, and won, air charters from the UK and Europe, Bermuda has banned them.

Just as dozens of Caribbean islands sought to become ports of call to as many revenue-earning cruise ships as possible, Bermuda eschewed the chance and put a ceiling on cruise ship visits.

Many destinations have also allowed a welter of hotel developments. Bermuda's building freeze is still firmly on after at least eight years.

And its government has ruled no building is allowed to be taller than the cathedral of the Most Holy Trinity in the capital Hamilton.

Not for Bermuda is the garish glare of neon signs or advertising hoardings. Both are banned as the island continues to develop its image of pastel-coloured respectability.

Families are only allowed one car per household in order to prevent massive congestion on such a small island and the inevitable pollution that would go with it. And tourists cannot hire a car as there are no rental facilities permitted.

Getting around – British style, on the left side of the road – is by taxi, frequent minibus services or by renting mopeds.

The maximum speed for all traffic on the island is 20 miles per hour.

Added rules for motorcycle riders are the compulsory wearing of crash helmets, and their machines must be parked in specially marked bays.

The island claims full employment, and, as a result, there is no poverty, low crime rates and virtually no crimes against tourists.

Tourism officials say the lack of unemployment and poverty – often workers are recruited from the Azores and other parts of the world – means a visitor-friendly atmosphere.

Bermuda Tourism UK director Derek Brightwell said: "There is no hawking allowed which means visitors are not pestered to buy trinkets the way they are in many parts of the Caribbean."

KEY TERMS

Environmental Impact Assessment (EIA): assessment of the impact (of a development) on the environment.

Environmental impact auditing: an ongoing system of monitoring impacts on the environment.

DID YOU KNOW?

British Airways produces an *Annual Environmental Report* as part of their efforts toward their 'Good neighbour' goal.

An important part of planning for new tourism developments at a destination, in some countries, is an assessment of the impact of the development on the environment. This is not a legal requirement in the UK, but is carried out by tourism planners as part of good practice. An Environmental Impact Assessment (EIA) means going through a check list of points that must be taken into consideration. These can then be assessed against the benefits of the development and compared against local policies before it is decided whether the development should go ahead.

While EIAs are one-off assessments, an **Environmental Audit** is the process of inspecting and checking the environment as an ongoing monitoring process. This is a process carried out by businesses as well as public bodies.

Visitor management

Visitor management is a term that has been used to cover any activity that is designed to attract (or deter) a tourist to a destination, to encourage specific types of tourists and to influence what they do when they are at the destination (it is, in fact, the destination that we manage in order to attract the visitor, so the term destination management is also used).

ACTIVITY

Discuss destination management methods a local authority could use. Consider how they could:

1 encourage more overnight stays
2 reduce traffic in the town centre
3 encourage tourists to spread more evenly around the city
4 reduce seasonality
5 encourage business or conference tourism
6 encourage visitor numbers
7 reduce visitor numbers
8 encourage visits to a particular site or attraction
9 encourage visits to several sites or attractions

Which of the above most closely match the aims of your city or town council? What are they doing to achieve those aims?

CASE STUDY *Destination management in Cambridge*

Cambridge is visited by 3.4 million tourists on average per annum. This generates around £195 million for local businesses and employs 6,650 people within the city. The tourist:resident ratio is 32:1 – with the result that destination management is an important part of the tourism strategy.

Cambridge has a wealth of historic buildings, 1,411 of which are listed. Most are privately owned by the University colleges. It is these resources – the colleges and buildings – that are the most popular feature with visitors. The historic centre of the city exists in a small area either side of the River Cam. It is based on a medieval street pattern, making for an attractive area. Pedestrian congestion is, however, a problem as many of the town shops as well as the majority of the town's students live within this area.

There has been much research carried out on numbers and types of visitors to Cambridge. Results show a high proportion of day visitors (38%). This is often thought to cause the major transport problems in the city as approximately 75% arrive by car or coach. There is also a trend to make more use of on-street parking, rather than using the multistorey car parks or one of the three park and ride schemes. Only 2% of coaches used the official car parks in 1997, causing severe congestion in the city on summer weekends.

The main purpose of visiting Cambridge is sight-seeing (55%). However, an increase in both VFR and business conference tourism is beginning to happen.

Cambridge has approximately 20,000 foreign language (EFL) students each year. The fact that they are predominantly of school age and, therefore, travel in July and August creates some host/guest conflict. Their lack of skill in riding bikes through the city is notorious (one Japanese student was found cycling down the fast lane of the M11 one summer).

With 32 tourists to every resident, tourism has a high profile in Cambridge. Recent surveys carried out by the council show that only just over half the residents think that the benefits outweigh the costs; 75% agree that tourism creates congestion and parking problems, 43% think that tourism does not enhance the quality of life.

Cambridge City council take an active role in destination management. Their 1996 Tourism Strategy is the fourth to be developed in Cambridge. It has four objectives aiming 'to reconcile the sometimes competing needs of residents, visitors and the environment' (*Cambridge Tourism Strategy 1996*, p. 12):

- To conserve (protect and enhance) the local life, beauty and character of Cambridge and the surrounding area.

- To ensure a satisfying and enjoyable experience for visitors to Cambridge.

- To support a prosperous local industry which can contribute significant long-term benefits to the local economy and local residents.

- To ensure reinvestment by the industry in the infrastructure on which tourism depends, including conservation of the environment.

ACTIVITY

In small groups establish the tourism problems and issues in Cambridge.

Discuss destination management techniques that could be used to ensure the city council achieve their objectives and make recommendations. Make sure you consider the number of visitors, congestion, small areas (e.g. parts of medieval city), traffic and parking, coaches and cars, the type of accommodation to be encouraged and language schools.

Check the Cambridge City Council website at www.cambridge.gov.uk for more information about the facilities available.

Compare the methods or ideas that you have thought of with some of the things that are being (or have been) done in Cambridge.

The key point about Cambridge City Council is that, unlike many other local authorities, it does not want more visitors. Instead it wishes to manage those that it does have in such a way that they spend more (maximising economic benefits) and cause less congestion and damage (minimising socio-cultural and environmental problems).

Marketing of Cambridge as a destination is, therefore, limited and highly selective. There is no general consumer advertising, although there is some advertising in the trade press. The RTB underplays Cambridge in its regional literature. Marketing is focused on overseas visitors, short breaks for domestic visitors and the conference market (overnight visitors and business tourists spend more money than day trippers!). An accommodation service exists at the TIC and a conference service has been established to encourage higher spending tourists to visit.

KEY TERM

Dispersal: encouraging tourists to spread themselves around the area, rather than stay at the main sites.

Dispersal is the visitor management technique used once the tourists have arrived. Guides, signposting and information points encourage the tourist away from the medieval city centre to other attractions. Dispersal is also achieved in a wider context – people staying overnight are encouraged to 'disperse' throughout the region by going to the cathedral city of Ely and the Duxford Air Museum, both within a 15 mile

Courtesy Couriers: couriers employed by Cambridge City Council to help local tourists, in particular coaches.

DID YOU KNOW?

Cambridge City Council estimate that the cost of providing tourism services amounts to £331,000 (1995 figures), i.e. £2.91 per resident.

radius. This eases the pressure on Cambridge (although it still benefits from the overnight stays).

The College Pass Scheme helps manage the tourists in the colleges. This has reduced the conflict that previously existed due to the large number of tourists wandering freely though the buildings that are essentially educational establishments.

Courtesy couriers meet coaches and allocate guides. In addition, Cambridge has built three park and ride schemes and two more are planned (to reduce traffic congestion), it has improved information provision and has moved the TIC into larger accommodation to provide a better service. They have also invested in public toilets (£168,000 in 1987), information at car parks, improved coach parking and signs to show where those parking areas are.

Cambridge City Council holds an annual Tourism Forum to ensure community and local business participation. The Council has produced a video and a code of conduct for foreign language school students. Both are focused on cycling in Cambridge.

ASSESSMENT

Discovering Lincoln

Lincoln is considered to be an undiscovered destination. This is predominantly due to its location. Lincoln lies 40 miles from the east coast of Britain, surrounded by a mainly agricultural area with a low population density. It is not on the main line rail route and the main north to south link (the A1) is reached by 25 miles of single track road. The nearest airports are Humberside and East Midlands.

Lincoln used to rely on its heavy manufacturing industry. The decline of this has led to high unemployment. 1998 statistics revealed an unemployment rate of 7.5% – this is the highest unemployment rate in any part of the county and is well above the national average.

There is limited statistical information about visitors to Lincoln. The City Council began to monitor enquiries to the TIC in 1994 and the Department of Tourism at the newly established University of Lincoln and Humberside carried out a survey for the council in 1997.

It is thought that tourism boomed in the late 1980s, but has since slowed down with approximately one million visitors to the city in late 1998, a figure that has been static for several years. The survey showed that most visitors were day visitors (about 75%). Of those staying overnight the majority (56%) only stayed one night. Not surprisingly, the majority (85%) came by car, with 10% on coach trips and only 5% by rail. 75% of the visitors were from the UK. The proximity of Hull and its ferry service to Rotterdam, however, was thought to have contributed to a good proportion of Dutch, Belgian and German visitors. Visitors enjoyed their visits with 49% stating their intention to return.

The main attractions were as follows:

ATTRACTION	NO. OF VISITORS
Lincoln cathedral	300,000
Lincoln Castle	300,000
The Lawn	80,000
Museum of Lincolnshire Life	47,000
Hartsholme Country Park	20–30,000
Usher Art Gallery	29,440

Source: Lincoln City Council, Facts and Figures, *August 1998*

The surveys revealed that visitors clearly liked the historic character of the city and its attractions. The only really negative comments were concerning its 'Steep Hill'.

Lincoln developed as a walled city on high defensible ground. The castle, cathedral and main historic attractions are located at the top of 'Steep Hill'. This is appropriately named! The commercial shopping district developed later, at the bottom of the city. Thus, the city essentially consists of two parts: an upper historic area and the lower commercial district. The positive consequence of this is that the historic area has been largely preserved. However, it also means that the tourists do not use the lower part of the town, where the shops are. Visitors tend to venture part of the way down the hill, but turn back early to avoid the long climb back.

The fact that tourists are unaware of the 'downhill attraction' may also contribute to them not venturing downhill. This may not matter, but for the fact that visitors to Lincoln spend significantly less during their visits than those visiting other comparable historic towns.

The local council wish to change this. They feel that the product needs developing and that a flagship attraction may be needed. New sites for hotel development have been discussed and major infrastructure initiatives are currently under way. Park and ride schemes are being trialled and there is a proposal to link the historic uphill and the commercial downhill districts. A people-mover, funicular, city hopper and Guide Friday have all been discussed as possible options.

Jordan: A developing destination

Background

The Hashemite Kingdom of Jordan became an independent sovereign state in 1946. It consists of a constitutional monarchy with a representative government. At the time of independence most of the country's 400,000 inhabitants were poor Bedouin. Despite remarkable progress in the last 50 years, Jordan still has many problems: a huge foreign debt, 15% unemployment and 25% of the population still living below the poverty line.

Jordan was one of the main economic victims of the Gulf War. The United Nations estimate that in the period from August 1990 to 1991 alone it cost Jordan $US8 billion in lost trade and lost incomes of those Jordanians working in the Gulf. However, the general economic outlook appears to be changing. Assistance from the International Monetary Fund (IMF) and a reform plan has boosted confidence and the country now has a healthy growth rate.

Although more westernised than most Arab countries, over 90% of Jordanians are Muslims.

Tourism

Tourism, together with agriculture, used to be a major source of income for Jordan. However, Jordan is placed in an area of immense conflict and in 1967 the Kingdom of Jordan lost its share of the city of Jerusalem to Israel. In tourism terms, the loss of this major historic and religious attraction was phenomenal. Tourist numbers were beginning to recover when the Gulf War struck in 1991.

The Peace Treaty with Israel in 1994 has had a positive effect on tourist numbers and confidence is growing. In 1996 and 1997 the growth in tourism then began to slow. This could be attributed to a stalemate in negotiations between the Arabs and Israelis, as well as terrorism (some against tourists) in Egypt.

YEAR	1989	1990	1991	1992	1993	1994	1995	1996	1997
Arrivals (in 000s)	644	577	439	669	775	858	1074	1103	1127
% annual change		−10.40%	−23.92%	52.39%	15.84%	10.71%	25.17%	2.70%	2.18%
Receipts (JD million)	314.6	339.8	216	314.3	390.2	406.4	462.5	527.2	548.8
% annual change		8.01%	−36.43%	45.51%	24.15%	4.15%	13.80%	13.99%	4.10%
Receipts (US$ million)	443.59	499.51	317.52	546.88	561.89	581.15	661.38	743.35	773.81
% annual change		12.61%	−36.43%	72.24%	2.74%	3.43%	13.80%	12.39%	4.10%

Tourist arrivals 1989–1998

Source: MOTA

A shift in the tourists' origins is evident. The number of arrivals from Arab countries showed an increase of 5.5%, while those from Europe decreased by 4.9%. The number of Israelis visiting Jordan shows a steady increase. Availability of accommodation has increased, especially in the four and five star categories:

CLASSIFICATION	1992	1993	1994	1995	1996	1997	1998	P.C.98–94
Deluxe *****	3	3	3	3	3	3	3	0.00%
*****	2	2	3	4	7	6	7	133.33%
****	10	10	6	9	9	11	13	116.67%
***	24	23	23	28	32	34	37	60.87%
**	38	40	43	47	48	52	53	23.26%
*	48	48	49	55	60	55	64	30.61%
Pensions	1	2	2	2	2	2	N.A.	N.A.

Accommodation 1992–1998

Source: MOTA

The Ministry of Tourism claim that there were 188 classified and 161 unclassified hotels operating in Jordan in 1997. Hotels employ 7,815 Jordanians and there are plans to build 58 new hotels throughout the country. The International Hotel chains of Sheraton, Hyatt-Regency, Holiday Inn and Four Seasons all have plans to open in Jordan within two years. Jordan is increasingly becoming a 'packaged' destination with an average of 3.9 nights being spent in the Kingdom.

Attractions

Tourists are attracted by Jordan's historical, religious and geographical attractions. The most renowned of these is Petra. Tucked away in mountains south of the Dead Sea, Petra is considered to be the most spectacular ancient city remaining. It is the primary attraction for most visitors to Jordan. An ancient city hewn out of solid rock, Petra was the capital of the Nabataeans – Arabs who dominated the area in pre-Roman times.

This city was unknown to the western world for 700 years and as a result Petra is still well preserved. Local Bedouins and Arab tradesmen knew of its existence but chose to remain silent! A Swiss explorer disguised as a pilgrim gained the confidence of the Bedouin and revealed their secret to the west. The Bedouins continued to occupy the area until 1984, when the Jordanian government relocated them to a neighbouring town. Their reason for doing this was given as 'concern for the monuments'. The Bedouins are still not happy with this arrangement.

Much of Petra's fascination comes from its location on the edge of Wadi Arabi. The rugged sandstone forms deep canyons – Petra is reached through one such canyon, varying from 5 to 200 metres wide. This helped keep the settlement a secret and now protects it visually from the hotels emerging in the surrounding area. Once inside the city, the hundreds of buildings that are cut into the rock fascinate tourists.

Petra today

Following is an extract from *Lonely Planet Syria and Jordan*, January 1997.

Not so long ago it was an arduous journey from Amman to Petra, only affordable by the lucky few. Now good bitumen roads link it with the outside world and from Amman it can be reached in three hours via the Desert Highway and Shobak, or five hours down the historic King's Highway. Awaiting you are all types of accommodation, ranging from the five star Forum Hotel to simple backpackers' digs.

Since Jordan and Israel ended their state of war, Petra has turned from a popular tourist destination into bedlam. The adjoining village of Wadi Musa is expanding apace as the rush continues to erect ever more hotels – whole hillsides look set to disappear at any moment under a thick layer of concrete.

Luckily, Petra itself is shielded from all the visual horrors, although with up to 3000 people entering every day, fears are growing that the tourist onslaught may not be sustainable. For some time now the authorities have been toying with the idea of imposing a daily ceiling of 1500 visitors.

For the moment, the bulk of visitors rush the place, spending a couple of hours taking happy snaps and then zooming off to the next place on their itinerary.

Assessment questions

Discovering Lincoln

In 1999 Lincoln produced its first tourism strategy. Its mission was 'to maximise the positive economic and environmental impacts of tourism in Lincoln and to achieve year on year growth in tourism volume and value to the city'.

TASK 1
a) Name four organisations that will be involved in the development of Lincoln as a tourism destination and explain their roles.
b) Discuss any conflicts that may exist between the agents of tourism development named above.

TASK 2
a) Give the profile of two types of visitors that Lincoln may try to attract in order to achieve growth in both 'volume and value to the city'. What facilities and amenities could the local authority provide in order to help attract these visitors?
b) The 'Steep Hill' has both positive and negative impacts on the city. Discuss these and make two recommendations to the city council that would be in line with their mission statement. Justify your recommendations.

Jordan: a devleoping destination

'Jordan believes tourism to be a driving force of its economy in the coming years, and is therefore working to exploit this dynamic sector to its maximum potential.'

TASK 3

One proposal considered by Jordan, Egypt and Israel is the development of a 'Red Sea Riviera', to include Aquaba, Eilat and Taba (in Egypt's Sinai). Outline five principles of sustainable tourism that should be applied in this development project.

TASK 4

a) The Bedouins are nomadic peoples renowned for their hospitality. It is part of their creed never to turn a traveller away. Write a code of conduct for visitors to the area. Advise them of this custom and the religious ways. Give guidelines to ensure that they do not take advantage of this custom or offend the Islamic religion.

b) Describe two destination management measures that the local authorities in Petra could take to ease some of the problems at the ancient city.

Key skills

In completing the assessment for this unit, you can achieve the following key skills. These will be accredited at the discretion of your tutor on the basis of the quality of the work you submit.

C3.2 Read and synthesise information from two extended documents about a complex subject. One of these documents should include at least one image.

CHAPTER **3**

Worldwide travel destinations

Aims and Objectives

At the end of this chapter you will:

- **be able to use a variety of research sources**
- **be able to use research skills to build up your knowledge and understanding of travel destinations**
- **be able to locate major travel destinations in continental Europe**
- **be able to locate major long haul travel and tourism destinations**
- **understand the different features that give these destinations appeal to visitors**
- **be able to identify the main routes and gateways that tourists use when travelling to tourist destinations**
- **understand how tourist destinations change in popularity**

KEY TERM

Market segmentation: dividing the market for a product into groups of people with similar characteristics.

Introduction

This chapter introduces you to major continental European and long haul destinations for UK tourists. You will study their location and their key features and you will find out how these destinations are accessed by tourists, locating the gateways and routes from the UK.

You will learn that destinations can be grouped into different types catering for differing holiday needs, for example, city breaks and seaside resorts. You will find out about the features of destinations from climate to accommodation and you will distinguish between natural and man-made features.

We will examine how different destinations appeal to different groups of customers, according to the particular features of the destination. This aspect of the chapter will link with Chapter 4 (Marketing) as you will gain a greater understanding of market segmentation.

KEY TERM

Tour representative: works for a tour operator, looking after guests in a resort.

A sound knowledge of popular destinations is of vital importance for anyone hoping to work in the travel and tourism industry. Travel agents must be able to advise their customers on all aspects of a destination. Business travel advisers must be able to recommend appropriate transport and accommodation to clients. Tour representatives must be knowledgeable about all resort features and facilities and should also be able to advise on other destinations offered by their company. Tour operators must be aware of their customers' needs and find destinations with features that match those needs. You will also learn why destinations change in popularity and identify examples of factors that lead to that change.

Within this chapter, it is not the intention to provide a comprehensive guide to all destinations. The major destinations will be identified and discussed, but it is more important that you learn how to use various sources to build up your own knowledge. For this reason, you will learn how to use research skills to find information and to sift that information, deciding what is of use to you and what is not.

This chapter also builds on Chapter 1 (Investigating travel and tourism) and links with Chapter 2 (Tourism development).

Research skills

As part of your course, you are expected to carry out research, both individually and in groups. Undertaking such research enables you to find relevant information for assessments and to develop the knowledge you need to forge a successful career in travel and tourism. Chapter 4 (Marketing) explains how professional market research is carried out, but here we will concentrate on the kind of research you can do now, as a student, and in the future, as an employee in travel and tourism. Your research must be ongoing, otherwise your information will not be accurate and up-to-date. Researching involves the following:

- being clear about what you are trying to find out
- knowing how to search for information
- deciding what might be useful
- collecting and presenting relevant information
- drawing conclusions about your findings
- acknowledging your sources

Being clear about what you are trying to find out

If you are doing an assessment you will have been given a written brief. Read this brief at least twice immediately. It will also be explained

Customer's Name		Today's Date		Booked with TC before?	Y / N
		Consultant's Name			

TRAVEL DETAILS			ALTERNATIVES (e.g. if first choice not available)		
Destination					
Departure Date					
Duration/Return Date					
Departure Point					

Total Party Size	No of Children		No of Infants		No of Adults
	Age(s) on return		Age(s) on return		

Accommodation	
Room Type/Meal Basis	

Budget Range		Form of Payment		Booking Today?	Y / N

Address		Postcode		Mobile Phone	
		Home Tel. No.		Notes	
		Work Tel. No.			

SPECIFIC NEEDS OF CUSTOMER *64# Short Haul *65# Long Haul	Quiet	Lively	Beach	Kids Clubs	Special Occasions
	Excursions	Nightlife	Activities	Other	

TYPE OF HOLIDAY REQUIRED/SPECIAL REQUESTS	ESSENTIAL & IMPORTANT DETAILS
What do you like to do when you are on holiday?	Nationality of all Party Members
	Passports held
	Vaccinations/Health
	Visa(s) required
	Insurance Cover
	Car Hire
	Holiday Money
	Overnight Hotel
	Car Parking

OUR RECOMMENDATION

Tour Operator		Departure Date	
Departure Point		Duration	
Destination		Flight Details	
Accommodation Name		Room Type & Facilities	
Meal Basis		Special Notes	

Costing

These suggested travel details are correct at the time of enquiry, but may later be subject to change and availability. This is not a confirmation of booking for any details shown on this form.

Thank you for your enquiry - if you have any questions, our telephone number is:

When you call, please ask for:

FOLLOW UP ☎	Y / N	REASONS/NOTES
1. Date		
Time		
2. Date		
Time		Value £

Confirmed ☐   Provisional ☐   Enquiry ☐

Figure 3.1 Thomas Cook customer requirements form

Source: Thomas Cook Holidays

verbally, so first of all, listen! Many hints and pointers will be given about what to look for and where to look. Take notes; do not expect to remember everything later. Take the opportunity to ask for help and clarification. Do not be shy about asking questions; remember that is why you are a student and your lecturer is there to help you. After the brief, start to plan – write a list of all the information you need to find out and start to think about where you will get it.

If you are dealing with a customer, you must ask questions and take notes. Travel agents have special forms for this purpose so that they are prompted to ask relevant questions. Remember to take a contact number in case you need to ask something else later. Figure 3.1 gives an example of an enquiry form.

Knowing how to search for information

KEY TERM

Secondary research: is done first, as the information is more readily available.

This means you must know your sources. You must know what is available, where it is and how to access it quickly. Sources may be:

- secondary – already available and published (e.g. books and atlases)
- primary – not published (e.g. people with relevant knowledge or your own observations on visiting a destination)

Later in this section we will examine the various sources available to you and practise their use.

Deciding what might be useful

You might expect that it will be difficult to find information. This is often not the case, particularly with information on destinations. Rather, the problem will be that there are vast amounts of information available and you do not know which to choose. Return to your original list of what information is needed and be ruthless. Discard anything that does not match up with your list or with your customers' needs. For example, if they have asked for self-catering accommodation, discard half-board hotels. You will also find that much information is available in several sources, for example, information on climate in a destination. Choose one comprehensive source, check briefly that the information in the other sources confirms your findings and then discard them. If you are still unsure about what is useful, check with a colleague.

Collecting and presenting relevant information

If you are doing an assessment, you may have been told how the information should be presented: for example, it may be in the form of a report or a display. This will help you, but you will still need a plan. Your plan gives your work a structure, enabling you to make sure you have covered everything and that it is presented in a logical order. When you are collecting your information, organise it as you collect it. If you are making notes from the Internet or from a book, group all the notes relating to a topic or point together. If you are photocopying or printing, highlight the relevant points immediately and, again, organise topics together. When you are ready to collate your information, check back to your brief and to your plan.

Always include an introduction, explaining what you are doing and why, and make sure you have covered everything asked for. If you are finding out information for customers, the same rules apply. Make sure you have all the information required (but not so much as to be confusing) and make sure you present it in a logical order. If you have information for an assessment that you have copied, you must attach it as an appendix to your work.

Everything that you write in your assessment must be in your own words, unless it is a direct quote, in which case you must acknowledge it with the source name and date. If you attach notes or pictures as appendices, make sure you refer to them in your work. For example: 'A map of Spain shows the main coastal resorts, see appendix 2'. If you are presenting information to customers, you may need visuals to help them understand what you are talking about. Brochures will commonly be used for this, with the pages clearly marked.

Drawing conclusions about your findings

In an assessment you must always have a conclusion. This is a brief summary of what you have found out. If you are giving an oral presentation, you are reminding your audience of what you have just told them. You will also need to do this with customers, to help them take in the information.

Acknowledging your sources

A bibliography should be included with an assessment. This is a list of every source you have used with titles, authors, publishers, dates, website addresses, as appropriate. In addition, any direct quotes should be acknowledged in the text itself. Photos, maps or graphs should be clearly labelled with the source and date. When dealing with customers, it will suffice to mention where you got your information. Remember that it lends you some authority if you mention your source.

KEY TERMS

Appendix: attachment to a report.

Bibliography: comprehensive list of resources used.

Sources of information

Secondary sources

It is important that you become used to using a variety of information sources. You are fortunate in studying travel and tourism, in that many resources are available. We will begin by examining some of the secondary sources.

The Internet

The most comprehensive source you have at your disposal is the Internet. However, there are so many sites that you will have to learn how to search the Internet to find what you want. For example, if you enter the search words 'travel' or 'tourism', you will find thousands of sites listed. It is worth spending an hour or two 'surfing' through these generally to find those which will be of future use. You will not have time to do this every time you undertake research.

If you have your own computer, you can simply bookmark the useful sites by adding them to your list of 'favourites'. Otherwise, note down the useful website addresses for future reference (you have already been introduced to some of these in Chapter 1). You may also wish to limit your search to UK sites, depending on what you want to know. Be aware though, that Internet access is quicker for us in the morning, before the US wakes up and comes on line.

When searching for information on worldwide destinations, there are several useful sites to begin with:

- www.excite.com/travel/destinations – gives information, such as fact sheets, where to stay, what to do and maps on destinations worldwide.

- www.odci.gov/cia/publications – this is the CIA World Factbook and gives general information. It differs from other sites in that it will also offer you facts and figures on economies, government or transport, rather than just tourist information.

- www.geographia.com – also has destination information.

- Some publishers have introduced websites supporting their travel books. These include **www.fodors.com** and **www.lonelyplanet.com**. They do not have all the information from the travel books on line but are still useful sources.

- www.worldatlas.com – is useful for maps and country information. Also try **www.infoplease.com/countries.html**.

If you are doing research on a particular destination, simply type in the name of the destination and you will hit lots of sites, including the official tourist information site for that destination.

ACTIVITY

Find the CIA World Factbook site at *www.odci.gov/cia/publications/factbook*. Find the country entry for Bermuda. Find out Bermuda's location. Print off a map. Note down Bermuda's natural resources.

Find out the population and compare it with that of the UK.

What is the noun for a person from Bermuda? What languages are spoken? What is the capital of Bermuda?

How important is tourism for Bermuda and where do the tourists come from?

Now find the entry for Iceland. Find Iceland's location and print off a map. What is unusual about Iceland's parliament?

What is the climate like? What are the country's natural resources?

What is the population, compared with Bermuda? What is the capital and what is the most important industry?

What forms of tourism are important? How might tourists arrive at the island?

Now find Iceland on www.geographia.com. Give details of flights from the UK to Iceland. How can tourists travel around Iceland? What is the currency?

Read about the history of Iceland.

Now try a general search for Iceland and see what other sites you can find.

Books, directories and brochures

Books are obviously a useful source of information on destinations. You will find many travel guides in bookshops and libraries. These are usually detailed, with maps, and are extremely beneficial to the tourist. However, they will not always contain statistical information that you might need.

The World Tourism Organisation directories are the most comprehensive source of tourism statistics (these might be in your library). WTO does have a website, but unless your institution is a subscriber, you will not be able to access the statistics. You will, however, be able to access general information about WTO.

Many directories are produced for the travel trade (these might also be available in your library). *The World Travel Guide* is probably the best known of these. It is updated annually and contains factual information on every country. The information includes transport, accommodation, visa requirements, health and a social profile. Following is an example of an entry for Botswana.

KEY TERM

World Travel Guide: a trade directory with information on destinations.

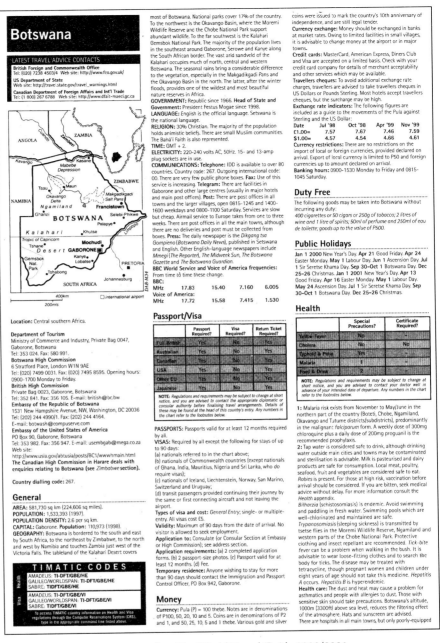

Figure 3.2 A page on Botswana from The World Travel Guide 2000/2001

Source: Columbus Publishing

It is essential that you have access to a good atlas. The *World Travel Atlas* (also Columbus Press) has been designed for the travel trade and for students (you should be able to find this in your library). It is also available on CD ROM with accompanying facts and figures.

Another guide that you would need if you were working in a travel agency is the *OAG World Airways Guide*. This gives details of airline routes and fares. It is quite complex to follow and a special training course is needed to understand it properly.

You will find brochures give you a lot of destination information. They are also visually appealing and easy to understand. You should not rely on these alone, however, as it must be remembered that they are a sales tool and therefore designed to attract the tourist to the resort. They will not contain any negative information.

Travel trade journals

Your library should have copies of travel trade journals – these give up-to-date features about the industry and you can buy them at a reduced price on a student subscription. *Travel Weekly* has regular features on specific destinations. The national and regional press also has very good coverage of destinations. Look for the Sunday newspaper travel supplements, in particular.

Primary sources

Primary sources of information will also help you. If you want to know about a destination, find someone who has been there. Whenever you go on holiday, collect photos, postcards and any literature that you come across. Visit the tourist office in the destination.

If you work in the travel trade you may get the opportunity to take part in educational visits. These are arranged so that the travel agents gain knowledge of a particular area.

PROFILE *Club Med Educationals*

Agents who return from educationals often complain about too many hotel visits and not enough free time. Club Med believes its familiarity trips are different because they focus on agents sampling the product. Before taking part, agents are expected to attend a training session. This two hour session offers an introduction to Club Med and is accompanied by a course book and a video. Once on the visit, agents take part in as many activities as they like. The only meeting they have to attend is the debriefing session where feedback is asked for. Agents then return home and train their own staff about the product. One such agent commented that 'the Club Med product is very specific, so on an educational you get to see what the holiday would be like for yourself'. Another said: 'Usually educationals are a bit more involved, whereas Club Med gives the agents more of a holiday, where they can actually sample the product themselves and gain an in-depth knowledge of a particular village or resort.'

Source: Adapted from Travel Weekly, *22 March 1999*

The location and features of major travel and tourism destinations in continental Europe

Continental Europe has a variety of travel and tourism destinations that can be grouped as follows:

- towns and cities

- seaside resorts

- purpose-built resorts

- countryside areas

- historical/cultural destinations

In this section you will locate the major destinations in each category and we will examine their particular features, identifying the types of visitors that will be attracted to each one.

Towns and cities

KEY TERM

Short break: a holiday of 2 or 3 days.

Cities such as Paris, Vienna, Madrid, Prague and Berlin are the most popular destinations for the short break market. This is the fastest growing sector in outbound holiday tourism. The market grew by 156% between 1989 and 1997 (source: UK Travel Survey, 1998). Research by Crystal Holidays in 1998 showed that Paris and Amsterdam were the top two city break destinations and had been for the previous three years. Copenhagen is the fastest growing short break destination with a growth of 37% in 1998. The tour operators Travelscene and Cresta reported that Lille and Stockholm were emerging city destinations. Lille is easily accessible to the British market by Eurostar and Stockholm is attractive as it was designated Europe's city of culture in 1998. It will also host the Eurovision song contest in 2000.

The UK Travel Survey found that short breaks abroad had rather different characteristics to those taken in the UK. For example, people are much more likely to use the travel trade to organise their break than go independently – 40% of breaks abroad are sold as inclusive tours. There is also a stronger reliance on public transport than with UK short breaks, although 31% travel by car. Two out of three short breaks include a channel crossing and France accounts for over half of all short breaks. Almost 80% of short breaks are to cities and towns.

ACTIVITY

Ensure you know the capital cities of all these countries:

UK	France	Spain
Greece	Portugal	Italy
Austria	Switzerland	Belgium
Bulgaria	Eire	Iceland
Finland	Germany	Poland
Romania	Hungary	Czech Republic
Slovakia	Sweden	Norway

Trace the following map of Europe and then locate all the above listed capital cities on it:

We have seen that Amsterdam and Paris are the most popular city destinations. It is interesting to consider why this is the case. You will probably come up with the following.

- Both cities are close to the UK.
- Both cities are easily accessible by air from many UK airports.
- 'No frills' airlines offer cheap fares to both cities.
- Paris is easily accessible by Eurostar.
- From London to Paris by car only takes about five hours.
- In Amsterdam the tourist can reasonably expect everyone to speak English.
- There are many attractions in both cities.

You might also have considered that these cities are also important as business destinations. Think about what information a business traveller might need on Amsterdam. Use the following criteria as a guide.

Business facts for Amsterdam

1 **General information**
   Local time: GMT + two hours.
   Driving: on the right, minimum age 18 years.
   Currency: guilder (about three guilders to the pound).
   International dialling code: 31.
   Language: Dutch.

2 **Business hours**
   Offices: 8.30am to 5pm, Monday to Friday.
   Shops: 9am to 5.30pm, Monday to Saturday.
   Banks: 9am to 4pm. Monday to Friday.

3 **Health**
   Free or reduced cost emergency health treatment on production of a valid E111 form.

4 **Transport**
   Airport: Amsterdam Schipol AMS, located 9 miles southwest of Amsterdam.
   Transport to city centre: bus takes 30 minutes. Taxi takes 20 minutes.

5 **Business hints**
   Appointments should be made in advance.
   Suits should be worn.
   It is customary to shake hands on meeting and taking leave. Business cards are exchanged on introduction.
   Most people speak English.

Note that a tourist will require the same general information but they will also want to know about attractions and what there is to do.

KEY TERM

'No frills' airline: low cost airline with few customer services, such as in-flight food.

KEY TERM

E111 form: available to UK residents from the post office, to enable them to obtain free or reduced cost medical treatment in EU countries.

ACTIVITY

Find out about attractions and other things to do for tourists in Amsterdam. Produce a fact sheet similar to the one above, but directed at tourists.

Find out the information a business traveller would need on Paris and produce a fact sheet similar to the example given for Amsterdam.

ACTIVITY

Study the map of Paris following. Note the location of these major attractions:

- Arc de Triomphe
- River Seine
- Sacre Coeur
- Cimetiere du Pere Lachaise
- Centre Georges Pompidou
- Musee du Louvre
- Avenue des Champs Elysees

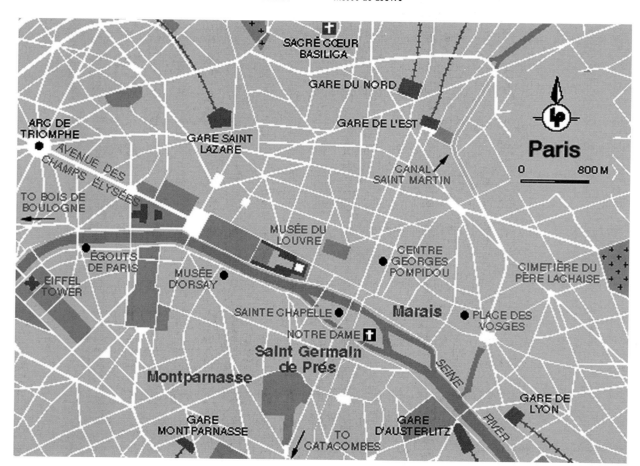

Source: Reproduced with the permission of Lonely Planet Publications

Find out about each of the attractions and say what the appeal of each is for tourists.

Airline magazines are a very good source of city information for both business travellers and tourists. The following extract is from *Red Hot*, the Virgin Express in-flight magazine. It is written in a lively and interesting manner and has a captive audience as it is distributed on the plane.

ACTIVITY

Read the extract on Madrid and find out similar information on a city of your choice. Produce an article suitable for inclusion in an airline in-flight magazine. You should use a desktop publishing package to produce your work.

Source: Red Hot, *November/December 1999, Premier magazines*

Tourists are also opting for breaks in more unusual and exotic places, such as Istanbul. The focus in Istanbul is very much on culture and shopping. There are many museums, palaces and mosques, depicting the Ottoman, Roman and Byzantine empires. The Grand Bazaar consists of 4,000 shops where carpets, jewellery, ceramics and leather are specialities. Boat cruises and city tours are also cheaply available.

Remember that city holidays are usually in addition to an annual holiday, they do not replace it. Tourists can take a city break with minimal or no time off work and many people are able to afford the cost of short breaks.

PROFILE *Cresta*

Cresta is one of the leading operators in the short break market. The company has been selling city breaks for more than 30 years. Cresta was acquired by Airtours in 1998, but continues to trade under the Cresta name. Its major competitors are Crystal, Thomson Holidays, Travelscene and British Airways Cities. Another competitor, Bridge Travel, is also owned by Airtours. Cresta is proud of the fact that they have been voted Best Short Break operator by UK travel agents every year since 1992. They offer over 100 destinations, mainly in Europe. Their top ten destinations in 1999 were:

1 Paris
2 Amsterdam
3 Dublin
4 Rome
5 Prague
6 Bruges
7 Brussels
8 Venice
9 New York
10 Vienna

Paris alone accounts for sales of 110,000 short breaks.

The company has introduced some new products, including short breaks to Havana in Cuba and trips to the annual Palio horse race in Siena, Italy. The company operates inclusive tour programmes for Eurotunnel and Eurostar, with a special day trip deal to Paris with Eurostar. Cresta claims that their holidays are not packages but are tailor made, that is, the customer chooses when to travel, where and for how long.

KEY TERMS

Short break: 2 or 3 nights away.

Holiday: 4+ nights away.

Tailor made: holidays organised by a tour operator to suit the customer's particular requirements.

1998*	47%	42%	11%	56%	31%	13%

Short haul *vs* long haul holiday type split

	Summer		Winter	
	Short haul	**Long haul**	**Short haul**	**Long haul**
1985	97%	3%	94%	6%
1990	91%	9%	88%	12%
1995	90%	10%	83%	17%
1997	87%	13%	78%	22%
1998*	89%	11%	80%	20%

Family/non-family split on package holidays

	Summer		Winter	
	Family	**Non-family**	**Family**	**Non-family**
1990	30%	70%	18%	82%
1995	40%	60%	20%	80%
1997	35%	66%	21%	79%
1998*	36%	64%	22%	78%

Destinations visited on a package holiday

	1990	**1995**	**1997**	**1998**
Spain	35%	42%	41%	43%
Greece	15%	15%	12%	9%
France	4%	5%	5%	6%
Turkey	2%	7%	8%	5%
Italy	4%	3%	4%	3%
Portugal	5%	4%	5%	4%
Cyprus	4%	4%	4%	4%
Malta	3%	2%	2%	2%
USA	6%	4%	5%	5%

*these 1998 figures from latest estimates

Figure 3.3 Thomson Holidays market information

Source: Thomson Holidays

Seaside resorts

When UK tourists plan their main holiday, they are more likely to opt for a seaside holiday than any other. The growth in long holidays abroad (4+ nights) since 1981 has occurred almost annually, reaching 29 million in 1998 (source: Thomson Holidays). This amounts to an annual increase of 4.7%. Spain and the Spanish islands continue to attract the largest numbers of British holiday-makers. Other popular destinations include France, Greece and the Greek islands (we will look at these particular destinations later in this section). Use your recommended Internet sites and brochures to research others that interest you. Figure 3.3 (Thomson Holidays market information) shows the most popular destinations from 1990 to 1998 for Thomson customers.

The British Travel Survey reports that France is the second most popular destination. Spain remains the number one choice in both surveys.

Seaside holidays provide something for all the family – lots of water, a beach and some form of entertainment, catering for everyone. Holiday-makers in Northern European areas, such as the UK, tend to travel south for a better climate. In the summer the Mediterranean resorts are ideal, as there is no need to travel further for the sun. In addition, the tourist authorities in these areas tend to be well funded and competent and a well developed infrastructure is in place.

Both mainland Spain and the islands attract large numbers of package holiday-makers. Most are looking for the sun and sand of the 'costas' (areas of coastline stretching along the Mediterranean).

DID YOU KNOW?

Spain attracts more than 40 million tourists each year. In 1998 there were 47.7 million, of which 12 million were British. The Spanish Tourist Board say people are attracted by sun, superb food, hospitality and joie de vivre.

KEY TERM

Infrastructure: roads, railway and sewage systems, utilities.

ACTIVITY

Mark the following 'costas' on a map of Spain:

Costa del Azahar	Costa Blanca
Costa Calida	Costa de Almeria
Costa del Sol	Costa Dorada
Costa de la Luz	Rias Altas
Costa Verde	Costa Vasca
Costa Cantabrica	Costa Brava

Study some summer holiday brochures and insert the main resorts onto your map.

KEY TERMS

Costas: areas of coastland in Spain.

Balearics: group of Spanish islands in the Mediterranean.

Canaries: group of Spanish islands in the Atlantic.

Mass market destination: area of intensive development attracting huge numbers of tourists.

DID YOU KNOW?

40% of Club 18 to 30 holiday bookings are to Ibiza. Its millenium party for 4,000 people was completely sold out!

You will find that most brochures concentrate on the Costa Brava (Lloret de Mar, Tossa de Mar and Callella), the Costa Dorada (Salou and Sitges), the Costa Blanca (Benidorm and Alicante) and the Costa del Sol (Marbella, Torremolinos and Fuengirola). These areas do differ, but their main attractions centre on sun, beach life and entertainment.

Also popular with British tourists are the Spanish islands. There are two groups of islands: the Balearics, located to the east of the mainland in the Mediterranean, and the Canaries, located off the coast of Africa in the Atlantic. Over three million UK tourists visited each set of islands in 1998.

The Balearic islands

The Balearics consist of Majorca, Minorca and Ibiza. Majorca had become a mass market destination with a reputation for cheap accommodation, food and drink and an appeal to 'lager louts'. However, major investment by the Balearic authorities has led to new promenades, parks, landscaping and clean beaches being created. Hotels have also been forced to improve or close. Tourists have gradually become aware that there are unspoilt, quieter areas on the island and that it is also a choice for many celebrities. These changes have led to increased appeal to families.

Minorca is a quieter island with no large resorts. Much of the accommodation is self-catering. Ibiza is famous for its club scene, although the island still has much to attract families to it. All of these islands can be reached directly by air. There is a fourth island, Formentera, which can only be reached by boat from Ibiza.

The Canary islands

The Canaries are a group of islands, with tourism concentrated on the four largest. These are: Tenerife, Gran Canaria, Lanzarote and Fuerteventura. The islands are dry with sparse vegetation, and are mainly volcanic. Fuerteventura has enormous beaches, but those on Tenerife are unappealing, consisting of black volcanic sand. The main attraction of these islands, therefore, is the year long, dry, hot climate. They are a very popular winter destination as they can be reached within four hours by air.

Features of Spanish destinations

Climate

The climate varies from region to region but tourists can expect up to ten hours of sun in the summer, with temperatures reaching the high twenties. Winters are cold in the interior, but Andalucia has warm winters as it is protected by the Sierra Nevada mountains. Skiing is popular in the mountain ranges of Sierra Nevada and in the Pyrenees.

Attractions

Natural attractions include beautiful coastlines (4,964 kilometres) and mountains, but there is a wealth of man-made attractions, for example, historical cities such as Granada, and the museums of Madrid and Barcelona.

Festivals

There are many religious festivals, especially around Holy Week, for tourists to enjoy. Bull fighting is the national sport and those with a strong stomach may choose to watch it.

KEY TERM

Paradores: hotels owned by the Spanish government.

Accommodation and eating out

There is a good choice of restaurants, cafés and bars serving reasonably priced, good food. Tourists particularly like tapas bars, which serve traditional snacks. Accommodation in Spain ranges from five star luxury hotels to self-catering apartments and the famous paradores. These are government-run hotels with traditional features in beautiful locations. There are 86 altogether, some in castles, monasteries and medieval palaces.

DID YOU KNOW?

There is a growing market for independent travel to Spain. This is due to the introduction of flights by low cost airlines to destinations such as Malaga and Barcelona. The Spanish Tourist Office is targeting these tourists in its UK advertising campaign.

Getting there and getting around

Flights are widely available to all parts of Spain from the UK, from regional airports as well as from London. Transport within the country is easy, via railways or bus. Car hire is also possible.

Tourism authorities are aware that most tourists are attracted by the recreational facilities of the seaside resorts, however, they are making efforts to promote tourism throughout the year by promoting cultural city festivals, historical sites, skiing and wine tours. Some tour operators, for example Citalia, specialise in offering 'the Real Spain', with accommodation in beautiful, historic areas.

Spain's appeal to UK tourists can be summarised as follows:

- It was the first overseas package holiday destination that was widely available.

- It is cheap.

- It has the traditional holiday attractions of sun and sea.

- It is easy to get to from many airports.

- There is little 'culture shock' on arrival – tourists can find British food and culture if they wish.

- Most people who work in tourism here speak some English.

resort report

Nerja

This picturesque fishing village has much to offer if you want to mix old and new Spain in one holiday. Typically Andalucian in style, with whitewashed houses climbing up the hillsides to the rocky mountains beyond, it has an unspoilt charm that's simply delightful. Lazy days can be passed on the main sandy beach or at some of the intimate coves that dot the coast around the resort. Discover Moorish style architecture and narrow alleyways waiting to be explored, and you are bound to find many tempting restaurants and cafe-bars everywhere you go.

Algeciras

This bustling resort is a port first and foremost and is ideal for getting a taste of typical Andalucian life. Set on the southern tip of Spain, it enjoys sweeping views over the Bay of Gibraltar. In the centre, you'll find plentiful interesting shops, welcoming restaurants and café-bars. When you fancy lying back and soaking up the sun, there are sandy beaches close at hand. The focal point of the town is the busy harbour where you can take a twice-daily hydrofoil to Tangier, just an hour's journey and a fabulous day out. Just a few kilometres from the Gibraltan border, Algeciras also makes a great base for day trips to the Rock. Whether you're an expert or novice windsurfer, the nearby resort of Tarifa is a young and popular surfing paradise, with great nightlife and long sandy beaches.

San Pedro de Alcantara

San Pedro de Alcantara has a restful pace of life and a very Spanish atmosphere. There are lots of hidden squares where you can sip coffee or enjoy tapas with a glass of chilled fino – the wonderfully pale local sherry – along with the locals, plus an enticing selection of shops where you can browse for Andalucian handicrafts such as ceramic plates and colourful handwoven rugs. The scenic beach with its darker sand and shingle is made all the better by the spectacular views of the Rock of Gibraltar looming on the horizon. In the near vicinity, you'll also find some intriguing Roman ruins to explore, whilst at night, San Pedro moves up a gear with some pleasant, low-key nightlife. The lovely town of Estepona with its daily fish auction and lively market is a few kilometres away, and also has a golf school where players can brush up their game. Other nearby attractions include Ronda, one of Spain's oldest whitewashed cities, and Puerto Banus, both easily reached by bus.

Puerto Banus

Just a few kilometres south of Marbella, this very smart resort has an ultra chic marina bobbing with luxury yachts and fringed with fine beaches, where most of its hotels can be found strung along the sands. The marina complex is a magnet for the jet set, so if you like the idea of people-watching, just take a seat at one of the innumerable waterfront cafes, order a plate of delicious tapas and soak up the goings-on around you. Shopping is on the stylish side too, with an array of tasteful boutiques and gift stores to explore, and when you want something slightly more strenuous, there's a full complement of watersports readily available as well as some magnificent golf courses. Later, as darkness falls, the place livens up even more, with several nightclubs where you can literally dance the night away. When you want even more designer shopping or simply a change of scene, Marbella, with its bright lights and beaches is comfortably close by.

Fuengirola

Only a few years ago, Fuengirola was a small fishing village – but a lot has happened since then! Now this well-designed and bubbly resort is absolutely ideal for families and couples seeking a sun-filled, fun-filled break. The 7 km long ribbon of pale sand that's got to be the best beach in the area. There's a wealth of shops and sports to get into, a water park for the kids, as well as the ever-present opportunity to meander around the yacht-filled marina and enjoy a typical local meal of paella, or even a few British dishes at the many good restaurants. The town's weekly market is another bustling attraction, and if you want to venture to other resorts, Marbella and Mijas can be reached by bus and Torremolinos by train.

Torremolinos

Bright, bold and packed with all the fun under the sun, Torremolinos, the most happening resort on this upbeat stretch of coast, is heaven if you want limitless entertainment on tap. If you can drag yourself away from the sandy beach, there's a wealth of enjoyment just waiting. The town's old El Cavario quarter is well worth a tour and if you want a taste of real Spain, you can see local fishermen put to sea in gaily-coloured boats from La Carihuela beach. Stick around and you'll be able to savour their catches at the bustling cafes overlooking the sands! Elsewhere, the town is jam-packed with gift shops, outdoor restaurants and bars, as well as excellent leisure amenities, so you can play tennis, ten-pin bowl, or splash out at a brilliant water park. And naturally, the whole place is jumping at night, with lively discos, nightspots and British pubs galore. It's easy to get to Gibraltar when you want a breather, and Ronda, is just a little inland.

Figure 3.5 Features of the Costa del Sol

Source: Cosmos brochure, Cosmoair plc

ACTIVITY

Answer the following questions on Spain:

1 In which city is the Prado museum?
2 Name one resort on each of these coasts: Costa Blanca, Costa del Sol, Costa Almeria and the Costa Brava.
3 Name the Balearic islands.
4 Which is the largest of the Canary islands?
5 In which city is the Alhambra palace?
6 Which city hosted the 1992 Olympic games?
7 Which country, popular for tourism, borders Spain to the west?
8 What is the native language of Barcelona?
9 Name two of Spain's mountain ranges.
10 Gibraltar is a territory of which country?

Greece

Greece is located in Southern Europe, bordering the Aegean sea, the Ionian Sea and the Mediterranean Sea, between Albania and Turkey.

Figure 3.6 Map of Greece

Source: Adapted from MegaSpider

Greece is the most popular destination for UK tourists, after France and Spain, with 5% of all overseas holidays taken there in 1997. Most tourists travel by air and take a package holiday. The most popular islands can be reached directly by air; others are reached by a ferry ride from the mainland.

The islands most visited by the British are Corfu, Rhodes and Crete. Crete is the largest and is mountainous. There are about 2,000 Greek islands, of which 166 are inhabited. Tourism is of great importance to the economy and some areas have suffered from the impact of tourism, so that the simplicity of landscape and culture which was once so attractive has somewhat been lost. However, as there are so many islands, tour operators are able to offer less developed destinations in their programmes. Greece enjoys a temperate climate with mild, wet winters and hot dry summers.

Attractions

The Greek islands have a lot to offer. The main appeal lies in the sunny climate and good beaches. The landscape is varied, with deserts in the Mani region and plains in Macedonia. There are still many traditional villages to be found, such as Aghios Stefanos in Corfu. There are also many historic sites, spanning thousands of years of civilisation. In Athens, the visitor can see many archaeological sites, including the Acropolis and the Parthenon.

Accommodation and eating out

Like Spain, Greece represents good value for money for the British and this adds to the appeal. Greek food is a big attraction, with dishes such as salads, feta cheese and traditional moussakas all cheaply available. A range of accommodation is on offer, including budget guest houses as well as more luxurious hotels. There are many cruise holidays operating around the Greek islands.

ACTIVITY

Using Internet sites and brochures, choose three Greek destinations to compare. You should compare one mainland destination, for example Halkidiki, and two islands, one which is well-known and accessible by air (for example, Rhodes), and one that is lesser known and only accessible by ferry (for example, Spetses).

Produce a chart comparing the resorts in terms of:

- accessibility
- climate
- natural features
- attractions
- type of accommodation
- food, drink and entertainment
- transport

State which destination you would prefer and why. Also state which destination older generations would prefer and why.

France

France is a popular destination for UK outbound tourists. France is suitable for many different kinds of holiday. We saw earlier that Paris is a popular city choice, however, like Spain and Greece, its main appeal to UK tourists lies in its seaside resorts. There are many regions offering beach holidays, the nearest of which is Normandy, which is easily accessible to us by crossing the Channel. Families also find the regions of Brittany, Vendées and the west coast attractive.

Climate

The climate in summer is much warmer than the UK and on the south coast (the Riviera) it is very hot indeed, with temperatures reaching 28 to 30 degrees.

Getting there and getting around

Driving is relatively easy in France, as the country has many autoroutes, although the motorist has to pay to use these. Due to easy access by ferry or Le Shuttle over the Channel and the internal access by road, many UK tourists choose to drive to France. This means that it tends to attract a rather different type of holiday-maker than Greece or Spain. The tourists tend to be more independent, relying less on package holidays and tending to make their own arrangements. Motorail allows tourists to take their car by train to the more southerly destinations. Sleeping cars are also provided so that tourists can travel overnight and arrive refreshed in the morning. Flights are available to many cities in France, particularly Paris and Nice.

Location

France is located in western Europe, southwest of Germany and north of Spain. Corsica, an island in the Mediterranean, is part of France. Mountain ranges border the country at the Italian, Spanish and Swiss borders. The Massif Central forms a plateau in the southern, central region. There are gentle lowlands and fertile river valleys, such as the Loire valley.

Attractions and features

Attractions include the many chateaux, particularly in the Loire valley, wine tours (as France leads the world in wine production), the battlefields of the first and second world wars in Normandy, and beautiful beaches and countryside. For lovers of good food and wine, the restaurants are excellent, each region having its own specialities. Transport is well provided for, with good roads and an excellent rail system.

Gîte: unsophisticated villa accommodation in France, often on farms.

Accommodation

There are different classes of hotels, ranging from the very luxurious on the Riviera and in traditional holiday resorts such as Deauville, to chains offering cheap overnight accommodation, for example, the Formula One chain. Business travellers often use the Sofitel and Mercure chains of hotels. Many families opt to stay self-catering in villas or 'gîtes'. Camping is also extremely popular. Sites have become very sophisticated with many facilities and far from basic accommodation, in pre-sited tents and mobile homes.

ACTIVITY

Locate the following towns and features on a map of France:

- Paris, Brest, Marseilles, Nice, Calais, Lyons, Nantes, Strasbourg, Biarritz, Ajaccio
- The Massif Central
- Seine, Loire, Dordogne
- Alps, Pyrenees

Find out the names of the airports serving Paris and the names of the Channel ferry ports.

Choose a resort, for example St. Tropez on the Riviera, or Benodet in Brittany, and write a fact file on it. Include details of climate, attractions, accommodation and facilities. Include also a map of your resort.

PROFILE *Happy campers*

The Parker family consists of Jerry Parker, a single parent, and his four children, ranging in age from 4 to 16 years. The family will take a camping holiday in France next summer. They have chosen to book with Keycamps, as this company was recommended by a friend. They have chosen to go to Royan on the west coast of France. They want a seaside holiday and they think Royan is far enough south to ensure sun. They will stay at a site set in a pine forest, next to a sheltered beach, called 'La Palmyre'.

Jerry thinks the site will be ideal for his family as there are discos for the older children as well as a teenage club. The little ones will be taken care of by the full-time children's club, leaving Jerry free to lie on the beach writing his novel. Lots of sports are available, including windsurfing, which the eldest child is keen to try. The family intends to camp in a luxury manner and they have chosen to stay in a mobile home, which is 34 feet long, with three bedrooms. They want to try some local restaurants, so will eat out, but there is a restaurant on the site if needed. Jerry's idea of cooking on holiday is shopping for croissants for breakfast and making some coffee.

They will drive to Dover to take an early morning sea crossing to Calais and then will pick up the autoroute for the long drive to Royan. Jerry has not booked any overnight accommodation. If he is too tired to drive all the way in a day, they will stay in a Formula One motel. He is looking forward to two weeks of bliss!

ACTIVITY

For this activity you will need to collect some holiday brochures. The most appropriate ones will be those featuring a range of summer and winter sun destinations. You might also look at brochures covering the 18 to 30 age group (there are a number of these on the market). Your task is to find suitable holidays for the following customers. All of the customers want a seaside holiday in Europe, but no particular countries are specified. For each customer, describe the resort chosen, the features of the holiday and say why it would appeal to that customer. You should also provide a costing for each holiday.

1   Joe and Ingrid Patel. This couple are in their 60s and retired. They dislike cold winters and wish to escape the UK winter for a period of four to six weeks. They have comfortable pensions and want to stay in a hotel. They would like breakfast to be included but will take your advice on other eating arrangements. They want some entertainment, but do not want to go clubbing!

2   Ms Jones is a travel and tourism lecturer. She is preparing an educational trip for 25 of her students. They are studying worldwide destinations and she wants them to have practical experience of a seaside resort in Europe. She expects them to visit a range of accommodation and facilities whilst away, but wants to stay in a hotel with half-board. The group will travel in May towards the end of their programme. The cost must not exceed £300 each for a week.

3   A group of 18 to 20 year olds have just finished their travel and tourism Vocational A Level. They have saved all year from their part-time jobs and wish to celebrate their success on their course. They are in the mood for sun, sea and clubs! They have to travel in July and want a two week holiday.

4   Joan and Jerry Smith have two small children and are very tired. Joan looks after the children (3 and 5 years old) and Jerry is a plumber, working long hours. They want to go abroad and need a rest in the sun. They can go outside of school holidays, probably in June. Joan refuses to go self-catering and insists on some kind of childcare facilities. Their budget for two weeks is £2,000.

Once you have gathered your information, present it to the rest of the group and compare findings.

DID YOU KNOW?

Butlins and Oasis are owned by the Rank Group.

Purpose-built resorts

The most well known example of a purpose-built resort is Disneyland, Paris. Others include holiday centres such as Center Parcs and Oasis. In the UK, holiday centres have been a tradition for family holidays for many years. Butlins and Pontins are famous and are still very successful. They feature accommodation, family entertainment and activities at a reasonable price. Center Parcs and Oasis are very similar in what they offer. They have a strong focus on being environmentally aware and are situated in forest locations where families can enjoy outdoor activities, as well as tropical domes featuring swimming pools and activities.

Center Parcs is the only one of these well-known British holiday centres to operate in the rest of Europe. The company runs 13 holiday villages in all. These are in the Netherlands, Britain, France and Germany. There are three villages located in the UK and these are currently much more successful than the European villages.

Most of the villages are in the Netherlands (five in total), which is not surprising as this is where they were first started in 1968. The first one in Britain opened in 1987. The villages have a particular appeal for families and it is possible to take either a full holiday or a short break.

The villages feature a central tropical dome which is maintained at a tropical 84°. Here, families can swim, use water rides, the jacuzzi, or relax amongst tropical plants. There are many sporting activities on offer, both indoor and outdoor. Accommodation is provided in villas and people are encouraged to travel around the site by bike rather than car (bikes can be hired). There are themed restaurants, as well as a supermarket for those who opt for self-catering. Three million guests visit Center Parcs each year.

ACTIVITY

Visit the Center Parcs website at www.centerparcs.com and find out what the company plans are for this millennium.

Club Mediterrannee

These holiday villages are all over the world and were probably the first all-inclusive resorts. They are in a range of locations, from beaches to mountains. For example, there are 11 snow villages where skiing is on offer. The accommodation is sometimes basic, in holiday huts, but can be in hotels. 'Club Med' gives each village a comfort rating, so that the tourist knows what to expect and in most villages there are children's clubs. Each age range is catered for so that parents can enjoy some freedom. Many activities, for example tennis and water sports, are available. Food and activities are included in the holiday price which may seem expensive, but there is nothing more to pay after the initial outlay.

DID YOU KNOW?

Disneyland, Paris has to pay royalties and management fees to Walt Disney World. In 1999, this amounted to 30.9 million euros, cutting into their income considerably. Prior to this, Disneyland, Paris had enjoyed a five year waiver of these fees (from 1994–1999) to help the company stabilise its financial situation.

Disneyland, Paris

This purpose-built resort is located in Marne la Vallee, near Paris. The location was chosen as it has easy access for millions of northern Europeans, by car or by public transport. Also, the French government was keen to bring employment to a depressed area. The resort has been very successful over the few years since its opening in 1992. In 1999, an income of 23.6 million euros was achieved. The park attracts over 12 million visitors each year.

Features of Disneyland, Paris

The main attraction is the Disneyland Park, known as the Magic Kingdom, which is divided into themed areas, each with rides, restaurants and shops. These areas are: Fantasyland, Frontierland, Adventureland and Discoveryland. Main Street, USA, also with shops and restaurants, links these areas.

Guests pay to visit the park and on any one day there may be 60 to 70 thousand visitors. Most of the attractions are targeted at families; there are only a couple of rides aimed at 'thrill seekers'. These are the Indiana Jones ride and Space Mountain. A parade takes place each day, depicting Disney films and characters.

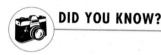

Accommodation is available in six themed hotels. The Newport Bay hotel is the biggest hotel in Europe and the Hotel Cheyenne has a wild west theme. All have their own restaurants and shops and two have swimming pools. Disney Village is an area of shops, restaurants, clubs and entertainment. Although open all day, it comes alive in the evening as people leave the park.

In autumn 2000, an international shopping centre, Val d'Europe, and a second railway station will open in Marne la Vallee, capitalising on the influx of tourists. There are also plans for 'Disney Studios', a second theme park, to be built on the same site. This requires an investment of 609.8 million euros. Disney will raise this with a shares issue to raise about 228 million and bank loans of around 380 million. The park should be ready in 2002.

Most visitors come from northern Europe. People may go to Disneyland for a short break or they may drop in for a day or two on their way to another holiday destination. The park has to cater for many different nationalities. This caused problems at first, as management tried to decide on products to suit different cultures. The family market is the most important, but there is also a strong corporate market. There are two convention centres at Disneyland, Paris and there are specialist staff catering for corporate clients. In winter there is an annual student convention, to bring in business out of season.

Countryside areas

We have seen that seaside holidays are the most popular, but there are a growing number of tourists who are looking for a different kind of holiday. Tour operators provide for this trend with specialist brochures, depicting countryside holidays.

They are usually advertised as 'Lakes and Mountains' holidays. Many of the resorts are in Austria and Switzerland, examples being St. Anton and Seefeld in Austria, and Interlaken and Wenden in Switzerland. Also very beautiful and appealing, are the areas around Italy's lakes: Como, Garda, Maggiore and Orta. As Slovenia has become safer, tourists are returning and countryside resorts are opening up here, for example in Bled. Bled is Slovenia's most popular resort, but only a few thousand UK tourists visit each year. The war in Kosovo meant that tourists were reluctant to travel to the area.

Figure 3.7 shows countryside resorts throughout Europe. These are the destinations offered by Inghams, but most operators have a similar range. Note the gateway airports to the resorts are also shown on the map.

Features of a countryside holiday

The temperature in the mountains is not as high as on the Mediterranean coast, but there are still sunny days suitable for walking in the

Figure 3.7 Countryside resorts in Europe

Source: Inghams Travel Lakes and Mountains brochure

mountains. People who choose countryside destinations are usually looking for some activity on holiday and do not want to lie in the sun. The attractions are the natural beauty of the area and the fresh air. There are plenty of restaurants and cafés, but customers are not looking for the lively nightlife that is often found in seaside resorts. Accommodation is usually in hotels and guest houses. Caravan parks are not found in the mountains due to the difficulty of access and the cold. Camping and caravanning is, however, popular around the Italian lakes.

These destinations tend to appeal to older people or those who particularly enjoy sightseeing and walking. In most resorts, special facilities for children are not provided, so families may prefer traditional beach holidays.

ACTIVITY

You will need a countryside brochure for this activity. Choose a resort in each of these countries:

- Switzerland
- Italy
- Austria
- Slovenia

For each resort note the gateway airport. Mark the chosen resorts and the airports on a map of Europe (ask your tutor to provide an outline map). Also mark natural features, such as mountains and lakes, near to your chosen resorts.

State what type of accommodation is available. How are transfers made to the resort? Note the particular attractions for each resort.

Draw up a profile of the likely customers for each resort. See Chapter 4 on marketing travel and tourism for help with this task.

The skiing industry is a very important market for countryside destinations. Skiing can be an expensive holiday choice as there are many extras to pay for which would not be needed on a seaside holiday. The customer needs skis, poles and ski wear. Ski passes have to be bought and many people opt to take lessons. All this has to be added to the usual costs of transport and accommodation. Many packages now include ski hire and passes so that customers can easily calculate the full cost of their holiday. The ski market is obviously dependent on snow and a lack of this seriously affects bookings. For this reason, many resorts have invested in snow-making equipment. The most popular destinations for UK skiers are shown in Figure 3.8. You will note that France is the most popular destination and that January is the most popular month for skiing holidays.

Families represent just over a quarter of the ski market, although the trend is now rising. The low percentage is due to families being tied to school holidays. The half term week in February is the most popular time for families to ski. As most regions of the UK take the same week, there is a lot of pressure on tour operators at this time, due to the high demand. It also means a premium price can be charged. By the Easter school holiday, snow conditions are not as good so families tend to go during this early half term break.

Examples of skiing resorts

There are some very large, famous resorts, such as Courchevel and Meribel in France. Kitzbuhel and Mayrhofen are examples in Austria. In Italy you might choose Claviere, a vast skiing area, or the quieter La Thuile. Andorra is also a popular destination. There are too many resorts to mention them all; what is important to note is that each resort has slopes suitable for the level of competence of the skier. Brochures give information on the types of runs in each resort and for whom they are suitable.

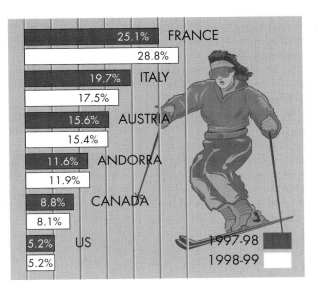

Figure 3.8 *Top winter package destinations*

Source: TTG News, *17 May 1999*

KEY TERMS

Après ski: eating, drinking and entertainment in the ski resort.

Snowboarding: a popular sport, like skateboarding on snow.

Snow blading: a technique that uses a type of short ski.

Off piste: experienced skiers may choose to abandon the dedicated ski runs and go for new powder snow.

Features of ski resorts

Accommodation may be in traditional chalets in a pre-alpine village. These villages are pretty and full of character, but may be at low altitude and a distance from the slopes. This means transport is necessary to reach the ski runs. There are many of these kinds of villages in Austria, for example Kitzbuhel. Ski buses are provided to allow skiers to reach the slopes here.

Some villages have grown with the demand for skiing, have improved ski facilities and added purpose-built accommodation to the resort. These purpose-built resorts may not be so attractive, but are ideal for the keen skier and incorporate the latest ski lifts. Many of these types of resorts are in France and Italy, built at high altitude – this means that the snow season is longer. It is also possible to rent accommodation with a dedicated chalet maid (male or female), who will clean and cook whilst you ski.

Skiing lessons are widely available and the 'Après ski' is an important aspect of a fun holiday. Most resorts have plenty of restaurants and bars providing evening entertainment. To attract the family market, tour operators feature children's facilities. These include crèches and ski schools. Those who have mastered skiing look for new options, for example snowboarding or snow-blading, both of which are growing in popularity. The more adventurous may choose to ski 'off piste'. This is only suitable for very experienced skiers.

 PROFILE *Which ski resort?*

The mixed-ability family

Resort: Les Gets, France

I had never been skiing before, and was a bit of a scaredy-cat about getting on the slopes. Les Gets is a village in the French Alps, and when we arrived, mid-evening in February, the whole place was lit up and covered in snow . . . like a magical fairyland.

The resort was perfect for all of us. My husband, Martyn, had skied before, and there were enough challenging slopes for him to enjoy, while I had lessons with the British Alpine Ski School, which was marvellous.

Our children, Amy, 9, and Katy, 5, simply adored the place. I never had the chance to go skiing when I was a child, so it was lovely to give my children the opportunity to do so. When Amy got her ski school badge, I blubbed!

The resort has a wonderful atmosphere – almost like a country park. People would go up the mountains and trudge through the snow with their dogs, so it seemed like you were staying in a proper community, rather than just in a holiday resort.

I was hooked on skiing immediately, even though I don't think I'm any good at it. I don't care, and it doesn't matter. This is definitely the best family activity I can think of. With other holidays we've tried, there has always been one of us who hasn't enjoyed it. But with skiing, it doesn't matter how good or bad you are, it's just such fun for everyone.

Women on their own

Resort: Soldeu, Andorra

Lifelong friends Avrell and Mary have turned their husbands into ski widowers because neither man enjoys the sport. They have been on skiing holidays before, but both agree that, for their age group and skiing ability, their experience at Soldeu was one of the best.

Avrell: It was the first time we had been on a skiing holiday together, and it was excellent because everything was so well organised by our two guides, Chris and Dave. They really managed to generate a great atmosphere. I've been on trips where you go to ski school one morning, then don't see your fellow students until the following day. But on this trip, there was much more of a group feeling. We had breakfast together, went to ski school together, lunched together and shared skiing experiences.

Mary: We both found it a really good trip. We had official ski lessons for two or three hours each day and the rest of the time, when we were free-skiing, we had a Ski Club guide with us. Although the guides aren't allowed to teach, they can give you tips on the best routes to follow, which was really helpful. You don't get that on some other ski holidays.

I've been on trips before where I've had two or three hours' instruction in broken English and that was it for the day. I was just left to look at the slopes and guess what I was capable of. Here, I didn't have to worry about making a mistake and ending up at the top of a ski lift only to find the way down is a red or black run that you can't attempt. Another good thing about this holiday was that I could ski with a group of people I already knew. I've tried all sorts of ski packages, from self-catering to full-board, and I think this was definitely the best. At our age, you just want to go skiing without any hassle, come home, shower and go out to dinner in pleasant company.

The expert

Resort: Whistler, Canada

I started skiing at 15 and until three years ago had always skied in Europe. Then I decided to try Whistler, which offers more extensive facilities than many American resorts. It also matches Europe in terms of scale and suits all abilities. My boyfriend was a beginner and there were slopes where he could learn, while I did the black runs.

The après-ski is very different from Europe's – not as rowdy or as in-your-face. There are three good nightclubs, but night-life is mostly geared around restaurants and bars. There isn't the shouting and dancing on tables you find in Europe. You can have a quiet drink in a piano bar, or opt for somewhere more lively. The town feels like a place where real people live, so entertainment isn't forced on you as in purpose-built resorts.

One of the best things about Whistler is that you are pretty much guaranteed snow. There's an average annual snowfall of 30 ft and you can ski right up until May. The ski school is outstanding, and the instructors really motivate people. I always found European ski schools very disappointing. Here, they really have fun, and they're especially good with children.

Source: Woman and Home, *January 2000*

ACTIVITY

Find out what the following terms mean. If you have been skiing, you may already be familiar with them.

- Altitude
- Langlauf
- Drag lift
- Chair lift
- Snow cannon
- Piste
- Snow line
- Mogul

KEY TERM

Gateway airport: first point of arrival from where transfers are arranged to resorts.

Getting there

Most skiers fly, taking package holidays. Tour operators include transfers to the resorts in the package. For those who drive, journeys can be long and hampered by adverse weather. Table 3.1 shows a comparison of transport methods to French ski resorts.

TRANSPORT	AIR	FERRY/CAR
SCHEDULE	A wide variety of scheduled and charter airlines fly to gateway airports such as Lyon and Geneva, which serve numerous French ski resorts.	Wide variety of daily services – most popular is Dover-Calais with a sailing time of 1 hr 30 mins.
TIME	Flying time is around 2 hrs with transfers of around 3 hrs by road.	Around 10 hrs from Calais.
COST	Most operators base their programmes on the cost of flying and then offer supplements or reductions for other modes of transport.	Inghams offer savings of up to around £125 per person based on five people in a car, Thomson and Airtours up to £140.
PROS	Even scheduled flights are cheaper than Eurostar, and with low-cost carriers entrance into the ski market prices can only get better; clients can fly from regional airports throughout UK.	Cheap; independence is upmost with clients having freedom of a car in resort.
CONS	Long check-in time; limited baggage allowance; long transfers by road.	Rough weather during winter, peak ski season, may cause cancellations; long journey; extra insurance required for car and petrol and road tolls.
CLIENT	Tends to be upmarket and are based throughout the whole of the UK.	Good for groups or families living in the South of England; great for those on a budget and for clients who want the freedom of exploring different resorts.

Table 3.1

Source: Travel Weekly, *24 February 1999*

Historical/cultural destinations

One of the policies of the European Union is to select one city each year to be the cultural capital of Europe. This has been happening for 15 years and provides a good boost for tourism in the city, because of the award's status and because the government will usually allocate funds for cultural development. There were nine cities in the running for 2000. They have all been elected cities of culture for the year. They will all be promoting the cultural aspects of their city and will hope to continue to attract tourists in the years to come. The cities are: Avignon, Bergen, Bologna, Brussels, Krakow, Helsinki, Prague, Reykjavik, and Santiago de Compostela.

European City of Culture 2000

As one of the nine European Cities of Culture for the millennium, Kraków will be hosting a year-long festival exploring various aspects of its history and cultural life. As well as numerous concerts, plays and exhibitions, major events include a festival devoted to Stanislaw Wyspiański, Kraków's influential playwright, painter and writer; a celebration of the 600th anniversary of the university, and the annual Jewish Culture Festival. You can discuss art and life over a cup of coffee at the Café Europa literary café, nod your head at the Fifth Summer Jazz Festival, and interact with the city's Romanesque inhabitants via a 'virtual' digital reconstruction. In June, Polish descendants of the Tartars will stage a peaceable raid on the city, and in December, a contest for the prettiest Christmas crib will be held.

Figure 3.9 *Krakow: one of the European cities of culture 2000*

Source: Cresta Journey Magazine

Earlier in this chapter we noted the growth in the city break market and that it was the cultural attractions of cities that held the most appeal. There are many groups of tourists, who have tired of sun and sand holidays, and who are looking for something of more interest, hence the growth in cultural tourism. Many other cultural options exist, outside of cities. There are tours of classical Greece, visits to the pyramids in Egypt, to Pompeii in Italy, and tours of ancient civilisations, such as the Aztecs in Mexico.

Many destinations also attract tourists through events and festivals. You may have heard of the Edinburgh Festival, but there are others all over the world. The more unusual ones include the Pushkar camel festival in India and the annual Galway oyster festival.

KEY TERM

European City of Culture: cities are elected to have this status for a year and may attract funding for cultural development.

ACTIVITY

You will need city brochures and access to the Internet for these tasks.

Choose two of the cities of culture from those mentioned previously. Locate them on an atlas. For each, find out what special activities and developments were planned for the year 2000.

Use your brochures to compare the cost of a two night break for two in each city. Compare your findings with those of the rest of the group.

The location and features of major overseas travel and tourism destinations

KEY TERMS

Long haul: flight of more than seven or eight hours.

VFR: visiting friends and relatives.

There has been a dramatic growth in the popularity of long haul destinations in recent years, as air travel has become quicker and cheaper. Tourists are also keen to visit new destinations and explore different cultures. Statistics from the *International Passenger Survey* (*IPS*) show that, between 1986 and 1996, visits to North America from the UK, rose by 208%. Table 3.2, an extract from the *IPS*, shows the numbers of visits to other areas of the world, outside of Europe.

UK TRAVELLERS ABROAD: VISITS (BY DESTINATION COUNTRIES/AREAS) 1986 TO 1996

PRINCIPAL COUNTRY VISITED	1986 ('000)	1987 ('000)	1988 ('000)	1989 ('000)	1990 ('000)	1991 ('000)	1992 ('000)	1993 ('000)	1994 ('000)	1995 ('000)	1996 ('000)	% CHANGE 1986/96	% SHARE 1996
Middle East	221	201	203	226	249	186	272	298	349	388	389	+76	1
North Africa	280	380	375	387	342	234	392	456	507	484	537	+92	1
South Africa	48	79	86	119	112	125	121	138	131	190	204	+325	*
Rest of Africa	176	197	222	247	292	280	289	318	373	381	350	+99	1
Eastern Europe**	194	225	300	323	418	507	599	784	721	596	655	+238	2
Japan	24	46	52	59	65	76	66	69	79	74	100	+317	*
Rest of Far East	489	557	648	648	720	707	789	948	1,138	1,207	1,370	+180	3
Australia	161	168	197	213	214	226	256	225	276	291	290	+80	1
New Zealand	27	36	39	37	52	46	55	68	70	71	90	+233	*
Latin America	49	53	77	94	119	95	102	140	154	212	314	+541	1
Others	237	270	286	331	392	406	405	502	531	508	632	+167	1
Rest of World**	1,905	2,210	2,486	2,684	2,975	2,888	3,347	3,947	4,328	4,404	4,931	+159	12
All Countries	24,949	27,446	28,828	31,030	31,150	30,808	33,836	36,720	39,630	41,345	42,569	+71	100

Note: Figures are rounded, so that component figures may not add up to totals.

   * less than 0.5%.

  ** Visits by travellers whose principal country of visit was the former East Germany are included with visits to Eastern Europe up to 1990.

Table 3.2 *Visits abroad by UK residents*

Source: British Tourist Authority

ACTIVITY

Study Table 3.2. Identify the three fastest growing long haul destinations. Locate each area on an atlas.

Identify the main cities/resorts and natural features of each area.

Draw a line graph, charting the rise in visits for each area, between 1986 and 1996.

Discuss the reasons for the growth in popularity of each area with a friend. Draw up a list.

In the next section, we will look at the major long haul destinations for UK tourists. You will have an opportunity to undertake research for your assessment.

North America

North America consists of the USA and Canada. The most popular destination for British tourists is Florida, although tourists visit all regions, as there are many business, independent and VFR tourists, as well as package holiday-makers.

INDEPENDENT HOLIDAYS	INCLUSIVE HOLIDAYS	BUSINESS	VISITS TO FRIENDS AND RELATIVES (VFR)	MISCELLANEOUS	ALL VISITS
1,405	868	672	590	62	3,597

Table 3.3 *Visits to North America by main purpose of visit, 1996 (Figures in '000)*

Why has America become so popular with UK tourists?

- There is no language barrier.

- We are familiar with the culture, through exposure to American films and television.

- There is a variety of spectacular scenery and tourist destinations.

- Fares are at their cheapest ever (at the time of writing).

- Florida is hot all year round, making it an ideal winter destination.

ACTIVITY

Familiarise yourself with the geography of the USA by tracing and then completing the map below.

United States of America

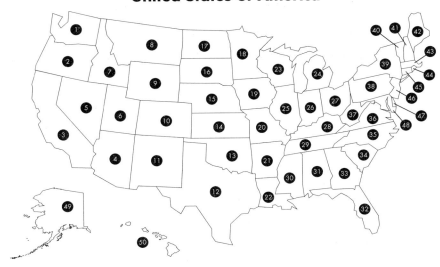

Name the State!

1	_____	13	_____	25	_____	37 _____
2	_____	14	_____	26	_____	38 _____
3	_____	15	_____	27	_____	39 _____
4	_____	16	_____	28	_____	40 _____
5	_____	17	_____	29	_____	41 _____
6	_____	18	_____	30	_____	42 _____
7	_____	19	_____	31	_____	43 _____
8	_____	20	_____	32	_____	44 _____
9	_____	21	_____	33	_____	45 _____
10	_____	22	_____	34	_____	46 _____
11	_____	23	_____	35	_____	47 _____
12	_____	24	_____	36	_____	48 _____

49 _____   50 _____

Where do tourists go in North America?

Whilst Florida is the number one destination, there has been growth in other regions too, particularly in California, Las Vegas and New York (see Figure 3.10).

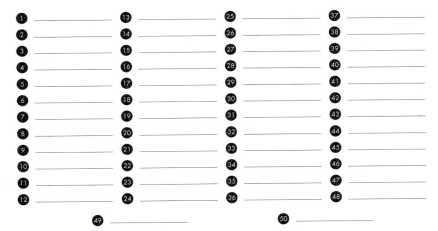

PREMIER'S TOP 20 SELLING STATES FOR 1999
(Last year's position in brackets)

1. Florida (1)
2. California (2)
3. Nevada (4)
4. New York (3)
5. Arizona (6)
6. Tennessee (5)
7. Massachusetts (7)

8. Louisiana (8)
9. Hawaii (9)
10. Virginia (10)
11. Illinois (10)
12. Utah (12)
13. South Carolina (14)
14. Wyoming (–)

15. Colorado (18)
16. Vermont (13)
17. North Carolina (16)
18. Pennsylvania (–)
19. New Hampshire (–)
20. Maine (–)

Figure 3.10 Premier Holidays' Top 20 selling states for 1999

Source: Travel Weekly, 18 October 1999

Florida

Most tourists fly into the gateway airports of Tampa, Orlando or Miami. Car hire and petrol are cheaper than in Europe, so many tourists hire cars to get around. There are many attractions in Florida. First time visitors head for Orlando, where the theme parks are located, including Disneyworld. Disneyworld in Orlando is on a much grander scale than Disneyland, Paris. It has many themed parks within it, including The Magic Kingdom, MGM Studios, the Epcot Centre and the Animal Kingdom. As the climate is so good, water parks are highly successful in Florida. Disneyworld has Typhoon Lagoon and Blizzard Beach.

There are many other theme parks in the area. Universal Studios opened their second in 1999. Seaworld and Wet and Wild are also based in Orlando. The Kennedy Space Centre is an easy drive from Orlando, as are the beaches of the east and west coasts (Daytona is the nearest beach).

Accommodation is available in a variety of hotels, motels and self-catering villas. 'Efficiencies' are an American form of self-catering, which combine the facilities of a hotel with those of traditional self-catering. Disneyworld has many themed hotels in Orlando, as has its partner in Paris. There are many more of these in Orlando and they are spread over a larger area. Free buses, and even boats, are provided for Disney guests to transport them around the various attractions.

It is usual for families to spend a week in Orlando and then spend a week at the beach. The resort of St. Petersburg on the west coast is a favourite with British tourists, but there are plenty of other options. The beaches are beautiful all along the west (Gulf) coast, and these include Longboat Key, Captiva and Sanibel Islands and Marco Island. The beaches on the wilder, east (Atlantic) coast are less popular, but are still very attractive, with more rugged beaches and dunes. Disney owns an hotel in the resort of Vero Beach on this east coast.

The Everglades are a protected area of National Park, covering over a million acres in the south of Florida. Here tourists can view the native wildlife, such as alligators and birds. They can also take boat trips through the marshlands and swamps. Further down are the beautiful Florida Keys. These are strings of islands linked by bridges, eventually leading to the southernmost point of the US, Key West. Key West is nearer to Cuba than to Miami, but US citizens and Cubans may not travel freely between the two countries.

Miami is an exciting destination on the east coast. It is a major centre for cruise ships, therefore, many cruise passengers fly into Miami to embark. Miami airport is a major international gateway for the Keys. The most famous beach in Miami is South Beach, with its beautiful art deco buildings, which have been renovated to their former glory in

DID YOU KNOW?

The longest bridge in the Florida Keys is seven miles long. You can see the bridge in the film *True Lies*, where Arnold Swarzenegger's character is involved in a dramatic car chase.

KEY TERMS

Everglades: national park.

Yosemite, Sequoia and Kings Canyon: more USA national parks.

Florida Keys: string of islands in the far south of the USA.

recent years. South Beach attracts the young and glamorous and celebrities. It is also known as a gay resort.

In Miami, you will find all signs are in English and in Spanish, reflecting the cosmopolitan nature of the area. Many Cubans live in Miami, having fled Cuba to escape the communist regime of Castro. You will hear Spanish spoken everywhere.

ACTIVITY

Insert the following resorts and features on a map of Florida (your teacher should be able to provide an outline to copy onto):

Daytona Beach, Cape Canaveral, Palm Beach, Miami, Orlando, St. Petersburg, Tampa, Marco Island, Vero Beach, Key West and Longboat Key.

Also mark the Everglades, and the gateway airports.

California and surrounding areas

California is an appealing destination for UK tourists, and for American tourists also, it is the leading tourist area. California consists of a long, narrow strip of land, along the west coast of the USA. Most of the population live in cities on this coast, the main coastal developments being between the cities of Los Angeles and San Diego. The climate is similar to that of the Mediterranean – hot and dry in the summer. Unfortunately, there can also be fog belts in the San Francisco area. The particular attractions of the region are Hollywood, Disneyland and Huntington Beach, the surfing capital of the world.

Away from the coast, there is a central valley. This is an important wine growing region and wine tours are, therefore, an attraction, especially in the Napa valley. There are also mountains, where visitors can ski, in season (the San Bernadino and the Rockies). Lake Tahoe is a well-known ski resort. Tourists may visit and camp in the area's national parks, Yosemite, Sequoia and Kings Canyon.

Las Vegas is the gambling capital of the world, attracting many tourists, including those who want to get married quickly at one of the many chapels. Tourists usually opt for a three or four night stay, combining the city with California or Arizona. Las Vegas is also a good base for trips to the Grand Canyon. The appeal of the city itself centres on shows, entertainment and gambling.

ACTIVITY

Find the Las Vegas website at www.vegasstrip.com. This is one of many websites devoted to Las Vegas, but this one has information and maps illustrating all the night life.

Explore the map. In the Debbie Reynolds link, find a French restaurant on the Strip.

Visit Caesar's palace and find out about current events. Find out how to play roulette. Name the two kinds of roulette played.

DID YOU KNOW?

The gay market is very appealing to tour operators. Gay couples often have two incomes and are less likely to have children, so they are thought to be big spenders. Targeting the gay community is known as targeting 'the pink pound'.

DID YOU KNOW?

Teenage heart throbs Enrique Iglesias and Ricky Martin both have houses in Miami. Tourists can take guided boat tours where celebrities' houses are pointed out!

KEY TERMS

Art deco: a style of architecture dating from the 1930s.

Fly-drive: a holiday including flight and a car.

DID YOU KNOW?

Las Vegas is known as the city of lights, because of all the neon signs. The 'Strip' or Las Vegas Boulevard, has four miles of hotels, nightclubs and casinos.

ACTIVITY

The Johnson family have booked a British Airways fly-drive holiday in California. Their itinerary is as follows:

Day 1: Fly from Heathrow to Los Angeles. Stay at an airport hotel.

Day 2: Pick up the car, explore LA and drive to Anaheim.

Day 3: Drive down the Pacific Coast highway to San Diego.

Day 4: Go to the Tijuana market (Mexico). Continue to Palm Springs.

Day 5: Drive to Phoenix.

Day 6: Visit Tucson, Tombstone, drive to the Grand Canyon.

Day 7: Visit the Grand Canyon and then drive through a Navajo Indian reservation.

Day 8: Drive to Las Vegas, stay here.

Day 9: Explore Las Vegas.

Day 10: Go to Death Valley. See Zabriskie Point.

Day 11: Follow the Tioga Pass to Yosemite National park.

FACT FILE:
YOSEMITE NATIONAL PARK

Location: about a 5 hr drive from Los Angeles or San Francisco.

Getting there: as traffic congestion in the park increases during the summer, alternative forms of transport to a car include scheduled Amtrak train and bus services from the West Coast. Flights are also available from San Francisco to Fresno–Yosemite Airport, south of the park, and to Merced Airport to the west.

Admission: $20 per car, payable on entry; $10 per person if hiking or biking.

Getting around: regular shuttle buses within the park are free and take passengers to all the main trails, viewing points, shops and the visitors' centre.

Recommended: a 2 hr valley floor guided tour from Yosemite Lodge which takes in many scenic points; a Glacier Point tour by bus, or in your own car, for spectacular views of Yosemite Valley and the Sierra Nevada, including the Half Dome.

Largest complex: Camp Curry, which also has a shop, restaurant and evening entertainment. Prices on site are very reasonable.

Source: Travel Weekly, *18 October 1999*

Day 12: Spend the day in the park.

Day 13: Drive to Lake Tahoe

Day 14: Drive to San Francisco. Explore the city.

Day 15: Fly from San Francisco to Heathrow.

Study the itinerary and find out about each destination on it. Use brochures or the Internet and write a paragraph on each destination, so that the Johnsons know what they are going to see.

Use an outline map of California and plot their route.

New York

New York City gives its name to the state of New York, the capital of which is Albany. The city is very large, with over seven million people. It is made up of five boroughs, the most familiar of which to tourists is Manhattan, as this is where most of the main tourist sights are. The other boroughs are the Bronx, Queens, Brooklyn and Staten Island. The city is a good base from which to visit Washington, Boston and even the famous Niagara Falls. Boston and Washington can be reached by train or by a short flight.

As city breaks become more popular and air travel becomes less expensive, New York is an increasingly popular choice. Airfares are at their cheapest and operators are offering many package deals. More than one million UK tourists visited New York in 1999. Shopping is a particular attraction, as prices for many goods are cheaper than in the UK, especially branded goods, clothes and CDs. Tourists can often expect to recoup the cost of their flight in savings on shopping. In addition, there is a wealth of culture, museums and theatre to be seen, and sights such as the Free Trade Centre and the Empire State Building.

There are three international airports serving New York City: JFK, Newark and La Guardia. UK tourists arrive at Newark or JFK. Once in New York, transport is good – there are plenty of buses and a subway system. The yellow taxis are famous, but as the traffic is busy and there are often traffic jams, these are not always the best form of transport.

New England

New England is famous for its 'fall colours'; the beautiful autumn colours of the countryside. Most tour operators offer tours or self-drive holidays to the region, often beginning in Boston. The season for such autumn trails is short, only about six weeks, so tourism organisations in New England are promoting the area as a year round destination. The focus is on fly-drives and coach tours and may include Boston, Maine, New Hampshire, Vermont, Rhode Island and Cape Cod.

ACTIVITY

Use brochures and travel guides to find out information on the following New England destinations: Massachusetts, Maine, Connecticut, New Hampshire, Rhode Island and Vermont. Produce an article suitable for the travel section of *The Sunday Times* newspaper. Include a paragraph on the attractions of each area, with pictures. Remember to lay out your information in news feature style, with an appropriate headline. It would be useful to include a small map so readers can see the location of each region. Make sure your readers are aware of the gateway airports and modes of transport.

Canada

Over 700,000 UK tourists visited Canada in 1998. The UK market is important to Canadian tourism as it was the only market outside the USA to increase between 1997 and 1998, although the increase was small, at 1.9%. There are three main categories of holidays of interest: city breaks (the flight time from the UK to Halifax is only five hours), tours and skiing holidays.

The country is vast, covering about four million square miles. Most of the population live in the area to the north of the Canadian/USA border, and most of the resorts chosen by tour operators are in this area.

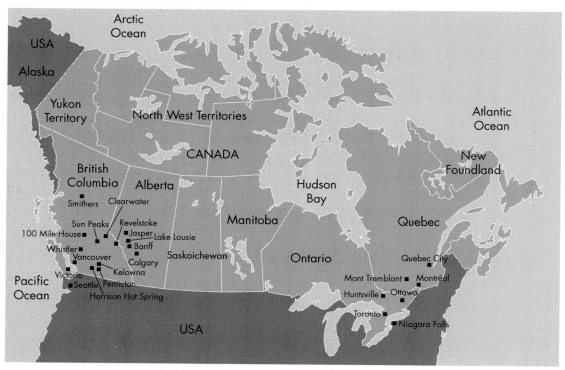

Figure 3.11 Map of Canada

KEY TERM

Niagara Falls: famous waterfall on the border between Canada and America.

DID YOU KNOW?

The CN Tower, in Toronto, is the world's tallest freestanding building. CN stands for Canadian National. The Skydome is built at the base of the tower and is a huge arena for basketball, football or concerts.

Canada has many natural attractions, including lakes, mountains, glaciers and waterfalls. The Niagara Falls are the most famous – these can be seen from the USA or from the Horseshoe Falls in Ontario. Also in Ontario is the Canadian capital city, Ottawa.

The Canadian government has spent thousands of dollars on parks, museums and culture to attract both tourists and business. Those who take long holidays, rather than a city break, usually opt for a tour of either the East or the West provinces. An Eastern tour will cover the provinces of Ontario and Quebec and include the major cities. These are Montreal and Quebec City in Quebec province, where French is the first language, although English is also spoken. Toronto is the country's largest city, situated on the north shore of Lake Ontario. Here, the tourist can visit the historic old town and attractions such as the CN Tower, the Skydome, the Ontario Parliament building and an underground shopping complex. Tourists may stay in hotels, or guesthouses, but an exciting option is a motor home rental where you take your accommodation with you!

Many skiers are taking holidays in Canada and the USA now, rather than in Europe. Prices are as affordable as a European destination, due to cheaper flights and a favourable exchange rate. Another attraction is that the resorts are less crowded than those in Europe and cater for families also. Whistler is a world renowned resort in British Columbia. Vermont has 20 alpine ski areas and 50 cross ski areas. The atmosphere is very traditional with small villages offering bed and breakfast accommodation in inns.

The Caribbean

The Caribbean islands are some of the most popular tourist destinations in the world. They became accessible to a wide British market in the 1980s with an increase in flights and a desire to travel to exotic countries. Table 3.3 gives a list of the islands with their arrival figures from 1993 to 1997. Please note these figures are for arrivals from all over the world.

(FIGURES IN THOUSANDS)	1993	1994	1995	1996	1997
CARIBBEAN	**12,833**	**13,707**	**14,037**	**14,385**	**15,286**
ANGUILLA	38	44	39	37	43
ANTIGUA, BARB	240	255	212	220	232
ARUBA	562	582	619	641	650
BAHAMAS	1,489	1,516	1,598	1,633	1,592
BARBADOS	396	426	442	447	472
BERMUDA	412	416	387	390	380
BONAIRE	55	56	59	63	63
BR. VIRGIN IS	200	239	219	244	251
CAYMAN ISLANDS	287	341	361	373	381
CUBA	544	617	742	999	1,153
CURAÇAO	223	238	232	219	209
DOMINICA	52	57	60	63	65
DOMINICAN REPUBLIC	1,609	1,717	1,776	1,926	2,211
GRENADA	94	109	108	108	111
GUADELOUPE	453	556	640	625	660
HAITI	77	70	145	150	152
JAMAICA	1,105	1,098	1,147	1,162	1,192
MARTINIQUE	366	419	457	477	513
MONTSERRAT	22	24	19	9	5
PUERTO RICO	2,854	3,055	3,132	3,095	3,249
SABA	25	29	10	10	10
SAINT EUSTATIUS	26	29	25	24	24
SAINT KITTS AND NEVIS	84	94	79	84	88
SAINT LUCIA	194	219	231	236	248
SAINT MAARTEN	503	568	445	365	439
ST. VINCENT, G	57	55	60	58	65
TRINIDAD TBG	249	266	260	266	324
TURKS, CAICOS	67	72	79	88	93
US. VIRGIN IS	550	540	454	373	411

Table 3.3 *Americas: Trends of tourist arrivals, 1993–1997*   *Source: Adapted from WTO data*

ACTIVITY

Locate the Caribbean islands on an atlas. Study the list of countries and figures and complete the following tasks:

Position as many islands as you can on the outline map. Note, you may not be able to locate the smaller islands. Which is the largest island? Which two countries share the second largest island?

Which islands form the Leewards? Which islands form the Windwards?

Which three islands have the most arrivals? Why do you think they have the most arrivals? Montserrat has the lowest arrivals. Why is this?

Find out which islands are Dutch. Find out which islands are French.

Locate Cancun (Mexico) on your map.

Barbados	187,700
Dominican Republic	156,287
Cuba	68,300
Cancun	65,144
Antigua	57,500
St. Lucia	51,000
Trinidad and Tobago	31,000
Cayman Islands	23,900
St. Kitts and Nevis	12,847
US Virgin Islands	4,000
Haiti	negligible

Table 3.4 *UK arrivals 1998 to Caribbean resorts*
Source: Figures extracted from travel press reports

There are too many Caribbean islands to look at in detail, so we will look briefly at a selection and examine the reasons for their popularity (or not) with the British tourist. First let us note the general appeal of the Caribbean:

- There are beautiful, perfect, white sandy beaches on most of the islands.

- The sea is warm and turquoise.

- The diving and snorkelling is some of the best in the world.

- The climate is tropical, consistently hot and sunny all year round (but watch out for the hurricane season).

- It is an ideal winter holiday destination to escape the British winter.

Barbados

This is the most popular island, with UK tourists and the number of UK visitors continuing to grow. It appeals to two socially distinct markets. The south coast has been extensively developed for mass tourism. It has many cheap hotels and lots of entertainment. Some would say it has been spoilt. The west coast of the island is more exclusive (and more expensive) with luxury hotels and a quieter nightlife.

The reasons for Barbados' popularity are clear. The island was formerly a British colony, although it is now independent. The island has, therefore, important ties with Britain. English is spoken and there are many English traditions, such as the love of cricket. There are many direct flights to Barbados, including charters, and Concorde also flies there.

Jamaica

This island has some similarities with Barbados, in that it was also a British colony, but is now independent. English is the native language. Jamaica also has easy access with many direct flights. It is a larger island and has more natural attractions, fantastic beaches, mountains and waterfalls. The nightlife is lively and there are good golf courses for sports fans. UK arrivals rose by 14% in 1999, although there had been problems the year before. Political problems led to riots and deaths of some locals in April 1999. Flights were cancelled for a week and the resulting publicity led to a short-term fall in UK arrivals.

Dominican Republic

This island has been beleaguered by problems in recent years. It opened up to tourism in the 1980s and quickly gained popularity due to its cheapness. Spanish is spoken but this did not deter UK tourists who were used to visiting Spain already. In 1997, the island suffered from negative reports on television and in the press due to hygiene problems in hotels. These problems were aggravated in September 1998 when damage was caused by Hurricane George.

Cuba

Cuba is the fastest growing Caribbean destination. It has the obvious attractions of sun and beaches, but also has a fascinating city, Havana, to explore. The main market in Cuba is for all-inclusive, beach front holidays in the resort of Varadero but specialist operators are diversifying into golf, diving and yacht holidays. International hotel chains, such as Sofitel and Novotel, are venturing into Havana and building new accommodation.

ACTIVITY

Research the history and politics of Cuba. Find out why relations with the USA are considered to be poor.

Cuba is expected to surpass the Dominican Republic in popularity in the coming years. Compare the two islands in terms of attractions, accessibility from the UK, accommodation and prices. Compare also the politics, recent history and the problems.

The Cayman Islands

The Cayman Islands are still a British colony. In spite of this, the island is not a major destination for UK tourists. Airlines reach the islands via Miami or Nassau and life on the island is very expensive. 50% of the accommodation is in villas or apartments and many of the tourists visit for the excellent diving.

St. Kitts and Nevis

St. Kitts is the main island with neighbouring Nevis only two miles away. These islands are growing in popularity with UK tourists,

DID YOU KNOW?

In 1997, Thomson evacuated an hotel in the Dominican Republic after 3 guests contracted typhoid. In January, 1998, an office was set up on the island with a team of Spanish speaking health inspectors. Over 8,500 workers in 70 hotels have been trained in good hygiene practice.

DID YOU KNOW?

A UK tourist office representative spoke about the hygiene scare in the Dominican Republic. He said he was puzzled why so many Britons became ill on holiday. There were few complaints from the Germans, French and Italians. One of the reasons he suggested was overindulgence!

DID YOU KNOW?

The Cayman Islands enjoy tax free status. The islands are the fifth largest financial centre in the world, with about 600 licensed banks. Not bad for a population of 36,000.

enjoying a 30% increase in visitors between 1997 and 1998. The islands were also hit by Hurricane George, but the airport and cruise port managed to open up again very quickly.

PROFILE *St. Kitts and Nevis*

Location: St Kitts and Nevis lie in the northern part of the Leeward Islands in the eastern Caribbean. Nevis is two miles south of main island St Kitts and is reached by air or ferry across the Narrows Channel.

Language: English.

Time: GMT −4 hrs.

Entry regulations: full British passport required. No visa is necessary.

Currency: Eastern Caribbean Dollar (EC$).

Flying time: 9 hrs.

Climate: hot and tropical climate. The driest period is from January to April.

Hotels: there are about 31 hotels, the majority being on St Kitts, including Allegro's Jack Tar Village. Nevis is well known for its heritage properties, many converted great houses and sugar mills on the old estates.

Self-catering: there are villas and apartments. A list is available from the tourist office.

Nightlife: very low key. Some hotels have live bands and dancing on Saturday nights and there is sometimes a disco. The Jack Tar Village has a casino, complete with slot machines, blackjack tables and roulette wheels.

Tour operators: a wide range of specialist operators feature the two islands, as well as one or two mass-market companies including First Choice.

Airlines: Caledonian flies nonstop once weekly from Gatwick. Regular British Airways' connections via Antigua and San Juan.

Contact: St Kitts and Nevis Tourist Office.

Source: Travel Weekly, *10 May 1999*

ACTIVITY

Choose two Caribbean islands to research (but do not choose Cuba or the Dominican Republic). Produce two profiles similar to the example on St. Kitts. A useful Internet site is: www.caribbeansupersite.com

Antigua

There is nothing spectacular about Antigua's landscape, but it is renowned for its beautiful coastline – it is always promoted with reference to its 365 beaches, one for each day of the year. The island is the largest of the Leewards and was also hit by Hurricane George. Only superficial damage was caused, fortunately, as the island had not long recovered from the devastation caused by Hurricane Luis in 1995. 75% of homes were damaged, however, and there was extensive damage to hotels and infrastructure.

Haiti

This is a country that is genuinely unspoilt and untouched by tourism. It shares an island with the Dominican Republic, although the two countries are very different. Haiti has a reputation for being a violent place with many political problems. It has a history of rule by dictators. Only a few intrepid travellers go there and they are mainly French, as that is the official language (only the educated speak French, however; others speak Creole). Haiti is the poorest country in the western hemisphere. Voodoo is widely practised and many Haitians believe in Zombies, the living dead, whose souls have left their bodies. It is wise to be well prepared, if you ever recommend this country or travel here yourself.

Cancun

Cancun is not an island, but it is a Caribbean resort on the mainland of Mexico. It has grown in importance as many UK tourists choose to go there for beach holidays, but also to use the area as a gateway to the rest of Mexico, visiting, for example, archeological sites. Holidays here can be combined with tours of other Latin American countries, such as Belize or Guatemala.

Australasia (Australia and New Zealand)

Australia

Figure 3.12 Map of Australia

Australia is about as long haul as it gets from the UK, right across the world. The UK has always had a strong VFR market to Australia, as many of us have family or friends who have emigrated there. It is also, however, a growing holiday destination for us as air fares have become cheaper. There was a great deal of interest in the Millennium celebrations in Sydney and in the 2000 Olympics. Sydney will also host the Gay Games in 2002 and the Rugby World Cup in 2003. These events have led to rapid hotel growth in Sydney to ensure there are enough beds to meet demand.

Most of the annual 470,000 UK arrivals in Australia want to visit Sydney. Sydney is the country's largest city, although the capital city is actually Canberra. Sydney is a cosmopolitan city with many attractions, including the Opera House, Sydney harbour, the Queen Victoria shopping centre and the beaches of Bondi, Manly and Cogee. Sydney is also a useful base to visit the Blue Mountains and the wine producing region of the Hunter Valley. Transport is efficient with a monorail, rail service and ferries serving Sydney. Petrol is cheap, so self-drive holidays can be cost effective.

The other area that is popular with first time visitors to Australia is Queensland, to see the Great Barrier Reef. Visitors can drive up to Cairns or take the train – there is a luxury service, the Great South Pacific Express. From Cairns, tourists can visit the Reef or the beaches, which are located a few minutes from Cairns by car. It is also possible to visit the tropical rainforest from Cairns or go on an ecology tour. Accommodation can be anything from a luxury resort to a camp site.

Repeat visitors may choose to go further afield and visit a different region. Wine, wildlife and outback tours of South Australia can be taken from Adelaide. On Kangaroo Island you can see kangaroos, koalas and pelicans. These tours are often by coach and some are particularly aimed at the youth market, taking in camp sites and lodges, rather than hotels. Although, as we have noted, flights to Australia are cheap, they are also long! Tourists may be flying for 21 hours with a fuel break in Singapore or Hong Kong. There are two ways to make the journey more bearable – travellers can choose a stopover for one or two nights in Singapore or Hong Kong, or, travel first class!

New Zealand

Figure 3.13 *Map of New Zealand*

New Zealand consists of two islands located in the South West Pacific, about three hours flight south east of Australia. The capital is Wellington, but Auckland is the major entry point for visitors by air. Cruise ships also call at Auckland. Those visitors who choose to tour the country may start at Auckland and finish at Christchurch in the south, flying home from there. New Zealand has not been as successful in attracting UK tourists as Australia, so the New Zealand Tourist Board is currently undertaking a major campaign aimed at the UK market.

KEY TERMS

Wellington: is the capital of New Zealand.

Auckland: is the major gateway to New Zealand.

Strapline: a catch phrase used by advertisers.

Fjord: a narrow channel of sea between high cliffs.

Ecotourism: a type of tourism that seeks to preserve and celebrate the environment.

PROFILE *New Zealand Tourist Board*

The role of the New Zealand Tourist Board is to develop, implement and promote strategies to market the New Zealand Tourist Industry. The board works closely with the country's tourism industry and also advises the government on strategy. A new website was launched in 1999 to promote tourism. In addition, a £1 million television and press campaign targets the UK, under the strapline '100% Pure New Zealand'.

New Zealand has a very beautiful landscape with vast mountain chains, volcanoes, fjords, rainforests and grassy plains. It is one of world's least populated countries and, therefore, is uncrowded and peaceful. The climate is mild and suitable for holidays all year round. It is also highly suitable for ecotourism and Taiaroa Head on the South Island is a top ecotourism destination, where visitors can see a colony of albatross, as well as penguins and seals. Other attractions include tours of the wine regions (the largest is Ratimera Bay, Marlborough Sounds).

Main travel and tourism gateways and routes

Access to departure gateways

In this section we will examine the options for access to the gateways for departure and the means of departure available to us. The choices are:

- road
- rail
- ferry
- air travel

People must consider cost, convenience and journey time when choosing how to travel.

Roads

The UK has a good network of motorways and we do not pay to use them. However, the busier motorways are frequently congested, particularly the M1, M6 and M25. As these roads are routes to our major airports, travellers must consider the time their journey might take very carefully. In addition, those people with a long distance to travel will also need to consider the cost implications, as petrol in the UK is very expensive. Figure 3.14 shows the UK motorway and major road network.

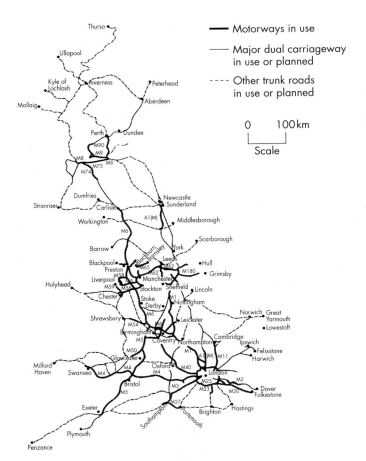

Figure 3.14 The UK's vast motorway and major road network

Railtrack: the organisation managing the complete rail network.

Train Operating Companies: these companies run the trains.

Tourists who wish to cross the channel or go to Ireland may want to take their car with them, so they will travel by road to their gateway port. Others may opt to use public transport and may choose rail, coach or air links.

Rail

The rail network in the UK is particularly complicated. Railtrack is the company responsible for all the railway tracks and systems. There are, however, 25 train operating companies covering the country, offering different fares and different levels of service. Examples include Great Eastern, Great Western, Central Trains and Virgin Trains.

PROFILE *Railtrack*

Railtrack is the organisation that manages the complete UK rail network. It provides access to the network of railways to the train operating companies, manages the allocation of train paths and plans and co-ordinates train movements. Railtrack runs the national rail infrastructure. It owns all the track, level crossings, viaducts and bridges and 2,500 stations. Most stations are leased to the Train Operating Companies, although the major ones are directly managed by Railtrack. Over 11,000 people work for Railtrack.

The railway companies have been heavily criticised in recent years and are making efforts to improve services. An Association of Train Operators represents the Train Operating Companies as there are so many of them. All the railway organisations have made common pledges to improve services. These are as follows:

● To have a £27 billion programme of investment, maintenance and repair over ten years.

● To renew or modernise over half of all passenger trains by 2002.

● 80% of stations to be refurbished by 2002.

It is possible to travel by train to all our gateway ports, but changing trains and stations, especially in London, means it is not the easiest of journeys for holiday-makers. There are, however, direct rail services from London to Gatwick and Heathrow:

1 **Gatwick Express**
  This trains runs every 15 minutes from Victoria and takes 30 minutes to reach Gatwick. Passengers of British Airways and American Airlines can check in at Gatwick.
2 **Heathrow Express**
  This train runs every 15 minutes from Paddington and started up in 1998 at a cost of £450 million. It takes only 15 minutes to reach Heathrow and passengers for more than 20 airlines can check in at Paddington.

Air

The third choice for reaching a departure point is air travel. This is most practical when a tourist intends to continue the journey by air. Internal flights are available to London airports from most regions but they are fairly expensive (Manchester to London, for example, costs around £120 return) and the tourist still has to travel to the regional airport.

DID YOU KNOW?

The British Airports Authority (BAA), who own Heathrow, aim to get 50% of travellers to Heathrow to use public transport, to ease congestion on the roads serving the airport.

Reaching your end destination

We have so far considered the travel options for travellers to reach the departure point for their trip. We will now look at the choices for reaching the travel and tourism destination. The categories once again include road, rail and air but we must also include ferries and cruises (the latter form of transport is the holiday itself). Table 3.5 shows visits made by air and sea for 1996.

PRINCIPAL COUNTRY VISITED	VISITS ('000) 1996		
	AIR	**SEA***	**TOTAL**
United States	3,066	23	3,089
Canada	506	2	508
North America	3,572	25	3,597
Belgium/Luxembourg	388	1,081	1,469
France	1,640	8,580	10,220
Germany (†)	1,218	699	1,918
Italy	1,236	333	1,569
Netherlands	884	660	1,543
Denmark	197	53	249
Irish Republic	1,456	1,713	3,169
Greece	1,450	12	1,461
Spain	6,839	715	7,554
Portugal	1,068	38	1,106
Austria	327	90	417
Finland	95	2	97
Sweden	237	45	282
Western Europe EU (†‡)	17,036	14,018	31,054

Note: * Travel by road and rail across the border with the Irish Republic is included with sea routes, as is travel by Channel Tunnel, hovercraft and jetfoil.

Table 3.5 *UK travellers abroad: method of transport (by destination countries/areas) 1986 and 1996*

Source: International Passenger Survey

Note that visitors to Belgium and France nearly all choose sea crossings. Sea travel is a popular choice for visits to Ireland also, but air travel is fast catching up. We will see why later in this chapter. For all other European destinations air is the major choice.

Road

The various channel crossings give access to the northern ports of Europe and the extensive motorway networks. Calais, for example, is situated right next to the motorway, so tourists can be on the road and completely bypass the town centre. Most camping operators expect their customers to be travelling by car and so provide information to help them. This can be in the form of a travel pack containing maps, guides and an itinerary with detailed directions. Also included are tips for driving in Europe and brochures containing mileage charts for destinations throughout Europe. Drivers must ensure they have adequate motor insurance. Tolls have to be paid on the autoroutes of France. Coach travel is a cheap option for travellers, but is becoming less popular as air fares fall.

Rail

Travellers can now take their car on the rail service Le Shuttle under the Channel. The journey can then be continued by road or by motorail to the south of France and Italy. Foot passengers can take the Eurostar train, which runs from Waterloo in London, to Paris, Brussels or Lille. There are Eurostar services to Disneyland, Paris also. The rail system in Western Europe is generally much better than in Britain. Trains travel at very high speeds so journey times are reduced and fares are reasonable as the public transport systems attract government subsidies.

Motorail is an option for those who travel to the Dordogne, Gascony or the Mediterranean. After the short channel crossing, the car is loaded onto a train at Calais and passengers travel in a couchette carriage on the same train.

Ferries

Ferry services across the Channel have been hit hard by the introduction of Eurotunnel. They cannot compete with the train on speed of crossing so they have to promote other aspects of their service. Ferry companies have, therefore, improved facilities on their ships to attract custom. They stress the fact that crossing by ferry is relaxing and that there is lots to do. These facilities include extensive shopping, good restaurants, bars and even cinemas on the longer crossings. Many holiday-makers enjoy the ferry trip as part of the holiday experience.

The ferry operators also ensure that prices are competitive, especially now duty free has been abolished. The day trip market was a lucrative one for ferry companies until the abolition of duty free in 1999 – travellers are no longer able to stock up on duty free alcohol and cigarettes on board. The companies have had to shift the focus to day trip shopping excursions to France, where prices for alcohol are much lower than the UK. The ferries and Le Shuttle also have Club Class services to entice business travellers.

KEY TERMS

Autoroute: a French motorway.

Motorail: a French train for passengers and cars.

ACTIVITY

Visit the Internet site for Le Shuttle at www.eurotunnel.com and find out what the costs and benefits of travelling Club Class are.

CASE STUDY *Channel crossings*

The competing ferry companies on the short route across the Channel are P&O Stena Line and Sea France. Both companies have responded to the competition from the tunnel by marketing the crossing as a 'cruise' style experience. A variety of lounges, eating areas, entertainment and shopping facilities are provided. Passengers can relax on deck (weather permitting). The crossing takes about 75 minutes plus load times.

Other options are the services run by Hoverspeed. They operate hovercraft up to 20 times a day on the Dover to Calais route. The crossing takes only 35 minutes. The hovercraft do not operate in adverse weather conditions. Hovercraft travel is more like air travel, in terms of meals and shopping, as food and drink is brought to your seat. Hoverspeed also has Seacat (a fast catamaran car ferry) services to Boulogne and to Ostend. The company has recently begun a Seacat service from Newhaven to Dieppe, hoping to appeal to travellers to Paris, as Dieppe is the nearest port to Paris. This crossing takes two hours.

Two services are available via the tunnel. These are Le Shuttle, a train service for cars and freight between Folkestone and Calais, and Eurostar, a passenger train service between London and Paris, Lille or Brussels. Le Shuttle passengers can drive straight onto the train and be in France in about 30 minutes. There will, however, be waiting times at busy periods. The service is quick and easy but there is nowhere to go and very little to do. In addition to these short sea crossings, Brittany Ferries, P&O and Condor Ferries offer longer crossings from Portsmouth and Plymouth to St. Malo, Le Havre, Cherbourg, Roscoff, Bilbao and Santander.

Source: Adapted from Insights, *November 1998, ETB/BTA*

ACTIVITY

You are working as a travel agent. Your manager has given you three customers to deal with. Each customer requires a channel crossing.

1   Ms Singh needs to travel to Paris on Monday morning to go to a trade show. She wants to leave the UK port at about 9am with her company car full of exhibition material. She will return on Friday evening.

2   The Gee family wishes to go to the Pyrenees for the summer. They want to drive through France on the first Saturday in August. However, they are not keen on the long drive back. They have been told that there is a sailing from Northern Spain. They would like to return on the Bank Holiday Monday at the end of August. They will need a cabin.

3   Helen wants to celebrate her birthday in style. She has decided to take her boyfriend to France for a weekend. While they are there they will buy wine for a big party on their return.

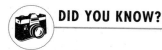

DID YOU KNOW?

The Princess Anne, a hovercraft from the Hoverspeed fleet, holds the record for the fastest crossing of the Channel, travelling the 23 miles between Dover and Calais on 14 September 1995 in 22 minutes.

Locate the UK and continental ferry ports on a map of UK and Europe coastlines (your teacher should be able to supply you with this). Mark the ferry routes available. Use appropriate brochures or websites to find a suitable crossing for each of the above customers. Make notes detailing the routes, costs and benefits of the service chosen, so that you can inform the customers.

It is important to note that there are many other crossings from the UK, apart from those across the Channel. P&O have a service from Hull to Rotterdam and from Hull to Zeebrugge. Crossings are overnight so cabins are provided. Swansea Cork Ferries, Stena Line and Irish Ferries operate from the ports of Holyhead, Pembroke, Fishguard and Stranraer to various destinations in Ireland. There are also services from our northern ports to Scandinavia, for example, Fjord Line's Newcastle to Bergen service.

Air travel

In Chapter 1 you learnt the difference between charter and scheduled flights. People who book a package holiday are likely to be travelling on a charter flight, often owned by the same company as the tour operator. Sometimes it is difficult for a passenger to know whether the airline is charter or scheduled, as the services on offer are very similar. Charter flights will be consolidated if they do not receive enough bookings to achieve their load factors. This means that a flight will be cancelled and passengers put onto another flight to fill it.

This does not happen with scheduled services, which run to a timetable. In fact, scheduled services may even be over booked at times. Passengers with full price tickets are then able to transfer their tickets to another flight if they wish. This means it is difficult to know exactly how many passengers will turn up for a flight. When over booking occurs some passengers have to be 'bumped off'. This means they are offered a later flight and some form of compensation for the inconvenience. On short journeys, tourists must decide whether flying is cheaper and more convenient than other alternatives.

Flight costs are currently very low and one of the reasons for this is the growth in low cost airlines.

KEY TERMS

Consolidation: merging passengers from two flights to one.

Load factor: percentage of seats sold on the aircraft.

'No frills airlines'

Several cut-price airlines have been developed in the last few years. The liberalisation of the European Union aviation market allows European airlines to start services in the EU without government permission. The low cost carriers will fly passengers safely to their destination but offer few, if any, services. These small airlines have to compete with the big carriers and although they have a price advantage, they find it difficult to obtain take off and landing slots at airports that are dominated by the larger airlines. Some of the big carriers have introduced their own low cost airlines to compete and perhaps drive away the competition. Examples include 'Go' (British Airways) and 'Buzz' (KLM). It is important to note that low cost carriers are not only taking business away from the competition, but are encouraging more people to fly to more and more destinations because of the low fares. This gives the whole of the travel and tourism industry a boost. Figure 3.15 shows how low cost airlines keep costs down to enable them to offer low fares.

PROFILE *Ryanair*

Ryanair claims to be Europe's leading low fares airline. It started as an independent Irish airline and was floated on the New York and Irish stock exchanges in 1997. Scheduled services began between Ireland and the UK in 1985 with one 15 seater aircraft. By 1990, Ryanair operated direct services between all major airports in Ireland and the UK. The number of people flying between London and Dublin doubled and fares were halved. Now the airline operates 34 different routes and carries almost six million passengers a year. In 1998, the company bought 45 new Boeing 707-800 aircraft. Over 1,000 people are employed by Ryanair.

Source: Adapted from the Ryanair website

ACTIVITY

You will find the travel advertising sections of newspapers and company websites helpful for this activity.

Identify the low cost airlines. For each of them state the base airport. Why are the airlines based at these airports? What are the advantages and disadvantages for the company?

Give details of the destinations served. Is there any overlap between the operators?

Give examples of fares. Are they competitive? Compare them with those of larger carriers.

What is meant by 'no frills'?

Traditionally, charter airlines offer a one class service, but they have recently begun to offer premium services. This is in recognition of the public's dislike of being treated 'en masse' and is an attempt to give a more tailor-made service. It is also an opportunity to increase profits.

How we do it!

easyJet offers a simple, no frills service at rock bottom fares. Fares can be offered at such good value due to the following 4 main reasons:

NO TRAVEL AGENTS
easyJet was the first airline not to pay a penny in commission to a travel agent. Even British Airways who originally copied us, have now succumbed to selling through agents. All bookings are made DIRECT with the **easyJet** reservations centre or booked direct on the Internet. Cutting out the middleman saves the commission fee paid to a travel agent.

NO TICKETS
easyJet is a ticketless airline. All you need to fly is proof of identity (passport for international flights).
This is less hassle for the customer who does not have to worry about collecting tickets before travelling, and cost effective for **easyJet**.

NO HEATHROW
easyJet uses uncongested, inexpensive airports with the cost advantages being passed on to travellers. Using uncongested airports also allows easyJet to get much better utilisation out of their aircraft rather that wasting time waiting for slots at a busy airport.

THERE'S NO SUCH THING AS A FREE LUNCH
... so **easyJet** does not offer one. Plastic trays of airline food only mean more expensive flights. **easyJet** passengers are given the choice as to whether they wish to buy themselves drinks or snacks from the in-flight easyKiosk. Our customer feedback illustrates that passengers do not want a meal on board a short-haul flight. They prefer to pay less for the flight and purchase snacks on board if desired.

This is why BA had to copy OUR IDEA

The lefthand side of the diagram shows the costs incurred by all airlines including **easyJet**

The righthand side of the diagram shows the additional costs incurred by big airlines, but NOT by **easyJet**.

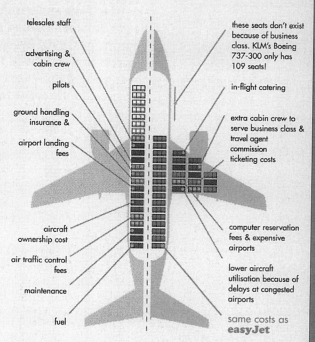

telesales staff

advertising & cabin crew

pilots

ground handling insurance &

airport landing fees

aircraft ownership cost

air traffic control fees

maintenance

fuel

these seats don't exist because of business class. KLM's Boeing 737-300 only has 109 seats!

in-flight catering

extra cabin crew to serve business class & travel agent commission ticketing costs

computer reservation fees & expensive airports

lower aircraft utilisation because of delays at congested airports

same costs as **easyJet**

This diagram approximately illustrates the number of seats **easyJet** needs to sell to cover each type of expense.

Figure 3.15 easyJet: 'no frills service' and low fares

Source: www.easyJet.com

KEY TERM

Premium service: extra facilities offered (for a fee).

Many business travellers are opting for low cost airlines in order to achieve cost savings. As a result, other airlines have increased their services to business travellers to compete. On long haul flights business people are likely to opt for first or club class travel as they need to arrive at their destination refreshed and ready to work, but here too, there is a lot of competition. First class passengers can expect gourmet meals, fully reclining seats or even beds, seat back screens with a choice of videos, amenity packs and telephones. On the ground they will have priority check in and exclusive lounges.

Cruises

Cruising has been one of the fastest growing segments of the travel and tourism industry in the last few years. The Passenger Shipping Association report an increase in the UK cruise market from 309,000 passengers in 1994 to 770,000 in 1999. Cruise passengers used to be mainly elderly, with plenty of time and money at their disposal. These groups still compose the main market but the advent of tour operators like Thomson and Airtours has made dramatic changes. They offer value for money cruises with the focus on families. Figure 3.16 shows how the age profile of passengers has changed over the last few years.

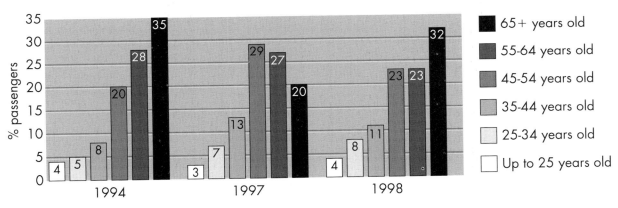

Figure 3.16 Age range of British cruisers

Source: *PSA-IRN Cruisestat*, Travel Weekly, *31 May 1999*

Cruises range from a few nights to a complete world tour lasting a few months. They take place in all areas of the world, from the Caribbean to the Mediterranean, across the Atlantic to New York or around the fjords of Scandinavia. The cost can vary from a few hundred pounds to thousands, for complete luxury, but overall prices have decreased due to intense competition.

DID YOU KNOW?

Crystal Cruises allocate passengers their own e-mail address before departure. They can pass it on to friends or business contacts before they leave.

The appeal of cruising lies in the fact that the tourist can see lots of different places with very little effort. There is no need to pack and unpack; no need to negotiate airports or railway stations. Everything except drinks and tips is included in the price of the cruise and the level of service is extremely high. Passengers can eat all day long, if they want to, and take part in many different activities. Accommodation may be cramped in a small cabin, or spacious in a suite, depending on what the tourist can afford.

Dawn Princess

Vessel: *Dawn Princess*.
Operator: Princess Cruises.
Built: 1997.
Tonnage: 77,000.
Passengers: 1,950 (double occupancy).
Crew/nationality: British and Italian officers and international crew/staff.
Cabins: apart from 38 suites/mini-suites with private verandahs and 19 wheelchair-accessible cabins, the size and amenities of the remaining 918 cabins are similar, with TVs, hairdryers and bathrobes standard. Storage space is adequate but bathrooms are on the small side. There are 372 inside cabins but the major development is the large proportion – nearly two-thirds – of outside cabins which each have their own private balcony.
Food and drink: the quality of the food and its presentation is a major step forward for a ship which can be catering for up to 2,250 passengers. There are two main dining rooms each operating the usual two sittings but there are also alternative evening dining options at a pizzeria and in the attractive Horizon Court, which is open 24 hrs a day. There is also a patisserie and an ice cream parlour. Drinks prices in the bars are on the high side but there is a good and reasonably-priced wine list in the restaurants.
Service: highly professional, mainly Italian staff in the various restaurants. Standards are patchier around the many bars and at the main reception.
Entertainment: the inclusion of a theatre as well as a standard cruise ship show lounge allows the line to stage more ambitious and original musical productions by its own on-board company. There is live music in most of the other bars and lounges and a disco. There is a good-sized but pleasingly unobtrusive casino, an excellent spa and fitness centre, several pools and Jacuzzis, plenty of deck space with a sports court, table tennis, golf course simulator, video arcade, play-room, and mini pool for children.
Comments: the quality of food, service and the lack of crowding on board a ship carrying 2,000 passengers is remarkable. The main criticisms are the lack of a separate observation lounge, which is particularly missed when the ship cruises to Alaska for the summer, and the in-cabin food service, which is below the high levels set elsewhere on the ship.

Figure 3.17 An example of what to expect on a cruise

Source: Travel Weekly, *14 June 1999*

Gateways

Airports

Air travel is the main form of long distance travel and the most rapidly expanding transport sector. To cope with increased demand for air travel, many gateway airports have had to expand their capacity. All our major airports have plans for expansion.

There are over 50 commercial airports in the UK, yet inter-regional air travel is still uncommon. No distance is so great as to make road travel unfeasible, unlike the USA, for example.

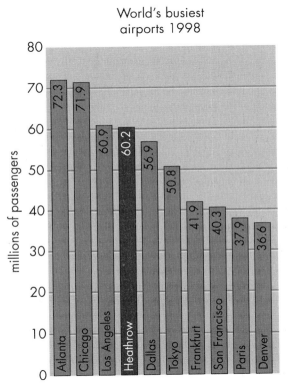

Figure 3.18 The world's busiest airports in 1998

Source: Travel Weekly, 17 May 1999

Note that six of the world's busiest airports are in the US and their passengers are travelling inter-state within the US. The busy international airports do not just deal with inbound passengers, but with transfer passengers (i.e. those who are using the airport to connect with another flight). For example, 2.8 million people, in 1998, flew from regional airports in the UK, to Amsterdam Schipol, where passengers then transfer to other flights.

KEY TERM

Transfer passengers: using the gateway to connect to another flight (or alternative mode of travel).

KEY TERM

Satellite terminal: smaller terminal linked by train to the main airport.

London airports

London has four major airports. These are Heathrow, the world's busiest international airport, Gatwick, Stansted and Luton. In addition, there is a small airport in the Docklands, City Airport. The latter caters mainly for business travellers. The British Airports Authority (BAA) owns 15 airports in the UK and these include Heathrow, Stansted and Gatwick. Luton airport is owned by Luton Borough Council. The BAA is a very profitable organisation. It has invested heavily in retail facilities at airports, realising that holiday-makers are in the mood to spend as soon as they reach the airport, considering their holiday to have already begun.

ACTIVITY

Find the BAA website at www.baa.co.uk. Find out which airports they own throughout the world.

How many destinations does Heathrow serve? How many passengers does Gatwick serve?

What is BAA's mission?

What is the CAA?

What is Terminal Five at Heathrow?

Look at the news releases section (2000). What development has BAA made into e-commerce and how much has been invested? What awards has BAA won?

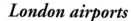

PROFILE *Stansted airport*

Stansted is London's newest and most modern airport, located off the M11 in Essex. The airport had a very successful year (1998–1999), making more than £18 million profit, a rise of 400%, and achieving a 35% growth in passenger figures to 7.5 million. Scheduled flights will make up 97% of the airport's traffic in the year 2000, serving 65 destinations. Ryanair is the busiest airline. Other airlines based at Stansted include, KLM UK, Go, Swissair, Alitalia and Virgin Express. The attraction for both the airlines and passengers is that the airport is less congested than Heathrow and Gatwick, and slots for take off and landing are easier to acquire. Routes to the airport are also quieter. The BAA has extensive expansion plans for Stansted, hoping to almost double the number of passengers by 2007. This will mean the addition of two more satellite terminals and an extension to the main terminal. The government gave permission, in 1999, for the level of air transport movements to be increased from 120,000 to 185,000. The BAA has invested more than £500 million in Stansted since 1986.

Other airports with plans for expansion are Heathrow, planning a fifth terminal, and Gatwick, where a £30 million extension to the north

KEY TERM

Gateway: point of departure or arrival leading to other destinations.

terminal will be completed by the end of 2001. This will give 50% more lounge space. At Manchester airport a second runway opens in 2000. At Birmingham, there is a new immigration hall and a new arrivals hall, as well as extra check in facilities. A new terminal is to be built at Liverpool airport to boost capacity and Edinburgh's new terminal opened in 1999, almost doubling passenger capacity.

At Luton Airport, a £170 million development programme is underway, funded by a partnership with the private sector. A new terminal building opened in 1999. One of Luton's major airlines stayed away from the opening. Stelios, the chairman of the airline, commented in the EasyJet magazine that he did not feel it appropriate to celebrate something that has been a costly mistake: 'The new management have (sic) raised the fees that they are charging to the airline to pay for the cost of the terminal. To meet these increased costs, EasyJet will have to raise fares to passengers.'

PROFILE *Business traveller*

Mr Harrison works in exports. He travels extensively throughout Europe, using the four major London airports regularly. He most often uses Stansted and Luton, taking advantage of the low cost airlines. His company pays the fares, but Mr Harrison feels a responsibility to keep costs down. He says he cannot get good deals with British Airways and Air France unless certain conditions are fulfilled, like staying over a Saturday night or booking well in advance. These deals simply do not give him the flexibility he needs.

DID YOU KNOW?

Three passengers travelling from Luton to Turkey had a wonderful surprise when they checked in. They were the first passengers to use the new terminal and were given champagne and a £1,000 holiday voucher!

He likes Stansted, saying the road access is good, parking is reasonably priced and the short-term car park is right next to the terminal: 'As it is not a multistorey, it is really easy and quick to park and get into the terminal. The flow through the airport is well organised, much better and quicker than the others, there are lots of check in desks and they are near to passport control. You can go straight through the duty free mall to the satellite train and do not have to go outside.' Mr Harrison does not like Luton as much; he thinks that the main disadvantage is that the airport is accessed via the M1, one of the busiest motorways. To get to the airport from anywhere else, travellers have to negotiate Luton town centre and, at peak times, the traffic from the workers at the Vauxhall motor plant. On the plus side, he says checking in is no problem with the new terminal, lots of new check ins have been provided. He does add, though, that 'I still have to walk from the new terminal through the old one, and I dislike having to go out onto the tarmac to board the plane, whatever the weather. It surprises me that some passengers do not end up on the wrong flight when there are several planes waiting to board.'

Embarkation: boarding.

Megaship: carries more than 2,000 passengers.

Ports

Ports are also important gateways for travellers. They are embarkation points for ferry services and also for cruise passengers. Cruise passengers may, for example, fly to a port to take their cruise. Miami is one of the busiest of these – in fact, it is known as the cruise capital of the world. It is home to 18 ships and is able to handle very large 'megaships', vessels capable of transporting more than 2,000 guests. In 1998, more than 2.9 million passengers used Miami's port.

Ports have to offer cruise lines a range of services, including:

- ship repairs
- immigration control
- security services
- duty free shops
- restaurants/bars
- foreign exchange
- first aid
- parking
- transport services

In the UK, Southampton is the major departure point for cruise ships. All the facilities mentioned above are available there.

The development of the Eurotunnel meant that two passenger terminals had to be built, one in Folkestone and one in Coquelles (Calais). These are modern buildings with lounge, shopping and restaurant facilities. There are also passport and customs controls at each site. At Coquelles, there has been extensive development as the tunnel has turned the area into a major tourist gateway. Around the terminal there are various leisure facilities, a cinema, hotels, a hypermarket and a new shopping centre, Cité Europe.

The changing popularity of tourist destinations

There are many factors that affect the popularity of tourist destinations, some of which we will examine here. The travel and tourism industry is constantly changing, so you should be aware of topical events which affect destinations currently, you can best do this by regularly reading newspapers.

Economic considerations

There is a vast range of destinations available to UK outbound tourists, so if costs are significantly higher in one area and do not represent value for money, the tourist will simply choose another destination. Holiday brochures often give examples of typical prices for drinks and meals.

The current exchange rate is also very important. When the pound is strong, we can buy more foreign currency for our money, and travel abroad is, therefore, more attractive. Of course, this means that Britain is more expensive for inbound tourists and our own tourist industry suffers.

Social and political considerations

Promotion of the destination

Interest grows in a destination when it is heavily promoted by tour operators or featured on travel programmes on television. Tourists on package tours can only choose destinations that operators include in their brochures. Even independent travellers depend on travel principals providing access to their destination. Tourist boards targeting the UK hope that their campaigns will bring about an increase in visitors.

Over commercialisation or exclusivity

As a resort grows and attracts large numbers of tourists (mass tourism), it loses much of its original appeal. Tourists want to move on and look for somewhere different and hopefully more exclusive. This is one of the factors accounting for the increased interest in destinations such as the Indian Ocean and the Far East. Tourists accustomed to long haul flights, having visited Florida or the Caribbean, for instance, feel confident about exploring new places. Some countries with a burgeoning tourist industry have a deliberate policy of exclusivity, keeping costs high and limiting the numbers of hotel beds. They aim to minimise the negative impacts of tourism with a low number of high spending visitors.

Crime

Few, if any, places are crime free, and tourists should always be wary of petty crime. High levels of crime dissuade tourists so it is in the interests of tourism managers to tackle crime. This was achieved with much success, a few years ago in Florida. Muggings and murders of tourists was deterring tourists from visiting the area. Although the incidences were not that high, they were gruesome and heavily publicised. Action was taken, with extra police and advice to tourists, and arrivals figures soon recovered.

South Africa is an emerging destination, hampered by its reputation for violent crime. Zimbabwe was also becoming a popular destination for tourists, but recent political turmoil and violence have deterred tourists.

The Foreign Office maintains an excellent website, giving detailed travel information. Tourists can look up destinations and find out exactly what to expect, not only in terms of crime, but also information on political clashes, terrorism and natural disasters.

Political instability

The Foreign Office warns British travellers against travel to certain areas of the world. These are not usually traditional tourist areas, but sometimes problems occur in tourist resorts. Current examples of problem areas include parts of Sri Lanka, where there is civil unrest, and danger from guerilla activity in Peru (although Peru is thought to be becoming safer and is increasingly attracting UK visitors). At times, unsuspecting tourists find themselves in the midst of violent outbreaks. This happened in January 2000, for example, when holiday-makers had to evacuate Lombok (Indonesia) when riots broke out.

Lombok latest

Holidaymakers forced to flee the riot-torn Indonesian island of Lombok were last week being put up at hotels on neighbouring Bali. No tourists were injured in the violence, which involved local Muslims and Christians.

Although close to Lombok, Bali is considered safe as it has a predominantly Hindu population and a history of religious tolerance. January is low season, so there have been few problems finding accommodation.

The Foreign Office (0171-238 4503; www.fco.gov.uk/travel) advises against travel to Lombok and warns of increasing instability in east Kalimantan, Maluku and Irian Jaya. On Lombok, bars have been burnt at the resort of Senggigi Beach. Hoteliers evacuated guests and Christian staff early last week.

The hotel industry in Bali is braced for a disastrous season, and tour operators say cut-price deals are likely to start appearing soon.

Figure 3.19 Tourists amidst violent riots in Lombok

Source: The Sunday Times, *23 January 2000*

ACTIVITY

Locate the Foreign Office website. Find out which countries it is currently advisable to avoid.

Look up the travel information for four countries of your choice. Try to choose countries in different parts of the world. Make notes on possible problems under the headings of:

- crime
- political situation
- health advice

 DID YOU KNOW?

Headlines such as 'Holiday Firm drops coral island "hell", caused the demise of hopes of becoming a popular tourist destination for the island of San Andres in the Caribbean. Tourists complained about gastric illnesses, including dysentery, and broken glass on the beaches. One honeymooner had scorpions in the bedroom and sludge pouring out of the taps. The tour operator had to drop the resort and offer alternatives to those who had booked.

Media coverage

Media coverage may be favourable or unfavourable; either way it is very powerful. We have already noted how the problems of the Dominican Republic and Florida were exacerbated by bad publicity.

Growth of independent travel and short breaks

Earlier in the chapter you studied the growth of the short break market. Tourists' interest in culture and their propensity to take more than one holiday a year, combined with the increase in low cost airlines, has led to greater city tourism, especially for Eastern European cities, some of which are new to the industry. For example, we saw that Krakow was one of the cities of culture for the year 2000, and Prague has been very successful over the last few years.

Environmental and geographical considerations

Accessibility

Accessibility to more gateway airports in the world means that surrounding areas can be accessed. For example, Bangkok is an important gateway to Vietnam, as Vietnam ventures into tourism. China is another country that is more accessible as the government relaxes its restrictions on the entry of visitors. Earlier, you saw that Ryanair, single-handedly, doubled air passenger traffic between the UK and Ireland with its increased services and low cost fares.

Pollution and natural disasters

As with outbreaks of violence, natural disasters are usually sudden and unpredictable. They may range from pollution to volcanic eruptions. A major oil spillage in December 1999 brought devastation to the coastline of parts of Brittany and the Vendee in France. As this is a major beach holiday area, the impact was severe. Earthquakes in Turkey, also in 1999, made tourists feel insecure and doubtful about booking holidays, even though the earthquakes were away from tourist regions. A violent storm in France in December 1999, caused problems all over the country, including Disneyland, in Paris, where they had to close the Davy Crockett Ranch camp site due to storm damage. Disney issued the following explanation to customers (see Figure 3.20).

Davy Crockett Ranch, arrivals scheduled January 1st to 31st inclusive

We regret to inform you that the Davy Crockett Ranch has been badly damaged by the storm of December 26th 1999 that hit France. As a result, we are unable to honour your reservation at the Davy Crockett Ranch when your initial arrival date was scheduled between 1 January 2000 and 31 January 2000 inclusive.

If you have booked with a travel agent, please contact your travel agency for further information.

If you have booked directly with us, we ask you to call us immediately on the telephone number indicated on your confirmation letter.

We sincerely regret this exceptional situation due to unusual and unforeseeable circumstances beyond our control, and we apologise for the inconvenience that you may experience.

Figure 3.20 *Statement from Disneyland*

Source: Disneyland® Paris Online

ACTIVITY

You should carry out this activity over a number of weeks.

Study newspapers regularly to find examples of any topical events that affect the number of tourists visiting a country. Read the last section of this chapter carefully so you know what to look for. Cut out the chosen extracts and keep them in a file or scrapbook. Make sure you write the date and source against every entry.

ASSESSMENT

You are to produce a fact file containing detailed information on four travel and tourism destinations. The fact file will be suitable for helping future students to study particular destinations in depth. Two of your destinations should be in Europe and two should be long haul. Try to choose destinations other than those studied in this chapter. Use the research sections of this chapter to help you.

Your fact file will include the following:

- An introduction to each destination, including a brief description and location on a map.

- Report on the number of UK visitors to the destination, supported by statistics.

- Report on the number of operators to the destination with examples and prices.

- Report on the travel routes and gateways to the destination and the travel principals used.

- Explanation of the appeal of each destination to UK tourists, ensuring you cover the features of climate, attractions, accommodation, events, food and drink and transport. Make sure you do not merely describe the features, but state why they appeal and which are the most important in attracting tourists.

- Description of trends in the popularity of the destinations over the last ten years, supported by statistics.

- Analysis of trends in the popularity of the destination, ensuring you identify factors that affect popularity.

Make sure you use a variety of resources for your research, note them all in a bibliography and include a contents page with your file.

Key skills

In completing the assessment for this unit, you can achieve the following key skills. These will be accredited at the discretion of your tutor on the basis of the quality of the work you submit.

N3.1 Plan, and interpret information from two different types of sources, including a large data set.

C3.1b Make a presentation about a complex subject, using at least one image to illustrate complex points.
C3.2 Read and synthesise information from two extended documents about a complex subject. One of these documents should include at least one image.
C3.3 Write two different types of documents about complex subjects. One piece of writing should be an extended document and include at least one image.

IT3.1 Plan, and use different sources to search for, and select, information required for two different purposes.
IT3.3 Present information from different sources for two different purposes and audiences. Include at least one example of text, one example of images and one example of numbers.

4

Marketing travel and tourism

Aims and objectives

At the end of this chapter you will:

- **understand why companies set missions and objectives**
- **be able to carry out a marketing audit using SWOT and PEST analyses**
- **understand why and how travel and tourism organisations segment the market**
- **describe and analyse marketing research techniques**
- **be able to describe the marketing mix and apply it to travel and tourism organisations**
- **understand the use of various marketing communication tools in travel and tourism**

Introduction

This unit introduces you to the basic principles of marketing. You will learn about the marketing process and how its use helps companies achieve their objectives. You will discover that marketing is a continuous process embracing all aspects of an organisation, not just the marketing department, and that marketing is a philosophy, a particular way of doing business that always focuses on the customer.

Marketing has great importance in the travel and tourism industry, as there is immense competition and customers' needs and expectations are constantly changing. In order to succeed, an organisation must take heed of these changes and produce products and services that meet customer requirements.

In this unit you will begin by gaining a clear understanding of the marketing concept, of how it means getting the right product to the right people, in the right place at the right time. You will examine company objectives and how the tools of marketing help to achieve them. You will learn how travel and tourism organisations undertake a marketing audit. This means they must carefully examine the strengths and weaknesses within their company and also be aware of external influences on their operations.

You will examine the ways in which a company segments its market and look at examples of different customer profiles, and how travel and tourism products appeal to those customers. Marketing research methods will be examined so that you can see how the needs of customers are identified and analysed through these methods.

The 'marketing mix' will be explained and you will examine each of its elements, known as the 4 Ps (product, price, promotion and place) in detail. You will learn how companies develop the marketing mix to fulfil customer needs and meet company objectives. The four Ps are interdependent, each one affecting the others.

Finally, you will examine marketing communication methods, that is, the promotion element of the mix, in detail. Advertising, direct marketing, public relations, sales promotion and sponsorship will all be studied so that you understand how these tools help an organisation reach its target customer and how it is crucial that the message is received at the right time.

As the focus of marketing is on the customer, this chapter has important links with Chapter 5: Customer service in travel and tourism. These two chapters complement each other. In addition, the skills and knowledge you gain in this chapter will help you succeed in Chapter 6: Travel and tourism in action.

What is marketing?

The Chartered Institute of Marketing provide the accepted definition of marketing as:

❛ The management process responsible for identifying, anticipating and satisfying customer requirements profitably. ❜

The concept of marketing was introduced in the 1960s in America, and was soon adopted in the UK. The idea that a business will achieve success if it caters for the customer's needs and desires is a very simple one, indeed you might think it common sense. However, there are still many companies who do not practise marketing. Instead they concentrate on producing goods and services because they have always done so, and promote the goods heavily to sell them. The result may be that the product they offer is not what the customer wants, in a changing market. Long-term success for this type of company is unlikely.

Selling concept

Produce goods/services → Sales effort → Profit through sales volume

Figure 4.1

In Figure 4.1 the focus is on producing goods and putting a huge effort into promoting and selling them. This will produce short-term profits, but unless customers are satisfied with the product they have bought, they will not come back for more.

Marketing concept

Identify customer needs → Production integrated with other marketing activities → Profit through customer satisfaction

Figure 4.2

The company that adopts the marketing concept is more likely to be successful, as it has developed all its products to suit its customers.

Conclusions

In the travel and tourism industry, marketing is very important, due to the amount of competition within every sector. If a company does not cater for the needs of the customer, the customer will be able to choose from others who do. A further difficulty is that there is often no physical product to be marketed in travel and tourism. Instead, there is an intangible service to be marketed and it is difficult for customers to gain product knowledge before they purchase. Also, tourism products and services are highly vulnerable to seasonality, making the timing of marketing activities crucial.

Remember that not all organisations are in business to make profits. Although this is a factor in the Chartered Institute of Marketing definition quoted at the start of this section, there are many organisations who practise marketing but who do not make a profit. These include charities, health educators and tourist boards. Their aim is to provide a public service and to inform and educate. Any money raised is ploughed back into the service.

DID YOU KNOW?

One of the biggest health education marketing campaigns concerns preventing heart disease. It aims to get the British public to change their diet.

The process of marketing

Marketing is a continuous process. If you imagine, for example, an entrepreneur starting up a business from scratch, then you can identify the different stages that must occur to ensure a successful operation.

Identify and research the market

First the successful entrepreneur will have identified a gap in the market. This means that a customer need that is not currently being met has been identified. Market research may uncover such gaps, but often it is simply a good idea that is then developed. Market research is essential to find out if consumers are receptive to the idea.

Product development

The next step is to develop the product, including its name or 'brand'. The product must have some quality that sets it apart from the competition – this is known as the unique selling proposition (USP). The product must have a price, it must be promoted so that the public knows about it, and the distribution channels must be determined. This stage can be summarised as the development of the marketing mix, and this will be considered in more detail later in this chapter.

'After-sales service'

If the marketing process has been effective, then sales will occur, but with the focus on customer satisfaction after-sales service becomes an important part of the process. Some organisations are proactive and telephone their customers after they have bought a product to ensure they are satisfied with it. This is a simple task for travel agents who can telephone their customers on return from their holiday and ask if they enjoyed it. The customer will be impressed by the personal touch and is likely to return to the agent to book again.

Research must take place at every stage of the marketing process to ensure that customer needs are being met. Constant monitoring of the marketing activities should also be a priority.

The organisation of marketing

Some companies think that, by employing a marketing manager, they are practising marketing, but this is not the case. Marketing must be a way of doing business that pervades the whole organisation. Every member of the company must understand that customer needs are a priority. This means that the marketing manager must have senior status and must meet regularly with other senior personnel to discuss objectives and strategy. The role of marketing personnel differs from one company to another – some job specifications are wholly concerned with collecting and analysing data on customers and the market. Others stress the importance of external communication and the public relations role.

Many large companies have marketing departments, but it is not necessary to have specific marketing personnel to practise the philosophy of

KEY TERMS

Gap in the market: a customer need that has not been met.

Intangible: cannot be physically touched, e.g. a holiday.

Unique selling proposition (USP): something special about the product that makes it stand out from the competition.

Seasonality: demand changes according to the time of the year.

Brand: the name given to a product or service that allows the consumer to identify it.

marketing. As long as the whole company is focussed on customer needs, the marketing concept is being applied.

The following organisation chart shows how the marketing function is organised in Canvas Holidays. Note that the Marketing Director reports directly to the Managing Director. You can also see the responsibilities of the marketing department.

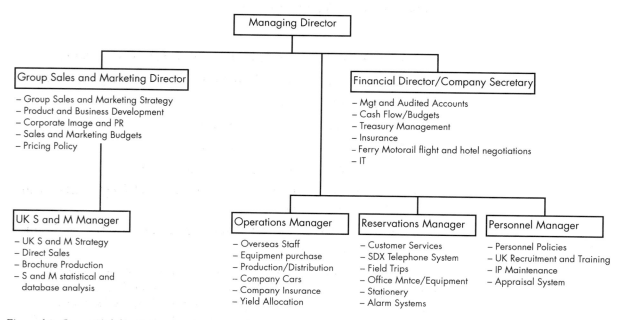

Figure 4.3 *Canvas Holidays Ltd. senior management team*

ACTIVITY

Collect the appointments pages of some national newspapers. The Sunday papers have relevant supplements and the dailies have one edition per week containing marketing appointments. Find at least four examples of marketing posts. Compare the advertisements, making notes under the following headings:

- main responsibilities of the post
- salary and benefits on offer
- education requirements
- experience requirements
- skills and knowledge required (e.g. numerate, knowledge of Excel)
- person specification (type of person, e.g. enthusiastic, outgoing)

When you have made these notes, select the job that interests you the most and say why it appeals to you.

PROFILE *Marketing Officer at Magic Holidays*

Magic Holidays is a tour operator specialising in activity holidays in the Red Sea area.

Name: **Judith Simmons**

Job title: **Marketing Officer**

Reporting to: **Marketing Manager**

Key tasks:

- **Implement marketing plan as directed by Marketing Manager.**
- **Develop strategies for implementation by marketing assistants.**
- **Oversee brochure production.**
- **Maximise promotional opportunities.**
- **Send out and monitor press releases.**
- **Maintain media relations and exhibition work.**
- **Oversee the co-ordination of information about Magic Holidays for inclusion in directories.**
- **Oversee marketing research and analysis in conjunction with the marketing manager.**

Judith has a Vocational A Level in Business Studies and a degree in Marketing from Huddersfield University. Before coming to Magic Holidays, she worked as a seasonal courier for Canvas Holidays, achieving a supervisory position. She hopes to attain a management position at Magic Holidays or elsewhere within the industry. She comments about her job: 'No two days are the same. I work long hours and it's often chaotic, but I love it!'

ACTIVITY

Carry out an interview with someone who works in marketing. This might be someone who works at your college who will talk to your group or it might be someone at your work placement or part-time job.

Find out how marketing is structured in their company. Find out what their job entails and what qualifications and experience were needed to get the job. Present your findings to the rest of your group for comparison.

Marketing objectives

Objectives are goals – they describe what the company is trying to achieve. It is important to have objectives so that the company knows where it is heading and what business it is in. For example, Virgin Atlantic does not consider itself to be just in the travel business but also in the entertainment business, entertaining customers whilst getting them from A to B.

Mission statements

It is common practice for a company to sum up its goals in a mission statement. This is a short statement, perhaps a few lines long, which states what it hopes to achieve in the next three to five years. The mission statement is usually published in company literature. You would expect there to be some mention of customer service in the mission statement, rather than the emphasis being on profit. The mission statement is useful as it defines the company's purpose and makes it clear to all employees.

The World Tourism Organisation's (WTO) global mission statement is:

❝ To support sustainable tourism development yielding wealth, creating employment, and promoting better understanding between races, religions, and human beings worldwide. ❞

'Yielding wealth' relates to the creation of wealth for nations where tourism is developed, it does not mean wealth for the WTO.

The English Tourism Council's (ETC) mission statement is:

❝ We will drive forward the quality, competitiveness and wise growth of England's tourism, by providing intelligence, setting standards, creating partnerships and ensuring coherence. ❞

These statements are fairly complex, but a mission statement need not be. Compare the above statements with that of Virgin Express that follows:

❝ Our mission is to make air travel the most simple, convenient and inexpensive form of transport in Europe. ❞

Some organisations now issue a vision statement in addition to a mission statement. This is a statement of very ambitious goals which the organisation would like to achieve, but it recognises that they are long-term and not likely to be achieved in a three to five year period.

The company objectives will reflect the company mission statement, but will be much more specific. Objectives may be strategic (general) and operational (broken down to specific targets). Examples of strategic objectives include:

- increasing sales
- increasing profits
- increasing market share
- reducing costs.

Each of these is valid but begs the question of how are they to be achieved? This is where managers must set very specific objectives for

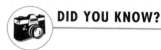

DID YOU KNOW?

The English Tourism Council is funded by the government and in turn, the ETC funds Regional Tourist Boards. As funding has been cut over the years the Tourist Information Offices have to find ways of raising income. They do this by opening souvenir shops and selling the services of guides. This means marketing skills have become more important to them.

each sector of the business. These objectives may be expressed in terms of the marketing mix. The marketing mix is the term used to describe the company goals for product, price, promotion and place. For example, a tour operator may set the objective of increasing the distribution of its brochures to new travel agents by 30%, with the ultimate objective of increasing sales. This objective would be part of the place mix.

Setting strategic objectives

To help set objectives, marketers should use the SMART approach. This means that objectives must be: specific, measurable, achievable, realistic and time constrained.

The ETC reflects its mission in its objectives. These objectives are SMART, as we will see. Try the SMART approach on setting your own targets during your course.

Example of objectives

The following is an extract from an ETC publication *Framework for Action*. It relates to one of the ETC's objectives derived from its mission statement:

❝ The ETC will report annually on progress made by RTBs, other agencies, the tourism industry and itself in delivering the strategy at the annual Tourism Summit to be established by the DCMS. ❞

A report will be made as follows.

- It is specific.
- It is measurable, progress will be detailed in the report.
- It is achievable within the time frame.
- It is realistic.
- It is time constrained as the report must be submitted to the annual Summit.

ACTIVITY

Read through the target above and note the abbreviations. Find out what they all stand for. Go to the ETC website and look for the other targets set out in *Framework for Action*.

ACTIVITY

Read this extract from *Travel Weekly* about Hungary. Write down the Hungarian National Tourist Office's main objective. State the measures that will be used to help achieve this objective. Analyse the targets according to the SMART approach. Say why each target is smart or not.

Hungary sets target of 500,000 visitors

THE HUNGARIAN National Tourist Office is launching a £300,000 advertising campaign in the UK next year with the aim of attracting 500,000 British visitors a year by 2003.

The HNTO expects 250,000 visitors from the UK this year, up from 213,000 in 1998. Some 85% of all visitors go to the capital, Budapest.

Deputy secretary of tourism Peter Kraft said the UK advertising budget for 2000 will be about four times bigger than this year.

It will be spent on advertising on 750 London buses – which will carry the slogan 'Hungary welcomes Britain' from January 1 – and adverts on Carlton TV. Also, August 20 has been set aside as Hungarian Day in the Millennium Dome.

Kraft admitted that the visitor target is ambitious, but said he was confident it could be achieved. "There is a lot of interest generally in eastern Europe, and Hungarian tourism is changing dramatically, with new restaurants and new and upgraded hotels in Budapest," he said.

Four Seasons, Le Meridien, Hilton and Holiday Inn are opening properties in the city over the next two years, while the first five-star hotel outside Budapest has just opened in Sasvar, 120 km from the capital. It cost $10 m to develop.

Kraft added that Budapest will be pitching to host the ABTA convention in 2001 and 2002.

"We hosted the convention in 1990 and saw a big increase in visitors as a result," he added.

Source: Travel Weekly, 17 November 1999

External influences on the marketing environment

PEST and SWOT analyses

Having determined its objectives, the travel and tourism organisation will implement them through the development of the marketing mix. Before this takes place, there must be a thorough analysis of the external influences which affect the company's operation. This is known as an environmental audit or PEST analysis, where PEST stands for: Political, Economic, Social and Technological influences.

These influences are sometimes beyond the control of the company management. In other circumstances they may be able to exert some control by lobbying through membership of an organisation, which exists to support travel and tourism businesses. We will look at some examples of these organisations later in this section.

The company must also undertake a thorough analysis of internal factors affecting operations. The strengths, weaknesses, opportunities and threats of the company are examined – this is known as a SWOT analysis. Many of the opportunities and threats will become apparent when the PEST analysis is carried out.

You need to understand how to carry out these analyses and how to make use of the information gathered. We will begin by looking at some examples of external factors that might currently affect travel and tourism companies.

Figure 4.4 *Ryanair advert protesting against government Air Passenger Duty*

Source: Ryanair/Sunday Times, 21 November 1999

KEY TERM

Lobbying: seeking to influence MPs on behalf of the industry.

Political factors

These often relate to changes in legislation introduced by the government. An area of contention is the levy of Air Passenger Duty on all flights. Currently, this adds £10 to the cost of an air ticket. Many airlines are unhappy about this tax and fear that the government may raise it further. Ryanair's attitude to the tax is clearly expressed in their advertising (see Figure 4.4).

Airlines lobby parliament to protest about the tax and prevent it rising any further. They send representatives to MPs to put forward the point-of-view of the industry. Another lobbying campaign, that took place in 1999, concerned the abolition of duty free sales within Europe. This campaign was unsuccessful and duty free finished in June 1999.

DID YOU KNOW?

The abolition of duty free had a big effect on sales for cross channel ferry companies who depended on duty free sales for much of their income. It also meant lost sales for airlines and for airport terminal shops.

DID YOU KNOW?

In South Africa in 1998, 82 people were killed in taxi wars. Taxi firms were hiring hit men to kill off their rivals and get rid of the competition.

KEY TERMS

Euro: the new currency introduced in Europe.

Euro zone: the 11 European Union countries who are adopting the euro.

Tour operators have to be aware of the political situation in their destinations. You may remember that some tourists were kidnapped and shot in the Yemen in 1999. This kind of occurrence may deter tour operators from using a destination. It also presents problems as it is unexpected and cannot be planned for. The war in Kosovo had an impact for holiday-makers, even though it was not a holiday destination. Air traffic controllers had to divert aircraft away from the air space for safety reasons and this meant delays occurred at airports.

Trying to monitor political changes is a very difficult business. Help is available through organisations like ABTA (Association of British Travel Agents), who keep their members informed of developments in the industry. The ETC will also represent the tourism industry to the government.

Economic factors

Changes in taxes affect tourism, as they can raise costs. Rises in interest rates affect a company's ability to repay its loans. The exchange rate can also dramatically affect a company's costs. For example, a tour operator with contracted accommodation in Spain will pay the hotelier in pesetas. A weak pound will mean less pesetas in the exchange and increased costs to the tour operator. The introduction of the Euro will have implications for businesses. The UK is not currently a member of the 'euro zone' (the countries that have agreed to adopt the euro). Until we join, the euro will be a foreign currency in the UK. However, a single euro currency in the eleven countries which have adopted it, will operate from July 2002.

Travel and tourism businesses will be affected when they have customers who come from euro zone countries and when they market their services in the euro zone. Companies are preparing by making sure that their financial systems can accept euros and by opening euro bank accounts. There is no doubt that there will be pressure on UK travel and tourism countries to trade in this currency.

Changes in taxes always affect prices. Tourists travelling to Australia, for example, will find that their trip is more expensive as the Australian government has introduced a new Goods and Services Tax (see Figure 4.5). Tour operators may lose business if tourists are aware of the increase and concerned about it.

New tax for Oz travellers

GETTING STUNG in Australia used to mean a close encounter with a spider or a jellyfish. Now the taxman is getting in on the act.

From July 1 next year – which means in good time for the start of the Sydney Olympics in September – a 10% Goods and Services Tax (GST) will be applied across the board, including drinks served in bars, meals in restaurants, hotel rooms and tours. Everyone will be affected by the tax, but Australians will be compensated by cuts in their personal taxes that will amount to a total of almost £5 billion.

There will be a few items on the tourist's shopping list that are exempt. One will be international flights and onward domestic flights booked and paid for outside Australia, so visitors who plan ahead will be able to save themselves a few dollars.

Figure 4.5 'New tax for Oz travellers' article

Source: Sunday Times, *21 November 1999*

Social factors

You should now be aware that travel and tourism businesses operate in a rapidly changing market. It is important that marketers take note of social changes affecting their customers. We have seen that people are living longer and are more financially secure, due to pension funds. This 'grey' market is a target for tour operators, but tastes also change. Holiday-makers want to try new destinations. They are also interested in taking short breaks as well as the traditional summer holiday. These trends represent opportunities for the travel trade. Campers may prefer the luxury of a mobile home rather than a tent, therefore, camping tour operators must provide them.

The public is becoming increasingly aware of the dangers of sun bathing and the links with skin cancer, If, in the future, they do not want to sunbathe, what are they going to do on holiday? There has already been a great increase in activity holidays and in cultural tourism, where excursions to sites of interest, museums and galleries are included. Our culture is influenced by the media – films make us aware of places and encourage us to visit. The recent film *Hideous Kinky* featured Morocco and Figure 4.6 describes the increase in trips to Tunisia following the film *Star Wars: The Phantom Menace.*

Explore Tunisia by train

In the wake of this year's *Star Wars* mania, more and more people are visiting Tunisia, where key scenes in *The Phantom Menace* were filmed. But few realise that the best and cheapest way of seeing the country is by train. The cost of a return ticket between the resort of Hammamet and Tunis, for example, is around £2 per person for the hour-long journey. First-class seats are just £4 return!

Figure 4.6 The influence of the media on travel and tourism

Source: Woman and Home

Technological factors

This is probably the area of greatest change, with rapid changes in technology. Consider all the new developments that the 1990s have seen. The creation of the Channel Tunnel meant competition for ferry operators on cross channel routes. Ferry companies might have to move their services to different locations, for example, crossings to Ireland, to compensate for lost business in the Channel. Aircraft are being developed that will hold many hundreds of passengers, presenting economies of scale to airlines and tour operators. It is not really necessary to have a pilot when flying can be fully computerised, although it is debatable whether many of us would be happy flying without one. Systems have been developed for tourists to hire cars from a vending machine, where payment is made and the keys are collected, the car is found in the car park, without any personal contact. Companies watch all technological advancements carefully and adapt accordingly.

The Internet presents a great opportunity to tour operators and airlines who are all developing and promoting on line booking systems. At the same time, travel agents are under threat from the Internet. If we can research on the web, see 'virtual' destinations, choose and book our holiday, why visit the travel agent? Those agencies who survive will be those who are ready for these changes and adapt their role so that they become advice centres with a high level of customer service rather than just a holiday booking service.

ACTIVITY

You have read many examples of PEST factors that can influence marketing in travel and tourism. Remember that these influences can occur at a local, national and international level.

Work with a partner and choose a tourist facility in your locality. This could be a tourist attraction, tourist office or a hotel. Describe the facility and its location. Consider its target market.

Now identify all the political, economic, social and technological influences that will impact on its future planning. You may need to research in local newspapers and government offices to find out what is happening in your area, as well as looking at the national outlook. Present your findings to your group and discuss the variations that occur.

It is usually easier to carry out the internal or SWOT analysis, as the information is readily available within the company. The factors to look at will include the financial status of the company, its market share, the quality of its products and its customer service. It is a good idea to carry out the SWOT in terms of the marketing mix as this will ensure a thorough analysis. The opportunities and threats should be apparent from the PEST analysis that was carried out previously. Having completed both these analyses, the company is in a position to make its marketing plans and adapt its marketing mix.

Example of a SWOT analysis

The easiest way to understand a SWOT analysis is to look at an example. Let us imagine a tourist attraction in the middle of England. It is located in beautiful countryside, yet near to major road networks. It has many thrilling rides that appeal to teenagers and has tamer rides which appeal to families with small children. Its facilities include restaurants, shops and it has recently added an hotel. It is regularly rated a top attraction in the country and its strengths are immediately apparent to you.

Its weaknesses are not so obvious, it is, after all, a successful organisation. However, many people complain about queues and when the weather is bad there is not as much for people to do. New rides are essential to attract repeat business but cost millions of pounds to build. You have probably visited somewhere like this yourself.

The opportunities and threats do not just come from inside the organisation. The hotel presents a wealth of opportunities in longer stay business and facilities for corporate entertainment. But, outside this company other attractions are developing, all over Europe, and making a play for the same market.

ACTIVITY

Think of a tourist facility or attraction in your locality. Visit and find out as much as you can about it. Carry out a SWOT and PEST analysis for this facility and then present the information in a table.

Market segmentation

The market for a product or service includes all customers and potential customers for that product. In order to effectively market their products, companies will segment the market. This means that the market is divided into groups of people with similar characteristics. Once the market is divided in this way, the company must then determine at which market it will aim. This is known as 'targeting', and the segment the company has chosen then becomes its 'target market'.

If a company chooses only one target market and specialises in a particular product, then it is practising what is known as 'niche marketing'. An example of this would be a company offering diving holidays, which are, by definition, offered to divers. It is more usual for a company to offer several different products, each of which is aimed at a particular market.

The example from First Choice Holidays in Figure 4.7 shows clearly how their different brands or brochures are targeted at different groups.

First Choice

This is the main volume brand (offering value for money holidays with a special emphasis on families)

Brochures produced within the First Choice brand are:

- Summer Sun
- Winter Sun
- Tropical
- All Inclusive
- Lakes and Mountains
- Flight Busters
- Greece
- Cyprus
- Turkey
- Portugal and Madeira
- Florida, USA and Canada
- Ski (incorporating SkiBound)

Sovereign

Our premium brand (provides stylish holidays with the emphasis on quality and service)

Brochures produced within the Sovereign product range include:

- Villa Collection
- Lakes and Mountains
- Summer Sunshine
- Winter Sunshine
- Cities
- Scanscape
- Small World

Eclipse Direct

This is our specialist direct sell brand, aimed at this small but important sector of the market providing an alternative for those choosing to shop direct from home.

Brochures within the Eclipse brand include:

- Direct Summer Sun
- Direct Winter Sun
- Direct Flights

Figure 4.7 Brochures offered by First Choice Holidays

There are many ways of segmenting the market. It is important to remember that an organisation will use not just one of these methods, but several, to draw up a detailed profile of the typical customer.

Demographic segmentation

Demographics is the study of the make-up of the population. Demographic trends illustrate how the population is changing. Factors that affect the make-up of the population are the birth rate and the life expectancy of people. When the market is segmented demographically, people are grouped according to one or more of the following:

- age
- sex
- race
- family life cycle

DID YOU KNOW?

The total population of the UK is 59 million and there are slightly more females than males.

The family life cycle refers to a person's stage in life. It is categorised as follows:

- young singles
- young married people
- full nest 1 (youngest child under 6)
- full nest 2 (youngest child 6 or over)
- full nest 3 (older, but still dependent children)
- empty nest 1 (children gone)
- empty nest 2 (children gone, parents retired)
- solitary survivor

These life stages do not always relate to age, for example, full nest 1 could be a couple in their twenties or forties. They are used in segmentation, as our needs and spending habits differ according to this life cycle. Empty nest 2, for example, is very important to the cruise market. You might think these categories are rather old fashioned, after all, not everyone gets married. The stages are, however, still relevant.

ACTIVITY

Work with a partner and try to think of travel and tourism products or services that are targeted demographically. An easy example to start you off is 18 to 30 holidays. Try to find an example for each stage of the family life cycle.

Socio-economic segmentation

Here the population is divided according to socio-economic grouping (SEG), income or occupation (see Table 4.1).

These groupings are based on occupation, not income. Researchers and advertisers use these classifications extensively.

DID YOU KNOW?

Royalty are not included in the socio-economic classifications. They are right off the scale!

Geographic segmentation

This is fairly simple to establish for travel agents and tour operators, when they want to know the geographic location of their existing customers, as their addresses will be held on the customer database. A travel agent or tourist attraction can establish its catchment area by researching where its customers have travelled from. The catchment area is the geographic area from which customers are drawn, for example, a tourist board in a destination will be interested to find out which countries visitors come from. This is expressed as the origin of tourists.

SOCIAL GRADE	SOCIAL STATUS	OCCUPATION
A	Upper middle class	Higher managerial, administrative or professional
B	Middle class	Intermediate managerial, administrative or professional
C1	Lower middle class	Supervisory or clerical, and junior managerial, administrative or professional
C2	Skilled working class	Skilled manual workers
D	Working class	Semi-skilled and unskilled manual workers
E	Those at lowest level of subsistence	State pensioners or widows (no other earner), casual or lowest grade workers.

Table 4.1 *Socio economic groupings*

Source: National Readership, Survey, ONS

Needs of customers will vary according to their geographic location, for example, airlines operating from London airports must consider the travel needs of customers far from London. Virgin offer connecting flights from regional airports and free limousines for business class customers. Companies that operate in international markets must have their sales literature professionally translated to appeal to different nationalities.

 **DID YOU KNOW?**

Over one fifth of European visitors to Britain come from France. The French are, after all, our nearest neighbours. France is the major destination for UK travellers also.

ACORN

ACORN (a classification of residential neighbourhoods) is a sophisticated method of segmentation that can be used for profiling buyer behaviour in different geographic locations of the UK. There are six basic categories, which are further subdivided into groups and neighbourhood types (see Figure 4.8). An area data report can be purchased from CACI Information Services (developers of ACORN) for any given area in the UK.

Categories	%Pop.	Groups	% Pop.
A Thriving	19.8	1 Wealthy achievers, suburban areas	15.1
		2 Affluent greys, rural communities	2.3
		3 Prosperous pensioners, retirement areas	2.3
B Expanding	11.6	4 Affluent executives, family areas	3.7
		5 Well-off workers, family areas	7.8
C Rising	7.5	6 Affluent urbanites, town and city areas	2.2
		7 Prosperous professionals, metropolitan areas	2.1
		8 Better-off executives, inner city areas	3.2
D Settling	24.1	9 Comfortable middle agers, mature home owning areas	13.4
		10 Skilled workers, home owning areas	10.7
E Aspiring	13.7	11 New home owners, mature communities	9.8
		12 White collar workers, better-off multi-ethnic areas	4.0
F Striving	22.8	13 Older people, less prosperous areas	3.6
		14 Council estate residents, better-off homes	11.6
		15 Council estate residents, high unemployment	2.7
		16 Council estate residents, greatest hardship	2.8
		17 People in multi-ethnic, low-income areas	2.1
Unclassified	0.5		0.5

Figure 4.8 The ACORN consumer targeting classification

Source: © CACI Limited, 1993 (Source: OPCS and GRO(S) © Crown Copyright 1991).
All rights reserved. ACORN is a registered trademark of CACI Limited.

Psychographic segmentation

This type of segmentation uses personality types, lifestyles and motivation to divide up the market. It is difficult to use accurately as it is not easy to measure someone's lifestyle. However, when it is done well, it can help in developing very effective marketing and advertising messages.

Many different methods of psychographic segmentation have been developed, an example being, the categorisation of Cross Cultural Consumer Characteristics, developed by the advertising agency Young and Rubicam. They suggest that the population can be divided into the following groups.

Mainstreamers

These are people who do not want to stand out from the crowd; who need to feel secure and will buy well-known products and services that they can trust.

Aspirers

This group aspires to success in life and want products and services which demonstrate that success, for example, designer brands or exotic holidays.

Succeeders

These people have already made it and they do not need to prove it. They will be looking for luxury and comfort and can afford to pay for it. They are likely to travel first class.

Reformers

A highly influential group, very well educated and the most likely to influence society. This group will be interested in eco tourism, due to their concern about the environment. They are also likely to travel independently rather than taking a package holiday.

Individualists

Determined to be different, this group is the most likely to try something new. They will dislike package holidays as they will hate to be part of a crowd.

PROFILE *Le Sport*

This resort unashamedly appeals to people who are looking for luxury and pampering on their holiday. The customer will be provided with luxury accommodation and an array of sporting activities. A health and relaxation centre also offers all kinds of treatments. In addition, the tourist is buying an all-inclusive package, so they do not have to consider how to get to their destination or even where to eat once they get there.

Le SPORT

All-Inclusive

◆ ◆ ◆ ◆

FREE WEEK – 2 FOR 1

FREE WEDDING

HONEYMOON SPECIAL

EARLY BOOKING OFFER

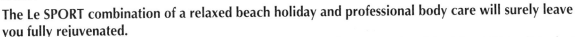

The Le SPORT combination of a relaxed beach holiday and professional body care will surely leave you fully rejuvenated.

Le SPORT is set in quiet seclusion at Cap Estate on the north-western tip of the island. This all-inclusive hotel offers all the amenities you would expect from a Caribbean beach resort, but with an emphasis on health, activity and relaxation. At the Oasis (access via a steep hill) you can enjoy a wide range of treatments such as seaweed wrap, massage, facials, aromatherapy and a full range of professionally taught fitness and relaxation classes.

Facilities

Swimming pool • Exercise pool • Hot & cold plunge pools • Open-air restaurant • Two bars • Tennis • Volleyball • Table tennis • Bicycle tours • Aqua aerobics • Archery • Fencing • Golf (at the 9-hole Cap Estate course, 5 mins away) • The Oasis – offers a full range of health treatments for adults only • Relaxation classes with stress management, yoga, Tai Chi and meditation • Shop • Watersports including scuba diving, snorkelling, waterskiing & windsurfing • Nightly entertainment.

Accommodation

Luxury Rooms (sleeping up to 2 adults & 1 child) with two twin or one four poster kingsize bed, air-conditioning, bath, shower, bathrobes, hairdryer, minifridge, clockradio, balcony/patio & partial seaview.

Premier Oceanview Rooms are as above but have a partial view of the sea and a pool view.

Luxury Oceanview Rooms are as above but have panoramic ocean views.

Luxury Oceanfront Rooms are as above but have marble floors and directly overlook the beach.

Meals Basis AI = All Inclusive

Average Transfer Time Approx 1 hr 30 mins

All-Inclusive Features

The all-inclusive features at Le Sport include:
Breakfast, lunch & dinner • Unlimited drinks by the glass (excluding champagne) • All land sports, inc. archery, bicycles, fencing, tennis, table tennis & volleyball • Watersports, inc. snorkelling, sunfish sailing, waterskiing & windsurfing (excl. deep sea fishing) • Scuba diving instruction • 9 hole golf course, golf school & green fees at Cap Estate 5 minutes away • Yoga, meditation, tai chi, aromatherapy & sauna • Individualised relaxation, fitness & restorative beauty programme • New therapeutic massage and reflexology facility at an approx charge of US$30 (excluding under 15 year olds) • Nightly entertainment • All gratuities.

Source: British Airways Holidays

PROFILE *Cresta Holidays*

Cresta Holidays have produced client profiles to help travel agents target sales of French holidays more effectively. They have used geographic regions of France as a basis and added different elements of segmentation.

Pas de Calais

Appeals to Mr and Mrs Weekender who live in the south of England. They are happy with a two star hotel, as they go for good food and a chance to explore colourful markets and cobbled streets. They might use Eurotunnel to take a short break.

Brittany

Appeals to the young family, mum, dad and two teenagers, who go for a week self-catering. Travel is during school holidays and is by ferry.

France's west coast

Popular with Mr and Mrs Sandcastle, who want to go to the beach for a couple of weeks. As they have small children, they prefer to take the ferry and drive so they can stock up the car.

Dordogne

Mr and Mrs Francophile, empty nesters, are to be found here. They want to do lots of sightseeing and wine tasting on holiday. They can travel off peak.

ACTIVITY

Study the two hotel descriptions below. For each one, draw up a profile of the target market. Remember to use demographics, socio-economic, geographic and psychographic segmentation. Use the hotel descriptions to help you write a summary of why you believe the holiday is targeted to your profiled customer.

PALMA NOVA

Or should we say "Super Nova" because there's an explosion of activities at this resort. With its massive beach and impressive water sports, it's no wonder it's a family favourite among the British. If vigorous activity is not your thing, shelter can be found among the bars and cafes or the beautiful marina and the nautical club. Palma Nova is a resort that offers something for all ages.

"BARS AND BEACHES"

In an ideal location about 60 m from the white sandy beach of Palma Nova, we discovered the Hotel Bermuda. The pool is one of the first things you notice as you arrive as it is right by reception, although you are so close to the beach, the choice of where you develop the tan is entirely up to you. The style of the hotel lends itself to a Majorcan theme with furnishings, tapestries and paintings continuing the idea. The rooms are a good size for such a central location and all have a balcony. The hotel offers live music a few times a week but there's no entertainment programme, being so well located, we assume you'll make your own.

Source: Virgin Holidays

Marketing research

Marketing research is a vital part of the marketing process. Without it how would marketers identify customer needs? How would a company know how its performance matched up to its competitors? How would market trends be identified? Marketing research must go on continuously throughout the marketing process. Depending on the complexity of the research to be carried out, a company might carry out the research itself or contract a research agency to do it for them. Research might be carried out in any of the following areas:

- product research
- price research
- promotional research
- place research
- market research

 DID YOU KNOW?

'Research is the collection and analysis of data from a sample of individuals or organisations relating to their characteristics, behaviour, attitudes, opinions or possessions.'

Source: Market Research Society

Product research

If the product is tangible, the research will involve testing the product, and making sure it performs as it should. For example, new cars are stringently tested on all safety aspects. A tour operator might carry out research into new destinations with a view to adding them to the product range.

Price research

It is important that the price charged for a product represents good value for both parties: the seller and the consumer. This research might include finding out what competitors charge for similar products or asking consumers what they are prepared to pay for a new product or service. Travel agencies are very conscious of deals offered by their competitors and will often match them.

Promotional research

Television advertisements, in particular, are very expensive to make. Research into the consumer's reaction to an advertisement will be carried out at each stage of its development. Researchers also test advertisement recall, showing a series of advertisements to a group of consumers and then asking questions about what they have seen.

Place research

This includes researching the different means by which the product reaches the consumer. For example, an airline might research into use of the Internet to determine whether sales can be made on line.

Market research

You will note that the term 'marketing research' has been used as an umbrella term for this section. Market research should be used when research into a specific market is undertaken. For example, a tour operator may need to know the size of the market for holidays to Florida, and then the size of their market share in relation to other operators.

ACTIVITY

Match up the following examples of research to the different categories of research areas outlined before:

A hotelier conducts research amongst it fitness suite users to find out what kind of equipment should be added to the gym.

A newly established tour operator collects data on travel agencies with a view to contacting them to place their holiday brochures.

An airline gives an employee the regular task of telephoning competitive airlines and asking for quotes for airfares on popular routes.

A tourist attraction monitors the local press and copies and records any features or mentions relating to their attraction.

A holiday company asks all its home-bound customers to complete a questionnaire. A question is added asking holiday-makers which other operators they have travelled with in the last two years.

The Marketing Research Process

Marketers must develop a logical procedure for research to ensure it is carried out effectively. The process involves the following stages:

1 Definition of problem.
2 Determination of research strategy.
3 Collection of data.
4 Analysis and interpretation of data.
5 Reporting on findings.

Definition of problem

There must be a reason for research. It may be triggered by a downturn in sales, for example, or by a need to develop the product range. An airline may find that business class sales are in decline. Management may suspect this is due to the competition from 'no frills' airlines, but will undertake research to test this theory.

Determination of research strategy

How is the research going to be carried out? Where will it be carried out? Who is going to do it? When will it be done? Who will the respondents be?

Quantitative data: facts and figures.

Qualitative data: attitudes and opinions.

Collection of data

What types of data should be collected? Quantitative data consists of easily measured facts and figures, for example, the number of visitors to a stately home in one day. Qualitative data is more difficult to obtain and analyse because it covers the consumer's attitudes and opinions to products. For example, we may know that 1,000 visitors came to the stately home in one day, but how do we know what their opinion of the experience was?

Analysis and interpretation of data

It is possible to analyse research data by hand and indeed you might do this when you carry out research for assignments. However, it would be unusual for a company to work in this way. Computer analysis is the most common technique and enables cross-tabulation of data. It is not usually possible to analyse qualitative data by computer due to the diversity of responses.

Reporting on findings

The findings should be reported in a formal written report. The report should be concise and must include recommendations so that the relevant personnel can action the report. It may be that further research will be undertaken as a result of the report but this is quite usual. Appendices will be attached and will include the full findings, a copy of the original questionnaire, if used, and any relevant charts and tables. An introduction will explain how the research was carried out.

Types of data

Secondary data

This refers to data that already exists and is available to the researcher. It may be internal or external to the organisation. Do not be confused by the term 'secondary' – it means second-hand information, but you do this research *first*. This type of research is sometimes called desk research, as it is easy to do it at your desk, computer or in a library.

Sources of secondary data include: internal and external.

Internal

- sales figures
- customer database
- costs
- profits
- load factors (airline)
- productivity of staff

External

- World Tourism Organisation (WTO) – statistics on worldwide tourism.

- Tourism organisations – e.g. Caribbean Tourism Organisation statistics and country facts.
- British Tourist Authority (BTA) – various statistics and reports.
- UK International Passenger Survey – statistics on inbound and outbound tourism.
- Central Intelligence Agency (CIA) Yearbook – a wealth of information on different countries.
- Cultural trends and social trends.
- Keynotes and Mintel – available to subscribers only, your library may subscribe, check this out. Keynotes and Mintel provide reports on different products and services.
- Government statistics published by HMSO (Her Majesty's Stationery Office) – available in libraries or on line.
- National Readership Survey – this gives readership figures for newspapers and other publications.
- www.bized.ac.uk – this site will help you find company information and government statistics.
- www.cabinet-office.gov.uk – find out government policies and link to other government sites.
- www.mapquest.com – an interactive maps site.
- www.travel.world.co.uk – an on line version of a travel agency, with links to UK tour operators.
- Travel and Tourism Intelligence – produce reports relating to the industry.

ACTIVITY

Use the Internet to find out answers to the following questions. You will need to visit the government statistics site, BTA's Star UK, Eurotunnel and First Choice. In each case find the most up-to-date information.

1 Find out the figures for international tourism arrivals for the US.
2 Find out the top five (paid entry) tourist attractions for last year.
3 How many long holidays (4 nights or more) were taken overseas?
4 Find out what percentage of the UK population is over retirement age.
5 How many people visited museums in the UK in the last year?
6 How many divorces were there last year?
7 What percentage of people in the UK attend a cinema at least once a year?
8 Which companies are in the First Choice portfolio?
9 How many cars and coaches can each Eurotunnel passenger shuttle hold?
10 Find out how many passengers/cars used the 'Shuttle' through Eurotunnel last year.
11 What awards has Eurotunnel won?

Secondary data: data that already exists, you just have to find it.

Primary data: data that you research for the first time.

Primary data

This is data that has been collected for the first time. Once desk research has been carried out, it should be apparent what further information is needed. Then, primary or field research will be carried out. There are many ways of undertaking primary research, some of which will be examined in this section.

Methods of collecting primary data

Questionnaires may be carried out person-to-person, by telephone or by post. There are many advantages of using a questionnaire to conduct a personal interview:

- The interviewer has the opportunity to explain any point that the respondent does not understand.
- The response rate is much higher than the other methods.
- The interviewer can use prompts if the respondent is not able to answer straightaway. This means the interviewer will be armed with a series of cards listing possible responses. These can be shown to the respondent to aid recall.
- Disadvantages are that personal interviews are time-consuming and expensive. Many interviewers must be employed to carry them out.

A telephone survey is fairly easy to administer. Many calls can be undertaken in a short period of time and interviewers can be easily supervised. The response rate is fairly good, however, people can hang up if they get bored. It is important, therefore, that the questionnaire is not too long and is varied enough to retain the respondent's interest. Interviewers have to rely on verbal contact; there are no visual prompts.

A postal questionnaire is the cheapest type of survey, however, the response rate is fairly low. It also relies on finding the most appropriate database to reach the correct target group.

Tour operators and hoteliers often provide questionnaires for self-completion by customers. These may be left in hotel rooms or may be given out on homeward bound flights.

DID YOU KNOW?

A recent MORI survey showed that 87% of holiday-makers were familiar with the ABTA (Association of British Travel Agents) name. This is because ABTA members display the logo in their windows and brochures.

Designing a questionnaire

Follow these rules:

1 Before you write any questions, make a list of what you want to find out.
2 Go through the list and discard anything that is not absolutely essential.
3 Go through the list again and try to order the information required in a sensible way. (continued on page 255)

QUESTIONNAIRE

Interviewer: Hello, my name is .... I am doing research into visitor attendance at Slaith Hall. Would you mind answering a few questions?

1. How many visits have you made to Slaith Hall in the last year?
   One
   Two
   Three   *closed question*
   More than three

2. What attracted you today to Slaith Hall? (Tick all that apply)
   Lambing event
   Jazz event
   Visit to the house
   Visit to the gardens
   Other (write in)

3. Have you visited the restaurant today?
   Yes
   No   *filter question*
   If no go to question 5

4. The service in the restaurant is excellent. Do you agree or disagree with this statement?
Strongly agree ☐   Agree ☐   Don't know ☐   Disagree ☐   Strongly disagree ☐

5. Do you recall seeing any press advertisements for Slaith Hall in the last month?

(Write in) _____

(If no response, show prompt card with examples of newspaper adverts)   *prompt*

6. Do you have any comments you would like to make about Slaith Hall?

_____   *open question*

Male   Female

Age   16–25_____   26–35_____   36–45_____   46–55_____   over 55_____

Occupation _____   SEG _____   *classification data*

Thank you for your help, goodbye.

Figure 4.9 Example of a questionnaire

ACTIVITY

Look at the example of a questionnaire following. What do you think are the objectives of this research? Analyse the types of questions asked in the questionnaire. Are they open-ended or closed questions? What are the reasons for using these question types?

Note that there is no classification data. What is the disadvantage of omitting this data? What other comments can you make about this questionnaire?

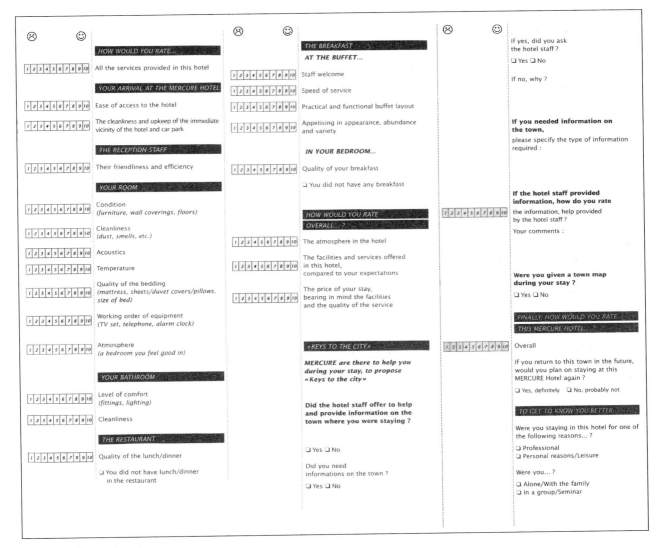

Example of a questionnaire

4 Write the questions, moving from general questions to more specific ones.

5 Never ask more than one thing in a question.

6 Avoid bias in questions.

7 Try to use closed questions, i.e. those with a limited range of answers. These will be easier to analyse.

8 Use open questions if you need to investigate the respondent's opinions.

9 Use a filter question if the respondent does not need to answer every question. This consists of an instruction to the respondent. For example 'If you answer YES to question 4, proceed to question 7'.

10 Always put classification data at the end. This is important, as it is not a good idea to start your questionnaire by asking age and occupation. The exception to this rule is when you need to establish whether the respondent fits your quota. Classification data includes: gender, age group and occupation of the respondent. The occupation will be used later to determine their socio-economic group.

ACTIVITY

Design a questionnaire to find out what activities your fellow students got up to at the weekend. Find out what sports and social activities were undertaken and where. Try to include some of the features that have been described. Above all keep your questionnaire simple.

'Mystery shopper' method

This is a method of observational research. It is regularly used by the *Travel Trade Gazette* to report on the performance of travel agencies. Companies may also use the method themselves to check on customer service in branches. The 'mystery shopper' goes to the branch and asks for information, then reports back on the standard of service received. It is a very simple and yet effective research method.

Focus groups

It is easy to assume that primary research means questionnaires. However, there are many other interesting ways of collecting primary data, a focus group being one. A group of people is invited to an office or even a home and led through a discussion by a group leader, who may be a trained psychologist. The intention is to discover the group's attitudes toward a product or service. For example, an airline wishing to improve its business service may invite a group of frequent business travellers to the discussion. An incentive will be given for attending, perhaps a small payment. Sometimes the discussion is observed by researchers or recorded. Some useful interview techniques exist, which can be incorporated into a focus group discussion:

● **Playing the devil's advocate** – we all know people who do this. The group leader deliberately expresses an extreme point-of-view so that the group will react and reveal their own opinions.

● **Sympathetic silence** – when a group member expresses a view, do not respond. Wait with a sympathetic expression on your face, and they are sure to expand. Watch out for chat show hosts doing this.

- **Sophisticated naiveté** – the leader pretends not to understand the point being made. Again, the respondent will have to expand.
- **Closed book technique** – towards the end of the interview, the leader switches off the tape recorder or closes their notebook. The group relaxes, thinking the session is over. This is when they may reveal interesting attitudes, as they think no one is really listening.

In-depth discussion

This is similar to a focus group, but takes place on a one-to-one basis. As there is only one respondent at a time, it is expensive and the results may also be unreliable. Several interviews need to be carried out to overcome this.

Projective techniques

These techniques use psychology and are useful for attitude research. A problem of research is that people do not always tell the truth; they prefer to give answers which make a good impression. For example, if you carry out research asking people how much they drink per week, they are likely to significantly reduce the amount imbued. Projective techniques get around this problem by asking about someone else!

Our first example is the 'third person test'. The classic example of this is the research into instant coffee in the 1950s. Two groups of housewives took part in the research and each group was given a shopping list. The lists were identical apart from one item. One group had instant coffee on the list; the other ground coffee. The women were asked to describe the woman who had written the list. The instant coffee group said the list writer was poor, slovenly, and a bad homemaker. The ground coffee group found their shopper to be caring and a good homemaker. The research revealed the housewives' attitudes to instant coffee.

Another example of a projective technique is a word association test. This is useful for testing brand names. The respondents simply say whatever comes immediately into their heads on hearing your prompt word. For example, if you were thinking of calling your new holiday company 'Cyclone', word association might reveal some disturbing connotations.

Our last example is a technique known as 'story completion'. The first sentence or two of a story are given and the respondent must complete the story. Again, this will reveal the respondent's attitudes.

KEY TERMS

Prompts: a device used by an interviewer to aid recall.

Respondent: the person answering the questionnaire.

ACTIVITY

Carry out a focus group discussion among fellow students. Decide who is going to lead the discussion. The leader should try to use some of the techniques described in the text.

It may be a good idea to designate a student as an observer. They can report back on how successfully the techniques are used and note the main points emanating from the discussion. The suggested research topic is: 'Young people's views on Ibiza as a tourist destination'. You can, of course, choose a different topic if you wish.

Sampling methods

It is often impossible to ask all the people whose views would be useful to respond to a survey. For example, a tour operator might wish to carry out a questionnaire on its customers' experiences on holiday. The total number of their customers is known as the **population**. If they did manage to question every single customer, this would be called a **census**. Due to the expense and difficulty involved in conducting a census, the company is likely to take a sample of customers. This sample should represent the whole body of customers, otherwise the research results will be biased.

Random probability sampling

With this method, every customer has an equal chance of being selected. The company would use their customer database as the source of respondents and a percentage of these would be selected at random and interviewed. When a national survey is required, respondents can be randomly selected from the electoral register.

Quota sampling

This is the most common form of sampling used in research. The respondents are not selected at random. The interviewer has a quota to fulfil, usually based on factors such as age, gender and socio-economic group. Quota sampling is appropriate where a survey is conducted among people with a common experience. For example, if the tour operator wants to question people about their Greek holidays, a random sample will not work, as it will come up with people from all holiday destinations.

Stratified random sampling

A random sample could be taken among the holiday-makers who went to Greece, and this is known as stratified random sampling. The population has been divided into strata, which are groups of people with similar characteristics.

The marketing mix

This term describes the key elements that an organisation uses to achieve its objectives and attract customers. These elements are commonly known as the four Ps:

- product
- price
- place
- promotion

The four Ps are interdependent. They must be carefully developed and balanced in order to meet the needs of the target market. It is, therefore, vital that the company has established the target market before determining the marketing mix.

Product

❛ A product is anything that can be offered to a market for attention, acquisition, use or consumption that might satisfy a want or need. It includes physical objects, services, persons, places, organisations and ideas ❜.

Source: Principles of Marketing, *Kotler and Armstrong*

This definition is useful, as it shows that a service is also considered to be a product, and, in travel and tourism, businesses are predominantly concerned with the marketing of services. The marketing for services may be different from that of a simple physical product as it is highly dependent on the people delivering the service. A fifth element, 'People' is, therefore, often added to the marketing mix for services.

Tangibility of product

A product can be tangible or intangible, or a combination of both. An example of a tangible product is a suitcase – you can touch it, pick it up, admire it and take it home with you. Having bought it, you own it. A visit to a theme park is an intangible product – you are buying a fun day out, full of thrills and excitement. All you take home with you are your memories and photographs. An airline seat can be both tangible and intangible – you can touch it, (you cannot take it home), but what you are hoping to buy is a comfortable travel experience, taking you from one place to another.

Product features

Another way of looking at products is to examine the product features and benefits. The product features represent the core value of the product. For example, the features or core of a package holiday are the accommodation and transport. There will be a whole range of added features, depending on the holiday chosen. These might include food, sports facilities and entertainment. The benefits on offer may be relaxation, the opportunity to see sights or to learn a new skill.

Companies are always looking for new features to add to their products to give further benefits to the customer and to maintain a competitive advantage. Thus, theme parks must introduce new rides, restaurants must offer new dishes and cinemas must sell ice cream and offer pre-booking facilities. Marketers hope to find a 'unique selling proposition' (USP), something that makes their product different and stand out from the competition.

KEY TERM

Tangible: can be physically touched.

Thomson unveils its new perks

THOMSON'S summer holidays for next year go on sale on July 29. Here are some examples of its new "reinvented package" approach:

- Late check-out rooms – varies by hotel, but costs between £20–£30.
- Fan and fridge hire from £1.50 a night.
- Premium seats from £30 short-haul; £60 on long-haul flights.
- Check-in the night before flying from the UK – £10 per person. Also, check-out at the hotel on "Platinum" holidays.

THE company is also extending the range of options in resorts, away from the traditional coach tours. They include swimming with dolphins, helicopter rides and hot-air balloon flights.

In the main Summer Sun brochure, extras include prebookable playpens, beach toys and nappy packs.

- Breakfast parties for children will also give parents some time alone. For between £2–£5, kids will be collected at 8 am and kept occupied with games, videos and other activities for two hours.

The breakfast breaks will feature in 32 resorts across the Mediterranean and Canary Islands. Holiday prices start at £259 per adult for a week-long stay in a one-bedroom apartment in Majorca.

- Thomson will also introduce pagers for parents who leave their children in crèches while they are out and about sightseeing.
- As with credit-card companies, Thomson has adopted gold, even platinum, labels in a marketing attempt to brand holidays – and charge top prices.
  "Gold hotel" service, for couples only, has been introduced in nine resorts in the Med and Canaries. Choice of 200 extras, including towels, pillows and interior design.
- The "Platinum" brochure, featuring hotels in the Canaries, boasts satellite TV and videos in the rooms – with extras including a double bed.

Figure 4.10 Newspaper extract showing how Thomson introduced new product features for the year 2000.

Source: The Times Weekend, *24 July 1999*

KEY TERMS

Core value: main product features.

USP: unique selling proposition.

Branding

The brand is the name that identifies the product, and it may suggest something about the product itself. Examples include the travel agency, Going Places, and the tour operator, First Choice. Conversely, other brand names, such as Thomson, do not suggest a type of product, but still work, as they have been established over many years and have built up a reputable image with consumers. Within these 'family brands', many other smaller brands are on offer.

Sometimes a company takes the decision to re-brand all its products. This usually occurs when a company is having problems and wishes to project a totally new image. A recent example was the introduction of the JMC brand by Thomas Cook, in 1999, which was marketed as 'A new and genuinely different approach to holidays'.

The product life cycle

This concept is used to show how a product moves through different stages in its life until it becomes obsolete. It is useful in marketing, as the stage of the life cycle will have an impact on how the product should be marketed. It is also important that a company has products in each stage of the life cycle. If all the products were in the stage of decline, a company would soon go out of business.

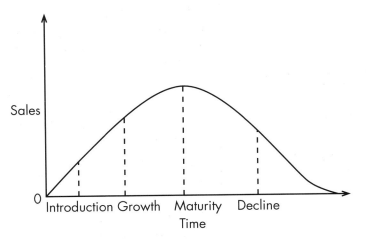

Figure 4.11 *Product life cycle*

1 **Introduction**

The launch of a new product is a very exciting, but tense period in its life. Consumers have never heard of the product, so a great deal has to be spent on advertising to let them know it exists. Developing the product will have involved an investment of both time and money. For these reasons, no profits are expected in the introduction stage. Rather, it is hoped that the product is successful and that some contribution to costs will be made. The type of people likely to buy the new product are 'innovators', that is, those who like to be the first to try something different. The price charged is often high – this appeals to innovators, who do not mind paying for exclusivity – and it helps to recoup costs. Some products never get beyond this stage.

2 **Growth**

Growth is the most profitable stage in the product's life cycle and companies are eager to reap these profits while they can. Word of mouth promotion is important as consumers hear about the new product and wish to try it. Competitors will rapidly enter the market, copying the new idea. Due to increased competition, it is important for companies to try and build up brand loyalty, and the promotional budget will be devoted to stressing the product's benefits over those of the competition. Internet services and mobile telephones are currently in growth stages of their life cycles.

DID YOU KNOW?

Nine out of ten new products fail.

3 Maturity

Competition is at its most intense at this stage. Weaker competitors will be squeezed out of the market. Debonair, one of the early low cost airlines, failed in 1999, in the face of aggressive competition. Marketing efforts are aimed at maintaining a competitive position. Sales promotions are common, often directed at dealers, in the form of incentives to sell the product. This might mean increased commission for travel agencies for tourism products. This stage of the cycle is usually the longest.

4 Decline

Sales and profits start to fall at this point. Marketers must recognise when products are likely to move into this stage, as they must decide if it is worth staying in the market. An organisation should be diversifying into other products or markets at the beginning of the decline stage, to ensure survival. It is sometimes possible to reap profits by staying with a product or service that other companies have abandoned.

5 Obsolescence

A product that is obsolete no longer exists.

Successful companies have products at each stage of the product life cycle. It is difficult to predict how long each stage will last, as many external factors affect the product's life. In travel and tourism the life cycle can be applied to products or destinations.

ACTIVITY

Draw the product life cycle. Try to determine which holiday destinations are in each stage.

Consider only the holiday destinations of UK outbound tourists and compare your ideas with other members of your group. Check your findings against BTA (British Tourist Authority) statistics on holiday destinations.

Repeat the exercise above, but instead of using holiday destinations, use types of holidays, for example, skiing or activity holidays.

KEY TERM

Brainstorming: a technique for generating new ideas.

New product development

New products are rarely brand new; they are usually a variation on what has gone before. The important thing is that the consumer detects 'newness', and, therefore, wants to try the new product. Companies go through several stages in developing their new ideas, carefully screening at each stage, in the hope of avoiding failure.

1 Idea generation

As many new ideas as possible are generated and these ideas may come from various sources. Employees are a useful source, especially those who have direct customer contact. 'Brainstorming' is a technique that is used to collect a diversity of ideas. This is where a group of people from the organisation generate all the ideas they can think of. No criticism of ideas is allowed; the purpose is quantity not quality at this early stage. It may be that the wildest ideas are those that eventually succeed.

2 Screening

All the ideas are screened to see if they help fulfil the company objectives. If not, they are abandoned, and some ideas will be left for further development.

3 Business analysis

Will the idea fit in with the product mix? How much will it cost? How much can it be sold for? Answering these questions helps determine if the product is likely to make a profit and how it will impact on sales of existing products. The development team must also consider whether the resources exist to make or supply the product. If not, can they be acquired? For example, a travel company may decide that offering trips to the island of St. Helena is a good idea. However, transport links to the island are very poor, with infrequent boats and no air links.

4 Product development

The product is actually made or a package is put together. The brand is determined and the packaging or brochure is decided on.

5 Test marketing

A true test market is where all aspects of the marketing mix are tried out together in one location. It is an expensive stage, but worthwhile if it avoids a full launch of a product that might fail. It may be that problems are identified that can easily be corrected before a full launch takes place.

6 Full launch

The product is fully launched on the public and hopefully succeeds.

Price

The second element of the four Ps of the marketing mix is pricing. Prices must be set that allow the company to meet its objectives. Incorrect pricing policies will mean the company fails to make a profit. The simplest approach to pricing is the 'cost plus' method. This is where the organisation calculates the costs of producing the product and adds a percentage for profit. Although this is simple, it is not a marketing approach to pricing and will not lead to long-term success. This is because it ignores the basic premise of marketing, identifying customer needs. Every approach to pricing should start with considering the principle of 'what is the customer prepared to pay?' There are many different strategies in pricing that a company can adopt. The strategy chosen for each product will depend on the stage in the product life cycle and the amount of competition in the market.

ACTIVITY

The following article describes a one day skiing trip, which is a new product from Airtours and is one of several day trips on offer. Read the article and answer the following questions:

- What is the core value of the product?
- What are the added features of the product?
- What are the benefits of the product?
- At whom is the product aimed?
- Why do you think Airtours developed this product?
- Do you think it will be a success or not? Give reasons for your answer.

03.45: Wake-up call – it seems like I've been asleep only five minutes. This better be worth it.

04.30: The cab arrives for Gatwick.

05.20: Check-in at the Airtours desk then wander off in a daze around duty-free shops.

06.45: We board the aircraft but I'm starving.

07.07: Take off – only seven minutes behind schedule. I discover I'm sat next to an extreme skier who's planning to tackle Chamonix's famous off-piste runs – I start to get a little nervous.

07.23: Bucks Fizz is served to calm my butterflies. How very civilised.

07.33: Breakfast of orange juice, sausage, scrambled egg and hash browns.

08.00: The Airtours representative explains the day's procedure, weather conditions, ski equipment hire, and when we get our lift passes. Now I'm really starting to get excited – and at last I feel completely awake.

08.08: First view of the Alps, bathed in sunshine. Realise it's going to be perfect skiing conditions.

09.21 (local time): Touch-down in Geneva and by 10.00 we've collected all our equipment and we're on the coach.

10.03: Airtours' Chamonix head rep, Jo, tells us more about conditions in the resort. Apparently they've got the most snow since 1967 – and most of that fell in 48 hours.

Jo runs through the itinerary in more detail, explaining where we change, meet for lunch and for beers at the end of the day – glad to see they've got their priorities right.

11.15: Coach pulls up in Chamonix and the group splits into intermediate, advanced and extreme skiers.

The daredevils head off for Les Grandes Montets to check out the off-piste action, while the rest of us take the cable car to Les Brevants.

It's exactly midday when we make our first descent. The conditions are superb and it's hard to believe we were in London just a few hours earlier.

We ski for nearly 90 minutes in the vicinity of the mountain restaurant before meeting for lunch.

14.15: Back on piste and ski right through without a break until 17.15. End up in a village called Flegeres – five minutes bus journey away from Chamonix centre.

17.30: We've done some tough skiing and I'm desperate to get out of my ski gear. I end up doing a quick change upstairs, then head down for a welcome beer and the obligatory schnapps.

18.45: We're back on the bus to Geneva. The flight is delayed about 30 minutes and we eventually get back to the UK at about 22.00 (local time) – not that I noticed. I was asleep for most of the journey.

Conclusion: Aside from returning totally shattered, Airtours' new ski day trips are a fantastic product which will suit corporate and incentive travellers – as well as hard core skiers.

● The trip to Chamonix on February 4 was the second such one-day event organised by Airtours.

The operator plans to introduce more one-day skiing trips next year to Chamonix. Dates will be revealed soon.

Source: Travel Trade Gazette, 15 March 1999

PROFILE *Bath Spa Project*

A state of the art new spa will open in Bath in the year 2001. It will be the only place in the UK where you can bathe in natural, hot spring water. Parts of the building are Roman, Medieval, Georgian and Victorian. The new part of the building will be clad in Bath stone and encased with an outer envelope of glass. The facilities will include an open air rooftop pool, a main spa pool with whirlpool, steam rooms, massage rooms, treatment rooms, solarium and gymnasium. There will be a 'Preventorium' – a medical treatment centre providing physiotherapy, hydrotherapy, acupuncture and massage.

Source: Bath Spa project (image by Nicholas Grimshaw & Partners)

A project team was set up to see the project through and this was set up by Bath Tourism Bureau, a local government organisation. Many other bodies are involved, including archaeologists, for excavation of the site, architects, to develop plans, and planners, to approve them. Construction began in October 1999 and is expected to be completed by 2001. The scheme is a 'Millennium Project' and as such attracted nearly £7 million pounds of funding from the Millennium Commission. The Millennium Commission is one of the organisations that distributes funds raised by the National Lottery. See also *www.bathspa.co.uk* for more information.

Market skimming

This strategy normally applies to a new product. When the product is launched, costs are high and the company needs to recoup these as soon as it can. The new product appeals to innovators who are prepared to pay a premium price for it. The high price lends an air of exclusivity to the product, but may later be lowered to attract new users. The millennium celebrations produced many examples of market skimming. Taxi drivers were charging treble rates for transport on New Years Eve. Entrance to clubs could reach hundreds of pounds. Tour operators raised their prices to take advantage of anticipated demand for holidays over the millennium period. By late November, prices were tumbling as consumers proved less gullible than the tour operators expected, refusing to pay millennium supplements. The article from *Travel Weekly* (see Figure 4.12) describes how 'Panorama' raised prices.

Panorama hikes up 2000 prices in bid to profit from millennium rush

PANORAMA Holidays has become the latest operator to cash in on the millennium with its decision to increase prices by up to 30% across its Wintersun programme.

The increase comes as the company targets 15% growth in its dedicated Tunisia brochure – taking capacity to 30,000 – and 20% in Wintersun to 20,000.

Sales and marketing director Martin Young said: "We delayed the launch of brochures so we could be certain we had millennium rates from hoteliers."

Young said the rates had become more realistic over the last few months as demand cooled for New Year breaks.

Long-stay holidays have been added to the Tunisia programme with prices leading in at £199 per person for 21 nights' half-board at the Hotel Dalia in Hammamet.

Millennium prices start at £499 for seven nights' half-board at the Hotel Miramar. New to Wintersun are Lanzarote and Fuerteventura along with a four-day desert safari.

Young said demand for the Canaries from the UK is so strong hoteliers are demanding up to 10% more from operators. He said: "We are resisting these demands and prices have risen by 3%."

Figure 4.12 *Increasing prices to cash in on the Millennium*

Source: Travel Weekly, *19 April 1999*

Market penetration

Again, this is a common strategy for the introduction of a new product. It takes the opposite approach from market skimming, by entering the market with a low price in a bid to gain market share quickly. It is often used for products termed as fast-moving consumer goods (FMCG). These are household goods, such as detergents and groceries. It can also be used in travel and tourism. It was the strategy adopted by the airline, Go, when it was launched in May 1998. The airline is a subsidiary of British Airways and was set up to compete with cheap operators such as Ryanair and EasyJet. Very low prices were charged because of the competitive nature of the market, resulting in heavy losses for Go – £20 million in the first year of operation. Go claims it will make a profit within its first three years of operation.

Competitive pricing

This is a similar strategy to market penetration but is used in a competitive market, where consumers are very sensitive to price and will switch brands to get the cheapest price. Tour operators and airlines watch their competitors closely and react quickly to price changes. It can be a dangerous strategy, as prices might fall so low that weak companies fail.

Odd pricing

This is a simple strategy, which persuades consumers that they are paying a cheaper price than they think – for example, £99 sounds cheaper than £100 (see Figure 4.13). It is very common, but no one yet knows if it really works.

Promotional pricing

This is where the price is linked to a special promotion for a limited period of time. It is most often used by tourist attractions in an attempt to attract new customers (see Figure 4.13).

Discounted pricing

Different prices are charged for different groups of people, for example, in museums and cinemas, students and senior citizens can expect to receive a discount. Further examples would be an organisation's employees enjoying special rates or tourist attractions offering discounts for groups and schools (the Millennium Dome price structure shows how prices favour those who visit in groups and families). Note, also, that tickets offering discounts can sometimes be booked over the Internet.

Seasonal pricing

This is particularly important in the tourism industry. The whole season is divided into three broad seasons. Peak season always coincides with school holidays and prices are set at their highest. People travelling without children, who travel at off peak times, get the best deals. Similarly, transport operators charge the highest prices at peak commuting times, for example, rail fare prices are most expensive during rush hours and at weekends. Airlines charge the highest prices on Friday evenings and Monday mornings to take advantage of commuting business travellers.

DID YOU KNOW?

The New Millennium Experience Company website is designed to process up to 24,000 Dome tickets per hour.

Figure 4.13 Ski saver advert: a good example of promotional and odd pricing

Source: © SeaFrance 1999

ACTIVITY

The following extract is an example of seasonal pricing throughout one summer season. Two other pricing strategies are evident. Can you identify them?

PRICES PER PERSON BASED ON 2 ADULTS SHARING	7 NTS		14 NTS	
	ADULT	CHILD	ADULT	CHILD
02 MAY '99–11 MAY	399	99	569	99
12 MAY–18 MAY	419	99	579	99
19 MAY–25 MAY	469	199	639	219
26 MAY–01 JUNE	499	279	639	299
02 JUNE–08 JUNE	459	199	609	229
09 JUNE–22 JUNE	469	199	619	229
23 JUNE–29 JUNE	479	199	629	229
30 JUNE–06 JULY	489	199	689	239
07 JULY–13 JULY	539	229	759	279
14 JULY – 20 JULY	569	269	779	299
21 JULY – 17 AUG	599	299	799	319
18 AUG – 24 AUG	569	279	779	299
25 AUG–31 AUG	549	249	759	269
01 SEPT – 07 SEPT	519	199	739	219
08 SEPT–14 SEPT	519	199	729	219
15 SEPT–28 SEPT	499	199	719	219
29 SEPT–05 OCT	499	99	719	199
06 OCT–19 OCT	419	99	549	99
20 OCT–24 OCT	429	99	N/A	N/A

Child price available up to and including 12 years old

Supplements per person per week	Single Adult	£119 7/7–5/10 £84 All other times
Reductions per week	3rd Adult Sharing	£49 7/7–5/10 £35 All other times

Source: Virgin Holidays

KEY TERMS

Channel of distribution: the means of getting the product to the consumer.

Principal: supplier to the travel trade, e.g. airline or hotel.

Place

This is the aspect of the marketing mix that entails getting the product to the customer in the right place. The means of getting the product to the customer is known as the channel of distribution. With travel and tourism products, the process is complicated by the fact that there is no tangible product to pass through the channel of distribution. Agents do not buy and resell, but take a commission on what is sold. Thus, a travel agent receives a percentage of the price of the holiday sold from the tour operator or airline (principal). Likewise, a theatre booking agency receives a commission on tickets sold.

Tour operators have few options in the place mix. They can sell through travel agents or they can sell direct to the public, reaching potential customers through the media, teletext or via the Internet. In any case, the tour operator will have to invest heavily in brochure production as this is still the accepted method of displaying the product to the customer.

Advantages of selling through travel agents include:

- Gives the tour operator a High Street presence in every town.
- Travel agent can give personal advice on the products.
- It is easy for customers to visit a travel agent.
- Consumers expect to buy holidays through travel agents.

Disadvantages of selling through travel agents include:

- A commission must be paid to the travel agent.
- The agent decides how to rack the brochures, but may not give prominence to your product.
- No control over the quality or method of selling.
- Travel agents will not sell your insurance, they sell their own policies.

Advantages of direct sell include:

- Control over how the product is sold.
- No commission to be paid to a third party.
- No problem with brochure racking.

Disadvantages of direct sell include:

- No High Street presence.
- High cost of advertising to reach customers.
- Call centre operation needed.

DID YOU KNOW?

Over 90% of package holidays sold in the UK are currently sold through travel agents.

In order to retain the advantages of using travel agents without incurring the disadvantages, some tour operators have started their own travel agency chains. These include Going Places (owned by Airtours) and Lunn Poly (owned by Thomson). This is known as horizontal integration and was discussed in Chapter 1.

Tourist attractions have different considerations in respect of the place mix. To enjoy their products, customers must come to them. This means the location of the attraction is important, as it must be accessible. Alton Towers is fortunate in its location in the middle of the UK, enjoying close proximity to major road networks. However, channels of distribution are still essential to provide a network of locations where tickets may be ordered or bought. Tourist attractions use tourist offices and agencies to sell tickets. They also market to coach operators and educational establishments to ensure a steady flow of groups to the attraction.

Figure 4.14 shows how complex distribution channels can be.

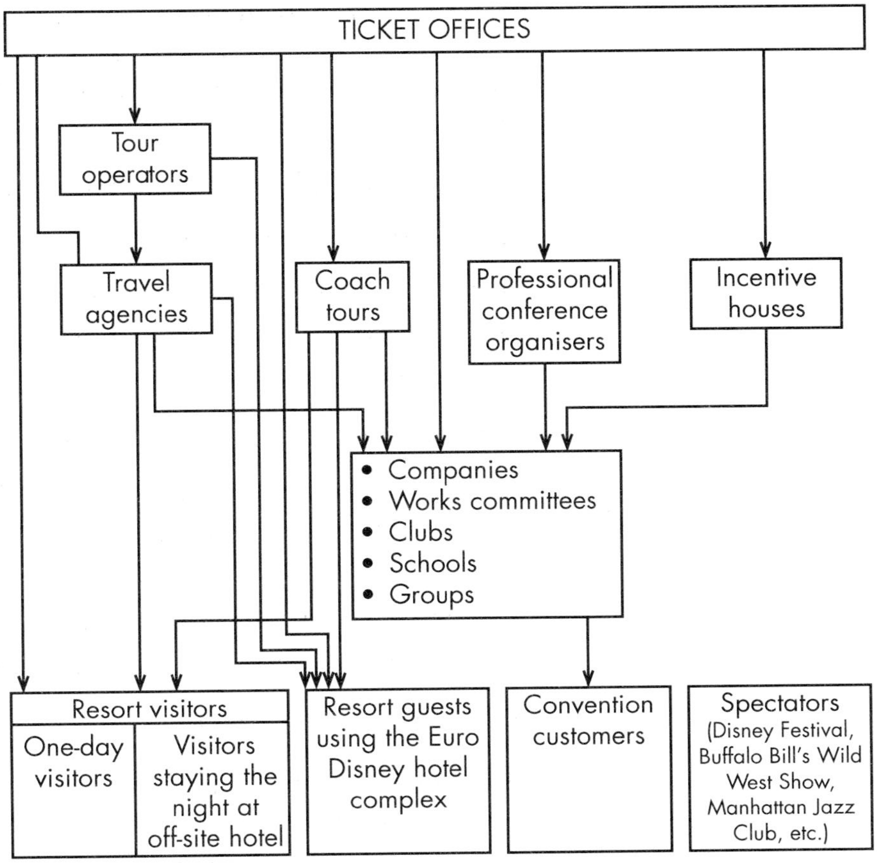

* Influencers and prescribers: airlines, tourist boards (especially Paris), local authorities (e.g. town halls in respect to senior citizens), major newspapers, etc.

Figure 4.14 *Distribution channels at Disneyland Paris*

Promotion

The fourth element of the mix is promotion, which includes advertising, sales promotion, selling, public relations, sponsorship and direct mail. A company may use any or all of these in its promotional mix. These aspects of promotion will be examined in detail in the section on marketing communications.

CASE STUDY *National Centre for Popular Music*

Museum for pop music open with a fanfare

'Previously unfashionable Sheffield reinvents itself as the home of pop. The National Centre for Popular Music will open its doors on 1 March 1999. The city that gave us Heaven 17, Human League and Pulp will present a range of music, past, present and future, in the new centre.

The idea was conceived ten years ago, but only received funding four years ago. The £15 million project was awarded £11 million from the Arts Council National Lottery Fund. Another grant came from the English Regional Development Board. £8 million was spent on the new building, which resembles four giant stainless steel drums, each housing a different exhibition area. The building is situated in the Cultural Industries Quarter, a rejuvenated industrial area. £2.5 million has been spent on state of the art sound systems, video and computer effects.

In "Perspectives", you will hear snatches of pop songs and be surrounded by video images. There are interactive activities, the chance to learn how pop music is recorded, edit a pop video or design an album sleeve. There are cafés and bars and a shop to complete the day out.

The centre is expected to attract 400,000 visitors a year. Stuart Rogers, the centre's chief executive, describes it as "A celebration of what popular music has meant to people's lives. Perhaps the centre will do for music in Sheffield what the Full Monty did for film".'

PRICES	STANDARD	OFF PEAK
Adults	£7.25	£5.95
Children	£4.50	£4.00
Families	£21.00	£18.00
Concessions	£5.50	£4.75

Note: Groups and schools attract special rates.

CASE STUDY *Bankruptcy threatens National Centre for Popular Music*

'The National Centre for Popular Music was in crisis yesterday as insolvency advisors were called in. PricewaterhouseCoopers are hoping to complete a restructuring plan to save the Centre from closure. The Arts Council, Yorkshire Arts and Sheffield City Council have reached an agreement on a package of revenue funding for the next six months.

The £15 million centre opened in March and hoped to attract 400,000 visitors per year. However, after the first six months this figure is now expected to be as low as 130,000. A representative from Pricewaterhouse said the centre's troubles stemmed from overly optimistic predictions of visitor numbers: "You have to remember that this is Sheffield – it's the fourth largest city in the UK, but it is not a major tourist attraction." "We are not closing down", said a member of staff at the centre, "it's business as usual as far as we are concerned".'

ACTIVITY

Study the two Case Studies on the National Centre for Popular Music and answer the following questions:

- Identify the strategies for the marketing mix in the Centre. If you require further information, visit the website for the National Centre for Popular Music.
- Why do you think the location, Sheffield, was chosen?
- What do you think were the causes of the problems facing the Centre?
- Find out the difference between capital and revenue funding.
- What else do you think should be done to save the Centre?
- There are many lottery funded projects. Research one in your area and report on its development and current success.

Marketing communications

In order to achieve their marketing objectives, travel and tourism enterprises must make both customers and trade aware of their products and services. The tools they use to do this are collectively known as 'promotion' and form part of the marketing mix.

Promotion may include some or all of the following:

- advertising
- direct marketing
- public relations
- sales promotion
- sponsorship

The objectives of promotion must help fulfil the marketing objectives. They might be:

- to inform the public about a new product
- to inform the public about a change to the product or company
- to increase sales
- to increase awareness of the company
- to give reassurance to existing customers
- to increase market share

Whatever the objective, it will only be achieved by choosing the right promotional mix and the right medium to reach the target market. It is also important that the message reaches the target at the right time, that is, at the time when the purchaser is at the stage of deciding what to buy. You will notice that most television advertising for holiday products occurs just after Christmas. This shows good timing, as, once the excitement of Christmas is over, consumers' thoughts turn to planning their summer holiday.

Many marketers use the AIDA model to help plan their promotion. A successful promotional campaign will lead the consumer through the above stages. First, the promotion must attract the attention of the consumer. Having being made aware of it there must be something about it that captures the consumer's interest. Hopefully, the campaign is so good that the product is desirable and the most important stage is the last one, action, where the action is the purchase.

KEY TERM

AIDA: an acronym for **A**ttention, **I**nterest, **D**esire, **A**ction.

PROFILE *Oblivion*

Alton Towers is a theme park situated in Staffordshire. It is Britain's most visited, paid for, tourist attraction, attracting nearly three million visitors per year. 28.9% of its visitors are in the 18 to 24 year old category and 19.2% in the 13 to 17 year old category (*Alton Towers Student Information Pack*, 1999). It is very important that Alton Towers continues to attract the teenage market and their product development strategy takes this into account, introducing more and more thrilling rides. In fact, Alton Towers describes the target for these rides as the 'teenage thrill seekers'. In March 1998, the attraction launched a new ride, 'Oblivion'. It was described as the world's first vertical drop ride and cost £12 million to develop. Much of Alton Towers' £5 million marketing budget was

devoted to the launch of Oblivion. The objectives of the campaign were:

- **to attract teenage thrill seekers**
- **to communicate the magic of Alton Towers**
- **to achieve an 80% reach**

(*Note:* 'Reach' is the total number of people that see an advertisement.)

The advertising agency, J. Walter Thompson, was chosen to handle the campaign and the medium chosen for advertising was television. An advertisement was made and shown on television leading up to the launch of the ride. Information was also fed to the press, little by little.

Advertising

The Advertising Association describes advertising as 'messages paid for by those who send them, intended to inform or influence people who receive them'.

Advertising is placed in the media. Other examples of media are: television, radio, newspapers, magazines, cinema, the Internet and outdoor advertising (for example, billboards). All advertising is paid for – this is important to remember, as it will help you distinguish between advertising and public relations.

Television advertising

Television and radio are known as broadcast media. In Britain, the Independent Television Commission (ITC) is responsible for licensing and regulating all television services. This excludes the British Broadcasting Corporation (BBC). There is no advertising on BBC, as the programmes are paid for by licence fees. Independent television pays for its programmes by selling advertising time. There is a wealth of choice for advertisers wishing to select a television channel, as there are 15 ITV companies, covering the country by region, as well as GMTV, Channel 4 and Channel 5, and the many cable and satellite channels.

Television advertising is sold by the 'slot', and a slot may be a few seconds or even a minute. The price of a slot varies according to region, as there is a vast difference in the number of homes in a region (for example, there are over five million homes in the Greater London region). Cost also varies according to the time of day – 'peak time' is from about 5.30 pm to 10.30 pm. An advertiser may buy a package that includes some peak and some off peak slots.

There is a seven minute per hour limit on advertising in Britain and it must be easy for the viewer to distinguish between the programme and the advertising. This gap between programmes is called the commercial

KEY TERMS

Slot: period of advertising time on TV or radio.

Broadcast media: radio and television.

Press media: newspapers and magazines.

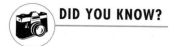

break. Rates for slots rise if a particularly popular programme is shown, for example the World Cup attracts many viewers. The millennium attracted great competition for slots (see Figure 4.15).

The £1m millennium ads

THE firm which owns some of Britain's best-known drinks brands has paid an estimated £1 million to ring out 1999 and ring in the new millennium on television.

Diageo has bought all of the final ITV advertising breaks before midnight on December 31 and the whole of the first break of 2000 to promote its products. An advert for Guinness will be the last of 1999 while the first TV commercial of the new millennium will be for Bell's Whisky. Each will share the three-minute advertising breaks with other Diageo brands, such as Smirnoff vodka, Archer's peach schnapps, Bailey's, Sheridan's and Malibu.

The Diageo deal covers the London, Granada, Yorkshire and Tyne Tees regions.

Firms had been rumoured to be bidding up to £500,000 for each 30-second slot.

The normal cost of a half-minute peak-time commercial across the ITV network is about £100,000.

One advertising insider said: 'There has been competition for the first and last ad breaks on ITV because of the significance of the time this year.

'When the nation is in a celebratory mood, it's a bit of a coup for a drinks firm to secure the first and last advertising slots of this millennium and the next.'

Anita Andrews, marketing manager for Guinness, said: 'After a century of award-winning advertising, it seemed right that we should have the last word.'

Figure 4.15 Television advertising produces high competition for prime time slots

Source: Daily Mail, *15 December 1999*

Television is a very useful medium for advertising. It reaches a mass audience, although it is possible to target a particular area as the companies are divided into regions. It has movement, colour and sound and can, therefore, hold our attention. It is ideal for advertising holidays as it can demonstrate the product very well, however, it is expensive. The cost of making a good commercial can be hundreds of thousands of pounds, on top of the cost of the advertising slots.

Since 1991, sponsorship of TV programmes has been allowed. Sponsors pay to be associated with the programme and will be credited at the beginning and the end. For example, the travel agency Going Places sponsors the popular programme *Blind Date*. There is a code regulating this type of sponsorship, which will be discussed later in the book.

DID YOU KNOW?

Spending on advertising in the UK in 1998 was £14.3 billion, of which 28% was spent on television advertising. (*1999 Advertising Statistics Yearbook*)

DID YOU KNOW?

Capital FM has nearly 3.75 million listeners each week – Chris Tarrant has over 2 million listeners per week for his breakfast show.

ACTIVITY

Find other examples of sponsorship on television. For each example, consider why the sponsor has chosen that programme. Note the advertisements shown in the commercial breaks of these programmes.

Do you think that the advertiser is aiming for the same target market that the programme appeals to?

Teletext is a popular way of advertising on television for travel and tourism companies. Printed information is given on the television screen and viewers are invited to telephone for further details of products.

Radio advertising

If you wish to advertise on the radio, you must advertise on commercial radio. BBC Radio is funded by the same licence fee as television. There are many local, commercial radio stations and you will probably be aware of those in your area. There are few national, commercial radio stations. Some stations that are very well-known are: Virgin Radio, Capital Radio and Classic FM.

Radio stations are regulated by the Radio Authority. The Radio Authority has to plan frequencies, to appoint licensees and to regulate programming and advertising. The Radio Advertising Bureau is an independent company that markets commercial radio. It gives information on advertising matters to both its members and to advertisers. The Bureau is funded by a levy on all national radio advertising and their aim is to promote radio advertising.

The advantages of choosing radio for advertising are that national coverage can be achieved if you want it, but it is particularly appropriate for local advertising. It is also very flexible – it does not have to be planned a long time in advance. If the target is young people, radio is very useful, as 81% of 15 to 24 year olds tune in every week (Rajar, 1999). It is also important to choose the right listening time – more people listen to the radio in the morning than watch television, but this changes in the late afternoon. Radio is much less expensive than television, particularly to produce the advertisement itself.

Airtime is sold in slots like television time. Travel and tourism companies spent £19 million on radio advertising between 1998 and 1999, however, they were not the biggest spenders. Companies who spent the most on radio advertising in this period included Vodaphone, Camelot and Dixons.

Audience research for radio is carried out by Rajar, Radio Joint Audience Research Limited. They produce a wealth of information on who listens, when they listen and how much revenue is made through advertising. You can look in detail at Rajar's findings by visiting their website. Radio commercials have to be carefully vetted before they go on air. Scripts are examined and approved by the Radio Advertising Clearance Centre.

PROFILE *Air UK (now KLM UK)*

Radio was used to support TV advertising in Air UK's campaign. There were two objectives of the campaign: to promote Stansted in preference to other London airports and to increase market share. They also used press and posters to advertise.

PROFILE *Lufthansa*

This airline used a mix of radio, television and press for a promotion named 'Best Price'. Radio out-performed both television and press in generation of response. The cost per reply was much lower for radio than for other media.

Advertising in national newspapers

Newspapers and magazines are known as press media. There are national and regional newspapers and consumer and trade magazines.

There are eleven daily (dailies) and eleven Sunday national newspapers, distributed all over the UK. Most of the Sunday papers include a colour magazine. The most popular national newspaper in the UK is *The Sun*, with a circulation of 3.7 million copies per day. The *Financial Times* sells approximately 168,000 copies per day. The *News of the World* is the most popular Sunday paper, selling 4 million copies, compared with *The Sunday Times* at 1.2 million. The circulation and readership figures are produced by the National Readership Survey. Circulation refers to the number of copies sold, whilst readership is three times that figure, as the assumption is, that each newspaper is read by three people.

It is possible to place a small classified advertisement in a newspaper. This is relatively inexpensive, however, it may not attract much attention. Advertising is sold by the page, half page or column and prices vary according to the position of the advert. Obviously, the front page is very expensive – *The Sun*, for example, commands high advertising rates as it has the highest circulation. As most British people read newspapers, they are useful media for advertising, and, as each newspaper has a particular profile of reader, targeting can be extremely precise. Press advertisements were placed in the national press for the launch of the new airline 'Buzz', in 1999. These appeared on different pages throughout the papers so that readers were constantly reminded about Buzz as they turned the pages. Each time a little bit more information was offered and the advertisements were brightly coloured to attract attention.

KEY TERMS

Circulation: number of people who buy a publication.

Readership: circulation × 3.

ACTIVITY

Work with a partner and see if you can name all the national and Sunday newspapers. Find out the circulation figures for each one. A publication called 'The Media Pocket Book' will help you (ask for it in your library).

Choose four of the newspapers to compare and draw up a profile of the type of reader for each one. Refer to the section in this chapter on market segmentation to help you.

DID YOU KNOW?

Nine out of ten adults read a regional newspaper every week.

DID YOU KNOW?

The London *Evening Standard* has a circulation of 409,000 each day. It is one of the most popular evening papers in the country and can also be bought at many railway stations outside London. It is sent up on the trains in the afternoon.

Regional and local newspapers

There are hundreds of local newspapers and eighteen morning regional papers, for example, the *Yorkshire post*. Some of the local papers have very small circulations but if a company wants to advertise in one locality, the local paper will suit their purpose. The advertising will be relatively cheap and an advantage is that weekly newspapers are often kept all week, so that the advertisement has more than one opportunity of being noticed. Most advertising is in black and white.

Magazines

There are two broad categories of magazines:

- consumer magazines
- trade magazines

Within the two categories the spread is enormous. Consumer magazines include all the women's titles, home magazines, general interest and hundreds of specialist titles, such as computer magazines, fishing, caravanning and titles catering for any specialist interest you care to imagine. There are many travel and holiday magazines aimed at consumers for example.

The trade magazines are of interest to people working in a particular industry, for example building, banking or travel. You will already be familiar with the *Travel Trade Gazette* and *Travel Weekly*. You might also have read *Marketing* and *Marketing Week*.

Magazines are very useful to advertisers, as they can be targeted very precisely to particular groups of people. Potential advertisers can receive detailed readership information from the magazine to help them decide whether it matches their target market. The advertiser will also receive a rate card detailing prices of different pages or parts of a page. Some travel companies have their own magazines. This is a very good idea as they are able to use their database of customers as a mailing list and communicate directly through the magazine.

PROFILE *Thomas Cook*

Thomas Cook has a magazine, entitled *The Thomas Cook Magazine*. The circulation is small – approximately 260,000 – but is very specific. It is sent to their regular customers, who are claimed to be ABC1, affluent homeowners. The magazine is of interest to advertisers who want to target these affluent Thomas Cook customers. They can place adverts in the magazine at a cost of £4,000 for a full colour page. *The Thomas Cook Magazine* comes out three times a year and is timed to coincide with the times when customers are likely to be planning their holidays. The magazine is mailed direct to customers' homes and covers a wide range of travel features and personal travel accounts.

Another way of using magazines is to place an insert. You will have noticed lots of these when you have bought magazines. There is often a pile of them inserted loosely inside. Inserts can be distributed in chosen regions if required.

Cinema advertising

The cinema is probably the most exciting medium for advertising. The cinema audience is in place waiting for the film to start and the advertisements become part of the pre-film entertainment. They are on the big screen and the audience is highly receptive, ready to enjoy themselves. There are no distractions, for example channel hopping or making a cup of tea. The sound and vision are usually of the highest quality.

Cinema is ideal for reaching a young audience as most cinema goers are 16 to 30 years old. It is easy to target regionally as advertising time can be bought locally, regionally or nationally. The advertising can also be linked to categories of film, such as 'U' or '18'. It is possible for local advertisers with a small budget to use their local cinema by displaying a still picture advert before the main advertisements start.

Advertising on postcards

Most people like to receive something for free and postcards are now available free in many locations, as a form of advertising. You can take as many as you like and send them to your friends. Figure 4.16 shows a clever example that not only advertises Zanzibar, but also directs you to a website for more information.

Figure 4.16 Postcard advertising

Source: © ZanzibarNet

ACTIVITY

Carry out some advertising awareness research amongst your colleagues or friends. Find out which cinema advertisements they remember and what it was that made them memorable.

Collate the results and see what the most remembered advertisements are. Next time you go to the cinema, make a point of noting all the advertisements, including the stills. How effective are the adverts, in terms of AIDA? Do they make you want to purchase the product?

 **DID YOU KNOW?**

Media mogul Chris Evans created Ginger Online. It is part of the Ginger Media Group and develops Virgin Radio and TFI Friday on line. You can, of course, buy advertising on line to reach Ginger's audience.

Internet advertising

A new and exciting form of advertising is available and growing fast – Internet advertising. You may have noticed that many Internet service providers have become free over the last year. Perhaps you wondered how they were able to do this when previously, rental charges were between £5 and £10 per month. The reason is, they attract a lot of advertisers who bring in revenue and are able to target customers in the same way as with established media. Advertisers can also find out if you are responding to their messages. They do this by sending you a 'cookie'. The cookie is a tracking device which monitors when a computer is tuned in to their advertising site. If you respond often, you will be sent more advertising messages.

Medium	Slot	Cost
Daily Mail	Full colour page	£32,000
The Sun	Full colour page	£338,500
The Mirror	Full colour page	£29,500
Capital Radio	30 sec prime time slot	£150 to £200
TV ITV (30 sec)	Coronation Street	£120,000
TV ITV (30 sec)	The Bill	£85,000
TV Channel 4 (30 sec)	Brookside	£35,000

Table 4.2 *Media advertising costs*

As soon as you do a search on the Internet you will notice advertising messages. For example, a general search for travel brought up advertising for 'Dollar, Rent a Car'. 'Amazon books', and a company called 'Fare Compare'.

Outdoor advertising

This refers mainly to billboards. If a travel company wants to advertise on billboards, they do not have to go around the country renting individual sites. They will approach a company, such as Mills and Allen, who sell billboard space. Billboard advertising is often used as a back up to a television or press campaign.

It is not possible to have a lot of text, as people do not have time to read it as they are usually driving when they see the advertisement. The exception to this is the advertising on billboards in the underground. If you are waiting for the tube, then there is ample time to read the advertising or the writing on the wall! Transport advertising is another form of outdoor advertising, with taxis and buses being used to display very distinctive campaigns.

You will find current media prices in a publication called *British Rate and Data* (*BRAD*, ask for it in your library).

Direct marketing

Direct mail

Direct mail is a form of direct marketing, where advertising comes direct by mail, addressed to you. It is sometimes referred to (but not by advertisers) as junk mail. This is because we receive so much of it and throw a lot of it away. Research undertaken by the Direct Mail Information Service showed that 91% of people opened and read travel-related direct mail. This figure is very high but it does not mean that the mailing is successful. Only 27% actually responded to the mail.

Direct response

This form of direct marketing does not depend on the mail, it can be used in all the same media as advertising. The difference is that a response is solicited. For example, the reader is invited to send for more information or a brochure. The value of direct marketing is that it is much easier to monitor than advertising. You are always able to measure the rate of response and you get important customer information with every response.

Lists

With direct mail, a mailing list is needed and there are companies whose primary trade is the sale of these lists. They charge a fee per name and address. Other companies have lists of people who have responded to some kind of promotion and can make money by selling these lists on. Whenever you respond to a promotion, look out for a box that asks if you wish *not* to receive information from other companies. You have to tick this box if you do not want your personal details to be passed on in a list.

Public relations (PR)

This is a major part of the promotion mix and is of particular importance for travel and tourism companies who have small marketing budgets. This is because public relations activities are much cheaper than other forms of promotion. Like advertising, PR can be carried out in house or it can be contracted out to a PR agency. PR can cover a wealth of activities, including newsletters, exhibitions and internal communications. there may also be some overlap with other marketing activities.

The Press and Public Relations Office
The Press and Public Relations Office forms part of the Assistant Chief Executive's Division within the Chief Executive's Department.

It is responsible for:
- Press and media liaison, including handling enquiries and generating Press releases
- Formulating and implementing public relations campaigns
- Publication of the Civic newspaper
- Corporate publication production
- Promoting Oldham Town Centre as shopping/visitor destination jointly with the Town Centre Manager
- Event organisation
- The Council's Corporate Identity

The Office comprises the Press and Public Relations Officer, Assistant Press and Public Relations Officer and Press and Public Relations Assistant.
Publications produced by the office, all of which can be accessed via this website, include:
- Weekly output of all Press Releases
- The latest issue of the Civic newspaper, Council News
- Know Your Councillor
- The Performance Indicators for 1996/97

Figure 4.17 Responsibilities of a Press and Public Relations office

Source: www.oldham.gov.uk

Figure 4.17 shows the responsibilities of the PR office at Oldham Metropolitan Borough Council. This is a public sector organisation, one of whose responsibilities is promoting tourism in the town. You will note that an important feature of their work is the generation of press releases, as much publicity can be gained from a press release. You may have used them already, but if not, you will get an opportunity later in this book (see Chapter 6).

Newspapers and magazines are bombarded with press releases and select what they want to use. If an event is planned, then hopefully, the newspaper will be sufficiently interested to cover the event and take photos. Of course, the danger is that there is no control over what is eventually written, unlike in advertising. Someone did once say, however, 'there is no such thing as bad publicity'.

Aussie visitors study Oldham's Best Value operations

4 October, 1999 KG/PR/COMP/6/99

Oldham Council is playing host to a group of managers from 'down under' who are visiting the Borough to find out more about the Council's pioneering work on 'Best Value'. The five Australians are members of the Municipal Engineering Foundation in Victoria and had Oldham's initiative highlighted to them as a good example in Best Value policy and implementation.

Director of Operational Services Mike Kelly said a full day's meeting has been organised to give the visitors an insight into how Oldham is tackling the issues relating to Best Value. Council officers will also have the opportunity to set out the progress made so far and the various service innovations already in place.

"Oldham has been highlighted as a leading authority in introducing Best Value practices into all areas of its service provision.

"We are pleased to be able to share this expertise and give guidance to others. We are keen to give our visitors the opportunity to find out more about our experiences and discuss the practical issues surrounding implementing 'Best Value' standards and practices," he said.

Oldham Council was selected as one of 37 local authorities to pilot the Government's new 'Best Value' initiative. It is seen as a leading authority in introducing 'Best Value' practices and policy into its service delivery to bring about an improved quality of service for local residents. A number of services are now subject to Best Value practice in the Chadderton area.

Figure 4.18 Press release

Source: www.oldham.gov.uk

Figure 4.18 shows an example of one of the press releases sent out by Oldham Metropolitan Borough Council to local newspapers. A good press release must have the following features:

- It should be targeted at the right audience, via the right media.
- It should be written so that a journalist can use it as they wish. This saves work.
- There should be an attention-grabbing headline.
- The press release must be dated.
- If an event is being publicised, the venue, date and time must be given.
- A photo can be sent for publication.
- Always give a name and number for further information.

ACTIVITY

First, identify all the above listed features in the Oldham press release. Then write a press release of your own. Your press release should be directed to your local newspaper. Imagine you are to put on an exhibition of student work in your college. Put all the details in your press release.

KEY TERMS

Direct mail: advertising material, personally addressed and sent in the mail.

Loyalty scheme: promotional activity aimed at regular customers.

Sales promotion

Sales promotion covers activities that bring about an early or extra purchase of a product. For example, when you shop at a supermarket you may be tempted to buy something that is on special offer or comes with a free gift. These kinds of promotions are used extensively in travel and tourism. Many companies operate 'loyalty' schemes to attract business customers. The traveller is rewarded with loyalty points every time they use the service. The most well-known of these is the Air Miles scheme. Special promotions are often directed at members of the loyalty scheme. An example is given in Figure 4.19.

Promotions are sometimes run in conjunction with a partner with related interests, so the cost of the promotion will be shared. Sales promotions are very useful for boosting sales in the short-term. They will normally run for a few weeks only, otherwise interest will wane.

Trade promotions are very common in the travel industry, and will often take the form of incentives to agents to sell more. The incentive might be financial, so that an increased commission is given, or it may take the form of a competition.

With *Who Joins Wins* you could become an *Air Miles* millionaire.

As an Executive Club member who currently collects *Air Miles* you're already enjoying the benefits that *Air Miles* bring you. And if you join *Air Miles* through Sainsbury's, Vodafone, Amerada, Scottish Hydro-Electric or NatWest, for the first time, by 31st October 1999, you'll be even better off.

Just by joining one of these partners, you will get off to a flying start, winning a guaranteed prize with *Who Joins Wins* from *Air Miles*.

There are thousands of prizes to be won with *Who Joins Wins* – the top prize being 1 million *Air Miles* – enough for you to jet off around the world whenever you want. A selection of other prizes are shown overleaf.

Figure 4.19 Air miles promotion

Source: Air Miles Travel Promotions

Sponsorship

Sponsorship of television programmes has already been discussed. It is possible to sponsor an event or an organisation and the sponsorship is usually financial. Funds are given to the organisation and in return the company's name and logo are given exposure and promoted. Sometimes the sponsorship is in material form, for example, building materials could be given to a venue in return for publicity. Public and voluntary sector organisations rely heavily on sponsorship as they have a limited income and need to provide a community service. In the arts and sports sectors, sponsorship is also common. Cigarette manufacturers are keen on sponsorship as they are heavily restricted in the forms of advertising they are allowed to undertake. It is ironic that cigarette companies often sponsor high profile sports. This, however, will be phased out in the next few years, following European legislation.

CASE STUDY *Cambridge Arts Picture House Launch*

On 9 August 1999, a new cinema open in Cambridge. The cinema was the latest in the City Screen Limited group, a company that has existed for 20 years. All their cinemas are in city centres and tend to be located in university towns. The new cinema has three screens and shows 'Arthouse' films. This means the policy is to show films from world cinema rather than American blockbusters. They try to show a wide range of films, up to 17 in a week across the three screens. Many are foreign films with subtitles.

There is an education department, providing workshops for children and adults and film making courses. A bar for ticket holders gives an atmospheric setting for relaxing drinks before or after the film. The cinema is a commercial venture, but receives funding from local councils for educational facilities. A grant was also awarded from the National Lottery, via the Arts Council, to set up production equipment, including an editing suite and digital cameras.

The promotion mix for the opening was carefully planned, relying mainly on PR activities, as the budget for advertising was limited. The management considered word-of-mouth to be the best form of production and with this in mind, they laid on three launch parties. The first was for UK film distributors, the second for local councillors, university personnel and media studies lecturers. The third party was for around 400 members of 'Friends of the cinema'.

Each week a film preview was shown for the local press. A mailshot was sent out using the database of customers from the previous Arthouse cinema, which had closed down. Press releases were sent out to local press, radio and television, including details of the 'Friends of the cinema' membership scheme. The article below was the result of one of these.

FILM fans from across Cambridge will be given a glimpse behind the big screen, thanks to a cash boost from the National Lottery.

Cambridge Arts Picture House has been awarded £99,000 to fund a host of innovative projects, as well as better educational facilities.

The boost, from the Arts Council of England, will be used to encourage budding film makers and pay for the third auditorium at the city's brand new cinema.

The cinema, in St Andrew's Street, has plans not only to show a diverse array of movies but also to work alongside local schools and colleges.

It will not just be young film enthusiasts who will get the chance to explore the magic of movies but the city's over-60s as well.

Nigel Arthur, the cinema's communications manager, said: "While we are committed to ensuring children become film fans at a young age, there will be classes for the over-60s, when they will learn the basics of film making.

"Films like Stephen Spielberg's *Saving Private Ryan* obviously have historical implications and schools with media studies departments can work with us on projects like that."

Mr Arthur added local film makers would also get to use the cinema as a forum for development and as a centre to show their films.

Sarah Gibson, education co-ordinator at the Arts Picture House, said: "This money will enable us to have the most up to date digital video production equipment, so we can provide the opportunity for budding film makers to make short films, taking participants through all the stages of film production from script to screen."

ACTIVITY

Consider the promotion mix described in the Cambridge Arts Picture House Case Study. What do you think was the purpose of each activity?

Describe the product mix for this cinema and compare it with your local cinema. Why were the guests at each launch party chosen?

Write the press release that might have resulted in the newspaper article shown.

Find examples of projects in your area that have received lottery funding. How much money did they receive and why?

Legislation affecting marketing communications

Advertising and promotion are carefully regulated in the UK. It is in the advertiser's interest to comply with the regulations. Failure to do so results in bad publicity and can end with costly court cases. Some controls affecting marketing communications are imposed by legislation; others are regulations introduced by the advertising industry. Travel and tourism organisations must be aware of and comply with, both sets of controls. First, we will consider the legislation relating to advertising.

Trade Descriptions Act 1968

This act is one of the most important pieces of consumer legislation and section 14 is the most relevant part for travel and tourism. This section deals with the supply of goods and services. It states that it is an offence to make a statement that is known to be false or to recklessly make a statement which is false. This applies to the provision of services, facilities and accommodation, the nature of services, facilities and accommodation and the location of amenities of any accommodation. An offence can be committed even when there is no intention to deceive the customer.

Consumer Protection Act 1987

This act makes it an offence to give customers a misleading price indication about goods and services. It lays down rules about use of terms such as 'reduced' and 'bargain'. Price indications given verbally are also covered. In travel and tourism care must be taken with brochures as well as with advertising.

Data Protection Act 1984

This act provides rights for individuals who have information held about them on computer. It also requires those who record and use personal information on computer to follow sound practice. An individual can have access to information held about them on computer and, if necessary, have it corrected or deleted. The act is administered by the Data Protection Registrar, an independent officer who reports directly to Parliament. If you want to have access to information you must make a written request to the holder of the information. This act is very important as so much information is held about us. Travel and tourism companies hold a lot of customer information, which must be revealed if the customer requests it.

Advertising regulations

The British Code of Advertising

This code covers all advertising, except radio, television and cable commercials. It states that:

- all advertisements should be legal, decent, honest and truthful
- all advertisements should be prepared with a sense of responsibility to consumers and society
- all advertisements should respect the principles of fair competition generally accepted in business
- no advertisements should bring advertising into disrepute
- advertisements must conform with the code

A similar code exists covering sales promotions.

The Advertising Standards Authority (ASA)

The Advertising Standards Authority (ASA) investigates complaints and undertakes research. The codes are very detailed and cover many different areas, for example, advertising aimed at children. There are too many advertisements to have a system where they are all checked before publication, so the ASA deals with complaints from the public. If it is decided the advertiser has broken the rules of the code, then the ASA can ask for the advert to be changed or even withdrawn. Figure 4.20 gives an example of an adjudication made by the ASA following a complaint from the public.

Media: Regional press
Agency: AMV.BBDO
Sector: Holidays and travel
Complaint from: London

Complaint: Objection to a regional press advertisement, offering flights to Shannon for £89 return, that claimed "Fly to Ireland with Aer Lingus and spend the weekend unwinding". The complainant, who was unsuccessful in her attempts to take advantage of the offer, challenged the availability of flights for a weekend at the advertised price.

Adjudication: Complaint not upheld. The advertisers said the offer was available on selected flights only, as was stated in the advertisement. They point out that, although there was a minimum stay requirement of Saturday night, the offer was not limited to travel over weekends. The advertisers did not provide proof of flights sold over a weekend but supplied documents that showed the total number of flights that were available for the offer and demonstrated that outward return flights were available over weekends throughout the period of the offer. Because of the minimum stay requirement, the Authority considered that the advertisement would not generally be seen to offer flights specifically at weekends. The Authority noted the complainant had been unable to get a weekend flight and was concerned that the advertisers were not able to produce evidence of flights sold. It was satisfied, however, that flights were available throughout the offer period for travel both throughout the week and at weekends.

Figure 4.20 *AJA adjudication on Aer Lingus Ltd.*

Source: www.ash.org.uk, November 1998

The Independent Television Commission (ITC)

This organisation controls all the independent television companies, Channel 4, GMTV, Channel 5, and cable and satellite television. It has its own Code of Advertising Standards and Practice, which is similar to that governing non-broadcast media. The full code is available from the ITC. Some things cannot be advertised on television, including cigarettes and gambling. All commercials are checked to make sure they comply with the code. If there are still complaints, after these checks, the ITC will investigate. The following extract from the ITC website states exactly what the organisation does:

Under its powers, derived from the Broadcasting Acts of 1990 and 1996, the ITC:

- issues licences that allow commercial television companies to broadcast in and from the UK – whether the services are received by conventional aerials, cable or satellite; and whether delivered by analogue or digital means. These licences vary according to the type of service, but they all set out conditions on matters such as standards of programmes and advertising;
- regulates these services by monitoring broadcasters' performance against the requirements of the ITC's published licences and codes and guidelines on programme content, advertising and sponsorship and technical performance. There is a range of penalties for failure to comply with them;
- has a duty to ensure that a wide range of television services is available throughout the UK and that, taken as a whole, these are of a high quality and appeal to a range of tastes and interests;
- has a duty to ensure fair and effective competition in the provision of these services;
- investigates complaints and regularly publishes its findings.

Source: www.itc.org.uk

DID YOU KNOW?

Anyone who appears in a commercial for an alcoholic drink must be, and appear to be, over 25 years old.

The ITC also has a Code of Programme Sponsorship. A sponsor is an advertiser who funds any part of the cost of production or transmission of a programme. The sponsor must be clearly identified at the beginning and end of a programme.

The Radio Authority

The Radio Authority also has a Code of Advertising Standards. Advertisements broadcast by a national advertiser must be checked by the Radio Advertising Clearance Centre.

ASSESSMENT

Study the following information on JMC Holidays Ltd.

JMC is a member of the Thomas Cook Group. This new brand was launched in September 1999. Its mission is to become the number one customer-focused package holiday company in the UK.

Objectives

- To create a new mainstream holiday brand.
- To bring distinctive and contrasting attributes to the holiday experience.
- To put the customer first, treating every customer as a valued individual.
- To provide help and information to help holiday-makers make the most of their holiday.
- To set high standards, then strive to exceed them.
- To be clear, efficient and helpful.

- To actively listen to consumers and implement a programme of constant improvement.
- To obtain an advertising reach of over 30 million in the UK by January 2000.

Background

The Thomas Cook Travel Group incorporates Neilson Activity Holidays, Style Holidays, Club 18–30 and JMC. The company is vertically integrated with is own airline and over 750 travel shops in the UK. The tour operating and airline divisions have been consolidated to produce JMC Holidays Ltd. and JMC Airlines Ltd. The same branding and livery will be used to develop a strong corporate image and to provide a seamless link between tour operating and airline divisions. The Thomas Cook Group was financially sound at the time of writing with profits in 1998 of £51.4 million. The group carries over three million passengers per year. £200 million is being invested over a five year period in JMC. The name JMC comes from the initials of John Mason Cook, son of Thomas Cook. The company employs 4772 staff.

Competition

Major rivals in tour operating are 'the big three': Airtours, Thomson Holidays and First Choice. First Choice was itself the result of a major re-branding exercise in 1994, replacing the 'Owners Abroad' brand. The market shares of these operators for 1998 are as follows: (Source: Thomson Holidays Market Information)

1 Thomson – 21%
2 Airtours – 10%
3 First Choice – 6%

Marketing

The products are branded as follows:

- Summersun
- Cyprus
- Wintersun
- Essentials Summer
- All-Inclusive
- Goa
- Portugal
- Tropical
- Turkey

- Beach Villas
- Essentials Canaries
- Family
- Florida
- Lakes and Mountains
- Golden Circle
- Select
- Tunisia

This is an extensive range of products, mostly branded according to destination. The 'Essentials' range is a very basic, low cost product, whilst 'Select' is at the top end of the market with a more luxurious product. 'Golden Circle' is aimed at over 50s.

Mission

In order to achieve its mission, the company has adopted the following strategies:

1 Extensive research into customer expectations, including a 1000 member consumer panel, whose views were sought to find out how holidays can be improved. The panel is to be repeated annually. The panel completed questionnaires before and after their holiday. Focus groups were organised to seek consumer opinion.
2 The airline has a fleet of 33 planes and is investing money into buying new aircraft, to ensure the fleet is one of the youngest in the charter airline business.
3 Holiday-makers receive free resort guides with articles by local experts. They are given emergency contact cards to keep in touch with the resort office.
4 There is a free pre-allocated seat service so that families can be sure they will sit together on a flight.
5 Brochures have simple descriptions and clear photos. They are endorsed by the Plain English Campaign.

6   A £6 million advertising campaign is underway, with television advertising, newspaper adverts and outdoor posters.

Marketing research

The following market research information gives key facts about British holidays abroad extracted from the British National Travel Survey 1997. During 1997, the British took an estimated 57.25 million long holidays. (Note: a long holiday is of 4 or more nights) This is an increase of 6.5%, compared to 1996. Of these long holidays, 30 million were taken in Britain and 27.25 were taken overseas.

Spending on long holidays abroad increased by 16% from £14,880 million to £17,220 million. In 1997, 31% of the British population took one main holiday and 26% took two or more holidays. 38% of long holidays are started in July or August.

Source: www.statistics.gov.UK

Having read the material in this assessment, you should spend some time doing additional research before you attempt the tasks below.

TASK 1

Describe the Strengths, Weaknesses, Opportunities and Threats for JMC Holidays and airlines. Explain how this SWOT analysis will be of use to JMC.

TASK 2

Identify and explain the Political, Economic, Social and Technological factors influencing JMC.

TASK 3

Describe the sources of secondary information that might aid JMC with marketing research.

Visits abroad by UK residents

Number of visits (millions)	24.9	27.4	42.1	46.0
of which:				
Total business	3.2	3.6	6.9	7.2
Total leisure	21.7	23.8	35.2	38.8
Total to N. America	1.2	1.6	3.6	3.6
Total to W. Europe	21.9	23.7	33.6	37.1
Total to rest of world	1.9	2.2	4.9	5.3
Number of nights (millions)	310.2	347.3	449.8	463.5

Explain why they are of use.

Describe two methods of market research, using primary information sources, which could be used to help JMC achieve their mission of being the number one customer-focused tour operator.

TASK 4

Explain how you would develop the marketing mix to help JMC achieve its objectives.

Key skills

In completing the assessment for this unit, you can achieve the following key skills. These will be accredited at the discretion of your tutor on the basis of the quality of the work you submit.

C3.1b Make a presentation about a complex subject, using at least one image to illustrate complex points.

C3.2 Read and synthesise information from two extended documents about a complex subject. One of these documents should include at least one image.

CHAPTER 5

Customer service in travel and tourism

....

Aims and Objectives

At the end of this chapter you will:

- **understand why excellent customer service is important**
- **know how to present yourself**
- **recognise that different customers have different needs**
- **be able to deal with customers in different situations**
- **have developed your own selling skills**
- **deal with complaints in an effective manner**
- **know how different organisations assess their own customer service**

Introduction

Customer service is perhaps the most important skill that you are going to need to pursue a career in the travel and tourism industry. Some people find that the ability to provide good customer service comes naturally. For these people, appearing cheerful, looking professional, smiling, working efficiently and meeting the customers' needs may not be too challenging. For others, however, providing these services is more difficult.

There are skills and techniques to be learnt by us all. Furthermore, we must all remember that we are not simply aiming to provide good customer service; we must always aim for excellence, providing customers with services and goods that exceed their expectations.

Travel and tourism businesses depend on their staff providing good customer service. Many of these businesses provide similar travel products and services. Consequently, customers can easily move to another company to purchase their hotel room, package holiday or flight, should they receive poor service at their first choice. For the company with poor customer service, this can result in loss of sales, profits and so potentially the business may fail. Good customer service is, therefore, the key to a successful business.

To prepare yourself for future employment, you must learn how to present yourself, in order to create a professional image. First impressions are vital, as in most businesses, the way you dress and speak, your attitude towards customers and colleagues and your personality, all influence the customer's view of your company. You must also develop an awareness of the needs of different customers. You will already know that, for example, when you go on holiday, your own needs differ from those of your parents or grandparents. In this chapter we will also compare the needs of people who do not speak English, people from different cultures or groups, and people with specific needs.

Within the travel and tourism industry, you will deal with people on the telephone, face to face and also in writing. You may be selling them products and services, providing information or giving advice. We will examine the techniques used for all these aspects of customer service.

Not all customers are easy to deal with. People do complain and this may often be justified. As an employee, you must develop skills to deal with complaints in such a way as to win the customer over and maintain the professional image of both yourself and your company.

Finally, all organisations must assess how good they are at providing customer service. We will examine how and why organisations measure and monitor their customer service levels and look at examples within the industry.

KEY TERMS

Market share: proportion of the company's share of the total sales available.

Competitive edge: being marginally ahead of the competitors.

Why excellent customer service is important

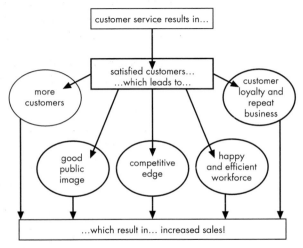

Figure 5.1

Satisfied customers

Without customers, no businesses could exist. All organisations, whether public, private or voluntary, depend on their customers in order to survive. Satisfied customers in turn, can increase business. The ultimate aim of many organisations, therefore, is to satisfy their customers' needs. As we will go on to discuss, all other business objectives (for example increased sales and profits, positive public image and an efficient workforce) will follow, provided the customer is satisfied.

It may seem rather obvious, but the idea of businesses depending on customers (rather than customers being dependent on the business) is in fact a relatively new concept. The importance of the customer is now recognised as being central to every organisation's success and is usually a part of most organisations' objectives. Many state it as part of their mission statement. For example, British Airways aims 'to excel in anticipating and quickly responding to customer needs and competitor activity', while Center Parcs aims 'to give . . . guests a truly memorable holiday experience which greatly exceeds their expectations'.

OUR PURPOSE . . .

To make Thomas Cook Holidays the most respected Tour Operator in the UK, in the eyes of our customers, competitors, suppliers and staff, and to be the most profitable. To demonstrate a 100% commitment to serving our customers, recognising that the Thomas Cook Shops, Thomas Cook Direct and the Travel Agents who sell us, as well as the people who go on our holidays, are our customers.

OUR GOALS . . .

We all play a part in achieving the highest customer satisfaction whether we are individually in daily contact with out customers or not. Achieving excellence in everything we do, doing things right first time, every time, ultimately benefits the customer – our number one goal. We must ensure we respond to our customer needs and establish a rapport based on honesty and trust to ensure our customers return to Thomas Cook Holidays time and time again.

This applies to both sets of customers – the staff who sell our holidays in the Thomas Cook shops and Thomas Cook Direct, as well as the clients who travel on them!

Figure 5.2 Extract from Thomas Cook Holidays: Our Purpose and Goals

Organisations, like Thomas Cook, recognise that satisfied customers will result in:

- increased sales
- more customers
- improved public image
- having an edge over the competition
- a happier and more efficient workforce
- customer loyalty and repeat business

ACTIVITY

Organisations often outline their customer focus in their mission statement.

Examine the British Airways, Center Parcs and Thomas Cook Holidays mission statements. Choose five other travel and tourism organisations. Investigate and compare their customer service aims.

What do we mean by customer satisfaction?

The best way to answer this question is to consider your own experiences.

ACTIVITY

Work in pairs and think about the last time your purchased something that you really wanted. Then think about the last time you enquired about something or asked for information. Did you receive good or poor service?

Identify those aspects of the service that made it good or poor.

Satisfied customers are those who have experienced polite and cheerful service in a clean environment by well-presented staff, and who feel that their needs have been met or even exceeded. They leave satisfied and will return. Their comments to their friends will also be positive!

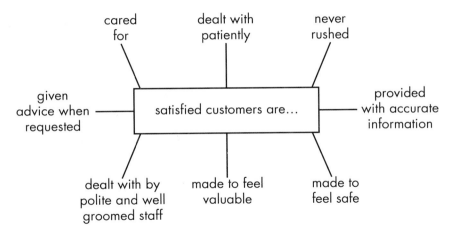

Figure 5.3

ACTIVITY

Using your own criteria, devise a check list against which customer service can be measured (e.g. politeness of staff or cleanliness of uniform).

Divide your class into small groups and analyse the levels and types of customer service that exist within your college. You could, for example, investigate the levels of service in reception, the learning resource centre, the computer area or the departmental office. For each criterion, give a score of between one and ten.

Give a short presentation to your colleagues, discussing the areas with the best and the worst customer service levels. Justify your comments and make recommendations for improvement.

Customer loyalty and repeat business

Satisfied customers will often return to buy their goods from the same place. It is arguable that the travel market is currently highly price sensitive (i.e. for many people, price determines where they buy a holiday). However, for some people, good customer service will be the main determining factor. These people would rather purchase their annual package holidays at agents where good service is provided, or fly with an airline with which they have previously been highly satisfied. When there is no price differential, service standards are even more important to the customer.

Customer loyalty schemes

Many organisations have developed customer loyalty schemes. This increases the likelihood of repeat business. For example, the air miles schemes developed by British Airways in the 1990s meant that customers had to fly with BA in order to collect air miles. These could then be exchanged for flights and used to take their families on holiday.

Most airlines now offer frequent flyer schemes with different levels of perks, according to the number of flights purchased. You may also be familiar with the supermarkets' loyalty cards, through which customers can accumulate points and eventually reduce their shopping bill. Some tour operators offer similar schemes whereby travel agents invite loyal customers to promotional evenings and mail shot any specific offers to their regular customers first.

All passengers who flew with Go during their first year of operation were sent a £20 gift voucher to be used against a subsequent flight

The objective of such loyalty schemes is to maintain existing customers. This results in more business (i.e. repeat business) and, therefore, more sales.

 DID YOU KNOW?

Research shows that it costs five times as much to attract a new customer as to retain an existing one.

 DID YOU KNOW?

Some schemes encourage you to give them the names and addresses of your friends. In exchange, your own name may be put forward for a prize draw.

 ACTIVITY

Identify three customer loyalty schemes with which you are familiar. Investigate how each scheme works.

Prepare a short fact sheet detailing the features of one scheme.

More customers

In addition to keeping existing customers, most organisations also wish to increase their market share (i.e they are always looking to attract new customers). This will result in increased sales and profits.

How businesses attract new customers varies from organisation to organisation. In January, tour operators spend millions of pounds on TV advertising, on costly brochures with beautiful images and on promotions aimed at persuading us to buy from a particular travel agent. The cheapest form of advertising, however, is word of mouth – and it is also the most effective!

DID YOU KNOW?

Many organisations use mail shots to attract new customers. These have a very low response rate – sometimes as low as 2%.

Improved public image

Certain organisations may produce particular mental pictures for you. This is known as an organisation's public image, meaning how you the customer views them. As discussed in Chapter 4, the role of marketing is to create a positive image that entices the customer to buy. Much of this image, however, is determined by the service received when buying.

Imagine you are booking a package holiday through a tour operator. You will form your own image of the company over a period of time. Its public image may already have been created by its reputation, or by the booking process itself or through your own personal experience of them.

Images can be created by the media but the appearance and window display of a travel agency may also determine its image and the quality of cabin crew uniforms may determine the image of the airline.

How is a tour operator's image produced

BEFORE BOOKING	• word of mouth/reputation • advertising
AT TIME OF BOOKING	• speed of service • efficiency • friendliness of reservation staff • product knowledge of reservation staff • being sold a 'suitable' holiday
ON HOLIDAY	• standard of hotel • friendliness of representative • efficiency of representative • accuracy of brochure

Table 5.1

ACTIVITY

What images do you associate with the following:

● Virgin Atlantic
● Club 18–30
● Saga Holidays
● Tesco or Asda

Identify three organisations that have a positive image to you. How were these images created.

Having a competitive edge

Many travel companies try to sell similar products. Very often it makes little difference where you buy your flight, package holiday or insurance as the products are so similar.

Travel companies are therefore forever trying to provide something that their competitors do not – to have an advantage, or edge, over the competition. This is easy to quantify in physical attributes: a hotel's competitive edge may be its leisure suite; a restaurant's competitive edge may be its riverside location.

To quantify a competitive edge when providing a service is more difficult. A tour operator's competitive edge may be provided by its knowledgeable overseas representative and helpful reservations staff. In addition, it may offer extra services, such as a free river trip in Paris, a complimentary guide book, champagne on arrival or reduced price flights within the UK to the departure airport.

Cities

THOMSON
Breakaway

Complimentary Guidebook Offer

We are delighted to have got together with two of the world's leading travel guide publishers, AA Publishing and Insight Guides to offer you the opportunity of receiving a complimentary guidebook for your chosen destination.

Each full colour travel guide is crammed full of sights, tips on where to eat, drink, stay and shop along with recommended walks and tours. Maps are included in each guide.

To receive your complimentary copy, just call the Thomson Breakaway Hotline quoting your name, address, preferred book title and ISBN number along with booking reference.

If your destination is not listed, we will include alternative information with your tickets enabling you to make the most of your trip.

THOMSON BREAKAWAY CITIES

GUIDEBOOK HOTLINE: 01476 541040 (24hrs)

Regional Connecting Flights

Fly from your local airport and take advantage of our special low fares!

EXPLORE can offer flight connections from UK local airports to London from just £69 including taxes and service charges.

Figure 5.4 Trying to achieve that competitive edge   *Source: Explore Worldwide*

Superior service can give a travel agency a competitive edge, and may also be a result of:

- better technology
- answering telephones quickly
- uniformed staff
- staff product knowledge
- staff travel experience
- efficient administrative systems
- smart office

ACTIVITY

Select three comparable brochures from mass market tour operators. What services do each provide, in order to try to gain a competitive edge? Identify the one that you think is the most successful at doing this.

KEY TERMS

Internal customers: colleagues, people who work within the same organisation.

External customers: customers who are not part of the organisation.

A happy and efficient workforce

Dealing with satisfied customers is rewarding. Their positive feedback, and the pleasure and gratitude they express in having their needs met are rewarding to whoever is providing the customer service. This results in job satisfaction and a feeling of wellbeing, which in turn makes it easier to deal with customers' demands (there is also the possibility that bonuses and incentives may be received as a result of satisfying customers).

Colleagues also help to create a happy and efficient workforce. If everyone within the organisation treats colleagues as customers, a happy and efficient workforce will be the result.

Colleagues are known as internal customers, while people outside the organisation are external customers. While we will concentrate on

customer care for our external customers, it is important to realise the effect your attitude and behaviour can have on your colleagues.

Within an organisation, everyone depends on each other. While you may aim to work in a position dealing with the external customer, you will be dependent upon many people within the organisation who will ensure that everything runs smoothly behind the scenes. This is essential if you are to provide excellent external customer service.

CASE STUDY *Sue and her internal customers*

Sue is a very efficient travel consultant in a small independent travel agency, called Breakaway. She is always being complimented by customers on her excellent customer service skills and in particular her friendliness and efficiency. While she knows that she is very good at her job, she thinks that it is unfair that she gets all the praise from the external customers. She feels others should be acknowledged for doing their jobs well, as this also makes it easier to do her share. In particular she is grateful to:

● Sam, her supervisor. Sam is very organised. Breaks are scheduled at the beginning of every day and are always fair. Her working hours are planned well ahead of time so that she can organise her social life. As she has to work most Saturdays and has varying weekdays off, this is very important.

● Bill in the finance department deals with refunds to clients very quickly. Cheques are acknowledged the same day and Sue's own requests for petty cash refunds have always been dealt with promptly.

● Her friend and close colleague is Emma, who works in the back office. Sue and Emma have very different skills but they work well together and help each other. When necessary, they take each others calls and cover breaks in emergencies. They make a good team.

The customers only see Sam, and so it is she who gets the praise. She is aware that she can only do her job well because everyone in the organisation treats one another as though they were customers.

ACTIVITY

What could Sue (or her supervisor) do to ensure that her colleagues know that they are appreciated?

Think about your own part-time job, or if you do not have one, one of your parents' jobs. Name their internal customers. How are they treated? Are they a happy and efficient workforce?

Increased sales

The aim of all private sector organisations is to make a profit. Increased sales can be the result of:

- repeat business from satisfied customers
- satisfied customers who not only return to buy (customer loyalty) but also buy more
- new customers who hear about the good service
- new customers who hear about the good reputation of the company
- new customers who are impressed by the happy workforce

KEY TERM

Market share: proportion of the company's share of the total sales available.

The results of excellent customer service

The results of excellent customer service are interlinked. Satisfied customers will return to the same company to purchase goods and services. They will also tell their friends and so bring new customers. This, in turn, increases sales for the company. Increased sales may motivate the staff, and make them happier as they may get a wage rise. Employees will feel proud to be working for their company. The public image can be improved, as increased sales means the premises can be refurbished, uniforms can be renewed and extra services can be offered to clients. Market share will gradually increase and sales will continue to grow.

CASE STUDY *Happy customers and motivated staff at Thomas Cook*

Thomas Cook is very pleased with its agency in Sheffield's Meadow Hall shopping centre. It continues to win prizes and a few a years ago tripled its profits in one year (from £150,000 in 1996 to over £500,000 in 1997).

Having decided a shake-up was needed, the shop's manager, carried out a survey of all existing customers. In addition, a focus group, exit polls, a mystery shopper survey and customer service questionnaires helped them to establish their customers' needs and expectations.

Through this research, Thomas Cook established repeat booking patterns, customer types, favourite destinations and customer care problem areas.

As a result, they took several measures to improve their service:

1 Students were employed to offer a meet and greet service.
2 Clients are now shown to a seating area and offered refreshments while waiting to be served.
3 Clients are shown the late availability board and given a folder featuring special offers, while they wait.
4 The 'late cards' in the shop are updated regularly and made more legible.
5 A back office deals with all telephone enquiries so that consultants are not interrupted when dealing with clients face to face.
6 An appointment service is available for all staff within Meadow Hall.
7 A privilege service is available to all loyal customers. This entitles them to parking discounts at the shopping centre, commission free foreign exchange and a magazine featuring favoured destinations.
8 Finally, a £10 booking fee is now charged to all new clients with bookings under £150.

Their revamped service has resulted in increased sales. Profits have tripled and the agency has won the Meadow Hall Customer Service Award, which has promoted a positive image locally.

In addition, the agency has won the Thomas Cook Shop of the Year award, earning all of its 34 staff a weekend break in Jersey. Their pride and job satisfaction are evident to all who visit the agency.

 **DID YOU KNOW?**

It is estimated that dissatisfied customers tell between six and eight other people about their experiences while satisfied customers tell one.

The results of poor customer service

The results of poor customer service are not simply the opposite of the results of good customer service; they can be far worse. Poor customer service can result in the failure of a business.

Some foreign countries are not as naturally welcoming to their tourist 'customers' as others.

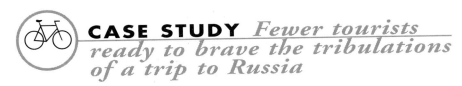

CASE STUDY *Fewer tourists ready to brave the tribulations of a trip to Russia*

ALTHOUGH Russia is a treasure trove of breath-taking historical monuments, its intake of tourists is dwindling because of incompetence and hostility.

Eight years after Russia opened up to Western visitors the number of tourists is falling. In 1997, a total of 2.2 million visited; a year later it was only 1.9 million. Even Sergei Shpilko, deputy head of the Tourism Ministry, admitted recently: "It will be a long time before Russia attracts ordinary tourists."

The Hermitage Museum ranks alongside the Louvre in Paris and the Metropolitan in New York as one of the world's greatest art museums. Cathedrals within the Kremlin rival Rome's finest churches. Top-class orchestras can be seen for less than a pound.

So what went wrong? First, the stress involved in getting here. You can spend up to three mornings queuing at the Russian Embassy in London for a visa, unless you want to pay the heavy costs of a courier. On arrival at the airport, delays can be long, staff are surly and the aggressive taxi mafia charge up to £60 for a ride into the city.

There are no reasonably priced hotels with good service and most services charge foreigners more than they do Russians. At the Mariinsky Theatre in St Petersburg, staff prefer to have empty seats than to let foreigners pay less than ten times the Russian price.

Once you are out sightseeing, there are no tourist information offices. Some of the country's top attractions have basic facilities. Once inside the Kremlin, there is nowhere to get a drink or a snack. The vast Hermitage is disgraced by its shoddy café selling greasy chicken legs.

The lack of the necessities of life makes for a trip that is as exhausting as it is exciting. "It's not organised. At one palace we had to queue miles for a toilet and then find a dollar and squeeze four people in one", said Christine Whitley, 60, who came to Russia on an organised boat trip. "There's nowhere for a cup of tea or a sit down. You laugh about it, but it's not what you expect."

The funnier side of sightseeing is provided by the *babushki*, the elderly women who are the backbone of this country. They reign in every museum or gallery, and can make or break your visit.

When I visited museums recently with friends, *babushki* ran after us switching lights off and on in every room because the museums can't pay their electricity bills. In the Mayakovsky Museum a tiny woman insisted on delivering paeans to the handsome poet. Some are very kind: one grandmother brought my flagging mother a cup of tea.

Things are changing, very slowly. For now, only those with plenty of stamina and a keen appreciation of the ridiculous will visit Russia.

Source: The Times, 13 August 1999

ACTIVITY

What aspects of customer service contribute to Russia's declining numbers? Consider 'pre-departure' as well as 'on-holiday' experiences.

How could these issues be addressed?

Would you like to go to Russia on holiday? Justify your answer.

KEY TERMS

Personality: those characteristics and traits which make a person unique.

Body language: the ways in which we communicate without using words (also known as non-verbal communication).

Attitude: how you present your moods or emotions.

DID YOU KNOW?

You never get a second chance to make a first impression!

Personal presentation

How you choose to present yourself conveys how you feel about yourself and your customers. Personal presentation directly affects a customer's confidence in you and enjoyment of the service. In an industry that is very much a 'people business', it is essential that due attention is paid to personal presentation and the impact that has on customers. While this is important in every customer service situation, it is vital if you are the only person that the customers will meet from the company. You literally will become the 'face of the company'.

PROFILE *Overseas staff: the face of the company*

Customers usually book a package holiday without ever meeting or speaking with anyone from the tour operator. It is often all done through the travel agent. Upon arrival in a resort, customers meet 'the company'. The resort representative is the first (and sometimes the only) person that holiday-makers will actually meet from a tour operator. Their role as ambassador is vital – it is usually the 'rep' who determines the success, or otherwise, of a holiday. Their excellent customer service skills are essential and are often the most important single aspect that will ensure repeat business for the tour operator.

Customers will judge employees as soon as they see them. They will form their first impressions based on:

- what you are wearing
- how you look after yourself – personal hygiene
- your personality
- how you express yourself – attitude and body language

Impressions are also created by taking care of the equipment used, for example, brochures, stationery and uniform.

PROFILE *Virgin Atlantic*

'The ongoing success of Virgin Atlantic Airways depends upon the service we offer and the care and concern we extend to our passengers. They will judge us in the first ten seconds of boarding an aircraft. Have they been acknowledged? Have they received a genuine smile? Are the crew giving out positive body language? Has sufficient eye contact been used? Is the appearance and grooming of the crew perfect?'

Source: Extract from 'Introductory Manual Preparing Ab-initio Crew for Training',
Virgin Atlantic

TYPICAL OVERSEAS REP. UNIFORM

MALE	FEMALE
1 jacket	1 jacket
3 shirts	3 dresses
2 ties	2 skirts
2 pairs of trousers	3 blouses
1 belt	1 belt
1 pair shorts (guiding)	1 pair shorts (guiding)
2 polo shirts (guiding)	2 polo shirts (guiding)
1 badge	1 badge
1 briefcase	1 briefcase
1 clipboard	1 clipboard

DID YOU KNOW?

Virgin Atlantic produce a 17 page booklet entitled _Grooming Regulations_, which is given to all their staff, both on the ground and in the air.

The importance of personal presentation is not limited to first impressions. A consistently high level is required throughout dealings with customers.

Dress – what you are wearing

Many jobs will provide a uniform and guidelines regarding personal grooming. For travel agents, this usually consists of a blouse and skirt for females and shirt, trousers and tie for males. Jackets are also sometimes included. A much more extensive uniform is provided for overseas staff.

The extent of the uniform provided indicates that the company is keen to have a smart, consistent and professional image. This benefits the customers in several ways:

- staff are easily identifiable
- corporate image is developed
- staff are helped in providing an excellent first impression
- it helps to make staff feel part of a team.

Employees' responsibility, in terms of their appearance, is often restricted to caring for the uniform and wearing appropriate accessories. Guidelines regarding accessories usually cover jewellery, hair, body piercing and make-up.

MALE STAFF	FEMALE STAFF
• uniform to be clean and ironed at all times	• uniform to be clean and ironed at all times
• hair must not exceed collar length	• hair must be clean and tidy at all times – it must be kept away from the face
• one plain ring may be worn	
• if a neck chain must be worn, this must be kept under the shirt	• jewellery should be kept to a minimum – only stud earrings may be worn (max. one pair)
• earrings, or any other form of body piercing, are not permitted	• no other visible body piercing permitted
• nails must be clean	• ankle chains must not be worn
• beards and moustaches must be kept trimmed	• nails must be clean and, if painted, varnish must be subtle and not chipped
• staff must cover tattoos wherever possible; refrain from having more	• make-up must be moderate
	• staff must cover tattoos wherever possible; refrain from having more

Table 5.2 _Guidelines for uniformed staff_

DID YOU KNOW?

A young man with a pony tail won his case against an employer, who refused to interview him due to the fact that he had long hair. He won his case on the grounds of sex discrimination – several young women with long hair were already employed.

Employers currently provide separate dress code guidelines for male and female staff. Examples for overseas representatives were shown in Table 5.2.

Shoes are not mentioned in the guidelines, but their suitability must not be forgotten. They must be sensible, allowing you to walk comfortably for long distances and they must be well polished.

ACTIVITY

Consider the guidelines in Table 5.2. Do you think they are reasonable, too restrictive or too lax?

How do you think such guidelines have changed in the past ten years?

How do you think the guidelines would differ for differing jobs? For example, consider cabin crew, travel agent, overseas representative or hotel receptionist.

How do you think the guidelines would differ for different companies? Compare possible staff uniforms for British Airways and Easyjet; Saga and Club 18–30.

Although many roles within the travel industry deal directly with customers, others do not. In some cases companies do not provide a uniform. They may, however, still wish to maintain a high standard of dress code.

DRESS CODE

TCH employees do not have a uniform, however, we do expect our staff to have a smart and business like appearance at all times. Please note – men should not wear earrings and women are discouraged from wearing the following items: nose studs, knee high boots, short dresses and T-shirts. Please remember you represent the Signature Brand, therefore it is important to look professional at all times. On Saturdays casual dress is acceptable.

Figure 5.5 *Dress code at Thomas Cook Holidays*

Source: Thomas Cook Holidays Induction Booklet

Personal hygiene

Immaculate personal hygiene is essential at all times in the travel and tourism industry. How you care for yourself conveys a lot about yourself and your attitudes. It reflects your opinion towards the organisation and the customers. Nothing will put your customers off more than poor personal hygiene:

● shower daily

● keep your nails immaculate

● keep your hair clean

- if you have smelly feet, have two pairs of shoes and use them on alternate days
- use appropriate hygiene products, if necessary
- wear clean socks or stockings every day
- avoid garlic – halitosis (bad breath) is very unpleasant!

When working in a customer care environment it is a good idea to have a full length mirror somewhere in your home that you can walk past before leaving in the morning. Check your appearance before leaving the house, and then check it regularly throughout the day.

DID YOU KNOW?

Some people argue that we are born with particular personality traits. Others believe that we acquire our personality as we go through life. This is known as the nature v. nurture argument.

Personality

There can be no doubt that we acquire some of our personality through our parents, whether it be because we inherit their genes or because we simply have lived with them during our early years and have copied their behaviour. As a result, many people are naturally able to deal with customers in an appropriate manner; others find it more difficult and have to learn the skills required. While it is arguable that you cannot 'learn' a personality, it has been proven that you can learn the skills needed to present yourself well to the customers.

Different roles will require different personality traits. While representatives in resorts for the twenties age group may need to be entertaining, bubbly and witty, this is not necessarily required of business travel consultants! Furthermore, it is important to remember that a successful team is made up of many different types of people. If we all had similar traits, not only would life become dull and predictable, it has also been proven that those teams would not be so productive. You will learn more about this in Chapter 6: travel and tourism in action.

ACTIVITY

friendly	happy	witty
consistent	sulky	dull
bubbly	quick tempered	kind
moody	boring	entertaining
lazy	caring	

Consider the adjectives listed above. These are often used to describe different personalities.

Put a tick against those that best describe yourself.

Put a line through those traits that should never be apparent to a customer.

Consider your ideal job. List the personality traits that an employer will look for (take some from the list above and add your own.) Do you possess most of these traits?

Our personalities are conveyed through our behaviour and will also be reflected in our attitudes. We must learn the skills needed to present a positive attitude, even though this may not be how we are actually feeling.

Attitude

Out attitude towards ourselves, our work and our customers is conveyed by how we dress, care for ourselves and our surroundings, and what we say and do. A far more subtle (and yet revealing) way of knowing someone's attitude is through their:

- posture – how they sit or stand
- tone of voice – how they say something
- the gestures used – how they use their arms and legs
- eye contact – do they avoid eye contact or stare?
- facial expressions – a key to someone's mood

The above are known as non-verbal forms of communication or body language. It is now recognised that as much as 93% of what we say is conveyed through our tone of voice and body language, rather than speech alone.

Your voice reveals your attitude clearly. You can use the same words, but appear impatient and cross, or caring and concerned, merely by changing the tone, speed, pitch and volume of your voice. This may remind you of the many times you have heard the expression 'it is not what you say, but how you say it'.

DID YOU KNOW?

Your own body language reveals your attitude. For example, it is easy for your lecturer to tell when you are not concentrating!

ACTIVITY

Work in pairs. Try ten different ways of saying the word 'no'.

What does each way of saying 'no' really say (i.e. what is the tone of voice implying)?

Research shows that voice and body language are the most important aspects of communication (see Figure 5.6).

If someone is providing customer care, it is important to be aware of the importance of body language. It is important also to develop the skills needed to read customers' body language. The following aspects of body language may already be familiar to you.

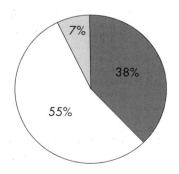

□ Words
■ Voice
□ Body language

Figure 5.6 Aspects of communication

	BODY LANGUAGE	INTERPRETATION
posture	• slouching • sitting up straight and leaning forward	• bored or tired • attentive or interested
gestures	• thumbs up • arms in air	• OK! • joy or excitement
eye contact	• avoiding eye contact • staring	• shyness or dishonesty • anger
facial expressions	• smiling • frowning	• happiness • worried or confused

Table 5.3

ACTIVITY

We all give many indications of how we are feeling. Take it in turns to act out the adjectives listed below. Add more of your own – remember you are interpreting body language, and so must not use words.

joy	**dismay**	**confusion**
anger	**excitement**	**sorrow**
boredom	**frustration**	

Create your own table of postures, expressions and what they might mean, using the table below as a guide:

BODY LANGUAGE	WHAT DOES IT MEAN?
arms crossed frowning/sighing	bored/cross confused

In order to provide excellent customer service, it is essential to be aware of body language and learn to monitor it so that a positive attitude is always conveyed.

KEY TERMS

Internal customers: colleagues, people who work within the same organisation.

External customers: customers who are not part of the organisation.

Homogenous: made up of similar parts.

Types of customers

We have identified that there are both internal and external customers. Organisations tend to focus their customer care on their external customers – after all, it is their satisfaction which will ultimately ensure the success of the business. However, the external customer is not simply one homogenous group; rather it is many different types of customers, all of whom have specific needs. It is only when we have established a customer's needs that we are able to offer products and services that can meet, or even exceed, their expectations.

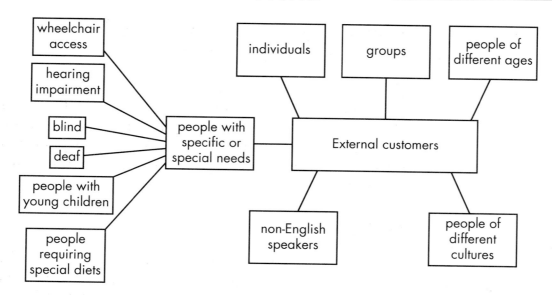

Figure 5.7 External customers

Individuals and groups

Individuals

Some individuals may book holidays by themselves because they wish to travel alone, explore, or meet new people and be independent. Others may have no choice. Bereaved, divorced or simply without friends who wish to do the same thing, these single people may be travelling alone reluctantly. Tour operators must try to meet the diverse needs of such individuals.

Groups

As well as respecting the person who wishes to travel alone, agents must try to ensure that the individuals who want to be part of a group are also catered for. This can be done through:

- offering a 'share scheme' (people of the same sex can be put in touch with each other before departure and arrange to share, thereby avoiding a single room charge)
- welcome meetings or introductions
- group meals
- excursion programme
- the representative

In any of these circumstances, it is the representative (the face of the company) who has the greatest ability to introduce single people to each other and ensure that they are catered for at all times. Tour operators must also cater for large groups of people who choose to travel together, as their requirements may be totally different. They may need:

- a group of rooms next to each other and on the same floor

- meals to be organised so that they can eat together
- an exclusive activity programme.

Special interest customers

If the group is a special interest group they will have additional demands. For example, if the group is on a diving, climbing, walking, bungee jumping or safari holiday, their group needs may include: transportation together, safety talks, group photographs, equipment hire and extra insurance.

Different age groups

Although different age groups may have different needs, the golden rule is not to make any assumptions and always establish client needs by asking 'open questions' (see section on selling skills on page 333).

Different age groups regularly travel together and so allowances may have to be made, for example young children and teenagers travelling with adults. The requirements of each age group are usually different but you must not assume that a sixteen year old does not want to go hill walking with his parents, or that his parents do not want to go clubbing! Travel and tourism customers are often put into one of the following general categories:

- young
- young, single, with no children
- young couple with child(ren) under six
- young couple with child(ren) over six
- couple, with children over eighteen living at home
- older couple with no children living at home
- older, single person

Scuba diving is an activity for different age groups

Source: Corbis

One of the biggest problems is organising activities for such a wide age range. Sometimes different activities are arranged for different age groups; other activities involve everyone, with the older ones acting as helpers. To ensure all the different customer types are satisfied, the Canvas Holiday Couriers are reminded:

- not to preach to the children – ask them what they would like to do
- that it is their role to make the holiday a success
- to be aware of the different needs of different ages and abilities
- that the service is both for children and parents – even if only one child turns up, he or she is the customer, so they must adapt the activities to suit his or her demands

Source: Adapted from Canvas Holiday Ltd. Courier Manual, 1999

ACTIVITY

Divide the class into small groups. Imagine that you work as a representative in a beach resort. Select one of the age or family categories described previously. Discuss what their needs might be.

Establish an evening entertainment programme for one of the age groups discussed.

KEY TERM

Culture: ideas, beliefs and values.

A tourist sign printed in several languages to aid understanding

Source: Life File/Emma Lee

Different cultures

The ability to recognise the different ideas, beliefs and values of different cultures will be acquired with experience. Once again, the important thing is to not make any assumptions about the differing needs of those cultures. A basic understanding of differing cultures will help you ask appropriate questions, through which the specific needs can then be established.

Non-English speakers

Misunderstandings and frustration can easily occur where a language barrier exists. To avoid this, and to provide good service, some travel and tourism jobs require that a second language is spoken by staff. This is particularly true of cabin crew, some TICs and hotel reception staff.

PROFILE *Welcome Programme*

The Regional Tourist Boards offer a series of training programmes, aiming to improve customer care. One of these two day programmes aims to provide basic skills in several languages. It is hoped that this will help attractions, TICs hotels and others to provide a better service to overseas customers.

Attractions very often provide leaflets in several European languages and Japanese literature is becoming increasingly available. Alternatively, symbols can be used – these are universally recognised and are commonly used at airports and major attractions. Should leaflets or symbols not be available, gestures and positive body language become essential and a dictionary may also prove useful!

DID YOU KNOW?

Black and yellow are the easiest colours for the visually impaired to recognise.

Other specific or special needs

Many people may have specific requirements that require additional care and attention. Such people expect the same level of excellent customer service as everyone else – in order to achieve this, you must pay particular consideration to their specific needs. As your role is to assess needs and then exceed them, this should also be possible for special needs. It simply requires sensitivity. Remember, the most important thing is not to presume you already know what a person needs, and never make customers with specific needs feel that they are 'different'. It is your job, in the provision of customer service, to provide whatever is required without making the customer feel that they are being a nuisance.

Examples of specific needs could include:

- dietary (e.g. vegan passenger on a flight)
- physical (e.g. child in a wheelchair visiting a museum)
- hearing (e.g. a deaf or hard of hearing man wanting to book a holiday)
- visual (e.g. partially sighted teenager wishing to take part in beach games)
- assistance (e.g. a single parent with young children)

PROFILE *Catering for specific needs at Stansted Airport*

All airports have to deal with the specific needs of a variety of passengers. Stansted Airport has been particularly successful in this area. The terminal offers the following features:

1 A multi-faith chapel, aiming to cater for all religions. Special care has been taken with the decoration and furniture to ensure that no single religion is dominant (for example, there is an altar but there are also prayer mats).

2 All directional signs are in black and yellow.

3 Many areas are 'looped', to aid those with hearing impairment.

4 All security staff take part in a disability awareness training programme. They can finger spell, lead a blind person and know how to deal courteously with a wheelchair passenger. They are often required to search passengers. The need for sensitivity is paramount.

5 The entire airport is wheelchair accessible – for the car parks to the terminal and for flights. Even the internal transit system is 'gap free'.

6 The airport employs an Aviation and Airport Service – a company who provide physical assistance to those passengers who need it (e.g. to push a wheelchair, or to help a single parent with young children).

7 A representative from the airport is employed to ensure all aspects of the Disability Discrimination Act are adhered to.

As a result of their care and sensitivity in recognising the specific needs of passengers, Stansted Airport won the Queen Elizabeth Foundation Access Award in 1998.

Golden rules when assessing customer needs:

- Never presume you know what a customer needs.
- Never react with surprise to a customer's request.
- Never make a customer feel 'different'.
- If you cannot meet a customer's needs, always explain why and offer an alternative.

ACTIVITY

Work in pairs and imagine you work in a hotel reception. Assess how you would react in the following situations. Discuss your answers and decide on the most sensitive questions and their solutions.

A well dressed lady in a wheel-chair is struggling to move up the slight slope leading towards the reception desk.

A group of Japanese basketball players are all standing in reception. You think that they are waiting to be checked in. Your Japanese speaking colleague is in a meeting, but will be available in 15 minutes. You do not speak Japanese.

A young mother is sitting in reception, drinking tea. She seems unable to cope with her two young children, who are disturbing other guests.

A gentleman with a slight hearing impairment has been staying in the hotel for a week. He keeps coming over to chat to you and is obviously lonely. However, you keep having to interrupt conversations with him to deal with guests at reception.

A gentleman asks about the different facilities for worship within the hotel. You do not know his religion.

Face to face: dealing directly with a customer, in person.

E-mail: electronic mail.

Dealing with customers

In all dealings with customers your objectives are to:

- identify the customer's needs
- meet the customer's needs quickly and efficiently
- exceed their expectations
- produce a satisfied customer

This can only be achieved through effective communication.

What is effective communication?

- the message is clear and accurate
- the information can be understood (no jargon used)
- the information is reinforced by body language
- the correct medium is used (telephone, letter or face to face)

When communicating effectively with someone, the information that you mean to give is understood exactly. However, communication can often be ineffective, in that it may be:

KEY TERM

Effective communication: means that the message sent is the same as the one received

- muddled
- garbled
- inaccurate
- too brief
- too long
- contradicted by body language
- spelt badly (if written).

ACTIVITY

Work in small groups. Each of you must try to remember three communication problems you have experienced at home, at college or with friends. Describe how the ineffective communication occurred and what happened as a result.

Communication is an important part of life and in a service industry, such as travel and tourism, excellent communication skills are needed. Employees must be able to communicate in many different ways, for example:

- dealing with colleagues and customers face to face
- on the telephone to customers and colleagues
- writing letters, memos and E-mails
- producing posters, notices, signs and window displays.

Face to face communication

Face to face communication is perhaps the easiest form of communication. When talking directly to a customer, you can see their reaction and use body language to reinforce your message. Personal appearance can be used to create a positive first impression and a warm, enthusiastic attitude can be portrayed by way of smile and tone of voice.

Within a high street travel agency, TIC or hotel, face to face communication is the most common way of dealing with customers. Travel consultants are encouraged to:

- get up from behind their desks and approach customers, to offer assistance
- ask open questions, e.g. 'How can I help you?', not 'Can I help you?'
- be smartly dressed
- smile
- use eye contact
- when searching for holidays, show the customers the computer screen, to make them feel more involved
- note full client details and use the client's name
- acknowledge other customers who are waiting, but not serve more than one customer at a time
- ask the customer if they mind, before answering a telephone (if no other consultants are available)
- give clients a personal business card before they leave, so that they can easily get back in touch with you.

One-to-one communication

One-to-one situations can be highly rewarding, and are common in the daily business of a travel agent. With care and effort, the travel consultant will hopefully be able to find an appropriate holiday, exceed expectations and satisfy customers. They will then benefit themselves from increased job satisfaction – especially when the satisfied customer returns. In this situation, customers may expect you to remember their names and where they have been on holiday, and although this may be difficult, you should try to remember! Even if you cannot remember a customer's name, your non-verbal communication can indicate that you recognise them and it is always relevant to ask if they enjoyed their holiday.

Group communication

Group situations occur frequently for tour guides and resort representatives and require a different approach. Whilst it is important to make everyone feel that they are being treated as an individual, it may be impossible or impractical to speak to everyone individually about matters such as fire procedures, excursions or airport transfer arrangements. It is important, therefore, to follow the guidelines given in Table 5.4, to ensure that communications are as effective as possible:

1 Choose an appropriate place.	Background noise can stop people hearing information. Tour managers often give basic information on a coach – clients are less likely to be distracted and a microphone helps them to be heard.
2 Timing is important.	Tell people about places and things, when they can see them. Do not try to give people important information when they are either very hungry or very tired (e.g. the 0500 hours coach transfer after a night flight is not the time to be talking about excursions!). Simply give them a time for the welcome meeting the next day, and remind them of that time as they get off the coach.
3 Structure your talk and vary you tone of voice.	Chatting to groups on holiday is very much like giving a presentation – make sure the information is presented in a logical order and is signposted (e.g. '. . . and now I want to tell you about . . .'.
4 Give opportunities for individuals to talk to you.	Within a group, some people may have special needs, or may have misunderstood or not heard part of your talk. Always ask if anyone has any questions at the end – this allows everyone to benefit from your answer (you may have missed something out or have been unclear). In addition, always provide an opportunity for individuals to approach you and ask specific questions. This can be done easily (e.g. 'I will be in the bar for about half an hour once we get back to the hotel, so if anyone has any questions, do feel free to see me there.'
5 Be enthusiastic about your subject!	

Table 5.4

Telephone communication

Communicating by telephone relies on good use of language and listening skills. It is particularly important to communicate clearly and check that the message sent is the same as the one received, people cannot read facial expressions and other non-verbal signals while on the telephone.

Although use of the telephone may be on the decline, with the development of E-mail, it remains an essential method of passing on information. Your skills in this area, therefore, must be finely tuned to avoid poor communication and any problems that this might create.

ACTIVITY

Consider any telephone calls that you have recently made to companies.

How was your call handled? Were you impressed with or disappointed by the service? Why was this? Identify the criteria that created a positive or negative impression of the customer service of these companies.

Good telephone techniques involve:

- conveying a positive impression on the telephone
- using words carefully, to communicate clearly
- using the tone of voice to create a positive image

Conveying a positive impression

First impressions also count on the telephone. When calling customers, it is important always to identify who you are and then clearly state why you are calling. If you are not used to using the telephone in a business environment, you may wish to write down the key points of information that you need to convey to your customer, before dialling.

At the end of the call it is always a good idea to recap on the key points discussed, before ending the conversation, as this can help to avoid any misunderstanding. Always have a notebook and pen beside you so that you can make notes while speaking to the customer. This also helps you recap correctly at the end, and pass on messages later.

Telephone communication involves handling incoming calls as well as making calls. In order to create a positive image, many companies now insist that all incoming calls are answered in the same way, for example:

❛ Good morning/afternoon, Breakaway Holidays, Lauren speaking. How may I help you? ❜

Although lengthy, this greeting guarantees a positive first impression, and the caller also knows that she has got the correct number and knows exactly who he or she is speaking to.

Using words to communicate clearly

Clear speech is vital for telephone conversations, because the listener cannot lip-read if they are unsure of what is being said. Remember to:

- be clear (use short sentences or phrases)

- do not use jargon
- be concise
- speak clearly (pronounce your words properly)
- speak slowly
- if possible, eliminate all background noise
- make sure you are speaking directly into the telephone mouthpiece

---

Words

Politeness	Politeness on the telephone is essential on incoming and outgoing calls. Not faked politeness, but real politeness. The 'please' and 'thank you' and 'I'm sorry you are upset' that rarely get said on the telephone. We are good at saying things face to face, but we tend to forget them when using the telephone. Good manners, thoughtfulness and the use of a person's name can all help to change the effects of attitude.
Vocabulary	We should always use vocabulary that is easily understood by the person we are talking to. Try not to use words that are 'over-worked'. Avoid technical terms and never use slang on the telephone. Do not use words for the sake of showing that you know them or that you are intelligent. Express ideas clearly and simply.
Speed of Speech	Adapt the rate of speech to that of the person on the other end of the telephone. A moderate rate is best. So we must speak slowly and distinctly, forming words carefully and not omitting syllables. When we speak slowly and clearly, and with frequent pauses, we are able to design our sentences or our thoughts more logically and the person at the other end is, therefore, able to understand us more clearly. Remember a person cannot lip-read over the telephone, therefore, your rate of speech must be such that the person on the other end can assimilate what you are saying as quickly as you say it.
Ask Yourself These Questions	1. Do I Speak clearly? 2. Is my voice interesting? 3. Are my words correct and understandable? 4. Do I sound enthusiastic? 5. Is there a 'smile' in my voice?

Figure 5.8 Extract from An Effective Telephone Selling Workshop for Thomas Cook Holidays

Using tone of voice to create a positive image

We have discussed how the voice determines 38% of the communication in face to face communication. On the telephone this percentage is greater, as it is impossible to interpret body language.

Voice

Impression	An important factor in the use of the telephone is voice. If it is flat and uninteresting, people will not listen. To gain someone's attention at the beginning of the call your voice must be pleasant to listen to, varied of tone, clear and sincere. Remember, we only get one opportunity to make a good first impression.
Pitch	Keep the pitch even and low. One of the best transmitting sounds is the lower range of the female voice. Many female voices tend to become shrill when upset, whereas a man's can become loud and dictatorial.
Smile as you Dial	'Smile as you Dial' idea was designed for people on the telephone. We can hear a smile in someone's voice – this is because of the use of the cheek muscles.
Colour	A dull monotonous voice on the telephone is very boring and when we are bored we do not listen. It is, therefore, essential to develop a good telephone voice. It is important to remember that the person on the other end of the telephone cannot see us, we cannot, therefore, rely on 'body language' to help us get our point across. We are relying, utterly, on our voice to project our enthusiasm. Callers telephoning your company or you telephoning them, the first impression they get is the way in which your voice comes over. An efficient communicator must develop a good telephone voice in order to project a pleasing personality.
Aids to Assist Effectiveness	Good posture is essential for proper breathing. The majority of us slouch when at our desk and this does affect the tone of our voice. Deep breathing is essential – shallow breathing causes breathlessness and interrupts the flow of words. Deep breathing is also essential to bring the brain back to clear thoughts after we have been upset. If after an upsetting telephone call, we take a few deep breaths, we mix the adrenaline that goes into our blood stream with oxygen, this enables us to think more clearly.

Figure 5.9 *Extract from An Effective Telephone Selling Workshop for Thomas Cook Holidays*

ACTIVITY

Work in groups of three. Two people must sit with their backs to each other (so that they cannot see one another's body language) while the other one observes. Role play the following two conversations.

1 James is calling his regular travel agent to enquire about a weekend break with his friend Sarah. He has already been to Prague this summer on business and now wants a sun holiday.

2 Liz wants to complain to a tour operator that the all-inclusive holiday she has just been on was not all-inclusive at all.

Ensure you see the guidelines regarding positive impact, words and voice, to ensure you have an effective telephone conversation.

Written communication

Written communication with external customers is usually by letter, however, it may also include faxes and use of E-mail. Internal customer communications will include all of these, plus memos, telephone messages and handwritten notes.

Other forms of written communications will also help to determine the image of the company, and all of these require faultless presentation. They include:

- brochures
- holiday itineraries, invoices and other computer printed information
- posters and notices
- advertisements
- timetables
- tickets

ACTIVITY

Gather three formal business letters from home. What image does each create of the organisation? Choose from some of the descriptions listed below:

- trendy
- clear
- scruffy
- efficient

- disorganised
- muddled
- stiff/formal

- friendly
- old fashioned
- pompous

How are these images portrayed?

Many companies send letters that lack a personal, friendly approach. These still use standard phrases that were developed a long time ago. Although written communication today is usually formal, its tone can vary.

ACTIVITY

Compare the following introductory sentences:

1 'Our records show that I have not yet received the final balance for your forthcoming holiday.'
2 'Despite my letter of 6 January, I still do not appear to have received the final balance for your forthcoming holiday.
3 'This is to give you a final warning that unless you final balance is received by . . .'.

What impression does each of the above give of the sender's mood?

Clear written communication must be well-structured. Good grammar and perfect spelling are essential (if necessary, have yours checked by someone else).

Your address

Recipient's address

(Date)

Dear Mrs Jawoski
or
Dear Sir/Madam

Re: (what this letter is about)

Beginning
State why you are writing e.g. 'Thank you for your application for the position of . . .'
I am very sorry to hear that your holiday in Ibiza was . . .'
Despite 2 previous reminders, I still have not received the final balance . . .'

Middle
Set out what information the reader requires, or what you require from them:
• use paragraphs
• be concise
• ensure all information is relevant

End
State what should happen next or conclude simply e.g. 'I will investigate your complaint fully and be in touch with you within ten days.' or: 'I hope this provides all the information you need.'

Yours sincerely
or
Yours faithfully

Sarah Bell

Figure 5.10 *Example of formal written communication*

Note in Figure 5.10, that if you use a person's name at the beginning you must sign off with 'Yours sincerely'. For Sir or madam, use 'Yours faithfully'.

ACTIVITY

Jenny Bell has left a message on your office answering machine. She wants to take her two children, James (13) and Sarah (11) on an activity holiday next summer. Investigate possible holidays and write a letter to her outlining three possible options.

Revenue: income.

Tourism concern: a pressure group, concerned with the impacts of tourism.

Selling skills

Selling products and services is just one of the many customer service situations you might become involved in, within the travel and tourism industry. It may be an important part of your job, in terms of both the company's profits and your own salary. As most travel and tourism organisations are private sector companies, the level of sales determines the success of the company. We will, therefore, cover this area, before examining other customer service situations.

Why is selling important?

Selling generates revenue, which creates profits for private sector companies (for example travel agencies, hotels and tour operators). In addition, provided customers are receiving what they want (or more than what they want), sales can produce the following benefits:

- new customers
- repeat customers
- an edge over the competition
- a happy and efficient workforce
- customer loyalty and repeat business

These benefits are relevant to all the industry sectors: public, private and voluntary. The National Trust for example, being part of the voluntary sector, is keen to attract more members and visitors to its properties. Although it is not aiming to make a profit, the income will enable it to spend more on maintenance and other purchases. A further example is Tourism Concern, which aims to increase membership sales to help fund campaigns concerning the negative impacts of tourism on host communities, in particular in the developing world. Museums and amenities, in the public sector, may wish to increase visitor numbers to ensure their survival.

You will see that the benefits of sales are also the benefits of satisfied customers (see page 298) – good selling will result in a satisfied customer (naturally this will only be the case if you are meeting your customers' needs and selling them something that meets or exceeds their expectations). A satisfied customer can have many positive impacts on an organisation.

Selling services

Purchasing a holiday, or any other service within this industry, differs from buying physical goods. Imagine that you have been given £200 to spend on new clothes one weekend. You will go out on Saturday to try on new clothes, feel their quality, see how well they fit you, and compare them with lots of other similar items, before you eventually decide on how to spend your money.

If you are given money to spend on a holiday however, and therefore go to a travel agent instead, you will not be able to see your purchase, assess its quality or know if it suits you before you pay. You will be buying your holiday based on the image portrayed in the brochures and on the advice of the travel consultant.

Selling travel and tourism services differs from selling physical goods in the following ways:

1 The purchaser cannot test the goods, as a holiday is not tangible. Unlike clothes, it cannot be tested out or tried on. The customer is buying an experience. Thus, the selling of holidays is often referred to as 'selling a dream'.
2 Each customer buys a unique experience. Although two people may be on the same holiday together, they may each experience it differently. This can depend on their personality, whether they like the people they meet, or even on whether they have suitable weather.
3 The people who are selling the holiday and the staff the customers meet on holiday (for example the holiday representative or the hotel staff) are all part of the holiday experience. It is the level of service that can often determine how enjoyable a holiday is. Although the hotel cleanliness, the quality of food and the standards of rooms are important; the receptionist, chambermaid and waiter are equally so, in determining customer satisfaction.

These factors apply to all travel and tourism products bought in travel agencies and hotels, or from airlines.

The importance of product knowledge

It is essential to have an extensive knowledge of the product in order to sell it successfully. This is why companies spend huge amounts of time and money on staff training. Sales techniques and communication skills can indeed be taught and will improve with practise. Product knowledge does, however, need to be learnt quickly. It is an area in which the seller must be highly proactive.

ACTIVITY

Imagine that you have been fully trained, and are about to start a new job in one of the following positions:

- aircraft cabin crew
- travel agency consultant
- resort representative
- hotel receptionist
- theme park ride attendant

For each position, list the product knowledge you would need in order to maintain high levels of company sales (and customer service).

Tour operators recognise the importance of the travel agent's product knowledge for their own sales. They regularly run familiarisation trips for staff, or 'fam trips' as they are known in the trade. These are considered by many travel agency staff to be some of the 'perks' of the jobs – a free trip, the objective of which is for the travel agents to have fun, learn about a product or destination and sell it on their return to their agency.

DID YOU KNOW?

Familiarisation trips are also called 'educationals'.

Other methods used by tour operators to train travel agents in product knowledge include: providing training packs (see Figure 5.11) and sending someone from the tour operator to visit the travel agent and conduct a training session. Many travel agents do not open until 9:30 a.m. or 10:00 a.m. one day per week, in order to allow for regular training and updates by tour operators.

Product Knowledge and Unique Selling Points

Product Knowledge does not mean just reading out what it says in the duty free magazine! Passengers invariably ask questions about products before they buy them and to give them confidence in the product you have to have the answers.

Product Knowledge is also a good way of opening a conversation, for example, 'Have you tried the new CKBe fragrance?' This would then need to be followed up with your own personal recommendation. Another, 'We have the latest skin care range from Clarins, have you read about it in all the women's magazines?'

Product Knowledge is a very valuable selling tool. You are offering information on a product, not asking someone if they want to buy it, which leads to the passenger's perception of service and not sales.

Figure 5.11 Product knowledge and unique selling points

Source: Service Training Onboard Reference Manual 1999, Virgin Atlantic

PROFILE *Improving product knowledge at Travel Destinations*

Travel Destinations is a small, but highly successful travel agent. It is situated in a small town within commuting distance of London. The key to its success has been the combination of a good location and the development of niche markets. The Manager, Pamela Relph, joined the agency in 1999. Although sales were good, she was aware that many local people booked holidays elsewhere and she suspected that this was in London, during their lunch hours, and increasingly, on the Internet.

Concerned about the security of her own job, she analysed sales to establish the main products and destinations. 60% of bookings of over two weeks' duration were long haul and these were spread evenly over the year. Ski bookings were negligible, but there had been a marked increase in cruise bookings over the last three years. Short European city breaks amounted to about 20% of revenue. Pamela decided that increased product knowledge would help Travel Destinations become more specialised. In the first year, she selected winter sun, cruising and short breaks as products to develop.

She asked all staff to come in to work at 8:30 a.m. on a Wednesday for a six month period. She used the first hour of the day to train the staff in the different products. Approximately every other week, a representative from a tour operator would come in to the agency and talk to the staff about their new products. On other weeks, Pamela did the training herself. This included travel geography and brochure quizzes. Staff were told which brochure they would be tested on and were expected to prepare in advance.

The main thing that Pamela noticed after the initial six month training period, was an increase in staff confidence. Everyone appeared to be making more sales and, as a result, they seemed happier in their jobs. Sales had certainly improved. Although no figures had been published, Pamela was aware that the shop was busier and sales had increased (she estimated by about 30%). Two 'fam trips' were offered to the agency, by different tour operators, in recognition of increased sales – a cruise and a weekend break in Prague.

A	Attention	• raise customer awareness
		• establish rapport with the customer
I	Interest	• investigate customer needs
D	Desire	• present the product or service
A	Action	• close the sale
		• deliver after sales service

Table 5.5

The AIDA technique: a reminder

The sales process

The AIDA technique, as discussed in Chapter 4, Marketing travel and tourism, is an established sales technique. Put simply, it is essential to attract customer's **attention** before you can investigate their needs (raise their interest), create the **desire** to purchase (by showing it to them or explaining its features and benefits) and then to sell (**action**).

KEY TERMS

Linked selling: selling complimentary goods and services (e.g. insurance with a package holiday).

Rapport: a positive relationship and understanding.

DID YOU KNOW?

In 1984, when Virgin Atlantic first started operating, their entire duty free range consisted of 40 items. In 1999, it featured 198 items, with prices ranging from £5 to £325, generating a turnover of £11 million.

DID YOU KNOW?

In 1998, duty free contributed 6% to Virgin Atlantic's profits. Duty free is the only revenue-generating service in-flight; meals, drinks and amenity kits are a cost to the company.

DID YOU KNOW?

It is estimated that our tone of voice and body language account for 93% of our methods of communication.

Raising customer awareness

Methods of raising customer awareness have already been covered in Chapter 4, Marketing travel and tourism. They include:

- Advertising – TV, newspapers, billboards, posters, window displays, brochures and leaflets.
- Sales promotions – special offers, free gifts, loyalty incentives.
- Public relations – press releases, sponsorship.
- Direct marketing – catalogues, direct mail, media direct response, E-shopping.
- Personal selling.

Any of the above examples may make a potential consumer aware of a new product or simply remind him or her of the fact that they want or need the product in question.

There are other simple methods of raising awareness that can also increase sales. All organisations are eager to sell complimentary products to further increase sales. Leaflets for car hire, airport car parking and overnight accommodation at airports can be given to clients when booking holidays. Tour operators can offer internal flights within the UK, to accompany the booking of an early morning departure on a long haul holiday, and travel agents will always offer insurance in addition to your flight or accommodation booking.

Linked selling is the name given to the process whereby the sales person offers complimentary products. The customer may not have thought about buying other products, but once made aware, may be tempted to buy. For example, an air steward, having sold a necklace as part of their duty free range, could then offer to sell the customer matching earrings.

ACTIVITY

Work in small groups. Consider the last large purchase that either you or a member of your family made. What other products and/or services were offered to you when you made that purchase?

Identify a tourism organisation within your local area. List all the techniques used to raise awareness of products or services

Establishing rapport with the customer

Establishing rapport is about creating a situation in which the customer feels at ease and relaxed. The customer must not feel under any pressure to buy. He or she will be confident in the sales person's ability, and feel able to ask any questions that they wish. Trust will be established between the sales person and the customer (see Figure 5.12).

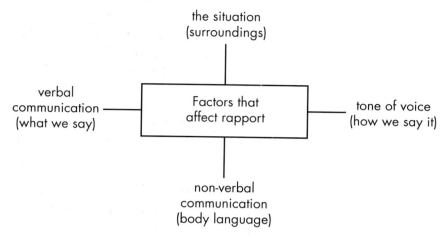

Figure 5.12 Rapport

We have already investigated how our tone of voice and body language contribute to communicating. Personal image is also a part of our non-verbal communication and is an indication of our attitude towards ourselves and our customers.

The environment in which we work contributes to making a customer feel relaxed and confident in our abilities. For example, when visiting a travel agency, it is to be expected that:

- it is clean
- there are no consultants eating at their desks
- coffee cups are hidden away
- staff do not have personal conversations or telephone calls in front of clients
- desks are tidy
- telephones are answered quickly
- the level of noise is acceptable
- computers and other electronic equipment is working properly

Rapport is established by:

- creating a positive first impression – smiling, professional appearance and a warm greeting
- offering clients a seat
- serving clients quickly and efficiently
- not allowing oneself to be distracted
- making good eye contact
- positive non-verbal communication throughout
- a professional working environment

Investigating customers' needs

It has been established that there are many different types of clients, all of which have different needs. The most challenging part of the sales process is to establish exactly what it is the customer wants. As a sales person, it is important to remember that some needs might be hidden. For example, a couple might be embarrassed by their limited budget; a single person might be uncomfortable about the fact that she is travelling alone.

Questions must be carefully phrased, body language must be observed and understanding checked. Throughout, it is important to pay careful attention to both verbal and non-verbal forms of communication!

In order to establish a customer's needs, you must not only ask for the correct information: you must also consider how to ask the questions. An effective questioning technique will involve asking different types of questions (*Source:* Adapted from *An Effective Telephone Workshop for Thomas Cook Holidays*):

1 Open questions – allow for long answers. They always begin with 'who', 'what', 'when', 'where', 'why', 'which' or 'how'. They will give you lots of information that you may not have asked for (e.g. 'What is it you most want to get out of this holiday?').
2 Leading questions – give information and facts. They will start with 'who', 'what', 'when', 'where', 'why', 'which' or 'how', but will produce specific answers (e.g. 'Where have you been in the past, that you really enjoyed?').
3 Closed questions – will produce a 'yes' or 'no' response. They can be used to confirm information (e.g. 'Have you ever been in a Club 18–30 holiday before?').

Active listening is essential. This encourages the client to keep on giving you information. This may involve:

- nodding
- saying encouraging things
- repeating key words (this encourages the speaker to expand on specific points)

Following are some guidelines for establishing customer needs:

- use open questions (e.g. 'what?', 'why?', 'when?' or 'how?')
- use positive language
- use statements of feeling to build rapport (e.g. 'I see' or 'I understand')
- check understanding (e.g. 'So what you really want is . . . ?')
- actively listen (e.g. say 'OK', nod or make notes)

- maintain good eye contact
- make sure your working environment is professional (i.e. neat, tidy and clean)

ACTIVITY

Work in pairs and role-play a travel agency situation. Use open, leading and closed questions to establish your client's needs and use active listening techniques throughout.

Repeat the exercise using inactive listening techniques (e.g. looking away, not concentrating). How did the use of inactive listening make your client feel?

Presenting the product or service

Once the customer's needs have been established, sales staff must use their product knowledge to find something that matches the expectations of the customer. As discussed on page 328, product knowledge is vital for successful selling. Although some employers provide a lot of training and much of the knowledge will be acquired with experience, new staff must also take some of the responsibility for increasing their own product knowledge.

The key to presenting the product is to identify the three or four things that are most important to the client, and to first of all explain why this product matches their needs.

You may recall the section on features and benefits, in Chapter 4 Marketing travel and tourism. It is important to consider the features of the product and its benefits, before you present it to clients. For example, the features of a two day weekend break in Prague might include: local flights and accommodation in a 5 star hotel with a sports centre. The benefits to the customer include: not having to take time off work, relaxation and the opportunity to play some sport.

ACTIVITY

Liz and Tim have two children, aged 6 and 8 years old. The sales assistant has established that their maximum budget for a holiday is £800, and that they would like a beach holiday, with activities available for their kids. They wish to go abroad, but do not want to go to Spain. A half-board arrangement is preferred by Liz, although Tim thinks self-catering offers more flexibility. They do not mind when they travel and appreciate that the length of their stay may be restricted by their budget.

Find a suitable holiday for this couple. Role-play the presentation of this product to Liz and Tim, ensuring that you highlight the features of the holiday that match their needs, and the resulting benefits.

Customers will not always accept that the products offered match their needs. In this case, the sales person may not have paid enough care and attention in analysing the customer's requirements. Alternatively, the customer may need some reassurance as to the features and benefits of the product. Finally, the customer may simply be difficult to please. It is important to think of difficult customers as a challenge. Never respond aggressively to a customer and do not take it personally.

Techniques for handling objections include:

1 Accept the customer's objections, e.g. 'I can understand that you feel that this resort would be too busy'. This will defuse the situation and help you to understand what the real objection is. Some clients, for example, may find it easier to say a resort is too busy, rather than too expensive. In this situation, rephrase and clarify what you have said – you may then find out what the real objection is. If necessary, ask more open questions – try again to establish the customer's real needs.
2 Do not take objections personally. Stay calm and maintain positive non-verbal communication.
3 Overcome the objection by offering a solution or alternative. You can, however, only do this once you know what the objection is.

Closing the sale

Sales will come to a natural end when the customer decides that the product on offer is what they want (i.e. its features entirely match their needs). Under no circumstances should clients be rushed. Some people are happy to make quick decisions, while others may wish to consider, or discuss with friends or partners and will purchase later. The sales person must watch for these signs.

Positive responses, such as 'that seems fine' or 'OK, I will take that' are clear indications that a purchase is to be made. An appropriate response would be to reconfirm all details with the client, complete the paperwork and take payment. During the close, the sales person should again highlight the features of the holiday or product that meet the customer's requirements.

The customer may, however, simply need more time to come to a decision. Offering to 'hold' a holiday or flight on option, reassuring the customer that there is still plenty of availability, is part of a good sales technique. It is more likely to result in a satisfied customer than if the person(s) is rushed, buys and remains unsure as to whether they have purchased what they really want. If the customer does not purchase straight away, ensure that he or she knows your name and how to contact you before the end of the conversation.

After sales service

The extent to which an after sales service exists varies enormously from company to company. With some non-travel products, the type of after sales service which is required is quite clear (for example, after buying a new computer, after sales service may include free delivery and installation and a 24 hour helpline, plus collection and replacement if faulty).

Travel is different from the purchase of other goods, in that the purchase is often well in advance of the actual holiday. Thus, after sales service also includes all the queries about a holiday or flight that may arise after the sale, but before the departure. Most tour operators have a separate department to deal with existing customers (known either as administration or operations). Prior to departure, part of this service will include sending out information packs, tickets and itineraries. Other aspects of after sales service can include:

- contacting the client after the holiday, for feedback
- delivery of brochures in subsequent years
- mailing of special offers

KEY TERMS

Interpretation panels: large boards explaining what the site or attraction is.

Visitor centre: a building providing information and facilities for the visitor.

Customer service situations

We have established that customer service situations may require face to face, telephone or written responses and have examined in detail how to deal with a selling situation. We will now look at other customer service situations, which are common within the travel and tourism industry.

Providing information

The ability to provide correct information in a customer-friendly manner is vital to good customer service. Customers require information upon every encounter with an organisation and their requests will vary in complexity.

Some staff are employed only to provide information. For example, it is the primary role of the staff working in a Tourism Information Centre (TIC) to provide relevant, up-to-date and appropriate information on car parking, visitor attractions, transportation and accommodation, within the customer's local area. However, all roles have some element of information provision. Simple queries that could be asked of almost anyone within the industry include:

- How much does it cost?
- Where is the toilet?
- May I have a refund?
- Can I speak to your manager?
- When do you close?
- Are there any special offers?

Certain information, such as that provided by a TIC, can only be given on a face to face basis. This is expensive for organisations, as it means staff have to be employed to provide this high level of service. There is no doubt, however, that this is necessary in many cases, for example, in travel agencies or overseas resorts.

Other methods of providing information may answer some customers' questions and so eliminate the need for face to face contact. For example signs, notices and leaflets at a theme park can deal with many customer questions and web pages are increasingly being used to find out about local attractions instead of visiting a TIC. Such methods may mean that it is also not necessary to employ so many staff.

In addition to employing staff to provide information, other methods include:

Interpretative panels

Providing information on large panels about the attraction at its entrance can help customers to find what they are looking for. The necessity for guides is reduced and customers are more likely to leave the attraction feeling informed and satisfied. This may also contribute to a feeling of having received 'value for money'.

Interpretative panels can also be used outside, at nature reserves, in parks or on popular walks. They may provide educational information about the area, wildlife and history, or even the need to take litter home and respect the countryside.

Visitor centres

Visitor centres often have two objectives: to provide information and to offer services (e.g. toilets). They will usually have a shop and possibly a cafeteria, both of which will, of course, generate money. Private sector tourist attractions will always offer these facilities, both to increase visitor satisfaction and to generate revenue. Visitor centres are also found in remote areas, in National Parks and the Highlands of Scotland for example, where they are run by the local authorities. Here, they are used to attract and manage tourists. The information on offer at such centres will include maps, details of circular walks, weather reports and local advice. Public transportation timetables and details of local facilities will also be available.

Signs

At airports, theme parks, overseas resorts and in our local towns, signs provide us with information about the locality of toilets, information points, buses, trains, car parks and other essential details. Simple signs can provide us with information easily, without the need to search for staff to ask.

The brown tourist attraction signs seen from major roads clearly direct tourists to visitor attractions. Good road signs to and within destinations can contribute greatly to customer satisfaction – can you remember the last time that signs seemed to stop before you arrived at your destination, meaning that you were lost and how frustrating that was?

Published material (e.g. leaflets and brochures)

Most attractions print leaflets, both to advertise and to inform. These will be available at TICs and also at the attraction itself. They may include maps or information about the attraction, opening and closing times and how to get there. Brochures provide extensive information and are a tour operator's main selling tool.

Information packs

Tour operators send out information packs as part of their service. These may include details about the resort, health and safety information, emergency contracts, itineraries and luggage labels. Guide books and maps are also sometimes provided. There are many advantages to the holiday-maker being provided with such extensive information. Rather than the representative telling the customer face to face, or reservations staff giving them the details by telephone, the holiday-maker has a record to refer to. The tour operator also knows that essential information cannot be left out or forgotten – providing more information means that a more professional impression of the company will be given.

Timetables

Most UK rail, bus and airline companies now offer free timetables. Although costly to produce, they enable more customers to check their services from home, and so fewer staff are needed on the enquiries desks.

Web pages

There are cheap to produce, easy to update and increasingly being used by customers. More and more organisations are now recognising the value of setting up web pages.

Giving advice

Giving advice is usually done in a face to face situation, but it can be difficult! Consider some of the situations in which your friends have asked you for advice? You may have expressed your own feelings and regretted it afterwards. Whilst it is not advisable to give personal advice to a client (for example whether or not they should visit their mother for Christmas), giving advice on different resorts, operators and services is essential.

The key to giving good advice is to:

- listen carefully, so that you know exactly what the customer needs
- propose possible options (two or three), e.g. 'Well if you went on the 3.30 p.m. train, you would arrive for tea, whereas the later one would mean that you won't arrive until after dark'
- ensure that the information or advice you provide is accurate. Use referenced sources wherever possible, to check

- use the feedback from the client (verbal and non-verbal) to help him or her to select their own preferred option.

Remember, when people ask for advice, they usually only want enough information to help them reach their own conclusions!

Keeping records

Excellent administration skills are all part of providing good customer service. Legible, easily understood records that can be found immediately, convey an efficient and professional image. Keeping accurate and detailed records may be as simple as collecting a customer's name and address, completing a form or recording financial transactions. Just as the customer will judge you on your personal appearance, the state of your organisation's records will create an impression about the efficiency of an organisation, and also of you.

DID YOU KNOW?

When helping someone who is in a wheelchair, it is important not to lean over them. If possible, pull up a chair so that you are speaking to them on the same level and can have good eye contact with them.

Providing assistance

Always offer assistance before actually assisting. Do not presume – the customer may feel patronised. A person who is struggling with a wheelchair or a young mother trying to push a pram and carry a suitcase may not want assistance. It is good customer service to offer, but do not be overly enthusiastic in these circumstances.

Dealing with people with specific needs is a sensitive area – remember not to make people feel 'different' and always address them directly, not via their companions.

DID YOU KNOW?

One of the most common problems when dealing with people with disabilities is to only see the disability and not the person This is the 'does he want sugar?' situation.

Dealing with problems

Working in an environment with such a high level of person to person contact means that there will always be problems and complaints to handle. Complaints are dealt with in detail in the next section. Problems, such as lost luggage, delays or stolen goods, do not initially reflect badly on the company. Indeed, some of the problems may in fact be the customer's own fault. It is important to be aware, however, that these often result in complaints if they are not handled quickly and satisfactorily.

Problems provide an opportunity to excel in customer care, but also to fail. You must deal with a problem in exactly the same way as you would handle a complaint. Although the customer is less likely to be angry and, therefore, the situation is easier to overcome, exactly the same skills are needed. Examples of problems include the customer who:

- leaves their handbag in your travel agency by mistake
- falls asleep on a bus and the driver has to wake them at the terminal
- has a passport stolen in Paris
- misses a train (and has someone waiting to meet them at the other end)
- is anxious because their friend has not arrived for lunch at the hotel
- has a sick child on a coach journey.

ACTIVITY

Imagine that you are faced with each of the previously listed problems List the options that you could propose to the customer.

Work in pairs. Role-play those same situations. While none of the situations have occurred as a result of faults within your organisation (i.e. they are not complaints), it is up to you to do your utmost for the customer and ensure they are satisfied with the solution(s). Use the guidelines in the next section on handling complaints, to help you.

Handling complaints

As a member of an organisation selling products and services, your aim is to produce a satisfied customer. Most of the time this may be easy and dealing with customers is both positive and rewarding. However, even the most successful travel companies receive complaints. Sometimes these are justified, and sometimes they are not. In either case, knowledge of procedures will help you deal with the complaint efficiently and without becoming personally involved. Throughout any dealings with a complaint, it is important to view it as an opportunity to turn a customer around, i.e. to change a complaining customer into a satisfied customer. This is a challenge, but remember that it could ensure repeat business, customer loyalty and will give you job satisfaction.

Examples of complaints to a tour operator may include:

- telephones not being answered quickly
- reservation staff not advising of hotel changes to those advertised in the brochure
- hotels that are not clean
- local people not speaking good English
- representative(s) arriving late for every meeting
- flowers being sent to the honeymoon couple, that caused hayfever

- evening BBQ and disco not taking place
- excursion to local market being too busy and hot.

 ACTIVITY

Examine the list of complaints above. Put them into the following categories: 'justified' and 'not justified'.

Are there any circumstances when those you consider 'not justified' could be justified?

 PROFILE *Written complaints procedures at Explore Worldwide*

Explore Worldwide is a direct sell specialist tour operator, dealing in small group adventure holidays in 90 countries throughout the world.

Complaints are treated extremely seriously at Explore. They are actioned immediately, upon receipt, and the Operations Director takes an active role in ensuring appropriate, speedy and correct responses.

A daily meeting is held between the Operations Director and the Customer Services Manager. Any complaints received are divided into two piles: justified and not justified. All complaints receive a reply letter within three to five days, but the nature of the response varies according to the decision made.

Justified complaints are dealt with first. A letter is sent out within three to five days. This may be a 'holding letter', acknowledging the complaint and reassuring the client that the company will be investigating the problem and getting back in touch in the near future. Alternatively, if the company is aware of the problem or simply knows that they have made a mistake, a full response is sent straight away. This letter will offer an apology, an explanation and, if appropriate, some reimbursement.

Those complaints that are considered by the Operations Director to be unjustified, are then examined a second time. Some will be in the 'lets see if I can get some money back' category. These will receive a reply letter with clear, straight answers explaining why Explore Worldwide believe the complaint to be unjustified.

Other people's unjustified complaints, however, are made in the sincere belief that they are in fact justified. They may, for example, have misunderstood the brochure, not anticipated the problems of travelling in developing countries or underestimated their levels of fitness. These complaints require long and detailed explanations and reasoned answers. Much care is taken to acknowledge the comments, but also to explain why Explore Worldwide still consider the complaint(s) to be unjustified. In most cases, clients accept these

explanations and acknowledge their own misunderstanding. They also usually remain as customers of Explore Worldwide.

Pre-emptive action is also taken. If things do go wrong on a tour and the Operations Director knows that justified complaints are to follow, he will take action before he receives the letters. For example in the case of substantial flight delay, he writes to travellers with an apology and reimbursement, if appropriate, so that it is with them upon their arrival back in the UK.

KEY TERMS

Accept liability: accept that you are wrong and that compensation may be due.

Active listening: demonstrating, through phrases and non-verbal signals, that you are listening.

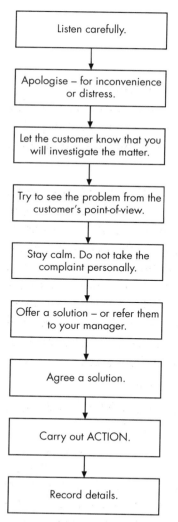

Figure 5.13 Handling verbal complaints

How to handle verbal complaints

Listen carefully

You must establish exactly what the complaint is about. Listening is not a passive activity. Use active listening techniques – this will reassure the customer that you are taking the complaint seriously. You may need to ask questions to get to the bottom of the matter. Let the customer voice their complaint first – do not interrupt and always look interested. If appropriate, make notes.

Apologise

While it may be appropriate to apologise and say 'I'm very sorry that you have been kept waiting for so long', it is important that you do not immediately accept liability (i.e. do not say 'We will obviously have to refund your excursion costs'). Apologise for the inconvenience caused and for the fact that the customer is cross. Use phrases such as: 'I am really sorry that your flight has been delayed'. 'You must be very tired' or 'I can see that this is really upsetting for you'. At this stage, you are trying to empathise with the customer, to reassure them and to manage a difficult situation.

Advise the customer that you will investigate the matter

An investigation can be as simple as finding out why towels were not changed, why tickets have not been received or why accommodation was altered unexpectedly. Longer investigations may be required, for example, a tour operator may have to write to hoteliers, airlines or car hire companies to establish the causes of the complaint or a travel agent may need to contact a tour operator. When telling a customer that you will investigate a matter, you must also tell them by which time or date you will get back to them.

Consider the customer's point-of-view

Many people save up for a long time to go on holiday. Their disappointment, therefore, often creates an unpleasant situation. It is important to try to imagine how the customer feels if they have spent the night at an airport, if they have received incorrect information or if they have been kept waiting. They may be afraid of flying, have argued or even have not slept the night before. Remember that such situations are stressful.

The flowchart in Figure 5.13 contains the following boxes:

- Listen carefully.
- Apologise – for inconvenience or distress.
- Let the customer know that you will investigate the matter.
- Try to see the problem from the customer's point-of-view.
- Stay calm. Do not take the complaint personally.
- Offer a solution – or refer them to your manager.
- Agree a solution.
- Carry out ACTION.
- Record details.

ACTIVITY

Try to recall the last time you complained about something. How did you feel and how did this make you behave?

Keep calm

Angry customers can be a shock! It is vital, therefore, that you do not take any complaint personally. You must not be defensive (accept the customer has the right to feel as he or she does) and under no circumstances should you contradict or argue with the customer. As a guide, when faced with a difficult customer, you should:

- maintain eye contact
- keep a positive, even, tone of voice
- use positive non-verbal body language
- listen actively
- let the client talk

Find a solution and agree it with the customer

There might be a clear solution that is within your authority to make. For example, a customer in a restaurant may be complaining of a draught from a window, and so they might be offered an alternative table.

It is important to always discuss the possible solution with the client first. Where solutions are obvious, and the client is agreeable, simply solve the problem, and you will produce a satisfied customer. Alternatively, the solution may be to fetch a manager. In this case, ask the customer if he or she would like to see the manager and take them to a quiet area out of earshot of all customers. Offer them a drink, if appropriate. Find the manager and brief them fully before they see the client. Sometimes, the simple fact of seeing the manager makes customers feel that they have been taken seriously, and so may defuse the problem. If it is a more serious complaint, the manager definitely needs to deal with this. If in doubt, refer the problem to your manager.

It can also be appropriate to ask the client for suggested solutions. Before doing this, however, be sure of your own authority.

Carry out ACTION

Whatever solution you agree with your customer, make sure that you carry it out, preferably immediately. Fast solutions create loyal customers. Be it a refund, letter, investigation or a simple replacement, make this a priority task. If you do not, there is the danger that you could end up with another complaint.

DID YOU KNOW?

If you resolve a complaint on the spot, 95% of customers will do business with you again.

DID YOU KNOW?

Most travel companies have a complaints procedure and appropriate forms.

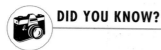

DID YOU KNOW?

Unfortunately, people are quicker to complain now than they were a decade ago. It may be that consumer affairs programmes have encouraged a complaints culture and that consumers now go on holiday armed with a notepad and video recorder, rather than towels and suntan lotion!

Record all the details

Record the complaint at the earliest moment possible. Within a short time, your memory will fade and the memorised information will not be as accurate. These records are needed so that your organisation can monitor their customer service levels. It may also be necessary to recall, if the client returns. Taking details of what happened, what was agreed and the subsequent action, creates a professional image to the customer.

Assessing the quality and effectiveness of customer service

At the start of this unit we investigated the benefits and importance of satisfied customers to organisations. These included:

- increased sales
- more customers
- an improved public image
- an edge over the competition
- a happier and more efficient workforce
- satisfied customers
- customer loyalty and repeat business

As all of these factors are so important, organisations should continually be checking that customers are satisfied – after all, this keeps commercial organisations in business and ahead of the competition. For non-commercial organisations, feedback from customers can help them to provide the best possible service for their customers.

Assessing and then improving customer service should be an ongoing process. In many travel and tourism organisations this is carried out formally through surveys, suggestion boxes, focus groups or mystery shoppers. However, some of the most useful feedback is gathered informally, through casual conversations or through overhearing comments. Both methods (informal and formal) are essential to an organisation if it is to maintain a customer-focused image, change its products regularly and update its services to meet changing customer needs.

Thus, the process of assessing the quality and effectiveness of customer service can be illustrated as a continuous loop (see Figure 5.14).

Ideally, the feedback back from customers should tell an organisation:

- to what extent customers are satisfied
- what they really think about products and services
- what aspects of the service they like
- what aspects of the service they dislike

Figure 5.14

- what are the most common complaints
- what suggestions customers have made for improvement.

Before an organisation is in a position to gather feedback, it must decide on which quality criteria are relevant and which methods are appropriate.

Quality criteria

KEY TERM

Accessibility: ease of travel from one location to another or the ease (or difficulty) of access for disabled people.

Figure 5.15 Examples of quality criteria

ACTIVITY

List the quality criteria which would be appropriate for the following organisations:

- a hotel
- a tourist attraction
- Eurostar

Price/value for money

Value for money is a great determinant of customer satisfaction. If a customer thinks that he or she has had a good meal, a wonderful day out or a fantastic weekend break, for the price paid, they are far more likely to be satisfied. This is the basis on which many people visit end of season sales or try to purchase late availability holidays – to experience the joy of finding a real bargain! Customers who feel that they have not had value for money are unlikely to return.

DID YOU KNOW?

The average delay for most charter airlines in 1998 was between 8 and 48 minutes. Between 5% and 22% of flights were more than one hour late.

Consistency/accuracy

Travel services running according to the timetable, literature being accurate and consistent levels of service from staff, are clear indications of good customer service. Some of these are easily measured, for example, numbers of trains leaving and/or arriving on time, and so often form the basis of setting customer service targets. The increasing number of published passenger charters also means that many organisations' performances are now measured by such information.

DID YOU KNOW?

Many organisations insist that telephones are answered within three rings.

Staffing – levels and quality

The amount of staff determines how quickly customers are dealt with. Lengths of queues and the time it takes to answer a telephone will be less if more staff are serving. Customer service skills and product knowledge (quality) also determine customer satisfaction. For example, while the number of reservation staff at a direct sell tour operator will determine how quickly telephones are answered, it is their knowledge of the resorts and selling their skills, which will help more to determine profitability and levels of customer satisfaction.

Enjoyment of experience

Selling a holiday is often referred to as 'the selling of dreams'. If the dream has been realised and the customer is happy, repeat business and customer loyalty are more likely to follow on. Enjoyment, however, is hard to quantify.

Health and safety

Health and safety is now a legal matter, as well as one which will determine customer satisfaction. Increasing legislation and consumers' awareness of their rights has helped to raise the standards of health and safety through the travel industry. To neglect these issues can result in the downfall of an organisation or a destination. As discussed in Chapter 1, the result of cholera outbreaks in the Dominican Republic in the mid-1990s caused a reduction in tourist numbers, resulting in considerable economic impacts on the local community.

Cleanliness and hygiene

Increasingly, we all expect immaculate standards, in terms of both cleanliness and hygiene. The simplest of accommodation and the most basic of restaurants should be expected to provide clean and hygienic facilities. Food scares within the UK have increased consumer awareness and corresponding legislation. In 1997 it became a legal requirement that all food handlers must have a reasonable understanding of food hygiene.

DID YOU KNOW?

Given the right conditions of warmth, food and moisture, some bacteria will multiply by 100% every ten minutes.

Accessibility and availability

Accessibility is often used to describe access for those with limited mobility. However, attractions and accommodation may also have limited or restricted access due to poor car parking facilities, or the distance from public transport. The accessibility of London Heathrow, for example, is often criticised, as it can take up to one hour on the underground system from central London. In contrast, good signposting of Alton Towers from the motorway has made it highly accessible and its location has become a positive quality criterion.

Availability of services, or lack of them, can greatly affect levels of customer satisfaction. Imagine being on holiday towards the end of the season, when the nightclubs are closing, half the bars are empty and the excursions do not run due to lack of customers. Your enjoyment may indeed be affected! On the positive side, the increasing availability of services, such as cashpoint machines, foreign exchange outlets, shops, bars, cafés and restaurants, has at least made the time prior to departures an enjoyable part of the holiday experience.

Provision for individual needs

We have established that customers are not one homogenous group; they consist of many different types of people who cannot easily be categorised. While organisations may try to segment their markets and cater for specific groups, it must not be forgotten that we all like to be treated as individuals. Good customer service, therefore, means that whatever the request, the provider should ideally be able to adapt their services to meet the customer's needs. For example, it would not be unreasonable for a hotel, airline, attraction or tour operator to offer specific facilities or services catering for:

- a gentleman who requests a vegan meal
- a father travelling alone with small children
- a baby
- an elderly lady who needs to visit the bathroom regularly
- an non-English speaker
- people of different religions who require worship facilities.

Methods of collecting feedback

Methods of gathering feedback from customers are identical to those used to gather customer information in order to segment a market. These have been discussed in detail in Chapter 4: Marketing travel and tourism, and include the following:

Informal feedback

The importance of informal feedback is increasingly being recognised. While someone may not wish to complain, their opinions are valid and you may find they are happier to give detailed information if they think it is of no consequence. Thus, the chats that a resort representative has with customers while on excursions may reveal more than the questionnaires circulated at the end of the holiday. Travel agents may overhear conversations regarding which destinations and tour operators clients do not wish to travel with, or even reveal comments on what other travel agencies have on offer. Such feedback is essential. Only through regular meetings with staff or another formal system, can managers become aware of this type of customer feedback.

Surveys

Questionnaires are sent out with tickets, by tour operators, or handed out by representatives in resorts. Tourist information centres conduct surveys of visitors for their local authorities and hoteliers may send out questionnaires to potential repeat customers who are on their mailing list.

Suggestion boxes

Used within many organisations, separate suggestion boxes are often available for staff and customers. Forms or cards are often provided to aid and encourage completion. Customers and staff can make suggestions regarding how to improve services. If they wish, this can be done anonymously.

DID YOU KNOW?

At Disney, regular meetings are held specifically to distribute the information or feedback that has been collected by staff while with clients.

DID YOU KNOW?

Suggestion boxes used to be called complaint boxes. The change in name is intended to encourage both positive and negative feedback.

Focus groups

Detailed feedback can be obtained from small groups of people using focus groups. These usually consist of a small group of 10 to 15 people, discussing products and being asked for information by an experienced interviewer. They are relatively time-consuming, expensive to run, require careful management and tend to be carried out only by large organisations who need to make fundamental changes to their products.

Mystery shoppers

An employee of the same company can be sent, unknown to the staff, to assess service quality in another part of the organisation. The mystery shoppers can assess service levels against quality criteria. His or her feedback regarding their own level of satisfaction can be highly influential.

Observation

Observing customer behaviour and purchasing patterns can be used to gather information. For example, in a theme park, it is useful to count the number of people in a queue and their response to queuing (i.e. whether they wait or move to another ride). It may suggest the need for another similar ride, to reduce the queues. CCTV is often used now, instead of people, to gather such information. Personal observation is, however, the easiest way to gather information about competitors' products and methods. Observing (and listening to) staff can also be a good indication of levels of service.

PROFILE *Quality Product Control (QPC) at Thomas Cook Holidays*

All calls into the Thomas Cook call centre in Peterborough are monitored. Each month, the reservation staff have one telephone call taped at random by a QPC analyst. The QPC analyst will then replay the call using a check list to ensure the call has met the standard required. Staff are then rewarded in the form of a payment, according to their performance. If they consistently perform below standard, additional training is instigated.

Benchmarking

While assessing the effectiveness of customer service demonstrates good practice in an organisation, it can only be useful if there is something to compare the results against. Most organisations have an established system. A modern word for one such system is 'benchmarking'. This simply means that standards are set and the results of the feedback (from surveys, suggestion boxes, focus groups or other methods) are compared against them. The Thomas Cook call centre operate a benchmarking system on a monthly basis, while, as you will discover in the Case Study following, Explore Worldwide do this at an annual meeting in February.

CASE STUDY *Assessment of customer service at Explore Worldwide*

Most tour operators use a questionnaire to assess customer satisfaction. Explore Worldwide, the small-group adventure tour operator, is no different. Their questionnaires are handed out by tour guides on the penultimate day of the tour and collected in on the final day, allowing customers plenty of time for completion. The tick box system is easy for customers to complete and simple for the Head Office to analyse statistically. Once the clients have left, the tour guides also write a report on each tour. This report details the services offered by hoteliers, restauranteurs, coach companies, guides and other service providers. Customer feedback is analysed and reacted upon at three levels within the organisation: locally in the resort after each departure, regularly at Head Office and annually by senior management.

Tour leaders read their own customers' reports once the customers have departed. If a pattern of dissatisfaction emerges from the questionnaires, it is important that this is dealt with before the next tour. Simple things, such as the type of cheese used in the packed lunches or the evening entertainment activities, can be dealt with by tour leaders immediately. More substantial complaints about suppliers will be dealt with from the UK. For example, should a pattern emerge whereby a hotel lowers its standards or does not meet the acceptable quality criteria, the Operations Director will simply change the hotel for the next tour. As hotels are not actually named in the brochure, they can be changed without affecting the customer. This degree of flexibility contributes to customer satisfaction and is highly advantageous.

The cycle of continuous improvement is completed each year in February when the senior management of Explore Worldwide meet with the four Product Managers from each department: the Middle East, Americas, Asia and Africa. Tour reports, questionnaires and clients' letters are examined. The questionnaires are statistically analysed and all suppliers (hotels, local guides, etc.) who fall below the average level are highlighted. Decisions are then made about each tour and supplier. Some will be dropped from the programme as a result of customers' and tour leaders' comments. These meetings decide the products to be published in the brochures the following year.

For the customers, the 'face' of Explore Worldwide is of course the tour leader. Although feedback is obtained from the questionnaires about their abilities after each tour, the leaders are also assessed on an annual basis by their managers. They are essentially assessed in two areas: their client handling (external customers) and their dealings with suppliers and the UK office (internal customers). Feedback is gathered from the tour reports, comments from suppliers and the people who administrate their paperwork in the UK. Each tour leader is graded on a ten point scale and their salary adjusted according to whether their score increases or decreases.

ACTIVITY

List the different methods used by Explore Worldwide to gather information about their products. Indicate which methods of gathering feedback use customers and which use other sources. What other methods could be used for assessing customer service? Why do you think these are not used by Explore Worldwide?

ASSESSMENT

Part 1: Travel Solutions

You work in Travel Solutions, a High Street travel agency in your home town. You only work on Saturdays, when the agency is most busy. The majority of the work involves providing information and advice to a variety of customers, who are searching for a suitable package holiday. You find this very rewarding. However, the paperwork, complaints, required selling skills, and the need to be positive at all times with both internal and external customers, makes the job very demanding.

This week you are faced with the following tasks. Graham and Susan Smythe have come into the agency. They wish to take their two children, Elizabeth and Nick, away for a two week holiday. They cannot agree on a destination and have come to you for help. They all appear to want different things. Susan wants to explore, find out about new cultures, to eat local foods and 'improve herself'. Graham also wants to be active, however, he would prefer to do water sports and is particularly keen to be near a beach. Elizabeth is 17 years old – she just wants to lie on the beach and meet other people her own age. Nick, aged 11, is only interested in football. His favourite foods are KFC and burgers.

Terry and June are regular clients. They had been in to the agency earlier in the week and said they would pop back on Saturday to book something. They usually travel abroad several times a year and know exactly what they like. They are looking for a European short break, in May. They have a total budget of £700 and want to get as much as possible for their money. They prefer three star, centrally located hotels and ideally would like to go to Prague, Barcelona or Krakow. They could, however, be persuaded to go elsewhere if it was a good deal. If absolutely necessary, they would accept two star accommodation.

Andrew Towers telephones the agency. He has just that morning returned from the Caribbean with his girlfriend and he is in a rage. Although it is difficult to hear him, because he is speaking so fast, you understand that the outbound flight was delayed, their room did not have a sea view (he claims he paid a supplement for this), there were cockroaches in their room and the staff were unfriendly. Apparently, he could not find the representative from Caribbean Exclusive (the tour operator) for the first four days and when he did find her, she was not interested. His girlfriend was also sick and it rained.

Assessment questions

Task 1

Find a suitable holiday for the Smythe family and then sell it to them. The family recognise that some compromises may have to be made. However, your aim is to match their original requirements as far as possible. They do not appear to have a budget restriction.

Task 2

You know that excellent research is required in the case of Terry and June, they will study all the brochures in detail themselves. Your product knowledge will also be tested. Try to find a few options that you can offer to them when they visit the agency later in the day.

Task 3

Deal with the telephone call from Andrew Towers. It is important that you have a record of this complaint, so make notes as you go, if possible. Write a memo to your manager at the end of the call, detailing all the issues, your responses and any action that you have taken. Make recommendations to the manager as to what should be done next.

Task 4

Write a 'holding letter' to Mr Towers and an appropriate letter to Caribbean Exclusive.

Part 2: Investigating the effectiveness of customer care

Your manager at Travel Solutions wants to set up a system within the agency to assess the quality and effectiveness of customer care. She has enlisted your help – you are to find out how the quality of customer care is assessed in two other organisations.

Investigate two other travel and tourism organisations. For each, you must (as a minimum):

- identify the key customer criteria
- investigate how the staff and managers achieve these criteria (i.e. what procedures and practices do they use?)
- conduct your own evaluation of their customer service, using appropriate methods.

Write a report detailing your findings in both organisations. You may also wish to compare each organisation's effectiveness of customer care, and recommend on how each of these could be improved.

Key skills

In completing the assessment for this unit, you can achieve the following key skills. These will be accredited at the discretion of your tutor on the basis of the quality of the work you submit.

C3.1a Contribute to a group discussion about a complex subject.
C3.1b Make a presentation about a complex subject, using at least one image to illustrate complex points.
C3.2 Read and synthesise information from two extended documents about a complex subject. One of these documents should include at least one image.

CHAPTER 6

Travel and tourism in action

Aims and Objectives

At the end of this chapter you will:

- **be able to plan, carry out and evaluate a real project**
- **apply the skills and knowledge you have learnt in previous chapters**
- **apply key skills to a project**
- **understand how to produce a business plan**
- **understand the importance of teamwork**
- **know how to evaluate a project**

Introduction

Now that you have studied five compulsory units, it is time for you to put what you have learnt into action! The assessment for this chapter involves working as part of a team to plan, carry out and evaluate a real project relating to travel and tourism. This chapter builds on the knowledge you gained in previous chapters, particularly the areas of marketing and customer service.

This is probably the most testing of chapters in that it demands highly practical skills. The more enthusiastic and motivated you are about your project, the more successful it will be and the more exciting and satisfying you will find its implementation.

The first section will demonstrate how to assess the feasibility of a project. In order to do this, you will learn how to put together and present a business plan. This is the first of many business skills you need to develop. In the plan, you will consider the aims and objectives of the project and all the resources needed to run it.

Developing effective teamwork skills is an important part of this chapter. Few projects or events can be entirely run by one person alone. We will examine the different types of teams and the factors that may influence their success, for example communication. We will then consider the other skills you need to run the project, including: understanding your role, keeping a log of your contribution and learning how meetings are conducted. You will find that these are valuable skills for later employment.

The final section of this chapter will look at the different ways of evaluating the project so that you are able to conduct a constructive evaluation of its success and of your own and others' performance.

In conducting the project, you will find out a lot about yourself and your strengths and weaknesses. You may find that you enjoy the unpredictability of running an event and respond well to the challenge of careful planning and problem solving. If so, you will be pleased to know that there are many job opportunities in event management, some of which are discussed in this chapter. You may even consider taking a degree course in event management, a fairly new discipline. Degree programmes are on offer at the universities of Leeds Metropolitan, Thames Valley and North London.

KEY TERMS

Feasibility study: involves matching and testing ideas against objectives to decide if the idea is worth pursuing.

Corporate image: the identity of a company, projected in logo, design and livery.

The feasibility of the project

Before you can plan your project, you will need to have some idea of the kind of project you would like to do. You and your colleagues will have to come up with ideas and decide which ones are likely to work and which ones are not. To some extent we do this in our daily lives – for example, you plan to go out one Saturday evening. The options are: the cinema, clubbing in London, clubbing locally or bowling. You automatically test the feasibility of these options and apply the following constraints:

- The cinema is not feasible, as there is nothing you want to see.
- Clubbing in London would be fun, but you are constrained by lack of cash.
- Clubbing locally is possible, but you cannot find anyone to go with.
- You telephone the bowling alley and it is fully booked.

As none of your options are feasible, you perhaps end up staying in and watching television!

That example was a simplistic one, but you will test your project in a similar way, applying more stringent criteria. Businesses have to do this constantly to ensure they remain efficient.

Idea generation

We saw that it is fairly easy to find ideas for a Saturday night out, but you have to plan a business project or an event. How do you know what to do? How do event organisers come up with ideas? There are various methods for doing this.

Brainstorming

This is a technique where a group of people sit together and state their ideas. The ideal group size is about 12 and the ideas are recorded. The ideas are not discussed at this stage, as it is very important that they are not criticised. Criticism inhibits people from putting their ideas forward, and also, it is sometimes the ideas that appear far fetched, which work. The aim is to get as many ideas as possible. Later on, most of them will be dismissed when tested for feasibility.

Customers

In business, customers may put forward their ideas, informally through suggestion, or formally through a consumer panel.

Staff

As part of a team planning events or proposing a new business project, staff are expected to come up with ideas.

Ask the experts

Find someone who has done a similar thing before and ask for ideas. Copy your competitor's idea and do it better.

ACTIVITY

Try the brainstorming technique in a group. Imagine you have been given enough money for a day trip at the end of your course. Come up with ideas for where to go. Remember not to criticise each other's ideas.

DID YOU KNOW?

You can ask your local banks for literature on business plans. They will have forms that you can complete and use for your own project. Another source of helpful information is your local Business Enterprise Unit.

Once you have some ideas, you will need to decide which ones to pursue. This is when a business plan should be produced. We will consider all the aspects of a business plan in this chapter.

Aims and objectives of the project

What does the project hope to achieve? This is the starting point of any business plan. The objectives may be commercial (to make money) or non-commercial (to provide a service or promote a company). Events often have public relations objectives, such as enhancing the corporate image or providing information. To give an example, students arranging an exchange programme with Dutch students for their 'Travel and Action' unit, came up with the following objectives:

1 To do well in the unit, to pass their Vocational A Level.
2 To develop business skills.
3 To develop team skills.
4 To learn about the Dutch culture.
5 To help the Dutch students with their English.
6 To show the Dutch students aspects of British culture.
7 To promote good European relations.
8 To project a good corporate image for their college.
9 To have fun!

You will note a number of points about these objectives. Firstly, there is no aim to make a profit. In fact, the students will need money to run the project. Also, there are lots of objectives, although some projects may have only one or two. It is important to enjoy the project, hence the students adding 'have fun'.

SMART

SMART is an acronym which helps set objectives. According to SMART, the objectives should be:

- Specific – that is, clearly and concisely stated.
- Measurable – so that we can see if they are achieved.
- Achievable – the team must agree the objectives and be sure they have the skills to achieve them.
- Realistic – there is no use in setting objectives that are overly ambitious.
- Timed – there must be deadlines by which to achieve the objectives.

The SMART objectives are recorded so that as the project goes along, they can be referred to, and students do not lose sight of their aims. At the end of the project you will need to revisit these objectives to assess whether they were achieved.

 CASE STUDY

Examine the non-commercial objectives of the following two events:

1 Glastonbury Festival

The Glastonbury Festival aims to encourage and stimulate youth culture from around the world in all its forms, including: pop music, dance music, jazz, folk music, fringe theatre, drama, mime, circus, cinema, poetry and all the creative forms of art and design, including painting, sculpture and textile art. The company aims to make a profit, which is then distributed to charity.

Source: www.glastonbury-festival.co.uk

2 Edinburgh Festival

The objectives of the annual Edinburgh Festival are stated as follows:

- To promote and encourage arts of the highest possible standard.

- To reflect international culture in presentation to Scottish audiences and to reflect Scottish culture in presentation to international audiences.

- To bring together a programme of events in an innovative way that cannot easily be achieved by other organisations.

- To offer equal opportunities for all sections of the public to experience and enjoy the arts.

- To promote the educational, cultural and economic wellbeing of the city and people of Edinburgh and Scotland.

ACTIVITY

Find out what events or acts are currently planned for each of the two festivals described. Consider their stated objectives and say whether you think the programme of events matches those objectives. You can find out about what is on at both festivals from the Internet or in newspapers, depending on the time of year. Write notes on your findings.

Notice that neither of these events has a commercial aim, and yet the Edinburgh Festival aims to promote the economic wellbeing of the city. Make notes on the ways in which the festivals can produce external economic benefits.

Meeting customer needs

You should be well aware of the importance of meeting customer needs, having studied Chapter 5 on Customer Service. In the course of your own project, you will have to plan how to give customer service. You will also have to decide who your customer is and draw up a profile of the target market.

Marketing

In your plan you must outline ideas for marketing your event. These will be constrained by the budget available, but you will be able to rely heavily on public relations activities for your own project. Local media are interested in student activities, therefore it would be wise to send them a press release. You might even contact television stations. Your success in promotion will depend on the newsworthiness of your project. Enlist the help of the college marketing manager and use Chapter 4 of this book to help you.

ACTIVITY

Draw up brief customer profiles for the following events/projects:

1 The foreign exchange described on page 356
2 Glastonbury Festival
3 Edinburgh Festival
4 A college-based travel agency
5 An exhibition of travel and tourism students' work
6 The London Marathon

KEY TERM

Physical resources: the rooms and equipment needed to run the project.

Resources

The resources will vary enormously according to your project. In all cases there will be the cost of the physical resources required. You must list these resources and then assess how much they will cost.

The venue

If you are planning an event, you will need a venue, and this can be expensive. To hire a hotel room, for example, will cost a few hundred pounds. You may have a college hall, like the fashion show team, and so this might be free, for a student event. If you are clever, you may be able to persuade a venue to let you use it for free. You could do this by promising publicity for them in your promotional material. Alternatively, you could persuade the venue management that they are providing a community benefit by letting students use their venue. In return, you can offer your specialist skills. For example, one group of students was loaned a major concert venue by their local council when they undertook a tourism research project in the town.

PROFILE *Earls Court Olympia*

Earls Court Olympia hosts around 270 events every year and is one of London's leading attractions, with over three million visitors each year. Earls Court and Olympia are separate venues, but are part of the same group, owned by Candover and the Morris family since October 1999. Both venues are renowned throughout the world. They are well-located in West London, with access to Heathrow and Gatwick, all major railway stations and motorways and the underground network. There are over 27,000 hotel beds within two kilometres of Earls Court, so visitors can easily find accommodation nearby.

There are five halls and two purpose-built conference centres at the venues, playing host to a wide variety of events. These include exhibitions, conferences, corporate events, pop concerts and world class sport. Famous examples include the Motor Show, the Great British Beer Festival and the World Travel Market.

There are four companies forming the Earls Court and Olympia Group. These are:

1 **Earls Court and Olympia Limited** – responsible for the day to day operation of the venues. This company is split into four basic areas:

- **sales, marketing and box office**
- **Event Management Team (work alongside event organisers)**
- **Operations Team (look after security, safety, cleaning and other services)**
- **Engineering Team (provide day-to-day maintenance of the venue)**

2 **Opex Exhibition Services** – the UK's leading supplier of services to exhibition and conference organisers. They provide equipment, such as stands, flooring, electrics and telephones.

3 **Beeton Rumford** – a leading corporate hospitality and specialist event caterer.

4 **Clarion Events** – an exhibition and event organiser. They organise about 20 shows at these venues.

The four companies, based at Earls Court, currently employ approximately 750 people. The *Exhibitor Survival Guide*, available free of charge, provides a reference to the facilities and services available in the locality of the venues. This guide is given to every exhibitor.

Source: Adapted from Earls Court literature and web site.

Equipment

Make a list of the equipment you need for your project. You will need access to computers, telephones, fax machines, etc. These will be available to you in college, but you should still record the expense of using them, to build up a realistic picture of costs. Depending on the type of project, you may need exhibition stands, lighting or sound equipment. Not only will you need funds to pay for these things, you will also have to find out where you can obtain them. *Yellow Pages* will help you find most of the things you need, but try also to think of any contacts you may have who might lend you the equipment.

Finance

You will be very fortunate if you are able to start up a project without any funds. It is likely that you will need to arrange funding yourself. In a business, this can be raised from various sources.

Share issue

KEY TERM

Acquisition strategy: a strategy of buying other companies.

A company will sell shares in its business to raise capital for starting up, for acquisition or for expansion. Airtours, for example, is a tour operator adopting an acquisition strategy. From time to time, new shares are issued to finance the purchase of new companies or assets, such as a new cruise ship. People will buy the shares, as Airtours is a profitable company, and the shareholders get a healthy dividend on their shares. You can sell shares in your project to staff, students in your group or parents. You will then have to give them a share of the profits, but you must also point out to shareholders that they risk losing their money if your project fails.

Loans

Banks loan money to small businesses, but they will normally expect some kind of security. There is, however, a government-backed loan guarantee scheme that enables banks to lend to companies without security. Enterprise agencies offer similar schemes.

Sponsorship

DID YOU KNOW?

The Edinburgh Festival raises over £31.5 million in sponsorship income. Sponsors include BT, Marks and Spencer, Scottish Power and Scottish Widows.

Non-profit making companies are unable to get bank loans, as they do not have the means to repay them. They may, therefore, invite sponsors to back their project to raise the necessary funds. The sponsors receive welcome publicity in return for their money.

As students, you cannot get bank loans for your project, but you can ask local companies for sponsorship. Banks may give you small amounts of money, shops may lend equipment or clothes and people may lend their services, all in return for publicity.

Friends

This source of funding is similar to sponsorship, but is available to individuals. It is usually in the form of a type of membership scheme where, for a fixed annual sum, participants receive newsletters and priority booking facilities.

Grants

Public sector companies may be eligible for grants. These may come from government bodies, such as the Arts Council, or from local government bodies. They will donate the money if they perceive some community or educational benefit from the project. The Prince's Trust is a start up agency in the voluntary sector. It provides grants to young people who need help to start up in business.

The Edinburgh International Festival Muses

Member: £15

- Three exclusive Muse newsletters and access to Muse events
- Regular information about Festival news and the Festival brochure mailed to you.
- Information on occasional special ticket offers.

Priority Member: £45

- Priority booking for all Festival events (maximum 4 tickets per event).
- 1st class mailing of the Festival brochure, posted the day before the festival programme launch.
- Exclusive late ticket offers to Priority Muses.
- Invitation to Festival Director's annual insight into the Festival programme.
- Special merchandise offers at local shops and restaurants.
- Invitations to exclusive Priority Muse events.
- And all Member benefits.

Associate Member: £95

- Priority booking for all Festival events (maximum total of 8 tickets per event).
- Opportunity to attend a preview performance (when available).
- Your personal copy of the Festival magazine posted to your home.
- The Festival's Annual Review posted to your home.
- And all Priority Member benefits.

NB: Please add £10 supplement for overseas postage if you live outside Europe.

Figure 6.1 *Edinburgh Festival membership scheme*

Source: Edinburgh International Festival Programme, 15 August to 5 September 1999

Lottery funding

Lottery funding is given for capital projects, that is for buildings and refurbishment; it is not given for one-off events or for starting new businesses, therefore, most projects would not be eligible. Lottery funding does not finance the whole of a project, so there must always be another source of funds.

European Union funding

If you are planning an exchange with another college you may be able to apply for a grant from the European Union. There are several schemes, with different conditions attached, so you would have to make sure you meet the criteria. Your tutors will have details of such schemes.

Promotional budget

Companies that plan events and exhibitions have finances set aside specifically for that purpose.

Fundraising

We usually associate fund raising with charities, but many public sector bodies have to undertake activities to finance projects. For example, the refurbishment of a council-owned venue would be an expensive project, which could not be financed by taxpayers money alone. Sponsorship, friends schemes and special events are possible additional sources of funds.

Students can fundraise for their projects in lots of ways. Successful schemes could include: a raffle, car washing, cake sales or sandwich making. Such activities could provide the start up costs for a project.

Sales revenue

It must not be forgotten that finance can be raised through sales. A student event might, for example, raise money through ticket sales. If you are counting on this revenue to finance the project, however, you are taking a risk – you need to be sure you can sell enough tickets at a price that will cover your costs.

KEY TERMS

Start up funding: the finance required to get a project up and running.

Security: some kind of physical asset that can be set against a loan (e.g. a house).

Sponsorship: a company provides funds or services in return for publicity.

Capital project: one that involves buildings, refurbishment or the purchase of major equipment.

ACTIVITY

Study the finance facts and figures, for the Edinburgh Festival below.

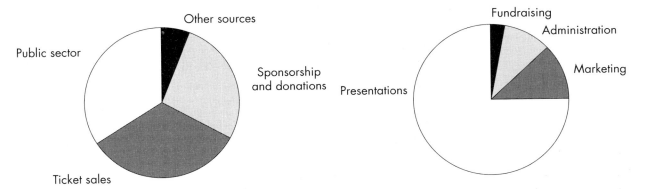

Figure 6.2 *Where the money comes from*

Figure 6.3 *How the money is spent*

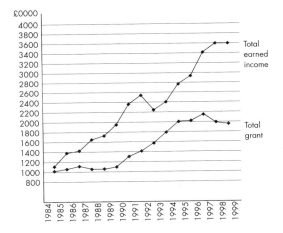

Figure 6.4 *The growth of earned income*

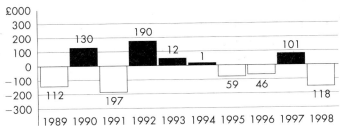

Figure 6.5 *The history of surplus and deficit*

Answer the following questions:

1 34% of the Festival's income comes from the public sector. What does this mean?
2 What expenses are included in paying for the presentations?
3 Explain the terms surplus and deficit.
4 Was there a surplus or a deficit in 1998?
5 Why have public sector grants decreased?

ACTIVITY

Find out about friends schemes in your own locality. Work with a partner and collect information on two schemes. Draw up a table and compare the two schemes in terms of costs and benefits.

Budgeting

You must estimate all your outgoings and revenue. It is important that these estimates are as accurate as possible, so you will have to carry out research into costs of equipment, venue, etc. You must also estimate any revenue you might receive in the way of sponsorship or sales. Budgeting in this way will help you to establish your break even point (the number of sales or ticket sales you need to make to cover expenses). Of course, it is possible that you are running a project that has no sales revenue, for example, organising an exhibition with free entry. In this case, you will still have to budget and ensure that you raise enough finance to cover your costs. Figure 6.6 is an example of a budgeting form extracted from a business plan. You might use this for your assessment later or design a similar one of your own.

Pricing

Calculating your break even point

Personal drawings _____   _____

Salaries/wages _____   _____

National Insurance _____   _____

Tax _____   _____

Stationary/postage/printing _____   _____

Management services fees payable to Franchisor _____   _____

Advertising _____   _____

Telephone _____   _____

Rent/rates/water _____   _____

Heating and lighting _____   _____

Vehicle depreciation _____   _____

Petrol _____   _____

Servicing _____   _____

Road Fund Tax _____   _____

Insurance _____   _____

Business insurance _____   _____

Bad debts _____   _____

Depreciation of equipment _____   _____

Bank loan _____   _____

Bank charge _____   _____

Accountants fees _____   _____

Direct/variable costs eg. raw materials _____   _____

Total costs _____   _____

I intend to charge £ _____ **per hour/per day/per item** (please delete as appropriate)

My break even point is _____   _____

Figure 6.6 Pricing form

Source: Barclays Business Plan: Small Business

CASE STUDY *Glastonbury Festival budget*

The Glastonbury Festival used to be free, but then it also lost money. The first festival was in 1970, but it was not until 1981 that a profit was made. 24,000 people attended and profits reached £20,000. Numbers today are limited by the size of the site, which will take around 100,000 people. The festival is, however, popular enough to sell many more tickets if there were room. Profits are donated to charity.

Bands	£600,000	Administration & Office Costs	£78,000
Theatre Performers	£240,000	Plant Hire	£360,000
Green Field	£96,000	Electricity	£198,000
Staging	£120,000	Water	£72,000
Cinema	£18,000	Licensing & Rates	£36,000
Litter-picking & Waste Disposal	£180,000	Catering	£60 000
Children's Areas	£36,000	National Insurance	£42,000
Wages	£600,000	Site Contractors	£120,000
Police	£432,000	Advertising	£60,000
Other Security	£240,000	Gate Costs	£48,000
Land use (neighbours)	£90,000	Communications & Telephones	£24,000
Fire services	£54,000	Car Parking	£36,000
Medical & Welfare	£36,000	Charitable Donations (at least)	£372,000
		Total Expenses	**£4,248,000**

Figure 6.7 Major components of total ex-VAT £4.25 million Glastonbury budget (round figures)

Source: Glastonbury Festival Leisure, January 2000

ACTIVITY

1 Draw a pie chart showing expenses relating to bands and entertainment (see first five items in Figure 6.7).

2 Find out which charities benefited from the Glastonbury Festival and what amount they received.

3 See if you can find examples of advertising for the festival (summer only).

Find out what the ticket price is for the festival this year and work out the estimated revenue, based on an audience of 100,000. Is the budget covered?

The Glastonbury website will help you with some of these questions. Alternatively, one of your group can write to the festival organisers for a student pack.

ACTIVITY

Using the pricing form as a guide, (see Figure 6.8) estimate the cost of holding a party for your friend's eighteenth birthday. You will have to change some of the headings on your form, as appropriate. You will also have to decide where it is to be held and how you will raise the money to fund it. Compare your estimates with those of other members of your group.

Staffing a project

Many different staff are needed to run a project. Immediate staffing needs will be fulfilled by members of the team, however, other staff may be needed to bring skills and expertise which the team does not have. It would be wise to consult your college marketing manager.

If you are putting on an event, you may need security and caretaking personnel. Remember that there may be financial costs associated with this level of staffing. You will go on to allocate staffing roles to members of your group during the course of your assessment.

Returning to the Glastonbury Festival example, we can see the numbers and types of staff needed to run the event:

The figures shown in 1997 and 1995 do include the many members of the team who are self employed but do not include the sub contractors such as the production teams, security companies, car parking teams and the local contractors who form an important part of the pre festival site workers. Neither does it include the voluntary workers, or people who exchange their time for a donation to the cause they support.

	1997	1995	1994	1993
Total	*1739	1335	476	399
Analysis				
Green litter	800	917		
Litter pickers	520	94	343	241
Theatre and circus	77	67	35	45
Markets	66	21	7	6
Site staff and offices	50	33	23	22
Pole painters	43	23	8	
Jazz	27	25	23	26
Green areas	27	25	10	13
Site safety	31	16	8	13
Comms.	23			
Dance area	22	26		
Pyramid	20	28	6	1
Staff catering	17	13	8	9
Press	7	6		
Recycling	5	6	8	11
Cinema	4	7		

*PAYE numbers 1598. 401 could be classed as local nb within about an hours travelling distance of the site.

Figure 6.8 Number of people employed by the Glastonbury Festival

Source: Glastonbury Festival Leisure

ACTIVITY

You are organising a fun run for charity. You have advertised the event and expect about 50 people to run. You have planned the route, which is on a disused airfield. You plan to have water available on the route and afterwards there will be freshly made burgers and hot dogs on sale. You have had some tee shirts printed with the name of the charity and these will be on sale too. There will also be a cake stall to raise more money. Each entrant will pay an entry fee of £3.

Decide on your staffing needs for this event. List the staff needed and state whether there will be any costs involved.

PROFILE *Event organiser*

What is a typical day in the life of an event organiser? This is difficult to define as it depends very much on how many projects are ongoing and the stage they have reached in their development. We tend either to be very busy indeed and working extremely long hours or quiet, when out of season. There are seldom periods of gentle, modest activity and this is something to be seriously considered if you are thinking of a career in the sector.

At SAS Event Management Ltd we provide event management support to third party clients – that is to say, we do not fund and organise events on our own behalf but, rather, provide whatever professional support is required to allow our clients to bring their own event plans to fruition. Our clients include charities, membership associations, local and central government as well as corporate organisations. We organise events of all kinds from exhibitions, conferences, seminars, workshops, product launches, roadshows, award ceremonies, competitions, social functions and corporate entertainment events such as golfing tours.

Working in the industry tends to give a very broad skill base as each project is a mini commercial enterprise in its own right. Each has to be evaluated and properly researched, a business plan needs to be prepared to include key elements of marketing, sales and financial matters as well as a sound and detailed plan for the execution of the project. Then comes the fun bit, the creative flair that sets the event apart from the crowd.

Our job falls into three main areas:

(1) High level planning and working with clients in an account management and consultancy role to understand their true aims and establish the feasibility of their plans
(2) Pre-event planning and post-event follow up work which tend to be largely, but not exclusively, office-based.
(3) On-site delivery which is such a small but crucial part of the process in terms of time but, without doubt, the most exhilarating and memorable part of the whole.

No one element can survive well without the others. It is a complex, interdependent system as many people have discovered to their cost! There is a tendency amongst the enthusiastic and inexperienced to launch into stage two without having given sufficient attention to stage one. Or, perhaps, to arrive at stage three expecting all to happen as if by magic without having prepared properly at stage two. Horror stories abound. It is the professional event manager's duty to ensure that clients understand the relative importance of each stage and allocate sufficient resources to them.

Source: SAS Event management

DID YOU KNOW?

It is so easy to book a flight over the Internet that some people are not sure they have actually succeeded and have been known to repeat the whole procedure by mistake. They then arrive at the airport and find they have booked duplicate seats. Airlines have started sending E-mail confirmations to reassure their customers.

Administration systems

You may need to take bookings or record sales during your project. To do this, you will have to set up efficient administration systems. These may be paper-based or on computer (sometimes it is useful to have both when you are inexperienced).

Businesses use many systems – they need order forms, invoices, advice notes and delivery notes. They may also need booking forms and receipts. Paper-based administration systems are more cumbersome than using computers, but essential in many situations, where it is not possible to access a pc.

ACTIVITY

Use your IT skills and design a simple database. Access or Microsoft Works are suitable programs to use. Enter the details of each member of your group, including, names, addresses, ages and favourite sport(s).

Try sorting your database alphabetically, by surname and then by town. Carry out some searches, for example, find all the students who are over 18, or all those who enjoy football. A business must have a system for logging expenditure and income. You should also use a paper-based system for your project, so that you are quite clear that you have made all the entries. A business is likely to use spreadsheets on computer for this purpose and an accounting package such as Sage.

ACTIVITY

Design a spreadsheet to show the following expenditure over four months, for a sporting event.

	ADMINISTRATION	ADVERTISING	VENUE	STAFF	CONTINGENCY
April	650	1,285		3,000	
May	750	1,000		3,000	
June	650	1,450		2,000	
July	855	1,300	5,500	2,000	1,100

Table 6.1

Enter formulae to calculate totals for each area of expense, for each month. Using your spreadsheet, create a pie chart showing all the expenses for July.

ACTIVITY

Design a form suitable for booking a sightseeing tour on holiday. Include information such as client details, destination, cost, dates and any additional information. Design a ticket and a receipt, as well as the booking form.

Much information will be held on computer on a database, particularly customer details. A database is useful for mailshots, enabling very specific targeting for events. Theatres and venues use their databases in this way, informing customers of events of specific interest to them. As e-commerce becomes more prevalent, companies are also using the Internet to take bookings and issue confirmations. It might be interesting to examine some airlines' websites to see how this works. Be careful that you do not actually make a booking.

Project timescales

When problems occur with student projects, they are usually due to poor time management. For example, a student agrees to undertake a task at a meeting, fails to do it, and so prevents the project from moving on. This is frustrating for the whole team and can throw the success of the project into jeopardy.

When planning a project, there will be a date by which the project must be up and running or, in the case of an event, a date when the event will happen. Although the team will be clear about these deadlines, there must also be deadlines by which individual tasks must be completed, during the preparatory stages.

One technique which is useful for planning is called critical path analysis. This can be a fairly complicated procedure involving network diagrams, and earliest and latest finishing times. You will study this method in your Key Skills (Numeracy) and may apply it to your project.

Critical path analysis

First, the different activities needed to complete the project are identified. Each one is analysed to see which other activities must be completed before this one can start. Each activity is identified by a letter and the time needed for each activity is estimated. A diagram is then drawn, showing how one activity depends upon another.

Another aid to planning is the Gantt chart. Each activity is shown as a bar on a chart, with activities labelled on the vertical axis and the timescale on the horizontal axis. (note that activities can be taking place simultaneously).

ACTIVITY

Your group is planning a day trip to London. The activities to be completed have been identified as:

- finding out how many students will go
- booking a coach
- arranging a tour guide
- publicising the trip
- collecting the money
- booking a restaurant in London
- obtaining permission for the trip
- completing internal paperwork for the trip
- informing students of arrangements

The trip is to take place five weeks from now. Plan these activities, detailing the time needed for each and which activities are dependent on others. Produce a simple diagram, showing how and when each activity will occur.

KEY TERMS

E-commerce: refers to businesses developed and run on the Internet.

Gantt chart and critical path analysis: aids to planning to help you achieve deadlines.

PROFILE *Timescale for power installation for 'Pop in the Park' concert*

3 months before the event

Request for power services arrives from concert organisers. Discuss requirements, agree fees, book plant.

1 month before event

Detailed plans produced of what goes where, the generators allocated.

3 weeks before event

Crew on site to start erection of lighting.

1 week before event

Generators arrive on site, are put into position, wired up and tested for safety.

The concert

Everything is under way, the generators have to be refuelled. The crew are on hand for maintenance.

You might devise your own system of planning to deadlines. Provided the whole team acknowledges the deadlines and sticks to them, the project has a good chance of success.

Legal aspects of the project

If your project is happening within the college environment, you will have few problems with health and safety, as these systems should already be in place. However, you should produce a check list of areas that might be affected by legislation and obtain advice for each one. Following is an example of a possible scenario.

A group of students has organised a college version of *Blind Date*, to take place in the college hall on a Friday evening. They have sold tickets to students, staff and friends and recorded the details of the customers on a database, so that they can inform them of future events. There will be an interval where they will sell wine and snacks. There will also be a raffle to boost revenue. They hope to sell 500 tickets. They have brought in lighting and sound equipment. They approach the college health and safety officer for advice and she advises them to check the following:

1 Hall capacity – it only has a capacity of 400.
2 Public entertainment licence – the college does not hold one, therefore students must apply and pay a one-off fee.
3 Drinks licence – the students cannot sell wine without a liquor licence.
4 Food safety laws – serving food introduces complications as there are a number of laws to be adhered to.
5 Fire regulations – the students must be aware of these and inform the audience of procedures before the show starts.
6 Data Protection Act – as they have recorded customer details on computer, they must comply with this Act.
7 Insurance – although the college has comprehensive insurance, the extra lighting and sound equipment is not covered by this.
8 Raffle – the students must check that their raffle complies with gaming laws.
9 Signature tune – The *Blind Date* theme tune will be played, so the students need to check performing rights.

You can see from this example that there is much to consider, in terms of the legal aspects of your project.

 ACTIVITY

Each member of the group should investigate an aspect of legislation or health and safety. Choose from the following:

- Data Protection Act
- Food Safety Act
- Fire Precautions Act
- Gaming Act
- Licensing Act
- Public entertainment licence
- Occupier's Liability Act
- Health and safety (first aid) regulations

DID YOU KNOW?

At Stansted airport there is a contingency planning manager. He has compiled a plan for all sectors of the airport, including fire service and operations. Drills are regularly carried out, so that when there is an emergency, such as a crash or a hijack, everyone immediately knows what to do.

Research your assigned Act or licence. Make notes and prepare a handout or overhead transparency for your fellow students. Present your information to the group. You may wish to add other pieces of legislation to the list, as relevant to your own projects.

Contingency plans

To ensure the success of your project you must have contingency plans in place. These are back-up plans, so that in the event of something going wrong, you know exactly what to do. Experienced event organisers always have contingency plans. They have learnt that, inevitably, whatever can go wrong, will go wrong. Contingency planning can also be vital for health and safety.

ACTIVITY

Following are some real examples of things that have gone wrong with past Vocational A Level student projects. For each one, think what the organisers could have done to prevent or solve the problem.

1 A trip to Alton Towers has been planned. The students arrive at 8.00 a.m., but there is no bus. It arrives at 9.40 a.m., having spent an hour waiting at the college's other site.
2 An evening fashion show is being held around a swimming pool. Rehearsals took place during the day, when the area was flooded with natural light. At 8 p.m. it gets dark.
3 A summer fête is held outside. It rains.
4 Another day, another trip. The bus turns up on time – it seats 49 people and there are 52 people waiting to embark.
5 A group of students are taking a trip to Paris. At the ferry port, customs officers get on the bus and ask to see their passports. They ask: 'Has everyone got a British passport'? A lone voice pipes up: 'No', and hands over an Australian passport. Australians need a visa to enter France, and so the student has to get off the bus.
6 Students staying in a hotel in Paris set fire to their room by accident. The hotel has to be evacuated.
7 At a seminar on travel and tourism for visiting foreign students. The first speaker fails to arrive.
8 Students are to give a presentation to their Principal, on the evaluation of their event. The one with the notes and handouts does not turn up. The two remaining students are left stranded.
9 At a fashion show the students cut all the labels off the garments, to prevent them from spoiling the appearance of the clothes. Afterwards, no one knows which item belongs to which shop.
10 At the same fashion show. All the borrowed shoes now have scuffed soles. The shop refuses to take them back.

Review and evaluation of the project

It is vital to consider how you will evaluate your project, before you carry it out. If you neglect this aspect, you will lose valuable opportunities to record or collect information. For example, you may want to ask your customers for their opinion on your performance. It is much more difficult to contact them later, so prepare a short questionnaire or comments sheet, which can be completed during the course of the project.

The steps in evaluation and review of a project are as follows:

1 Before the project, decide on evaluation criteria.
2 Before the project, decide on evaluation techniques.
3 During the project, collect feedback.
4 After the project, carry out de-briefing and evaluation.

Evaluation criteria

This is where you refer to the objectives recorded at the beginning of the project and decide if they have been met. In other words, the objectives become the evaluation criteria. For example:

- Did we raise £500?
- Did we reach an audience of 400 people?
- Did we pass our Travel and Tourism in Action unit?
- Did we gain Key Skills?
- Did we have fun?
- Did we develop new business skills?
- Did we stay within budget?

Evaluation techniques

This entails deciding which techniques will be used to prepare any documentation.

Group debrief

It would be very surprising if this did not take place for any project. For you, it is necessary to enable you to discuss your project as a group and determine your strengths and weaknesses. This will aid your personal development, in addition to helping with any future projects. You will also hear the views of your tutor or supervisor on your performance.

Self-appraisal

It is a good idea to reflect carefully on your own contribution to and performance throughout the project. You will have been working in a group where members have different qualities, and there will always be some people who were more willing to participate than others. You must decide, honestly, whether you have done your best and where you might have improved.

Your tutor might provide a form for this purpose, or you could design one for everyone to use. It should cover comments on the following:

- attendance
- punctuality
- motivation
- enthusiasm
- adherence to deadlines
- leadership
- completion of assigned role
- completion of non-assigned tasks
- support of team members
- outcomes
- improvements for the future

Peer appraisal

This is the most contentious of all the evaluation techniques, as students must appraise each other. You may be asked to appraise as individual-to-individual or group-to-group. It is a useful technique to practise, as peer appraisal often takes place in the workplace. You should design a form for the purpose covering similar areas to the one for self-appraisal. Once you have made your written comments, you should present them to the group that you are appraising (remember to be constructive).

Collecting feedback

The possibility of collecting feedback through questionnaires and opinion surveys has been discussed. Feedback does not have to be formal; listening to comments from visitors or customers can be equally useful. If you have an audience, watch their reactions closely. Staff at an exhibition, for example, will be able to comment on its success. During the course of your own project you too should keep a log of everything you do as this will help your evaluation.

Teamwork

It is very important, in this unit, that you develop effective teamwork skills. Your project will not succeed unless you are able to work together as a team. You are already a member of a group, but a team differs from a group in that members of the team work together to achieve common objectives. You can work as a team even when you are apart, contributing to a sequence of activities with a common aim. In your project, you will set objectives to work towards and you will allocate tasks amongst the team. The team may be the whole group, however it is likely that you will work more effectively by dividing it into smaller teams of three or four people.

The purpose of teams

Synergy: the sum of the parts is greater than the whole.

A good team will achieve synergy. This means that, together, you can achieve more than you can individually. You generate more ideas, energy and resources as a group than you do individually:

- The team can solve problems and make decisions together.
- The team allows a focus on priorities, with everyone working towards the same aim.
- The team provides a sense of belonging and gives you a sense of status.
- The team provides you with a support network.

Team structures

Formal teams

You may find formal teams in the workplace. They relate to the structure of an organisation and are planned in order to meet that organisation's objectives. The team will follow rules and regulations in its procedures, a good example being your teaching team. This team has come together formally with the common objective of helping you achieve your Vocational A Level and, as such, must follow college regulations in the way it operates. Team members must meet regularly and complete administrative procedures. Your own group can also be described as a formal team. You have been placed together because you share the common objective of achieving a Vocational A Level in travel and tourism.

Informal teams

These teams may work within or alongside formal teams. They are based on personal relationships between members, rather than on work roles. When you are asked to work with others on an assignment, you are often free to choose whom you wish to work with. You will choose to work with people that you like and who you know will contribute to the work and support you. These are called informal teams.

There are several theories of team structure and development, which may enable you to make your own team more effective. Tuckman (1965) identified four main stages of team development.

1 Forming – at this stage, team members form their first impressions of each other and establish identities. They are sounding each other out and finding out what is expected of them. They will be finding out information and resources.

2 Storming – the team has, by now, become more used to each other.

At this stage, members are prepared to put forward their ideas forcibly and openly. They are also prepared to disagree and so there may be some conflict and hostility.

3 Norming – the team now begins to establish co-operation. Conflict is controlled. Views are exchanged and new standards introduced.

4 Performing – the team is now working together, they begin to arrive at solutions and achieve their objectives.

Some sources suggest a fifth stage, 'mourning', where the team has disbanded and the members miss membership of the team.

ACTIVITY

Identify the different teams to which you belong (make a list). These may include sports teams, work teams, social or college teams.

For each team, use Tuckman's model and determine what stage each team conforms to. Give reasons for your decision in each case. Compare your findings with other group members.

Belbin outlined eight team roles necessary for a successful team. One person can represent more than one role, as most people have strengths in more than one area.

Belbin's roles

1 Chairperson/co-ordinator – the group leader, likely to be relaxed and extrovert, also likely to be a good communicator. Will use the strengths of team members and give them encouragement.

2 Plant – the ideas person in the team, a person who is creative in looking for solutions to problems, but not always good at details, and so may make careless mistakes.

3 Shaper – the task leader who unites ideas and effort. Needs to be dominant and extrovert in order to make things happen.

4 Monitor/evaluator – the team analyst, who is not so good at ideas but pays attention to detail, thus keeping the team directed towards its target.

5 Implementer – the organiser of the team, who is able to take the ideas of the plant and shaper and turn them into manageable and realistic tasks. A practical, stable and disciplined person.

6 Resource investigator – the person who always has a solution to problems, who is sociable and enthusiastic and good under pressure.

7 Team worker – a very people-oriented person, sensitive to others' needs. This person has good communication skills and will be good at motivating others. A natural mediator, who will deal with conflict within the team. Very good to have around in a crisis.

8 Finisher – a person who sticks to deadlines and likes to get on with things. Will probably be irritated by the more casual members of the team.

Belbin's roles acquire a different level of importance according to each stage in the team's life. At the beginning of a project the resource investigator and the plant will be important. At the end of the project, the roles of the monitor and the implementer will be more important.

ACTIVITY

First decide which of Belbin's roles you are most suited to. Then, consider the strengths and weaknesses of the different individuals in your group.

Decide which role each person is most suited to. Discuss this together and see if you can reach an agreement on each others' roles. You may be able to think of previous team projects where these roles were exemplified.

Roles and responsibilities of team members

In the course of your project, you must determine the roles and responsibilities of each team member. In order to do this, you must first identify the different jobs that need doing. You will find that there are several roles that are common to most projects and your own project may also have some specific job roles.

Job roles may include:

1 Chairperson – this is a very difficult role, requiring a strong personality. The chairperson takes an overview of the whole project and must steer it in the right direction. The chairperson must be able to motivate others and resolve conflict. They must be able to take control and make decisions when necessary. They should also be capable of multi-tasking as they must know what each team member is supposed to achieve, and should, therefore, offer support as needed. It is a good idea to elect the chairperson so that team members are happy with the choice. The chairperson will also have to chair meetings.

2 Finance manager – this person should be numerate and good at accounts. They should pay attention to detail and be totally honest. Depending on your project, the finance manager may be controlling large sums of money. If you have a project bank account, the bank will expect you to appoint two signatories to safeguard your funds. The finance manager will not make decisions about expenditure but will implement the decisions of the team.

3 Sales manager – an extrovert is needed to fill this position, as they will have to approach people and persuade them to buy your service or tickets to your event. They will be managing a team of sales people so they must be a good organiser to ensure comprehensive sales coverage and a good motivator.

KEY TERMS

Multi-tasking: the ability to carry out a number of tasks at once.

Signatory: a person authorised to sign cheques on a bank account.

4 Marketing manager – this individual should be dynamic and creative. They will have to oversee the marketing of the whole project. They will need good communication skills to liaise with people outside the team, such as journalists. They will be good motivators, as they will have to manage a team working on advertising material, press releases, etc.

5 Secretary – the secretary needs to have faultless English. It is essential that any written communication that comes from your team is spelt correctly and is free from grammatical errors, otherwise your professionalism may be undermined. The secretary will undertake tasks, such as writing letters, memos and faxes, on behalf of the team. They will also be responsible for taking minutes in meetings and distributing them to the team. An eye for detail is important.

6 Fundraiser – this role is needed if you do not have the start up finance needed for the project. The fundraiser needs to be an ideas person, as they are going to have to think of ideas for activities which will raise money. This is a very responsible role and needs to be carried out early, as aspects of the project will depend on the amount of finance acquired.

7 Venue co-ordinator – if you are planning a special event, you will need a venue. This person must be prepared to liaise with other people outside the team and approach venues to investigate facilities and costs. Again, this role needs to be undertaken early on in the project, as other decisions and arrangements will depend on the venue. The venue co-ordinator should be a good negotiator, in order to achieve the best possible deal.

This list of job roles should give you a good starting point when you are ready to begin your own project. You can of course add to them, with roles specific to your project. If you are working in a large group, allocate group members to different teams working for managers. Make sure that the team is allocated according to its strengths and weaknesses.

PROFILE *Keysites campsite courier team*

La Palmyre is a campsite on the west coast of France. Keysites is a UK-based camping tour operator who has a large number of pre-erected tents on this site. There are also about 20 mobile homes on the site. Keysites have a loyal customer base; many clients choose to holiday with the company, year after year. Keysites attribute this to the excellent customer service they offer. To ensure high standards of customer service, their couriers undergo extensive training and are monitored by area supervisors when they are on site.

An important element of the customer service training is teamwork. At La Palmyre, there are six couriers, whose role is to keep the customers happy. When they began the summer season, none of the couriers knew each other, but they now form a strong team.

One of the team, Becky, is a supervisor and she has responsibility for finance and managing the other couriers. Every Sunday night, she is to be found at the desk behind her tent, planning the next week's rota and struggling to balance the petty cash. The six couriers all have the same responsibilities, apart from Chris, who is a dedicated children's courier. This suits him very well as he is very good at his job and does not have to do as much tent cleaning as the others.

Cleaning is an important aspect of the couriers' jobs, as no client wants to arrive to a dirty tent or mobile home. Each courier is allocated a number of tents to clean each week. If, however, a client is due and the work is not done, everyone must pitch in to help. Other tasks include manning the reception area and providing information and advice to clients. There are set reception hours, but the couriers can be approached at any time as their tents are easily accessible to customers.

All new arrivals must be personally welcomed and shown around. The couriers are also expected to arrange parties and other activities for the clients and they must also take part in these. All the couriers appreciate the importance of good teamwork. They live in close proximity to each other and rely on each others' support to do a good job.

Team building and interaction

Team building is the process that enables a team to work together effectively and to meet their common goal. Team building may be instigated when there are signs that a team is not working well. These signs may include:

- reduction in the quality of work
- low morale and lack of enthusiasm
- people complaining
- conflict amongst team members
- absence from team meetings

Team building has become a big business in its own right, as companies invest in training courses to help their teams provide a quality service and to remain competitive.

Issues that are tackled on team building courses include:

- helping people to develop respect and trust for each other
- helping people to value each others' contributions
- getting people to communicate openly by sharing ideas and information

- encouraging the team to support and coach each other, to maximise potential.

The team building activities may take place in a specially developed centre and may not be related to work at all. It is possible that you have participated in such a course at an outward bound centre. Examples of the activities that are used to build teams include learning to sail an ocean yacht or taking part in conservation projects, such as creating a footpath or pruning a coppice. Participants in these types of courses live together during the course and share cooking and cleaning duties. The activities are combined with the development of interpersonal skills, such as planning and communication. Sometimes, a work-related activity is used to build teams, but participants are still housed away from the workplace, so that they can socialise as well as tackle work issues.

Factors influencing the success of a team

Communication

Open communication must be encouraged and ideas should be freely expressed. To enable this to happen, there should be a relaxed, friendly atmosphere. The way the chairs and tables are laid out is important, as there should be no visible barriers or hierarchy. Each team member should be encouraged to have their say and be listened to. There should be trust and support between team members. A good leader can encourage these points. It is also important to pay attention to body language.

Leadership

This is the process of motivating people to act in particular ways, so that the team can achieve its common goal. We have already identified the role of chairperson (this person should be leading the team). A leading authority on leadership is John Adair, a writer and management consultant. He has developed a three circle model of leadership, comprising the task, the team and the individual. The theory concerns balancing the needs of the team, the individual and getting the task done.

The task is about achieving the project goal. If too little attention is paid to the task, nothing will be achieved. If too much attention is paid to the task, then the team may not find a way of working effectively together.

Teams have to be able to work together. If too little attention is paid to the needs of the team, it will not function effectively. If too much attention is paid to the team, then the goal may be overlooked and the needs of the individual ignored.

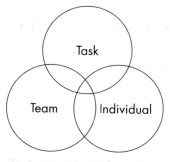

Figure 6.9 *Adair's three-circle model of leadership*

Teams are made up of individuals. Their needs must be met, to enable them to contribute. If too little attention is paid to the individual, then that person's contributions will be limited. If too much attention is paid to the individual, it will be difficult to achieve the team's goal. A good leader must inform, motivate and develop the team. This may occur through different styles of leadership, which we will now discuss.

Autocratic leadership

An autocratic leader makes all the decisions and announces them to the team. This person is the boss and so has full control. The advantages of this kind of leadership are that decisions are made quickly, as there is no consultation involved. The advantages include:

- A team that is immature or lacking in confidence will depend on the autocratic leader and gain security.
- New people can be accommodated quickly into the team.

The disadvantages include:

- It can be frustrating for the team to have to accept all decisions.
- There may not be room for the team to express creativity.
- There may be over-dependence on the leader (e.g. what happens if the leader is absent?).

Consultative leadership

Here, the leader still makes decisions, but discusses those decisions with the team. The advantages include:

- Everyone knows what is going on.
- Open discussion is encouraged.
- The leader spends time with the group.

The disadvantage is:

- The team may have the illusion of power, but they do not get to make the decisions.

Democratic leadership

With this style of leadership, decision making is shared amongst the team. The advantages include:

- The team has the opportunity to be creative, ideas are encouraged from everyone.
- There is greater commitment from team members.
- The team will be more supportive of the leader.
- The team know exactly what is happening.

The disadvantages include:

- An inexperienced team may not be able to cope with partaking in decisions.

- It can take a long time to reach agreement.
- The leader may not agree with the team's decisions.
- Powerful team members may take over.

CASE STUDY *John Clark*

John Clark is area supervisor for Magic Holidays, in the resort of Gran Canaria. He is responsible for a team of 12 holiday representatives. He spends every morning in the resort office, but likes to maintain as much customer contact as possible, so he visits hotels with different members of the team in the afternoon and sits in on the representatives' meeting time (when they are available for consultation with customers). John is in his forties and, therefore, much older than most of his team. He has held this supervisory position for two years, before which he worked for three years as a representative for a competitor. Prior to that, he served in the army.

He is fairly gruff in his approach to his staff and prides himself on 'not suffering fools gladly'. A very extrovert man, he is liked by customers, as they see him as the life and soul of their holiday. The following describes a typical day in the resort.

8.30 a.m. John arrives at the office. The official start time is 9 a.m. Judith and Meena arrive to take up their rota at the office at 8.35 a.m. They are disappointed to find that John is already there. They always try to get there just before him, and so are finding they are having to come in earlier and earlier.

9.00 a.m. John gives each of the women a list of tasks to complete for the morning. Judith has to complete some figures on tour numbers to fax to head office. She asks what happens to the figures when they reach the UK. John tells her she does not need to know that and to get on with the task.

9.20 a.m. Meena deals with a call from a sick client. She competently explains the procedure for reaching the doctor and tells the client she will call on them later in the day. John listens closely to the call and then tells her to remember to call on the client later in the day. She has already noted this in her diary and so feels annoyed.

10.00 a.m. Meena goes out to buy coffee for the office staff. John asks her to be quick, as she still has a lot of work to do. She purposefully dawdles and returns 20 minutes later.

11.00 a.m. A regular meeting takes place with another two representatives attending. The meeting is to discuss new day trips that can be offered for customers. The reps are very interested and spend half an hour putting forward their new ideas. they have produced itineraries and costings and become very excited at the possibilities. John takes some notes during the meeting and then announces that the new trip will be a half day boat tour to a secluded beach, with a picnic. He has already made the arrangements with a local boat operator. He tells Judith to prepare a leaflet for the trip.

4.00 p.m. John joins Judith at her welcome meeting for newly arrived holiday-makers. He is charming to the customers and hands round drinks. He sits by Judith during her presentation and every few minutes, interrupts her to add extra bits of information and selling points. Judith becomes fed up and so she drinks three glasses of wine.

5 p.m. John arrives at Meena's meeting point in one of her assigned hotels. She has just managed to calm down a complaining client and persuaded them to stay in their accommodation. John asks them loudly what the problem is and assures them that he can move them if they want.

11 p.m. All the resort staff are present at the weekly nightclub visit, accompanied by many customers. John is the centre of the customers' attention as he regales them with his fantastic resort knowledge and experience. The reps are still extremely fed up.

ACTIVITY

1 What type of leadership style does John Clark have? What do you think will happen to his team? How could John improve his approach to better motivate the team? Discuss your thoughts with your group.

2 Think about a part-time job or work placement you have had. Draw up a profile of your manager or supervisor, in terms of personality, attitude to work and attitude towards their team. Try to decide which leadership style they have adopted and give examples of how this manifests itself. Give your opinion of how effective their leadership is and suggest ways it could be improved. Present your findings to your group.

Personality clashes

At some stage in our lives, we all have to work with people we clash with or simply do not like. Such differences must, however, be put aside, for the team to work well together. One member of the team may dominate discussion. The chairperson must allow that person to have their say and then move firmly on to someone else. Unfair criticism of another team member should be discouraged by the group. Conflicts should be brought out into the open and dealt with before they escalate.

Tasks can be distributed between the team and then performed individually or in small groups. This will allow people to work with like-minded people. There may be team members who are reluctant to take on extra work and this problem should be openly discussed and a fair share of tasks agreed.

Access to resources and the working environment

Ideally, each team member will have equal access to resources. In practice, this may not be the case. In a working environment, each team member should have access to the required physical resources, but in planning an event, personal contacts will be very important and these will be different for everyone. When you are running your project you will find that many of you have different contacts who are able to help. You may also have different levels of access to resources. For example, those students with home computers may be able to spend more time on the production of artwork and materials.

Carrying out and evaluating the project

You are now almost ready to carry out your project. There are, however, a few more skills you need to cover to enable you to do this to the best of your ability. These include:

- chairing a meeting
- preparing an agenda
- writing minutes
- writing your own job description
- keeping a log
- writing a report on the project

Chairing a meeting

You may think that this does not apply to you, if you are not appointed chairperson of the project. In fact, for the purposes of meetings, it is possible to have what is known as a 'rotating chairperson', which means that each team member takes a turn at chairing a meeting and developing this important skill. The chairperson will prepare the agenda and control the meeting. The following check list will help you get through the first meeting for which you are chairperson.

1 Start the meeting on time.
2 Welcome the team to the meeting.
3 Inform the team if any apologies for non-attendance have been offered.
4 Agree the minutes of the last meeting (everyone should have a copy).
5 Go through each of the agenda items in turn, keeping an eye on the time.
6 Share information.

7 For each agenda item, agree action points and assign each to a team member.

8 Allow everyone to have their say.

9 Make sure that everyone speaks through the chairperson (i.e., when they wish to make a point, they raise their hand, the chairperson acknowledges this and then invites them to speak). This will allow you to retain control of the meeting.

10 Do not allow people to digress; bring them firmly back to the agenda.

11 Summarise the action points.

12 Agree the time and place for the next meeting.

13 Close the meeting on time.

Preparing an agenda

An agenda is a list of issues that need to be addressed in the meeting. It should be prepared and distributed in time for team members to study it and prepare in advance of the meeting. The team can also be invited to add points to the agenda. It should always start with an agreement of the minutes of the previous meeting. Following is an example:

Agenda for meeting of the student newspaper team, 14 January 2000.

1 Agree minutes of meeting on 20 January 2000.
2 Review progress on student residential feature (AH).
3 Agree deadline for copy for next edition.
4 Report on advertising placed (JF).
5 Appoint sports features writer.
6 Select photos from team's personal collections.
7 Ideas for future articles.
8 AOB
9 Time and venue of next meeting.

AOB means 'any other business', and is an opportunity for the team to raise other important issues. If there are many other agenda items to discuss, this section should be omitted. The agenda should be kept as short as possible, otherwise there will not be time to discuss everything thoroughly (one hour is long enough for a meeting). The initials in brackets after an item indicate that that person will be expected to report on the item and that they should be prepared for this.

ACTIVITY

Write the agenda for the first meeting of your project team. You will not have any previous minutes to agree. Show your agenda to the other members of your group. Compare agenda items and agree a final agenda to go forward to the next meeting.

Writing the minutes of a meeting

Earlier in this chapter, the role of minute writing was assigned to the secretary. It is, however, good practice for each team member to write minutes during your project, so that you all gain this experience in this area. The minutes will be your record of who agreed to do what, and, along with your log, will help you to complete your project report.

Start by recording any absences from the meeting (Note that there should be no absences without apologies). As each agenda item is discussed, make notes on what action is agreed and, importantly, who is going to do it. The date and place of the next meeting are then recorded. You will have plenty of opportunities to practise writing minutes in your project, but the following example will also help you.

Minutes of the student newspaper group, 14 January 2000.

1 Apologies: Penny
2 The minutes of the meeting on 7 January were agreed.
3 AH reported that the student residential feature was complete, but needed to be scanned and headlines added. **ACTION HJ** by 19 January.
4 The team agreed that the next copy deadline should be 19 February.
5 JF reported that there had been a marked increase in the number of advertisements placed for the next issue, but that another £500 revenue was needed to meet their target. The sales team would target named companies and try to reach the target. **ACTION sales team**. JF to provide contact names and co-ordinate sales drive. Sales drive to be completed by end of January.
6 After much discussion, it was decided that none of the team was sufficiently knowledgeable to write on sport. It was decided that an approach be made to Michael Wright (staff member), to help on the next issue. **ACTION KH**.
7 The team agreed on six photos for inclusion in the next edition. These were passed to the editing team.
8 A number of ideas were presented for the next issue. These were assigned to each team member for research and further discussion will follow at the next meeting. **ACTION all** by 21 January.
9 The date of the next meeting is 21 January, venue, in room 6.

Writing a job description

You may already have a job description for your part-time job, and when you enter employment you will also be given a job description. This is a document that lists all the responsibilities of the job and tells you who you report to. A job description is sent to applicants for a post so that they can see whether their experience matches the requirements and then tailor their CV or letter of application to that post.

The job description is often accompanied by a person specification. This differs from the job description in that it describes the kind of person who will be suitable for the job. It will use terms such as 'good communicator', 'team player' and 'self starter'. The descriptions of job roles earlier in this chapter give indications of the types of people who would be suitable for different roles. During your project, you will need to write your own job description and check it with the other members of the team.

Job description: Caterer for corporate events

Responsible to: Corporate event manager

Responsible for: Catering assistants, waiting staff and bar staff

Responsibilities:

- liaison with clients
- assessment of client needs
- menu planning and costing
- pre-ordering of food and drink, to budget
- preparation of food
- ordering of crockery, cutlery and table design materials
- supervision of staff and rotas
- appraisal of catering assistants
- hiring extra staff as required
- recording of expenditure with receipts

It is important to ensure that every aspect of a job is included in the job description, as an employer cannot easily add things later without negotiating them with the employee.

Examine the person specification for the caterer for corporate events, as follows.

Person specification: Caterer for corporate events

The appointee must have a degree in catering or food management with several years experience of dealing with corporate events. A knowledge of food safety legislation is vital and experience of budgeting is desirable. He or she must be a good communicator and be able to adapt to different environments. He or she must also be enthusiastic and self-motivated.

Keeping a log of your contribution to the project

You will be expected to produce a report at the end of the project and the log will remind you of what happened and what you did. It will also provide evidence of the tasks you carried out. The log can take the form of a diary, ideally completed daily throughout the duration of the project. You may decide as a group that everyone should complete their log in the same format. If so, the group should agree that format.

Figure 6.10 shows a suggested format and an example of a completed log for one day, for a student contributing to the student newspaper. She is called Marilyn, and is a member of the sales team, selling advertising space in the paper. You will see that the log is a very simple document, covering what the student had to do, who she needed to approach and problems she encountered on the way. You will see that when she did not have the information required, she had to use a 'contingency plan'.

When you complete your own log, remember to keep copies of minutes of meetings, letters, faxes or any other documentation you complete. You should also record any telephone calls you make, including the time and length of call.

DATE	TASK	PEOPLE INVOLVED	PROBLEMS	COMMENTS
15 January	Need to start contacting advertisers, as I have 2 hours free this afternoon.	JF (sales manager), contacts, tutor.	JF has not provided me with my contacts. Had to ask my tutor who I should contact. She gave me 3 possibilities.	Lost an hour because of JF, will raise this at the next meeting.
	Contacted the three companies, pleased to gain a sales interview with 2 of them; the other was not interested.		Still need more contacts, must prepare for the interviews with sales pitch and rates.	

Figure 6.10

Writing a report on a project

It is possible that you will be asked to complete a written report on your project. If so, you need to know how this should be presented, to make it look professional. Your report will contain the following sections:

- Title
- Introduction
- Information
- Conclusion
- Recommendations
- Appendices

Title

Keep this as simple as possible, for example, *A Report on the Student Newspaper Project 2000.*

Introduction

Explain why the project was carried out, and when, for example:

'Vocational A Level Travel and Tourism students were required to carry out a project, in order to achieve their Travel and Tourism in Action unit. Several business plans, for different ideas, were developed and presented. After discussion, the group opted to start a student newspaper. The project ran from January to June, 2000. Ms Harrison was the tutor in charge of the project.'

Information

This is the most detailed section of the report and will be subdivided under different headings, so that the points you make are in logical sections and are easy to understand. The sections will differ according to the project, but some possibilities are job roles, resources needed, procedures, contingency plans, the evaluation process and success. You should refer to any appendices in this section of the report and attach them at the end, clearly labelled. The appendices will include copies of your log and letters, etc.

The report should mainly detail your own contribution to the project otherwise it will become unmanageable, however, you do also need to include an overview of the project as a whole, and general comments on its success, so that the report makes sense to the reader. Following is an example of one part of the information section, appearing under the sub-heading 'Job roles'. The report is from Marilyn, whose log we read earlier (see Figure 6.10).

Job role

Each member of the team was allocated a job. Appendix 2 shows a list of the team and their roles. The role of advertising sales was given to me, reporting to JF, the sales manager. There were two other sales people, making a small team of four. Our combined role was to achieve sales targets agreed by the whole group by approaching potential advertisers and selling space in the newspaper. We had to do this for each of three issues of the paper and we were required to produce a detailed job description. As three of us had the same job, we produced this together.

Conclusion

When you have completed the information section of the report, you should write a conclusion. This is a brief summary of what you have said in the information section.

Recommendations

This is the last section of the report. It is important for your project, because this is where you have the opportunity to say how you would change things if you were to do the project all over again.

Your report should be word processed. If you want to write a formal report, then each section should be numbered so that the structure looks like this:

1	Introduction
2	Information
2.1	Job roles
2.1.1	Each member of the team was allocated a job . . .
2.1.2	The role of advertising sales was given to me . . .
2.1.3	We were required to produce . . .
2.2	Resources
3.0	Conclusion
4.0	Recommendations

KEY TERMS

Rotating chair: each member of the team takes it in turn to chair meetings.

Agenda: is a list of subjects for discussion at the meeting.

Minutes: are notes on what was agreed at the meeting.

Job description: sometimes named job specification, a list of the duties pertaining to the job.

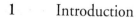

ASSESSMENT

You are now able to put all your knowledge and skills together into a practical project, and demonstrate how much you have learnt. This should be a real project, not a simulation, and possibly the hardest part, is to get started and decide what the project is going to be. Your group must decide for itself what to do, but this chapter does provide some examples of other groups' chosen projects. These included a student newspaper, a competition and other events. You might decide to put on an open day (e.g. exhibiting travel companies) or plan a trip or put on a fund raising event for charity. Make sure the project you choose relates to travel and tourism, and good luck! At all stages of the project, refer to the text to help you. Attendance at all stages and meetings of your project is essential – you cannot contribute if you are not there.

Part 1

Hold an informal meeting of your group and carry out a brainstorming session to come up with project ideas. Do not expect to do more than this at the first meeting. You do not need to minute this first meeting. Allocate these ideas to small teams or individuals for development. Each team will then be given a short period of time to produce a brief business plan for their allocated idea (a week should be sufficient for this). Each plan should include:

- objectives and timescale for the project (remembering the SMART approach)
- description of the project
- resources needed, with estimates of finance required
- consideration of the legal aspects of the project
- evaluation methods to be used.

You should produce a written plan, but also prepare materials for oral presentation to the group. Hold a second meeting, where each small team presents their plan and 'sells' it to the group. Following the presentations, you should discuss the plans and choose which project should be implemented.

Part 2

Having made your choice of project, the plan for that project should be developed further, so that all members of the group agree the objectives, timescale, etc. At this stage, you should use critical path analysis or a Gantt chart to help to plan timescales. Each member of the group should have a copy of the business plan.

You are now ready to start holding formal meetings and to allocate roles. Decide who is to chair the project, considering leadership styles as you do so. Allocate all the job roles for the project, considering each individual's strengths and weaknesses. Use the Belbin model to help you. Record all decisions in minutes.

Part 3

1 Write a detailed job description and person specification for your role.
2 Continue to hold meetings with prepared agendas and minutes, as necessary, for the duration of the project. Retain all this documentation as evidence.
3 Keep a log of your contributions to the project, with copies of any documents you produce. Use the log illustrated in this chapter or design your own.
4 Remember to collect feedback for evaluation.

Part 4

When the project is finished, you must carry out an evaluation. Your tutor will carry out a debriefing session. You should also carry out:

1 a self-evaluation
2 an evaluation of another individual or of the team
3 an evaluation of the whole project.

Use the section on evaluation in this chapter to help you, and design forms if you wish. You should have collected feedback during the project, so do not forget to include this.

Part 5

You have completed all stages of the project and are ready to write a report on the whole process. Again, use the relevant section of this chapter to help you. Attach all your appendices to the report, remembering to refer to them in the main body of the report.

Key skills

In completing the assessment for this unit, you can achieve the following key skills. These will be accredited at the discretion of your tutor on the basis of the quality of the work you submit.

C3.1a Contribute to a group discussion about a complex subject.

C3.1b Make a presentation about a complex subject, using at least one image to illustrate complex points.

C3.3 Write two different types of documents about complex subjects. One piece of writing should be an extended document and include at least one image.

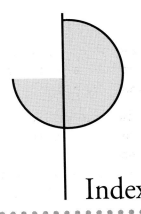

Index